The Passage

Memoir of a Boston Undercover Cop in the '60s

Phillip M Vitti

authorHOUSE®

AuthorHouse™
1663 Liberty Drive
Bloomington, IN 47403
www.authorhouse.com
Phone: 1-800-839-8640

Published by AuthorHouse 3/5/2012

ISBN: 978-1-4685-4333-9 (e)
ISBN: 978-1-4685-4334-6 (hc)
ISBN: 978-1-4685-4335-3 (sc)

Library of Congress Control Number: 2012900904

To my Aunt,
Mary Volante Morvan,
who taught me the difference
between right and wrong

and to my wife of 28 years,
Margaret 'Peggy' Vitti
1945 - 2004

Acknowledgments

I want to thank the following persons:

Christine Michalosky whose hard fought editorial expertise was invaluable to me;

Peter Flynn for his characterization of protest groups during the Vietnam era;

Brad Jones, Buddy Evans, Peter Ryan, Tom Mitchell, Gerry Vanderwood, Bill Bret for their memory of events;

Kevin McGuire, John Lydstone, Gary Wolf, Kim Morse, Nick Tranquillo, Paul Memos, Eddie Jesser, Mary and Dick Cash for their support;

The Whalens - Barbara, Debbie and Barbie for their patient listening;

A very special thanks to Connie Stahlman for her help on the final revision-

and especially my wife Peggy, an inspirationally vibrant, though very private person, who never failed to give me the right advice, even during the most intimate and difficult episodes. She never saw the book published, but it would never have happened without her support.

Thanks Peggy----

To the Reader

The Nineteen Sixties and early Seventies were an epochal time in America. The decade started off with a measured beat and ended up a crescendo. For anyone who lived during that age I don't have to remind them that it was a period of great social upheaval - perhaps the most tumultuous since the Civil War.

I was an undercover cop back in those times. Undercover cops are not born in a vacuum. They are formed and molded by the influences that affect them and the ravages of the times in which they work.

This story is a highly personal account of my experiences as an undercover operative for the Boston Police Department. It begins with the events that propelled me into the police service and ends several years later with an occurrence that would force me to choose, not between what was right from wrong, but what was right from right.

I have, on rare occasions, resorted to artistic license and in a few instances have altered descriptions and changed names to avoid embarrassment.

ONE

How empty learning, how vain is art,
But it mends the life and guides the heart.
------------ Young

One

I guess I could not have it three ways - go to Hollywood and get into the stunt man business, or migrate to the Village and drop out for a while, or do the boring thing, go home and pursue a conventional lifestyle. Those were exactly the three choices I was mulling over on that thirtieth day of January 1962, at the front gate of Camp Lejeune, North Carolina, fresh from receiving my honorable discharge from the United States Marines, or 'the crotch' as we referred to it. I cannot remember a greater feeling of elation before or after this event - free of it all - the relentless discipline of the Marines, and the unhappy childhood before that.

The Hollywood deal was in the making. Of course, I would not start off as a stunt man; this would take time, but I had the connection. My Marine Corps buddy, Mike Gardner, had an uncle who was a cameraman in Hollywood and he invited us there and promised us a job on the set. After that it would be only a matter of time before we would be getting paid to do stunts, not unlike some of the crazy things we already had done in the 'crotch'. We had done some risky cliff diving into shark infested waters, had gone over a waterfall in a barrel, and a few other nutty things that convinced us both that we had what it took. I can remember my pride when I was voted and crowned *King of the Animals* - any Marine will tell you that winning the platoon's confidence in the bestowal of such an honor is no small feat.

The problem with this first choice was time - the time, (Jan 30 until March 21) that it would take waiting for Mike to receive his discharge. One week short of two months is much too long to wait when you are twenty-two. So that was out.

The Greenwich Village thing, well, that was something else. Village people, artists, drop outs, beatniks, whatever one may wish to call them, their life style was appealing to me - independent, free floating, creative and peripatetic; they had it all and I was enchanted by it. The only problem was the lack of a pronounced talent that would legitimize my entry into this world. Don't get me wrong. I truly felt that with the proper training I could act or write well enough, but my spotty secondary education and *King of the Animals* experience did not provide me with the basics for the product of this inspiration. I disliked the idea of being labeled a phony beatnik. My trip down the road with Jack Kerouac would have to wait until later in life.

I got into a waiting cab, handed the cabby my boots in lieu of payment and directed him to the bus station in Jacksonville. A bus, a train, and on back to Boston; my adventures were over before they even started. If I had three lives I would have followed through on my other plans, but such was not the case, at least not in my religion. I enrolled in night school, flunked algebra for the fifth time and got a job at the Boston State Hospital where another kind of adventure was to begin - one that would take me to the realization that mental illness was among the most misunderstood and devastating sicknesses of all time. I don't mean to editorialize but it's true - it affects more people than simply the victim. What could possibly happen in the mind of a beautiful young woman to propel her off a building? Anyway, mental illness sucks, but let me get on with my story.

I worked at the hospital for a little over two and a half years, and it was the most carefree time of my life. In the beginning I lived in the male employees' residence situated in the middle of the grounds. I had my own room, and it included maid service. Her name was Reba. She made the bed, cleaned the room, emptied my ashtray and made sure my laundry was picked up and cleaned. All this for two dollars and forty cents that was deducted from my paycheck each week.

Every three months a new group of student nurses would intern at the hospital. As a result, I had an active social life. I did not make much, but considering my low expenses I was able to have a car and save twenty bucks a week out of the forty-eight I cleared. I was free, on my own. I could be alone or with someone should I choose. I could read, talk, and walk where I may, support myself, make love, argue political ideology, and all of this without fear of punishment or criticism. I met a great many interesting people. Some of them worked there; others were patients. They were all books to me, and I read them well.

I found the State Hospital to be an intensely intellectual place. Many of the attendants who worked the wards were students at various Boston area colleges, some of them on a graduate level. Northeastern University students especially, were represented as they utilized the Boston State Hospital as a job source for their co-op program. This program permitted students to help finance the cost of their education by alternating periods of employment and classroom instruction. The mix of students ranged from more conservative types, such as the few that attended Nazarene College, to more liberal types from Boston University and, in fewer instances, Harvard. There was always somebody around and good conversation took place throughout the three shifts, especially in the recreation room of the male employees' home. Good conversation remained an art form in the early Sixties. I recall being a member of a coffee shop in Harvard Square - between recitations of poetry and some folk music, talk was what happened.

During this time I met some of the brightest guys I have ever known. Ed Jesser was one of them - a slightly built, light complexioned, red-headed kid out of the streets of Dorchester. I liked him a lot because he had balls and brains. He was intrigued with politics, and at the time was an ardent Barry Goldwater supporter. (After a stint in Vietnam assigned to Army Intelligence he changed his political proclivity. I never found out the full story of his conversion, but I suspect it stemmed from a sudden awareness that conservatives were lying about the amount of body bags they were ordering.) Anyway, after his discharge he became involved with politics on the municipal level and on through to the national heights, eventually becoming a first string guy in the Carter White House. Jesser absorbs information quicker than a clam absorbs sea water and can spin out any number of outcomes, political outcomes of course, depending on intervening variables, which he can often times manipulate. He is known in political circles as one of the most important supporters that any candidate running for President can have. I didn't know that he would achieve all this at the time. To me he was simply an interesting guy that burned narrowly and bright. Was he a devil with a halo or an angel with horns? I have never known.

Paul Memos was an interesting contrast to Jesser. Regarded by some people as equally bright, he possessed an encyclopedic mind and enjoyed reading on a wide variety of subjects. I remember him commenting that the physical and biological sciences were moving in the direction of a unifying discipline, one that would someday evolve into a single science that would develop explanations for material existence. Paul acquired knowledge for its own sake. It was information to him; perhaps he used it for intellectual stimulation or understanding, but never for financial gain or personal aggrandizement. Paul was a short stocky Greek. Tough, both physically and mentally, he had an abiding belief in the natural processes of the physical world and completely rejected spiritual explanations for social or material phenomena. He held social scientists in disdain, believing they were frauds who engaged in the manipulation of data to pursue their own social agenda. He rejected egalitarian apologies for differences in racial behavior and believed that in the end the only thing that made a difference was the cold physical truth. He did not believe in the Godhead and failed to recognize his own leap of faith in embracing a belief that purported something could come from nothing. Paul Memos and Ed Jesser were brilliant and colorful characters who sparked my curiosity and stimulated my imagination. They demonstrated another level of existence that reached beyond the grimy streets of East Somerville where I had grown up. They were a source of education and nourishment and for sure, a continuous stream of entertainment.

The Boston State Hospital consisted of about forty-five mostly red brick buildings sprawled across 175 acres of rolling green land. There was a pronounced serenity to the grounds, a kind of calmness that effectively masked the human suffering concealed in its structures. Patients who were fortunate enough to have ground privileges, along with employees and visitors, kept the daytime in continual motion. It looked like a college campus to all but its inhabitants.

I was initially assigned to Reception Six, an admitting building close to the main entrance. It was here that patients in the acute stages of mental illness were first admitted. This was a good beginning point for a new, husky former Marine attendant - violent behavior occurred more frequently here. The concept of placing newly admitted patients together for purposes of evaluation was later abandoned because of this deleterious effect. I purchased my whites and underwent three days of orientation where I learned how to give shots, pills and enemas in addition to taking temperatures. (I never could understand why the mercury contained in the thermometer would not go down once the source of the heat was withdrawn.) Armed with this knowledge and confident of my professional abilities, I was ready to begin my first day.

The head nurse appeared relieved to have had me assigned to her ward. She didn't tell me this, but I sort of sensed it. I must confess that I did not always know exactly what Miss Ricci was thinking. I sensed a disparity between her words and inner emotions. It was almost as though she sensed my every thought and emotion and enjoyed the tension under which she placed me. Miss Ricci was a remarkably beautiful woman. About thirty-two years old, she reached about five feet three inches tall and her slightly plump curvaceous figure completely filled her uniform. Her eyes had the almond shape of a cat and her femininity housed an iron will. I found myself wishing to have her approval. She was mysterious and I liked her for that reason, but on this first day I knew that she was pleased.

About thirty patients were assigned to the ward, suffering from various forms of mental disorder. Many of them were classified as schizophrenic. I was not sure what that meant. I learned that it was an umbrella term that contained a variety of mental disorders that ranged from paranoia and delusions of grandeur to manic-depressive behavior. (It was explained to me that this form of disorder is characterized by serious mood swings from elation to depression.) I learned quickly that paranoid patients were the most unpredictable and potentially dangerous. I came to understand that the harder one attempted to gain their confidence, the more likely that it would arouse their suspicions, so I didn't press them too hard in hopes that at some point they would gesticulate toward me. Sometimes that would happen and I would experience a great sense of relief; other times it would not and a physical confrontation could well result. These confrontations often times ensued when one patient threatened or assaulted another, or when a patient was stopped from leaving the ward because he did not have ground privileges or in instances when he returned from the outside in possession of a temper or a weapon. The standard operating procedure for removing a knife from a reluctant patient involved more than one attendant pressing him into the wall with a mattress and forcibly removing the weapon.

The first patient that assaulted me was a woman. I was called over to the female ward on Reception Five to place an unruly woman into the seclusion room. This was a sort of solitary confinement that was used selectively to control a patient who was dangerous to herself or others. Unfortunately, it was used by some staff persons as a threat or a form of control over patients to induce conformity. I don't recall what the reason was in this case. I simply remember being ordered to place the woman inside this empty twelve by fourteen foot room that locked from the outside. It was also required that the woman's clothing be removed. My noble instincts resisted degrading her in this manner. I made a deal. I promised to look the other way and not forcibly engage her if, in exchange, she would voluntarily remove her clothing and hand the articles over to me. She consented and I was pleased that I had scored a victory so early in my psychiatric career. In fact, I wondered why the female aides assigned to the ward also couldn't have been so skillfully inclined. I questioned the rationale for my having to do this in the first place. If both male and female attendants earned the same amount, and if men were required to restrain male patients, why weren't women employees expected to do the same for their gender? As I was pondering all of this, my left hand was extended toward the patient in an effort to receive her garments and my eyes were turned away from her. I could hear the rustle of her clothing as she began to comply with our agreement when suddenly I heard her shout the name "Governor Volpe". I turned toward her but it was too late. The next thing I remember was lying on the floor writhing in agony from a well placed kick to my groin. It was literally a painful lesson and that was the end of my naiveté.

The next time I encountered an agitated woman involved a different set of circumstances. It was visitor's day in the Reception building and a young girl about twenty-two years old was standing in the outside hallway of the ward. The Reception building supervisor, a raw-boned, tough looking no nonsense nurse, ordered her inside because she still remained restricted to the ward. The patient became visibly upset and refused to obey Mrs. Benson's command. The young woman also refused to take her oral medication, in this case Thorazine, to calm her down. Faced with this increasing opposition and intensifying hysteria, the building boss prepared an injection of the drug and returned to the outer hallway and instructed me to physically place the subject on her stomach. The woman refused to go down and began striking me repeatedly. I countered this by placing her in an arm lock while simultaneously pressing the patient to the floor. Mrs. Benson pulled up the patient's dress, pulled down her panties, and injected her bare and exposed buttock in a clear view of a hall full of visitors and patients.

I vaguely felt that there was something wrong with this whole scene. Suddenly a very distressed and red hot angry man's face penetrated the confusion and stared directly into my eyes as I continued to forcibly hold down this young lady. I knew instantly that she was his daughter. I would have liked to have expressed my sympathy to him and have him understand that I was simply following orders, but knew this would be fruitless. Instead, I threatened him with permanent removal from the building if he intervened in any way. How many times does it happen that because of an individual's rash action, in this case Mrs. Benson's indiscreet decision to 'indignify' this young woman for her symptomatic failure to comply, that someone else is placed in an embarrassing situation or even worse, in harm's way? I was to learn much later that this also happens big time with wrongful political decisions.

There were other occasions of episodic violence. In one of them I came close to being suffocated. A patient who was not permitted to leave the ward became angry, placed my neck in an arm lock, and applied increasing pressure. The world started to blacken against a backdrop of blinking stars. The patient, a tall and very strong male mathematician, was standing over me. My neck and head were firmly imprisoned in the crook of his left arm while he continued to apply upward resistance using both arms. I was on my knees and was certain that my death was imminent unless I resisted with all the power in me. I reached up, and against a wall of pain inserted my thumbs in the soft tissue underneath his jaw and pushed up with all the strength I could muster. As quickly as he had subdued me he released me, throwing his arms up in the air and proclaiming surrender. I staggered up, assisted by another attendant who had been called to the scene by a patient, and placed my antagonist in the seclusion room. His final comment never ceased to amuse me. He said that I was a real strong guy. This patient never knew how close he came to murdering me that day. Oddly enough, we developed a mutual respect for one another - he increased my proficiency in math and became an ally.

I learned early on that allies were important in this environment. I entered into a friendship with a patient that lasted for the rest of the man's life. His name was Leo Bordier. The first time I recall Leo he was sitting in a chair with his back to the wall. He wore a blank expression on his face and appeared oblivious to his surroundings. Leo was four years my senior but he looked much older. He was good looking in a fierce sort of way, but his face was marred prematurely with wrinkles that hinted of the ageless knowledge he possessed. Leo appeared to be a lost soul, suffering deep in the fires of hell. He resided somewhere in his own psyche and I wanted to contact him. I learned that he was a writer, although he had never been published. Leo was sure to be an interesting guy and for three weeks I tried to prod him into conversation without any luck. He would sometimes look in my direction but would not respond. That is, not until we had a serious crisis on the ward!

In a scenario similar to the theatrical production, *One Flew Over The Cuckoo's Nest*, the resident psychiatrist who administered to the patients decided to punish them by locking the ward. This meant no one could leave and visitors were prohibited. Mail call was also suspended. This psychiatrist featured himself as tough guy because he hailed from the neighborhood of Blue Hill Avenue. He was pissed because a small multi-racial group of adolescents, led by a black, mildly retarded, diagnosed character disorder named Aaron, were raising havoc on the ward. They were stealing, lighting fires and intimidating other patients. I don't know what school of psychiatry would recommend closing the ward and punishing everyone, including the nurses and attendants, but that was the course of action the doctor chose. He, of course, did not remain to experience the effects of his treatment.

Once the door was locked the tension set in. Some of the residents were irked because of the trouble this youthful band of marauders had caused; others were increasingly more terrorized. The youths sensed this and grouped together. I knew I had to do something fast to regain my influence on this ward. Up until this point they had confined their disruptive behavior to times when I was not working. I think this was because of two reasons: one, they liked me, and two, they feared me. I deliberately fostered the false rumor that I was a Marine Corps trained karate expert. This fabrication bought me some respect, but that was beginning to crumble and I knew it. Something had to be done and done fast. The other attendant on the ward was a female - good with the talk but not the confrontational type. Nevertheless, I stood up and moved to the center of the room - in the direction where Aaron and his gang were standing.

Character disorders (as they were referred to in those days) were regarded as serious control problems. They presented a greater threat to the tranquility of the ward than did paranoid patients. The way I came to understand it, a character disorder does not act out because of unreasonable and exaggerated fears stemming from a misinterpretation of his environment, as in the case with the paranoid schizophrenic. In fact they are not psychotic at all. Individuals who are classified as psychotic suffer from some sort of reality split; they are simply, from time to time or all of the time, not fully engaged. The character disorder, conversely, violates the social order for different reasons - he is simply evil. Now the clinical world is not into making moral judgments. Rather than relying on such terms as good or evil, the dictates of the profession require the application of medical terminology and clinical explanations for this behavior. Hence, as Doctor Coggan would later instruct, the classical Freudian explanation would suggest that an underdeveloped superego or conscience is at the root of persistent anti-social behavior when other symptoms are lacking.

Coggan further explained that Freud postulated that the human mind/personality is comprised of three elemental forces, the most basic of which is the id. This is the earliest forming division and is comprised of two fundamental instincts that propel the individual towards sex or aggression. It has no sense of right or wrong, good or bad; it simply demands satiation. At some point in the early life of a human being there evolves a superego, part of which contains a code of conduct, a conscience, so to speak, that functions to prescribe behavior and limit the excesses of the id. Perhaps in the clinical sense Aaron could be described as an unregulated id, a psychopath or sociopath. All of this was new to me but it added up to the same thing - This patient was one dangerous son of a bitch! His being retarded further narrowed the region of rational contact.

I moved toward Aaron very slowly, reciting a whole litany of offenses as I made my approach.

"Aaron," I intoned, "I have warned you before. I have given you plenty of breaks. Time after time you have done things wrong, and each time I have forgiven you because you promised not to do them again - like when you left the ward without permission, or when you broke the candy machine downstairs because you lost your money. I didn't even get angry when you went over to Reception Five and gave Minnie a hard time. I told you to leave the student nurses alone, and besides, I liked Minnie and you knew that."

I stopped in the middle of my tracks, and not for one moment taking my eyes away from him, continued my recitation. "How about when you beat up the attendant on the second shift, (I forgot his name) or when you exposed yourself to Miss Ricci?"

Aaron became visibly upset. He glared back at me and began to breathe heavily. He knew that he would have to make a decision soon and I prayed that it would be to back off, even though it would mean defeat in front of his admirers. I resumed my slow progress toward him. (I had no idea how I would get out of this.) I became increasingly more fearful but continued my chanting.

"And now Aaron, you are really screwing up, stealing from other patients, lighting fires, robbing people and worst of all, I understand that you threw Jimmy off the wall, a kid with a broken leg to begin with. I am going to teach you a real lesson Aaron, right in front of all your friends because you're acting so badly."

There was only about four feet separating us now, and Aaron was in a high state of excitation. He inflated his six-foot, two hundred pound physique to its fullest capacity. He raised his arms slightly and nostrils flaring, began to groan amid short gasps of air. His face writhed in fear and a twitch developed underneath his left eye. He looked away from me for an instant, then took one step backwards.

I looked over my right shoulder to glimpse what captured his interest, and there was my ally, Leo Bordier, limping slightly but making his way in my direction. When he reached where I was standing he stopped. Leo was very serious; we both looked serious.

Aaron's friends began to walk away from him. They deserted him and he was frightfully aware of this. The tension lock was broken - Aaron continued his retreat, begging me not to strike him. I demanded that he apologize to each patient and to Miss Ricci, whom he had offended. He happily complied. I was happy, too - happy and relieved. I had called this bully's bluff. Aaron made his way around the ward apologizing to his victims, and to anyone else he encountered. I thanked Leo. On that day my cultural odyssey began.

Two

Chronic depression is a bummer. It darkens the mind and envelops the spirit. It can reduce a human being to his barest essentials. I remember Mr. Kaufman. Once jovial and rotund, I witnessed the dissolution of his body and soul. In a few brief months he lost one hundred and ten pounds. I attended him during this period.

In the beginning he was unhappy, but he managed to carry on conversations and crack a few jokes. The student nurses doted on him; they thought he was lovable. Initially I could not understand why he was admitted to the ward. He was suffering from depression, he said, but he appeared OK to me. He stopped cracking jokes one day and increasingly lost his appetite. The pounds dissolved and his body narrowed - even his head seemed smaller. I fed him small amounts of food until he refused to open his mouth. The day before he was transferred to the medical building to be fed intravenously he weighed in at ninety-seven pounds. I said so long and wished him well as I helped place him in the stretcher. He looked dolefully at me and after not talking for several days remarked, "Look, look at me. I am only a piece of skin and a little bit of hair." Mr. Kaufman died within a week; his heart stopped beating.

Leo began to emerge from his depression on the day that Aaron was diminished. That's the way it goes sometimes. Leo's presence on the ward added to my day. I enjoyed many fruitful conversations with him. As time went on he revealed more of himself to me. He believed that the fast life, attendant with the drugs and booze he consumed, put him in a depression. He added that it also had to do with two failed marriages. I never met Leo's first wife, but his second wife visited him on occasion. (He became noticeably stressed out during these calls). She was a pretty and feminine woman. She got pissed at him at lot and after a while she stopped coming in. There was a lot that Leo could not recall because he was dope and alcohol soaked so much of the time. Those were the days when drug addicts were drug addicts and drunks were drunks; Leo, by his own admission, was both. Uppers, downers, heroin and booze, he rode that roller coaster until it came off the tracks almost killing him. He was sick and depressed many times. Delirium tremors were nothing new to him. He got so bad that he almost died.

Once, while I was in the middle of a conversation with Leo, a forty year old Native American patient (we referred to them as Indians then) got up from his chair, walked to the middle of the floor and began jacking up a delusional car with an imaginary jack. By the time the other attendant could reach him and coax him away from the D.T.'s, he fell over, dead. The strain was too much on his heart. That or something akin could have done in Leo in a similar fashion, but it didn't.

I never read Leo's medical record book. I refused to because he was not just a case history to me. He told me that alcohol and drugs were at the center of his problems and I believed him. He had become a faithful and life-long member of Alcoholics Anonymous, to which he attributed his sobriety. Like I said earlier, I bought this explanation, but I suspected on occasion that his issues were rooted more deeply. I am not suggesting any pathology; I never did believe my friend to be crazy. Leo was an intellectual, similar to Jesser and Paul Memos. Neither of these guys were free from idiosyncratic behavior - most extremely bright people are not, intellectuals included. Leo was also a very serious artist, and in the total sense of the word. The art form for which he became known was writing but his interest and understanding covered the whole panoply of artistic endeavor - music, song, painting and sculpture. Leo was an artist in the fullest and most expansive sense. He viewed the world in painful and delightful ways and gleaned meaning from

15

the simplest sounds and physical arrangements. I believe the combination of these blessings of mind and skill can complicate life, and with booze and drugs, the results intensify.

Leo was a trip; he was my pal and I delighted in the times I spent with him. As he continued to improve our conversations became more frequent. Leo lifted me from the cultural abyss of my earlier conditioning, which had taken place mostly in the city of Somerville near the area of Sullivan Square Station, a large gray elevated train and bus terminal that straddled the borderline of Somerville and Charlestown, an older section of the City of Boston known for its historical treasures, wooden tenement houses and gangs. Somerville was in the record book as the most densely populated living area in the world, exceeding Tokyo, Japan. It managed, at its high point, to jam one hundred and four thousand people into four square miles.

There were a lot of kids around. My neighborhood was basically blue collar/working class. It was comprised mostly of first and second generation Irish and Italians, with the accent on the former. It held on to a strong work ethic, believing that success meant holding down a job, being married and having kids. Most of the people in my neighborhood were renters, but some owned and it was a point of pride when they did. A few of the kids did really well in life; they went on to college and into professional positions. One of them would became a priest, while another one would became known for the single savage act of killing four people in a bowling alley. He tied them up, smashed their heads in with a bowling pin and then, just to make sure they were dead, he shot each one in the skull. Most of the kids fell somewhere between these two extremes. What I can say, with no equivocation, is that the neighborhood males, especially the adolescents, were a lot heavier on the macho than the arts. I liked the tough guy image myself and later joined the Marine Corps to reinforce it. (*Battle Cry* by Leon Uris was the book that did it).

I enjoyed the theater, especially musical productions, and attended a few free college performances when I could, but never would I divulge this to my friends for fear of criticism - except for one friend, my life-long buddy Brian Gill. A tough guy, a 'good guy,' an athlete and scholar, he was unusual - more of him later. The point is this: I had a healthy curiosity concerning the arts, most pointedly good literature, but very few guides. My journey with Leo went beyond conversations on the ward and into some of the finest museums in the City of Boston.

On the grounds of the state hospital we discussed books - books were the love of Leo's life. He referred to the *Iliad* by the Greek poet Homer, which focused on the Trojan War. Leo believed it characterized life in its extremes - life, death, honor and dishonor, all against the background of a long war in which both Gods and men played prominent roles. He was deep into Graeco/Roman mythology and commented on the deities like they were old friends - Zeus, Athena, Jupiter, even Cupid. He was enthralled with William Shakespeare and particularly enjoyed *Hamlet* and *Othello*. He spoke volumes on John Milton's *Paradise Lost* and Miguel DeCervantes' *Don Quixote*. I enjoyed horror and was enchanted by his treatment of *Dracula* by Bram Stoker and Mary Shelley's *Frankenstein*. He loved Emerson and Thoreau and ventured into our times, elaborating on Jack Keroauc, the King of the Beat Generation and one of the great modern day writers. Leo knew Keroauc and recounted many stories of a personal nature with me. He had the same problems Leo had - brilliance, depth, talent, booze, drugs, and an early death.

Our museum visits were confined to my days off. By this time Leo had genuinely perked up and was awarded off-ground privileges. I knew very little about painting and I thought the Museum of Fine Arts would be a great place to begin - and so it was. My friend became completely alive and vibrant. He taught me the major differences among the various forms of art. *Cubism* was the geometrical compression of natural forms - kind of drab; *Expressionism*, an exaggeration of line, colors and shape; and *Impressionism* referred to the way the artist perceived the form and shape. Leo added "These terms could also apply to sculpture"

He seemed somewhat etched in the early Renaissance, and paintings expressing religious and mythological subjects held a certain fascination for him; Leonardo DaVinci, Michelangelo and Brother Van Eyck had been followed by post-Renaissance masters such as Rembrandt, Rubens and Van Dyck. With the passage of another hundred years, it was Chardin in France, and El Greco and Goya in Spain. Leo said that Pablo Picasso was regarded as one of the greatest painters of the twentieth century, a modern artist who largely abandoned the use of colors.

Van Gogh and Gauguin were roommates. Gauguin antagonized Van Gogh, who was a madman. Van Gogh had sliced off a part of his own ear, bandaged his head, and presented the severed portion to a prostitute.

Salvador Dali, another modern painter, had perfected the art form of *Surrealism* "The stuff of the unconscious" Leo said. Dali was influenced by Sigmund Freud's monumental work on the *Interpretation of Dreams*. The artist was able to capture the symbolism of the unconscious on canvas, hence the free-floating body parts and other severed and unrelated objects. His great work on time revealed the process of decay. I knew little about art, but I enjoyed Dali's work, especially the melting watches being devoured by ants. Time changes all things; eventually it results in death, and then another process begins and ends. The human body decays and becomes part of the earth; perhaps it comes back up as a flower. What happens to the life essence, where does it go?

My mind drifted back to the age of twelve. These painful thoughts overwhelmed me as I stood at the foot of my mother's grave. It happened so suddenly! I was totally unprepared. My mother was taken to the hospital for the treatment of pneumonia and pleurisy. That was a mis-diagnosis; she died within days of cancer of the lungs, unusual for a woman who neither drank nor smoked. She attended Mass and received Holy Communion every day of her life. Even more unusual, she left an identical twin sister who has at this time more than doubled the forty-two years my mother had lived. The only thing different about their lives was one single place of employment - the Watertown Arsenal, where my mother worked after my father died. He was twenty-eight when he passed; I was six months old. He died of a kidney ailment called Brights Disease (nobody dies of that anymore). He was a strong and powerful man who lived a clean life, but that's the way it goes. My mother never fully recovered from his death. She had to work and the Arsenal was where she found employment. It was during the Second World War and many thousands of women filled the men's jobs. I suspect that is where it happened, where she ingested increasing amounts of the microscopic killer agents that flew off the metal grinding machine she dutifully operated. I remember thinking she was back with my father whom she loved so much - but she left me.

Her sister took over the job of raising me. She believes to this day that the good Lord substituted me for the son she lost at birth. My Aunt Mary is one of the most remarkable women I have ever known. Full of love and loyalty, she kept the promise she made to my mother on her death bed and did her best to protect me against the excesses and abusive behavior of her husband, who could not understand why he had been saddled with someone else's kid. A good woman - she thought of herself as an underdog, a lot of ideals, a whole bunch of wisdom and one hell of a story teller.

"Hey, Phil, you're in a trance; it's time to go. You must really like Dali."

"Yeah, Leo, I do, but he is real fucking depressing."

I had intended to enter the University of Massachusetts pre-med program at Amherst and eventually to attend medical school, after which I contemplated a psychiatric residency. It would be necessary to work my way through. It was still possible in those days. Maybe it was wishful thinking, considering my problems with math, but I never had a chance to find out. The hospital denied my request to be transferred to Northampton State Hospital, preventing me from being within commuting distance of Amherst. I was bitterly disappointed and thought it odd that I failed to get a transfer to another hospital. It was done all the time and I knew there were jobs open.

Oh well! I would have to decide on something else and that something else became the Law Enforcement Program at Northeastern University's part-time college for adult education. A friend had recommended it to me because at that time it included a number of psychology courses in the curriculum. What a let-down!

I applied for the program, was accepted and submitted another routine request for a night shift job, working from eleven PM to seven AM. That way I would have time to get to early evening class and to work with plenty of time to spare, and I could do my homework on the ward. I was denied again. Miss Ricci recommended against it, and I further suspected it was she who stuck it to me on the Northampton transfer.

I couldn't believe it! I worked so hard for Miss Ricci. The ward was under control and was clean; I assigned the patients tasks; I enjoyed my work and went beyond the call of duty. On my own time I had searched for patients that escaped the hospital and coaxed them back. I even put on a play in the evening involving talented patients. It was a big hit with the doctors and nurses who had attended. Admittedly, the Master of Ceremonies got bummed out and went AWA (absent without authority) from the hospital and never returned and our prime comedienne, diagnosed with manic depressive psychosis, slipped down to the dark end of the spectrum on opening night and never performed.

But, it was also true that Andrianna Tranquillo, a professional opera singer, performed for the first time in years and knocked - them - dead! She sang *Ave Maria* by Schubert. She left the hospital fully recovered from her depression within two weeks after that.

As her official reason for keeping me on Reception Six, Miss Ricci used, 'More Supervision Required.' I was devastated! Miss Ricci could clearly read my pain when I approached her and requested that she explain her reasoning to me. She was unable to, but sometime during this period I figured it out. Miss Ricci wanted to keep me where I was; a transfer to nights meant another building altogether. Now, for the first time, she could leave the ward and not worry, and that's why she did not want me to leave. 'Pop' went Miss Ricci's mystique.

Three

Northeastern University was the first college on the East Coast to establish a college level Law Enforcement program (currently referred to as Criminal Justice). This occurred in 1961. I was scheduled to begin the program in the fall of 1962, and since it was only the beginning of June I still had plenty of time to get on the night shift. I buried my aspiring medical career and gradually became more enthusiastic about 'joining' the police department. I had thought about police work as a kid (what boy hasn't?) but had never given it serious consideration until now. The logical extension of the Law Enforcement program would naturally be some aspect of police science on a municipal, state or federal level. A good place to start would be the local police. Hey! Who knows? I could end up with the FBI or better still the CIA. A check with the Massachusetts Department of Civil Service revealed that I would have to wait until August to apply, so why not enjoy the promise of the coming summer.

At that time I had a girlfriend named Cindy. She was a student nurse at the Boston City Hospital and was doing her brief residency at the Boston State Hospital when I met her. She was assigned to the Reception Building. She volunteered to help me with the theatrical performance. There were several rehearsals and the students assisted me in the beginning. (This, of course, was in the evening time when they were off duty.) Gradually fewer of them showed up and, other than opening night, Cindy was the only one who was still around. I was very appreciative of this - I needed plenty of help.

The next night we went on a date and that got things started. She was comely, slightly short with soft skin and long velvet smooth brown hair that reached to the small of her back when it wasn't tied in a bun underneath her nurse's cap or carried in a ponytail - and a figure that she could not conceal - it was busting out all over. Cindy was the quietest person I had ever met. Even when she walked or moved she made little impact on her physical environment. She was exceedingly modest and appeared to lack any real need to project herself.

I was as garrulous as Cindy was quiet; some thought it a perfect match. Perhaps our personalities intersected at the appropriate points, but our aspirations did not. I was not ready for a committed relationship - apparently Cindy was. One night, just before dropping Cindy off at the nurses' residence on Mass. Avenue (she was finished with her residency and had returned to Boston City Hospital), I casually brought up the subject. I sensed that she wished to know my intentions. I was honest - very honest - believing, as young men often do, that truthfulness absolves them from insensitivity. I laid the whole thing out - lack of a fixed career, no dough, too young, and so on and so on.

We exited the car and walked to the front of the dormitory. I could see Cindy's face clearly in the lighted doorway - her eyes were moist. I kissed her lightly on the lips. She whispered, "Good Night," and that was the last time she ever spoke to me. She avoided me at every turn and refused to speak with me on the phone. One day I sat in my car at the front door of the nurses' residence knowing fully well that she returned there after her classes were over at 5:00 PM. After waiting about two hours, one of her friends informed me that Cindy had used an underground tunnel to reach the dorm.

I attended her graduation one year later - surely she would speak to me there. All I wished to do was apologize and bring this relationship to official closure. Her mother was the only other person present to see her graduate to RN status. I was with a big heavyset guy named Charlie Burleigh. Cindy saw me in the crowd and after the ceremony began to quietly approach me. I made the mistake of sharing my excitement with Charlie, explaining to him that Cindy apparently intended to speak with me after more than a year of avoidance. Charlie, in a gust of bravado, thought this was amusing and in a full and resonant voice commented, "So she hasn't spoken to you in a year, huh?"

Cindy heard this and turned abruptly in the opposite direction and disappeared somewhere with her mother. That was it; she was serious. I saw her one time after that and blew that too - but that was a couple of years down the road. Cindy was a nice girl. I will always remember her sitting so demurely in her nurse's uniform with her hands clasped over her knees giving Andrianna the quiet assurance she needed to stand up on that stage and permit her song to push away the darkness.

The way I figured it, the best way to avoid romantic entanglements in the future was a combination of up front honesty and willingness to discontinue dating once the student nurse returned to her respective hospital following completion of the residency requirement. The students came largely from three hospitals for psychiatric training: Boston City, St. Elizabeth's in Brighton, and St. Luke's in New Bedford. About ninety student nurses were merged in one class and domiciled for three months in the Nurses' Residence, located diagonally across from the male employees' home.

There were three major categories of male employee residents - students, homosexuals and drunks. From a strictly supply/demand dating model, straight non-alcoholic males enjoyed an advantage - willing and datable men were in short supply. This was a benefit I intended to enjoy, but I would definitely keep things light. There was a two week transitional period in the beginning when the girls could not be approached; they were too dammed scared. Most of these kids were the products of 1950's type homes - stable, enduring and protective, and all of a sudden they found themselves catapulted into the middle of madness.

There were about twenty-five hundred psyche patients residing at the hospital and many of them, especially the chronically ill, enjoyed ground privileges. On a warm summer day it seemed like most of them were outside. Some of them hallucinated, while others sat or stood in fixed positions gazing outward. They muttered, pointed and sometimes shouted or threatened the students. None of this made for a secure environment. The male employees, mostly college students, knew this and simply waited for the right approach time. (I know this sounds predatory but it's true.) The signal for this was at that precise point when the students began to walk to the cafeteria in small groups of two and three instead of clusters of ten and twenty. This meant they were settling in. Now the very same factors that raised their anxiety level produced the opposite effect; it lowered their resistance to male attention. Add this to the mix: they were away from home, away from the watchful eyes of their respective housemothers, and in some instances, their boyfriends. They were ready, and the dating began. There was a pregnancy on occasion, sometimes a marriage, a few broken hearts perhaps, but most of the time it was just - touch and go - the dance of the generations.

Summer unfolded across the acreage of the Boston State. The earth's spring had gradually pushed away the winter and the canvas of barren gray ground was replaced with a blanket of green. The periphery of the property became awash in the colors of wild flowers in full bloom. It also became witness to occasional acts of lovemaking among patients. This was a difficult problem to control and invariably produced a number of pregnancies by the time fall arrived. The hospital kept this quiet; the perspective mother would be transferred to some other institution and whatever happened, happened. I never knew.

New England is the place where summer happens best, and it had been five years since I had experienced it in its entirety, and as a free agent to boot. My obligations were minimal and my future was bright. It was a time to enjoy and a time to plan. My only major possession was a 1960 English Ford Consul that I purchased in 1962 for fourteen hundred dollars. It had only sixty-five hundred miles on it. It was a good deal, even then, in spite of its flamingo pink color. This was my first car and I was very fond of it; it had an almost human persona. Once or twice a week I would visit my aunt and her daughter, my cousin, (whom I have always regarded as my sister) in Somerville, and on occasion would drive to Cape Cod. More often than not, it was a dating vehicle and provided me an inexpensive access to Blue Hills Reservation, or some similar forested area where my date and I could hike, swim or make out. All I needed for props was a six-pack of Bud and a blanket. I mostly dated student nurses and assiduously avoided any serious involvement. Admittedly, I took advantage of the numbers situation and indulged in a party that seemed to never end. I rationalized this by recalling the long dry periods I had suffered in the Marines. Irresponsible perhaps, but I was making up for lost time and having an immense amount of fun doing it!

My network of co-workers continued to expand. There were a whole lot of characters working at the State Hospital, and most of them resided at the Male Home. There was Wilbur Beer, an intense red-headed Bible preaching Protestant fundamentalist, who appeared compelled at every encounter to spread what he sincerely believed to be the word of God. If he failed to communicate in person for any period he would place literature under his target's door. He never seemed very happy to me; it was as though he was acting out of some compulsion or rigidity of thought. I think most people who are convinced that they enjoy a monopoly on the truth share this characteristic. The senior elder, Father Sweeney, also dispensed advice to anyone who would listen. He advised me to save all my pay stubs from the Boston State and the Police Department, to justify any purchases that I might make in the future. (I saw this for what it was, camouflage for his belief that all cops were corrupt).

Then there were the brothers Joyce. John was a natural born businessman and eventually became a real estate developer. His brother Paul was awarded a minor judgeship. Mike Weinberg was a whimsical and gentle person who saw decency and goodness everywhere. Mike held the Junior Olympics world record for barrel jumping. He was also the first guy I ever knew who owned a Volkswagen Bug.

Not to forget Ben Cohen, the plump State Hospital Rabbi, who talked a lot about Martin Buber and his treatise of *I and Thou*. Ben was fired because he lacked the proper credentials, but in spite of this he was a pretty decent guy. Then there was Stephen Rosseta, a handsome Italian guy who went on to establish a chain of restaurants, and his friend, the likable Mike Mitropoulos, a weight lifter who was destined to live only a few more years. He died from cancer.

On the slick end of the scale, there was a group of very bright college students, some of whom went to jail for their part in a national larceny of motor vehicles scheme that centered on the theft of Volkswagens. They would decide on a vehicle, remove the ignition and insert their own device, drive the vehicle to another state, advertise it real cheap and sell it to the first person who came up with the cash.

One day the Feds were all over the property. They moved in quietly - no guns showing - but they made their presence known. Two of the suspect night attendants were pulled out of bed while others were summoned from the wards where they were assigned. In all, five guys were placed in custody and an outstanding warrant remained in effect for one other. The agents returned the following day to serve it. It was rumored, and later verified, that an undercover FBI agent had been working as an attendant nurse for several months and was involved with this investigation.

Jail time was in order and several potentially successful professional careers were cut short. One of the attendants was two months away from completing his first year at Harvard Medical School. They were smart asses who had ended up outsmarting themselves. (I wondered if the undercover agent was paid for both jobs.) This gave everyone something to talk about. Summer had arrived and many of the conversants moved to the benches in front of the Male Home - and the beat went on.

In August 1962 I filled out an eleven page application and questionnaire for the position of Boston Police Patrolman. I also attended a one month accelerated course on the content of the police exam (The Blue Book, a 194 page compendium of criminal law, police rules and regulations, and first aid procedures) at Donahue's Civil Service School on Boylston Street near downtown Boston. This involved a two-hour class, three nights a week. I had taken my first steps; now I simply would have to wait for the exam. I was on an inexorable path now and I knew it. I intended to do my level best to get on the police department, and the more I thought about it, the more enthused I became. The classroom was packed with similar aspirants and the lectures were delivered in a humdrum monotone. I was struck by the level of intensity with which a few of the students wished to become cops. It had been a lifetime, all-consuming drive for some of them. I have always been leery of people who are so singularly possessed. Cops are the most manifest symbols of power in our society. Was that the attraction? On the other hand, most of the guys I met in the classroom were just looking for a steady job with a pension.

I re-submitted my request for a transfer to the night shift. I sensed that Miss Ricci felt guilty about having blocked it in the first place. I was confident that it would be approved. I had some reservations about working in the 'back wards' as we referred to them. It was very different from the environment in the Admissions Building. The back ward buildings contained chronically ill patients who, for the most part, were beyond cure. There was a sense of hopelessness that prevailed in these wards. Many of the patients had been there for years and were totally resigned to their condition - this was their home. Their insanity had taken hold and worked its gruesome affect - their minds, spirit, and often times their bodies were permanently disfigured. Their general appearance declined and many of them had no wish to leave the ward. There was more predictability, less violence, reduced anxiety and a general lessening of pain. I believe that madness eventually rigidifies the mind and acts as its own balm.

Some of the patients suffered from catalepsy, a condition in which muscles become waxy stiff and leave limbs in the last position they are placed. Others were catatonic, another form of schizophrenia that drives the victim between stages of stupor and impulsiveness. They may sit perfectly quietly for months and then suddenly erupt into a long and repetitive tirade of verbal anger and aggression against some person, object or even body part.

Hallucinations, both auditory and visual, happened more frequently and Petit Mal seizures, a common occurrence in the Reception Building, became Grand Mal seizures (lasting over a minute) in the chronic wards. There were individuals who seized successively for hours, requiring the use of restraints. Electroshock therapy, in which patients were rendered unconscious after being jolted with fifty to ninety volts for one-tenth to two tenths of a second, would not be required here. Psychosis was permanent and irreversible. There was more pacing, staring, and vacant expression. The elemental life force that accounts for human differences, the personality, becomes diminished in this setting and eventually lost.

The time came. Miss Ricci informed me that my request for the night shift had been approved; I was to be reassigned September 5 to the H Building on nights, the eleven to seven shift. By some marvelous transformation I no longer required 'more supervision.' I knew that I would miss the ping-pong games and certain of the patients, especially Leo, but I wouldn't have to roll cigarettes for the patients anymore.

Four

people are, at the least, implicitly conscious of the passage of time. It is the curse of the Homosapien. Whole industries have developed around the effects of time on physical appearance, vitality and perception. I have always been conscious of even the most minuscule changes. Throughout my adolescence and early adult years I experienced a recurring dream that played out the ebb and flow of an endless summer evening. The content and the characters changed but the rhythm seemed infinite. Perhaps this was my mind's effort to isolate the joy and peace offered by a warm New England night. The earth was comfortable and the night was free of the day's tensions. These are times to savor and remember, and that is how I shall always recall the summer of '62.

I finished my last day on Reception Six. I said good-bye to Miss Ricci, the other ward personnel and the patients. I was surprised when the patients held a party for me. They generally did this only for student nurses. I was pleased with their gesture. I freely commented on my trepidation about leaving. For the most part I enjoyed the patients, and Leo and I had become good friends. I would miss our daily discussions. I was puzzled as to why Leo had remained a patient and had not been discharged. He was already well in excess of the ninety day limit for remaining in the Reception Building. After that, it meant either discharge or reassignment to a chronic ward. I encouraged Leo to seek state psychiatric evaluation and release.

I had two days off and I intended to enjoy them. I rose early in the AM and hiked the Ponkapoag trail alone. I enjoyed the quietude of the forest. Later that night I drove to Houghton's Pond, a part of the same reservation, with an auburn headed student nurse with long hemp-like hair twisted into a long braid who, initially, struck me as entirely rational. However, once she became aware that I had no intention of engaging her on an intellectual level, she completely flipped out. She lamented that men were more interested in her body than in her mind. She threw open the passenger door and ran about sixty feet to the pond's edge and threw herself into the water in an apparent suicidal frenzy, not once but three times. I rescued her each time. I began to think that I was immersed in some variation of water therapy, but this was not a patient. Once I was finally able to calm her, I coaxed her back to the car. I drove back to the nurses' residence and escorted her to the door. Standing at the threshold, she wrapped her arms around my waist and pulled me forward. Her short pants and halter were still wet. She pushed her firm body tightly against mine. She kissed me hungrily on the lips (a full sloppy one) and, not allowing me much wiggle room, asked when I would be seeing her again. I smiled and promised that I would call, as soon as I got off the night shift.

I learned that I was assigned to the H Building. It was situated nearer the Male Home and the cafeteria than the Reception Building, so it would be a quick walk to eat. (All employee meals were priced at thirty cents). It was a better draw than the I Building because there, many of the patients had a Zombie-like appearance.

I reported for work a half-hour early on my first night. (I never repeated that mistake again!) Whatever apprehension I was feeling at the time was quickly dissolved once I encountered the warm smile of Mrs. Marion Delaney, the RN in charge of the night shift. Her uniform was clean and crisp and her shoes were spotlessly white. Mrs. Delaney was heading toward sixty. She was tall and buxom. She was quick-witted and amazingly fast on her feet. I liked her immediately - Mrs. Delaney had charisma.

Mrs. Delaney informed me that I would be assigned to H-2, which was referred to as the 'Senile Ward.' It was comprised of about forty-five patients, most of whom were serving out the final wretched episode of their lives. Most of the patients were old and were suffering from "advanced stages of senility," she commented, and a few younger patients, between forty-five and fifty, were affected by "pre-senile psychosis." In any event, she remarked, "The end result is the same - they all require custodial care." She further explained that my basic functions would be to watch over them at night while they slept; check during the middle of the shift to see if anyone had died or messed their bed, and to get them up in the morning and sit them in chairs that were placed rectangularly around the ward. She sensed my disappointment with this assignment and promised that I would eventually be reassigned to an upstairs ward (probably just a little better). Mrs. Delaney was fair and took seniority into consideration. The last one assigned to the building won H-2, and then the attendant with the most time on H-2 was moved upstairs.

She escorted me to the ward and introduced me to Kevin Murphy, who would later become the Charge Attendant. The first olfactory sensation I experienced was the losing battle of stale disinfectant as it was overcome by the multiple odors of feces, urine and vomit. I had passed through this ward a couple of times when I worked days. I knew the depressing truth - it was a warehouse of 'fleshpots' that remained in position until death (or so I thought). This sucked, plain and simple. I shook Kevin's hand and thanked Mrs. Delaney for the time she had taken with me. She smiled and returned to the front office.

Kevin looked at me and smiled knowingly. He assured me that once I was there for awhile I would feel differently. I must have looked like I was ready to puke. Kevin was reassuring. I would learn later that was only one of his qualities. Kevin's medium build and soft blue eyes belied a keen intelligence and vibrant spirit. Kevin was a Northeastern University History Major. His ultimate goal was Law School, (he would serve as a Commissioned Officer in the Army first) but now he was simply an attendant, a slightly amused one perhaps. The mid-shift point arrived and Kevin and I moved around the sleeping ward. Whenever we discovered a wet patient, we changed both the patient and the sheets. Kevin insisted on performing this duty. I was not so sure that it was a good idea to wake the patient. I mean, what did the patient know of his condition - was it not better that he remain sleeping?

Kevin thought not! This Irishman was a conduit for human dignity, a bit obsessive perhaps, but thoroughly conscientious and reliable.

The next night, I met Ed Jesser for the first time. He was also assigned to H-2. Let's put it this way - he was a contrast to Kevin. Anyway, we finished out the night and when morning came we lifted the patients out of bed and placed them on their respective chairs. Most of them hardly acknowledged us. I never did eat breakfast that morning.

Ed Jesser arrived on his gray Vespa motor scooter the following evening. He parked it under a tree and made his entrance into the building. I was standing at the front door with Mrs. Delaney discussing building security during the change of shifts. Patients sometimes took advantage of the confusion generated during these periods to escape. He was late; he flashed a mischievous look at Mrs. Delaney. I could feel her warm almost immediately - she loved Jesser. I was to learn later that he reminded her of her youngest son, Francis. She introduced us. He shook my hand, made a disparaging remark about the Marine Corps, and joined Kevin on the ward. He was carrying a copy of *The Catcher in the Rye* by J.D. Salinger, a book that shaped much of the early thinking of the Sixties and Seventies. I vaguely recall seeing Jesser around the campus - but how did he know that I had been in the 'crotch'?

I joined them both a few minutes later. We would be the three attendants assigned to H-2. Each of us enjoyed different nights off. As a result, there would be only certain evenings that we all worked together and on some of those evenings it would be necessary for one of us to fill in on an upstairs ward to cover shortages.

The state hospital was permanently understaffed. Wards that theoretically required the assignment of three attendants on the night shift were routinely covered by one person. It became obvious to me that Jesser was selected more so than Kevin or me to cover these shortages. I found out that he had complained to Mrs. Delaney that he was allergic to the smell of urine. Everyone knew this was a preposterous lie, but it worked. Eventually he stopped pursuing this line. He explained that this was due to the much cleaner environment that H-2 had become over time. However, I think it had to do with the fact that he had to stay awake when he was alone on the upstairs wards. An attendant on the night shift who had fallen asleep in the Reception Building paid for this lapse with his life - a patient bashed his head in with a fire extinguisher. Jesser thought the first rule of the night shift was to cop as many zzzzs as possible, but he did not wish to have his hair parted in a similar fashion. Admittedly, the ward did get much cleaner. Mrs. Delaney insisted that the ward personnel assigned to days do their job and bring the ward up to standards. This, in addition to some new and more conscientious employees assigned to the day shift, resulted in H-2 becoming a far more pleasant place to work. Perhaps the truth was somewhere in the middle, but make no mistake about it - Ed Jesser was physically lazy.

One morning, as we were lifting a patient out of bed, he felt heavier than usual - his head fell over and his body was limp. His vital signs were absent. He was very, very, dead! This, of course, would occur on occasion and procedure required that the respective shift attendant clean and wash the body, place it in a body bag and deliver the corpse to the morgue. It was an unpleasant task but it had to be done. This man had been nasty in life, and in death he seeped from every body orifice. Compounding the problem, this had to be accomplished on our own time as we had discovered the body during the change of shift.

Let me tell you, Jesser panicked at the thought. He had no wish to be involved with this sickening process. He implored me to pretend that the patient was alive and to prop him up on a chair just like the others. "Let the day shift make the discovery," he demanded. I resisted this dereliction of duty and argued that the day personnel would know of this sham because once they tended to the patient his body would be cold.

"Not so!" Jesser argued. He then suggested that we prop the guy up next to the radiator and he would remain warm long enough for us to get relieved. We, of course, performed our responsibility and followed proper procedure, with Jesser verbally abusing me throughout. I got stuck with the paperwork. Conversely, given the same set of circumstances, Kevin would have given the guy a manicure. That was part of what made them different - one moved toward pleasure, the other absorbed pain. That was my first impression. Maturity slowly erodes the impulsive perceptions of young minds - but at the time I was comfortable with that notion.

I attended my first class at Northeastern University on Monday of the second week in September. I was uptight and had no idea of what to expect. I paid a visit to the Director of the Law Enforcement Program, Robert Sheehan, and his assistant Tim Moran, that morning. Believe it or not I was having second thoughts about the whole idea of a police career because I was concerned about the extent of corruption on the police department.

Any kid from the city knew the score - there was a lot of crap that went on with the cops. There was influence, money and politics: the whole shitten bit. Would I be compromised? That is what I needed to know. Clearly, I would be an unwilling participant. If there were some corruption built into the system, that would be one thing. I could reluctantly accept that condition as long as it didn't touch me. I was no goody-two-shoes. I knew a lot of racket guys and never held them in low esteem. At one point I had even considered booking numbers before I got into the service. I never did, but I had thought about it.

I had hung around a diner when I was growing up and the only adult I ever saw throwing money around was Henry the bookie. He was loaded. In fact, I had loan-sharked for about six months when I was in the military - you know, five for eight, ten for sixteen, etc. I stopped because I didn't like having to remain on the base on pay days to collect my money. There is nothing for nothing.

BUT THIS IS THE POINT. I WAS NOT OPTING TO BE A RACKET GUY. IF I WERE, I WOULD HAVE BEEN A GOOD ONE. I WISHED TO BECOME A COP, BUT I HAD NO INTENTION OF BECOMING A HYPOCRITE. COPS ARE COPS, AND CROOKS ARE CROOKS, AND I HAD NO DESIRE TO BLUR THE DISTINCTION.

I think that they were struck by the directness and poignancy of my question. Perhaps they were also amused. Corruption was not something that was mired in concrete; it could not be described in such an absolute manner as the question posed. In any event, both men made an honest attempt to answer the question, although neither one of them had ever had experience as a local police officer and I saw this as a limitation. Tim Moran was a former Massachusetts State Police Captain but that didn't qualify him as an expert.

I left with the impression that, to the extent that there was a corruption problem, programs like this one at Northeastern might be part of the solution. I felt pretty sprightly when I walked out of the office. I spent a good part of the day walking around campus and examining the buildings that made up this large urban university of students. I sat in the quadrangle for an hour, bought a light meal in the cafeteria and set out for my first class - English One, located in Hayden Hall.

I was registered for five courses - one class every night for each semester. At a cost of twenty-two dollars a semester credit that would add up to a total cost of eight hundred and eighty dollars for the year, not including books and fees. I had over two thousand dollars remaining from the thirty-five hundred I had managed to save in the Service (which, by the way, was exactly half of the seven thousand dollars in military pay that I had cleared during my four year hitch). I was all set.

It didn't take long before I developed a routine. Classes were either at six or eight PM. In either case I attended class and had plenty of time to report to work. As time went on I piggy-backed courses, doubling up on certain evenings, but that didn't present a problem either. Eventually I was to agree with another attendant to take turns driving Mrs. Hambleton, an elderly LPN assigned to H-3 (the female senile ward) back and forth to work. I earned five bucks for this. He soon tired of it and I assumed the job full-time for ten bucks, which paid for my gas. The down side of it was my having to take the same days off as her. Mondays and Tuesdays.

Actually I became quite fond of Mrs. Hambleton. Upon first meeting her, she struck me as a bossy, nasty old woman. As I grew to know her better it was evident that she was quite kind. She was an aging Canadian immigrant, seriously over-weight and suffering with a pair of deteriorating arthritic legs.

On Saturday mornings she would invite me to her second floor apartment on East Fourth Street in Southie and hobble around the kitchen to prepare me a full breakfast of coffee, bacon, eggs and thick Kasanov's Rye toast. She related endless stories of her deceased husband. I thought she must have loved him very much. She also told me about her son, and her daughter who was a practicing physician. Sometimes they would visit her, but because of their busy professional lives were unable to remain for long. I would sadly learn from her only friend that Mrs. Hambleton had never married and her children were born of fantasy. Lonely people sometimes go to great lengths to fill the void. I nevertheless enjoyed her tales.

I also enjoyed the political conversations that took place between my work mates - Kevin Murphy and Ed Jesser. Any night we were working together I waited eagerly for them to begin. Kevin argued classical liberal positions on various issues, and Ed countered with what he described as enlightened conservative responses. As one, then the other, would take the lead, I embarked on a political odyssey on the wings of these two birds - though they agreed on almost nothing, they transported me to the heights! They flew, then surged, then glided through the whole panorama of the human story. They passed through many phases of history, sometimes landing in ancient times.

I was surprised to learn that Socrates, a great philosopher and teacher, had never written a book. If it were not for Plato, a faithful disciple, history would not recall the *Socratic Method*, or the *Dialectic*, as Kevin referred to it. Socrates sought wisdom by walking around Athens asking questions, and for this he was executed. His detractors charged that he was corrupting youth (a familiar ring?).

Aristotle, when he was not collecting seashells, had fashioned the *Peripatetic System*. He lectured as he walked back and forth. He was 'beat'.

The Middle Ages witnessed St. Augustine developing the underlying *Doctrine of Christianity*. Voltaire regarded much of it as simple superstition that hampered human reasoning. John Locke could be thought of as the first liberal for his refutation of the *English Doctrine of Divine Right*. This avowed disapproval of absolute power being handed down through a majestic line heralded the beginning of a reform effort that would be further nourished by Rousseau, who was born in the decade following Locke's death, John Stuart Mill in the nineteenth century, and John Dewey in the twentieth.

Ed Jesser argued that it was present day conservatives who guarded the product of democracy's long growth, but Kevin Murphy maintained that it was the liberals. They seemed to only agree to disagree. I was puzzled as to how two well-read and very bright people could arrive at opposite poles on almost every major political issue. For example, each one of them strongly proclaimed his support for individual freedom, but for Ed that translated to economic freedom, or the right of the individual to pursue his personal financial interests. Kevin conversely regarded freedom as protection against arbitrary government, especially those rights included in the first ten amendments to the U.S. Constitution. Once I had read the two books they had referred me to, the first entitled *Conservatism* and the second *Liberalism*, it all started to jell. A lot of things were starting to jell. Northeastern too, was working its effect and I was enamored of the educational experience.

I was particularly amused by Ed Jesser. I had the sense that he modeled himself after Bill Buckley of the *National Review Magazine*, the voice of enlightened conservatism.

One night, just before dawn, I discovered that a baby squirrel had fallen through the open bars that covered the windows in a patient's room. The patient's name was Mike and he was not aware of this intrusion. I managed to capture the squirrel with a sheet that I flung over him as he attempted to scamper away. I decided to keep the animal as a pet, and as luck would have it, I found a suitable cage that an attendant in the Male Home was discarding. Thus began a peculiar relationship between a man and a squirrel. Mike Weinberg, another male attendant who was living in the Male Home at the time, was captivated by the squirrel and paid him a lot of attention. I named the squirrel Mike for this reason, and also because of the patient Mike, whose room he had invaded.

I took Mike with me wherever I went. I kept him on a leash and he became quite comfortable with me. He often slept in my left breast pocket. It was a sight to see; his tail hanging limply outside my shirt. When he grew larger I placed him in a small harness made for a Chihuahua and with the leash attached walked him down the middle of Blue Hill Avenue, a large boulevard that stretched from Mattapan to Roxbury. Cars would stop all over the avenue and the occupants, mostly young women, would dart out to get a closer look at Mike. Not a bad gimmick to meet chicks! He got me in trouble once. Here's how it happened.

Jesser had a girlfriend named Judy Delaney. She was tall, slender, and very bright. She was a St. Elizabeth nursing student, a senior who possessed the highest academic average in the class. I liked Dell. She was quiet, pretty and her eyes had that slight backward slant, sort of like Miss Ricci's. She had completed her residency but was continuing in her relationship with

Ed. He asked me if I would like to go out on a blind date. It was during the two week freeze period when the new class was 'settling in' and I was not currently dating a student. However, by this time I had branched out and was dating other girls beyond the environs of the institution - an RN at the Parker Hill Medical Center; a hair dresser from Blue Hill Avenue and when I felt like traveling, a petite little doll named Shelly from Milford, Connecticut whom I had met while in the service. In retrospect, if Jesser's hero was Bill Buckley, then mine was Dion's *Wanderer*.

In any event, I had no wish to go out on a blind date. Besides, I was leery as to who may show up. Ed was insistent. He assured me that I would not be disappointed, but I continued to refuse his offer. Finally he overcame my objection by allowing me to select any girl in the St. Elizabeth's class. He promised, just short of a personal guarantee, that Dell could deliver just about anyone I wished. Her top scholastic senior status carried with it prestige and influence with underclassmen. I ACCEPTED HIS CHALLENGE.

I specified the nurse I wished to date - she was short, cute, Italian and she came from Rutland, Vermont. Two days later he smugly confirmed her acceptance. I remained skeptical and wished to have more assurance. He excoriated me for my failure to comprehend the enormous odds against the likelihood of there being two cute little Italian girls from St. E's, in the same class, and both from Vermont. Ed Jesser learned a big lesson in the inviolate law of probability two nights later when Dell descended the front stairs of the nursing home with the 'other' cute little Italian student nurse from Rutland, Vermont.

There were two of them all right, and I had drawn the wrong one. I was stunned and she was clearly disappointed. The deteriorating situation was further exacerbated when Fran quickly seated herself in the front seat of the car and unknowingly tripped the leash to which Mike was attached, causing him to scamper out from underneath the front seat. He chose to run straight up Fran's left leg. I responded quickly, gingerly removing him from the nylon mesh to which he was clinging, but it was too late.

Fran was struck speechless. Her vocal cords were paralyzed with fear. She remained transfixed in a morbid state of silence for what seemed like an endless amount of time, but in actuality was more than likely two minutes. I profusely apologized, stumbling over my words to the point of incoherence. No explanation would suffice - her fear was gradually replaced with a stony silence. We, or I, or some combination of us, had permitted a rodent to run up her leg, and that was unforgivable. The evening was a BOMB! In the end I wished her a good night. She returned a venomous glance and walked in the front door of the nurses' home. About a week later I learned that I would have had a better shot with the 'other' cute little Italian girl from Vermont. Jesser never commented much about this episode.

On a pleasant Saturday afternoon, sometime toward the beginning of fall, I undertook the statewide Police Patrolman's Examination. It seemed like every classroom at Boston Latin High School was filled with faceless, nameless men, serious in their intent to score sufficiently well on the exam to get a job. Once the test was graded the candidate would be notified by mail of his score. Having passed, he would await the remaining portions of the entrance requirements - namely the strength test and physical. Once all parts were successfully completed the applicant would be placed numerically on a list according to his score (after adjusting for veteran status). Then the wait to be called would begin. The acquisition of a job depended on how many (if any) candidates were called and the assigned position of the individual on the list. It was simple enough in those days. The exam did not seem that difficult. It was based mostly on the Blue Book, which I had just about committed to memory. It was three hours in length. The most difficult part was the memory portion that challenged the testee to recall definitive intricacies and objects contained in a photograph displayed for a short period of time and then removed. I utilized the full three hours and left feeling reasonably confident that my studying had paid off. I would wait for the results.

Autumn blended into winter - I was so busy with school and adjusting to the night shift that I was hardly aware. After a period I conditioned myself to sleep well enough during the daytime to feel sufficiently refreshed. Just before turning in I would pull down the dark green shade over my window. I had pasted, on the inside flat portion, a fluorescent moon and star system whose glow obviated the conscious provoking effects of sunlight. I got the idea from reading a small article in the science section of the newspaper.

One afternoon, after awakening, I noticed that an official looking letter had been placed under my door. It was from the Massachusetts Civil Service Commission. I knew instantly that it contained the results of the Police Exam. I exerted my consciousness to its fullest state of alert and nervously opened the rear flap of the brown envelope. There it was - my score! I was delighted to learn that I achieved a 92.47 on the exam.

The following afternoon I visited the State House to view my examination responses. This right was offered to applicants for the purpose of possible appeal. The matronly looking, silver-haired clerk behind the reception desk commented to me that she had viewed all the grades and that it was her unofficial belief that I had achieved the highest score. I obtained a 98% on the objective portion of the exam. When combined with an experience mark, which measured experience in the police field, it fell to the ninety-second percentile. I felt jubilant! I passed the first big hurdle with flying colors. I thanked the clerk. I learned that her name was Eileen. I had a vague sense that she was proud of me, though I had never met her before. It was a strange feeling. I left from the rear of the State House and walked around the corner to Beacon Street. I descended the stone stairs into the Boston Common and rested on one of its green benches. It was cold but I hardly noticed it.

Five

1963 arrived and I was in good form. I ended the first semester with a 3.2 academic average. I became increasingly enmeshed in an advancing philosophy of police science that strove toward professionalism. Among its tenets were the eventual establishment of minimal educational requirements for entry onto the police department - first, an associate's degree, and later a baccalaureate. In five or ten years the police service would be transformed. This pioneering belief energized me and colored my existence. The seed was growing and soon its product would spread across the social spectrum. *Educated police officers*, hard hitting and articulate, that was the way the whole thing was heading. Jesser was astonished by all of this. He said he never heard of anyone going to college to become a fucking cop. But Jesser dreamed too - he dreamed of politics.

The Male Home continued to resonate with lively discourse - it was a free place, uncluttered by the real world's petty distractions. The cold winter ushered in the outside conversants and a couple of entrepreneurial patients set up a bacon and egg shop on the lower floor. It doubled as a kind of social center for male employees and selected patients to engage in endless chatter. I was able to resume my relationship with Leo and to involve him with some of my other friends, such as Paul Memos and Mike Weinberg. Imagine!

A 1960's type coffee shop, here, right here, at 591 Morton Street - in the middle of madness.

Speaking of food, by this time I had began to tire of straight cafeteria meals. It began to taste all the same. The price was right, but I needed some variation. I found what I was looking for and a whole lot more in the G & G Delicatessen on Blue Hill Avenue in the Mattapan section of Boston. It was located obliquely across from Johnston Road - a hop, skip and a jump from the front gate of the institution. It had a good selection of everything and my favorite dish was knockwurst and beans. The eatery was a legend in its own time. It sat in the middle of the largest Jewish neighborhood in the city. It was a working class ethnic enclave and served as positive proof that the stereotype of all Jews being rich was a false notion. The neighborhood was comprised of mostly two and three family houses with a number of one family houses closer to the Milton line. Although the Jewish migration was in the beginning phase of its southern expansion into Milton, Randolph, Canton, and Sharon, this area still remained a center of Jewish life.

The delicatessen itself remained open from early morning until late at night. It served as a meeting house for friends, family and neighbors. It was crammed full of characters, including an old woman who functioned as a matchmaker. She got a rundown on me right away - and it didn't discourage her from asking questions, even when I told her I was a Gentile of the Italian/Catholic variety. It was a place to kibitz and hang around. It was not necessary to purchase food but almost everyone did. The food was good, and inexpensive too. The G & G stood as a political symbol not only in the city but also in the nation.

Each election year it served as a stop for politicians at every level of government, including the Presidency itself. The hopefuls would stand on a large wooden platform erected near the front entrance and deliver their promises. JFK made a speech there in 1956. I later met Ted Kennedy on Blue Hill Avenue during one of these events. He was running for his first term in the U.S. Senate. I shook his hand; it was spongy-like. I looked at him very directly and commented that I could not in good conscience support him because, judging from his hand, he apparently never did a day's work in his life. His brother John had impressed me, but not him.

That is the way I was in those days, truthful to the point of pain. It would be only a short time later that I would remark to Shelby Scott, the first Boston based female news person that, while I liked her personally, I was having a problem adjusting to the elevated sound of the female broadcasting voice. Years later I would learn to enjoy the softer and more melodic sound of women over men - and Shelby was the Dean of broadcasting women. I was wrong about her anyway, but getting back to the G & G, it added infinitely to the life of the neighborhood and provided me with another recreational outlet.

Vinny Lopez was a big part of the neighborhood mix. A good looking, huskily built black cop, he exuded pride in what he did, and if he was a residuary of the declining practice of restricting 'colored' cops to walking beats, he masked it well. He never displayed any outward signs of animosity. He was resplendent in uniform and serious about his job. He worked nights and I would often run into him on the Avenue in the early evening. I respected Vinny and hinged on everything he said. I would continuously assail him with the same question.

"Vinny, have you heard anything about a list being established?"

"No, not yet, kid," and then we would branch off into conversation.

Once he elaborated on his police philosophy. I could sense he was feeling at the top of his game that evening. He pointed out the parameters of his walking beat on Blue Hill Avenue, citing the approximate number of businesses and people within its environs. He clearly understood the responsibility of his role and felt personally responsible for the safety of the neighborhood. "That is why you have to be out there," he would say, "because police visibility deters crime." He was clearly affronted by any assault against his protectorate.

Vinny was a good patrolman all right, like Officer Phillips was back in the East Somerville neighborhood where I grew up. George Phillips was a tall handsome man with a stately appearance. His premature gray hair lent dignity to his imposing figure. His beat was in and around the Sullivan Square end of Broadway. He could be seen everywhere - patrolling the neighborhood, talking to people, in and out of stores, getting kids and the elderly across the street, even tending to injured and frightened animals. It was rumored he was offered a detective's job but refused. He preferred the outside, he often said; it kept him healthy. It kept the neighborhood healthy too. I was not aware of it at the time but these effusive principles of personal presence and involvement, enunciated and demonstrated so well by these ordinary police officers, would provide the foci of professional police management more than three decades later. These officers would remain permanent fixtures in my mind, as they were in their respective neighborhoods. Of course, at the time I simply regarded their operation as one hell of a way to make a living.

In addition, for what it's worth, who could ever forget the Blue Hill Avenue Pizza war? Two family-owned pizzerias became engaged in a competitive price war that would drive the price of two slices of pizza and a coke down to twenty-five cents. At this price level, it was costing the owners money each time they made a sale. I rode the downward spiral to its lowest ebb. It fitted in fine with my modest income. I usually ate in the same place, and at some point I became fond of the owner, a weary looking guy named Mr. Lautman. I came to feel more like a predator than a customer. I pointed out to him the absurdity of this struggle. It was painfully clear to him. With his approval, I took it on my own to negotiate an agreement between the two competitors.

I proposed that they agree to a gradual and synchronous rise in prices over time to an eventual return to the half a buck for 'a coke and a slice of pizza' level. The plan was agreed to, and it was successful. They returned to their former price level. Surprisingly enough, the price war had generated new customers and their profit level increased. I knew there was a lesson to be learned in all of this. They both benefited but unfortunately I was forced to pay more - no breaks for the mediator.

Six

Winter grudgingly melted into spring. Buffeted by the rhythmical pulsation of a distant drum, I featured myself on the lower footage of a natural vine that stretched far into the heavens. In the beginning it would be crowded by the mass of humanity's aspirants. They would line up, vying with each other to gain a foothold, and then the ascent would begin. Some would tire early on, knocked off the net by their first encounter with resistance. Most would continue the struggle - pushing, climbing ever higher. One needed to be careful of his surrounding competitors. An unfair reach or a rapid pull of an arm or a leg could set the body hurtling into the abyss below. The ranks of adversaries would be thinned out at every elevation - fewer and fewer would reach the higher levels. One's progress was continuously slowed by the increasing intensity of resistance at each rung of the vine's network. Only the fewest of people would reach their terminal position. The higher one's objective, the more difficult it would be. It took foresight, preparation, discipline and endurance, but in the end the victor would enjoy the sweet product of his effort. I was just beginning the climb and another level of challenge was hurled at me - NOTIFICATION OF THE TIME AND PLACE OF THE POLICE DEPARTMENT STRENGTH TEST. It was delivered in the mail.

The strength test consisted of nine events. It was designed to measure muscular power, endurance and coordination. Many of the candidates, including myself, trained for it at the City of Cambridge YMCA, an old red brick building just outside of Central Square. The program was directed by a well-conditioned old timer who appeared as old as the building. He trained many generations of cops and he was still doing a laudable job. It was a worthwhile expenditure of money and effort. Repetitive practice sessions resulted in better technique and provided the candidate with a psychological advantage over the lesser trained. The most difficult parts involved a twenty-two foot hand-over-hand rope climb (feet could not be used), and the carrying of a one hundred and twenty-five pound dummy down an eighteen foot ladder. The other segments included a one hundred and twenty-five pound dummy lift, an eight foot broad jump, a dumbbell lift, a fence vault, a four hundred and forty yard run on an upwardly curved track, thirty abdominals and a hundred yard swim. It was not overwhelmingly challenging, but nevertheless, a slip on the ladder, a twisted ankle, or simply a bad day and WHAMMO, it was all over.

The day arrived. Curiously enough my anxiety level peaked just moments before the test was to begin. I stood on the gymnasium floor on the designated day and selectively surveyed some of the fewer out of shape and overweight bodies that were in the ready. I concentrated on the more rigorous training I had undergone in the Marine Corps. A strange calm enveloped me and I experienced an infusion of power. I riveted my mind on the job ahead and gradually came to feel as an Olympian might, competing at the Junior Varsity level. It was a mind game but it worked. I maxed out on every event but one, the four hundred and forty yard run. I ran it in eighty seconds instead of the seventy-five seconds necessary for a perfect score. I felt exhilarated and relieved all at the same time. I stood at the side of the track and cheered the remaining candidates over the finish line.

I was not prepared for the next development. True to the philosophy of the vine, I was unexpectedly jolted at the lower rung position by the delivery of another letter from the Civil Service Commission that contained distressing news. I was informed that I was no longer being considered for selection as I had been deemed an unsuitable candidate. I was wounded, doubly damaged, because I honestly anticipated that I was being notified of my position on the newly established eligibility list. If they were going to dump someone, I was under the impression that it occurred before the strength test and not after.

They did not give me a reason but I knew anyway. It was more than likely the result of my disclosure on the second page of the application entitled ARRESTS, SUMMONSES, ETC., of being taken into custody twice in Jacksonville, North Carolina, a small base town near Camp Lejeune, once for DRUNK in 1958 and the other time for DISORDERLY CONDUCT in 1959. The cops in this town, especially one of them, made a sport out of arresting young Marines. It was so bad for a period that the Commanding General of the Second Marine Division considered putting the town off limits. It was the 'especially one of them' that arrested me both times. He was a short, nasal sounding guy with a Napoleon complex, who enjoyed the tyranny he exercised over people. I once asked him, while he was in the process of arresting a Marine Corps buddy for a trivial offense, if he had ever heard of the Constitution. He didn't reply but he didn't forget either.

He got his shot at me one night. I was sitting in a honky-tonk bar and restaurant on the Jay-Ville strip. The waiter had just served me a B.L.T. and a side order of French Fries along with my first beer of the night. I spotted the battalion chef sitting about ten feet away in a booth. He casually remarked that I was starting in real early. I ranked him back, commenting over the loud music from the juke-box that, if the mess hall chow was any good I would have eaten at the base instead. The bartender overheard this. He was a kind of pansy looking guy; this was his first night on the job and he was pretty shaky. He thought we were arguing and that we might soon fight. He rushed into the street and returned with Officer Napoleon. I was ordered to leave the bar. I agreed, but I demanded a refund for the un-eaten food and drink. The bartender refused. Napoleon instructed me to finish eating and to leave as soon as I had done so. I agreed.

The officer left and returned in less than one minute with a plainclothes police officer. They pulled me from the bar, cuffed me and pushed me onto the street. Napoleon shoved me into the rear of a waiting cruiser between himself and another cop. He placed a twister on my right wrist and screwed it down on the way to the station. It hurt, but I would not give him the satisfaction of even a whimper. I was placed in a urine drenched cell where I spent a sleepless night. I had plenty of company as the night wore on and the bars emptied out. The judge placed the incident on file and I was released from court early the next morning.

The second time I got bagged I was simply in the wrong place at the wrong time. I was standing on the street outside a bar when a fight emptied out onto the street. The cops and the M.P.s hit the place en masse. I was a block away by the time they did but Officer Napoleon must have spotted me on the way down. He did his thing at the scene and when he was finished he came after me. I saw the cruiser coming at me; the blue dome light was flashing. As the car came to a screeching halt, Officer Napoleon stumbled out, and with his partner standing by, stuck it to me again. I paid an eight dollar cost of the court fee and was released the following AM. Here it was four years later and Officer Napoleon was still jacking me up.

The Civil Service System provided two appeals for rejected applicants. After these were exhausted, a court hearing would offer the final possible remedy. I filed my first appeal, thinking that surely this would do it. I mentally prepared my argument. I had no criminal or juvenile record, other than the two misdemeanor arrests in North Carolina, not even a parking or traffic violation. On top of this, I was an honorably discharged Marine with four years' regular service and a good conduct medal to boot. I was on the Dean's List at Northeastern University. I scored a high grade on the exam and I also worked for the State. Most of all, I could explain what led up to these false charges to begin with.

If I were not honest would I have made this disclosure at the start? Chances are they would never have found out. What I would not say, of course, is that I had agonized over this revelation before I decided to include it on my application. I was advised to divulge this shame by a Boston Police Sergeant who was admitted to Reception Six with Manic-Depressive Psychosis. His advice at the time sounded reasonable. "Tell the truth from the start and they can never come back at you."

Nor would I reveal that I had been taken into custody more than a dozen times by the Military Police - mostly for Disorderly Conduct. These arrests had not resulted in a criminal record. In fact, I was never brought up on Office Hours for any of them. The Marine Corps, as strict as it was, never paid much attention to off duty bouts of fighting and brawling. Boys would be boys - no permanent injuries - no permanent record. Like I have already said, being voted *King of the Animals* was no easy task. Performance was important and this sort of behavior was part of my repertoire.

My first appeal took place before a one man board. He was a portly gentleman with a sympathetic ear. He reminded me of Santa Claus. The tension ebbed from my body as soon as he introduced himself and invited me to sit down. He spoke in a soft and reassuring manner. The entire interview lasted less than an hour. I poured out my tale of 'justice perverted' and not surprisingly the Hearing Officer agreed that this simple disclosure should not have amounted to rejection. He commented that I was the best prepared candidate that he had interviewed so far and assured me that he would recommend that my unsuitability status be overturned. He concluded that the Civil Service Commission was probably trying to weed out people with alcohol problems, but in light of my explanation this fear was simply not relevant. I left the Hearing Office feeling very hopeful.

My relief was short lived. Two weeks later another letter brutishly intruded into my life, reaffirming my 'dead meat' status. My appeal was denied. Had the Hearing Officer been giving me a line of crap or had his recommendation been simply overruled? The deciding body had put me in a trick again and this time I was really mad. I filed my second appeal. This one would be in front of the full Civil Service Commission and I intended to get representation.

I would go to my State Representative, the colorful and flamboyant Julie Ansel, also known as the Mayor of Blue Hill Avenue. Julie was a Jewish offshoot of James Michael Curley, mischievous and magnanimous at the same time, a bit of a show-boater to be sure, but a tireless worker and advocate for the disadvantaged. Years later I would hear a story about Julie. He had been an elected official during the 'Curley Reign' and as a result of his close relationship with this revered Mayor was able to mimic his voice. He once phoned a meat distributor and ordered three hundred chickens to be delivered to a specific location. The distributor complied with the request and delivered the chickens. A short time later the real Mayor Curley called the same man and made the same solicitation. Once the confusion was cleared up, and Julie Ansel's deception was discovered, the original chickens had to be returned. The point of the story is that both of these men had ordered the poultry for the same reason, for distribution to the poor. That was the kind of guy Julie Ansel was, and true to form, he didn't disappoint me.

Julie was sick and in bed when I entered his Wales Street home. I had never met him before. His wife kindly admitted me and guided me to his bed. She wore the look of a woman who was all too accustomed to these endless visitations. Julie's small stature was clearly outlined under the blanket. He apologized for not feeling well and asked me my business. I related the entire depressing mess. He appeared clearly upset about the inequity of the whole thing. In a no nonsense fashion he instructed me to meet him outside the State House at 8:30 on the morning of the hearing date. I happily complied, and when the day arrived he showed up right on time. He reminded me of a Jimmy Cagney type tough guy. He shook my hand, and with a lot of bounce to his walk, brought me into the State House.

We approached the Hearing Room and he ordered me to remain outside and wait for him. Dressed in a suit and tie and looking really dapper, he opened the door and swaggered into the inquisition chamber. In less than five minutes he emerged. I breathlessly waited for his first remark. He looked me straight in the eye and without smiling or blinking, he commented, "You're all set kid, go in there and say hello."

My legs wobbled with relief. I thanked him profusely and walked into the room. The several members of the full Commission were just getting seated. One of them, probably the boss, was putting flowers on the table. Without asking me for any explanation he informed me that the board had ruled in my favor and apologized for any inconvenience that I had experienced. I learned something that day - the mighty power of politics and the kindly intercession of a truly memorable man.

Seven

The summer did not pass uneventfully. The ward continued to make significant improvements. Ed Jesser only asked to go upstairs when he could get into a card game with co-workers. Kevin became the charge attendant. Mike died, and a patient was killed. Kevin deserved the promotion, but Mike's untimely passage was precipitated by my personal failure. It was a mistake. I would never have done anything intentionally to harm that squirrel. Mike had become my everyday leisure time companion. I took him everywhere. I was genuinely attached to him. He was also attached to me; he thought I was his mother. After all, I had raised him since infancy. I humorously recall attempting to free him by removing his leash and placing him in a tree. I did this only because I was challenged to do so by a supposed animal lover who berated me for depriving Mike of his natural habitat. But Mike chose to leave the tree and follow me as I walked away. He did this not once, but twice. The witnesses, especially the animal advocate, were struck by this simple demonstration of animal fealty. I was convinced beyond any doubt that Mike preferred me to a tree, and that's the way we played it out.

One hot day, on the first day of my vacation, sometime around the middle of June I drove to Derry, New Hampshire with a friend to enjoy a day of swimming at Beaver Pond. Of course I brought Mike along, transporting him as I normally did, in a small open vinyl type travel bag that I placed on the floor of the car between my friend John and me. Mike was attached to a leash and remained in the bag for the duration of the one and a half hour trip. He stayed quiet.

Having arrived at the pond, I got out of the car and placed the travel bag containing Mike on a nearby picnic table. I removed him from the bag and I could immediately see that something was terribly wrong. He was frothing at the mouth and appeared disoriented and languid. I picked him up and placed him in the palms of my hands. His body was writhing and his front paws continuously moved in a forward fashion as though he were running. This went on for about one minute. He seized, and then died.

I believe my friend John, without the benefit of a necropsy, accurately diagnosed his fatal condition: heat exhaustion and asphyxiation, followed by heart failure. It must have been pretty hot sitting in a vinyl prison on the floor of a non air-conditioned car for that long a trip. Mike never bit me, even in the middle of his delirium. I was stunned, and hurt, and angry, very angry at myself for this pronounced act of stupidity. I buried Mike under a tree close to the pond and returned to Morton Street. Now, for the other misfortune.

Sometime in the early 1940's, a nonviolent sexual intrusion occurred during the night in one of the chronic wards of the Boston State Hospital. A seriously retarded young male patient (they referred to them as idiots then) climbed into the occupied bed of a just as seriously homo-phobic patient. The predictable result was swift and severe. The retarded man's primal drive for the warm touch of human flesh (anyone's flesh) was suddenly cut off by the intense physical pain from the beating that followed. The patients were transferred to other wards, in other buildings and twenty years passed. Institutions forget, and so it happened that both patients wound up on H-6, on the third floor of the H Building.

The summer vacation period further depressed the coverage levels of an already chronically understaffed state institution. Low paying jobs were plentiful in the early Sixties and employment at a massive mental institution was not generally regarded as an attractive option. Whatever the reasons, sometime during the late summer I reported to work and was assigned to cover two wards at the same time, H-5 and H-6. Mrs. Delaney and Ed Jesser were on vacation and Kevin was alone on H-2. I resented these frequent occasions of dual responsibilities. Instead of the four attendants who should have been divided between two wards that were separated by a hallway, there would be only one - me.

I decided to remain on H-5 and periodically check H-6 throughout the shift. That is how it was generally accomplished. I called my bed count to the front office and came up with one patient short. The outside replacement male supervisor panicked and ordered me downstairs to determine the patient's identity. I objected to having to leave my assignment, but complied with the order. I was downstairs when it happened. Richard, his infantile mind further stultified by the warehousing effects of an indifferent institution, suffered a chance encounter with his time elapsed homo-phobic antagonist. Still pained by the assault against his sexuality, the ancient foe knocked him to the ground and kicked him once in the head. One of the patients was a witness and immediately called downstairs and reported the incident. We raced upstairs, but the attack had already ended. Richard was unconscious. His face was bruised and his neck was swollen. His head appeared to have taken on the curious dimensions of a light bulb. He was rushed to the Medical Building, where he died the following day. The pressure exerted on his trachea caused by the thickening pool of blood in his neck cut off his breathing. The result: death by asphyxiation. At least that is the way the on-duty Doctor explained it to me.

Two State Police detectives investigated the homicide. They awakened me from a nightmare the following day. It would become a recurring dream for years into the future. In it I would look down at the bruised and swollen head of a man lying in the gutter. He looked like Richard. I would invariably bend down to retrieve him from the street, placing my arms and hands underneath his back and neck. I would strain to lift him up, and always the inevitable would occur, his bloated head would fall off his body and roll onto the street.

I explained to the investigators what happened, commenting that I was in the front office when the assault occurred. They didn't seem perturbed. I never informed them that I was ordered off the ward in spite of my opposition. I was no squealer. Besides, the supervisor had a family and had more to lose than I did. In spite of Kevin's sympathetic support, I took it pretty hard on a personal level and I worried that the incident might affect my status on the eligibility list. As it turned out it didn't make any difference. The state report amounted to a simple summary of the facts that led up to the patient's death. There was no blame directed at anyone, including the hospital for its understaffed condition.

Though I knew that I was not negligent, after all I was just following orders and I couldn't be in three places at one time, Marine Corps thinking would have it that it happened during my watch. I felt grief for this poor suffering bastard whose underdeveloped orb of a brain reduced his pleasure seeking capacity to food intake and excretory functions. That is what he was doing when he met his death, pissing into a urinal.

There was an inquest and a grand jury hearing. The judge ruled the homophobe unable to stand trial due to insanity. He was transferred to Bridgewater State Hospital for the criminally insane where, no doubt, he paid the unholy wage for his banality.

Northeastern's classrooms were stifling that summer. I asked myself why I would subject myself to this misery. Was I 'deferring gratification,' as Professor Coggan remarked? He said it was the most outstanding trait possessed by those who would achieve middle class success. That is what sociologists believed; I preferred to regard it as simple discipline. If I ever wanted to get out of college I had better keep my ass in gear. As far as middle class success was concerned, I thought I was already doing all right. I had plenty of girlfriends, a car, a room and no bills. In the event I didn't make it onto the police department I would have to do something else, perhaps law school. As it was, I was starting college late. I had no time to spare.

Sometime during the last week of the session a Southern Baptist Minister named Doctor Martin Luther King, a Boston University alumnus, organized a march in the nation's capital for jobs and freedom. About two hundred and fifty thousand, mostly young black people with a modest sprinkling of whites, assembled on the mall and demanded a two buck an hour minimum wage and an end to social injustice. I was inspired by his speech and didn't think he was asking for too much; short money; it amounted to a sawbuck more a week for me. The main brunt of the message had to do with equal treatment and simple human dignity.

During the speech, parts of which were broadcast on radio, I floated back to the Corps and recalled my friendship with Al Stroman, a tall, fastidious and excellently conditioned black Marine. In spite of our close relationship for four years, he had never been able to share a single night of liberty with me or any other white guy because of the South's segregated system. Stroman buried this humiliation deep inside himself but waged a silent protest against the system by refusing to go on liberty at all. For all the years and months he was stationed at Camp Lejeune, North Carolina, Al Stroman rarely ever stepped into a 'colored neighborhood.' When the speech was over I asked myself "Why was basic human respect so difficult to achieve?" Certainly well-meaning people could turn the whole thing around. Others didn't see it that way. They never do. The summer session ended and I enjoyed a brief respite before the Fall Semester began.

The vacations also ended and the staffing levels returned to normal. The ward took on an increasingly lighter atmosphere. The shroud of silence that once enveloped the night shift was punctuated with conversation and occasional laughter. Whenever the building enjoyed a full crew we would inevitably expect visitors. Two of the more memorable ones were Jim Martin and Grady Adams, two black, middle aged state waiver Licensed Practical Nurses who would supervise the shift during Mrs. Delaney's days off. Martin's hawk-like features hinted of a mixed Indian ancestry and correlated well with his razor sharp mind. State Hospital lore had it that he graduated 'Magna Cum Laude' from Harvard University in the early Fifties, the result of a full four year scholarship. He turned down a prestigious position with the United Nations and opened up a small aluminum siding business. The State Hospital was his second job. Upon first impression Martin appeared monosyllabic, but time would reveal the biting insights of a steel-trap mind.

They were both skeptics, sensitive to the vagaries of the system, but Grady exhibited a more relaxed and humorous brand of cynicism. He broke me up with the mental caricature he created of the old Southern Minister of his boyhood, slowly trudging along from door to door, begging for pork chops and preaching the word of the Lord. Grady Adams, like his friend Martin, concealed a keen sense of morality. His daughter Jacqueline would, many years later, become a well known Washington-based news correspondent. I remember a shy little girl with big eyes and a runny nose, standing behind the front aluminum screen door of her house, looking up at Jesser and me and wondering who the two white guys were who were visiting her father.

The most amazing development on the ward was the apparent emergence of unique individual traits and human personality styles that became manifest over time among the patients. Those, who at first had impressed me as 'fleshpots' awaiting the mercy of death, emerged as distinctive personality types peppered with layers of life's experience. Many of them, no doubt existed only in the isolation of their minds' remnants, cut off from reality by the encroachment of senility and what is now increasingly diagnosed as Alzheimer's Disease. But others were there because they were poor or the products of familial neglect.

Joe 'the blind man' was a victim of this social indifference. Joe was about eighty years old, totally blind and suffered from cancer of the stomach. He had difficulty sleeping and as a result would frequently grope his way through the hallway into the bathroom at night. It was his way of dealing with a restless night. Whenever I encountered him I would jokingly and affectionately remind Joe that he was supposed to be in bed. He would always challenge me and ask, "Who are you?"

I would respond, "The BOSS, Joe, I am the Boss."

Without fail he would retaliate by commenting, "Yeah! You the boss, you the boss of the buckoza." In Joe's mind - the shithouse.

The historical enmity between the Russians and the Poles would be played out repetitively throughout the early morning and day by two ethnic nationals. Ed (Jesser) and I would deliberately sit them next to each other. I can still vividly recall them sitting in their white johnnies, the Russian with a full head of white hair and the Pole completely bald, exchanging insults. "RUSKI, NO GOOD," followed by "POLSKI, NO GOOD," would be shouted alternately, first by one and then the other throughout the day. Perhaps the uninitiated would see this as a form of elderly exploitation, but on the contrary, the surfacing of this buried hostility provided these men with a final dose of life to the very end. Finally, when Polski died, Ruski cried.

One of the benefits of working H-2 was the lessened degree of violence. Most of the violence that did occur happened on other wards or in the hallway. I took a good shot in the stomach early in the AM one day by Big Tony, a two hundred and forty pound, seriously ill, hard hitting Italian guy from another ward. He was bent on walking out the front door. I tried to talk him out of it, but he wasn't listening. Jesser did one of his famous flying leaps from about five feet across the floor and tackled him somewhere around his ankles, slowing him up enough to permit me and another attendant named Yancy to bundle him up. Jesser couldn't fight worth a damn, but he knew how to use his body most usefully and the flying tackle was his specialty. He had employed it successfully on other occasions. Like I said earlier, "Ed Jesser had balls."

Most of the time it took no more than two attendants to forcibly restrain a patient. It was all a matter of technique. But not so with the patient Tarnisha, the most feared and notorious of all the State Hospital's female inhabitants, and for all of its history. Tarnisha was the focus of an international study for her remarkable ability to transform from a lithe and likable, five foot five, pretty black female into a raging inferno of a woman possessed of superhuman strength. During psychotic episodes her nimble body would become engorged with power. These physically destructive outbursts were usually directed against her surroundings, but on occasion she would fling around male attendants like they were rag dolls.

I witnessed a demonstration of her extraordinary strength only once, but I would never forget it. I was on the day shift at the time and I was called to the B Building to assist other attendants in placing a female patient in the seclusion room. By the time I arrived about five male attendants were standing around the patient who was perched on the top of a nearly immovable, massively thick and heavy wooden table in the middle of the ward. They were attempting to talk her into voluntarily admitting herself into the seclusion room. The patient was Tarnisha.

She looked directly at the hospital personnel and began to slowly disrobe, punctuating her movements with a slew of obscenities. Once fully unclothed she stood completely upright on the table and began to flex her body in a slow and deliberate manner. I remember thinking that she would have made a great stripper. She was tall, slender and perfectly proportioned. It was as though she were mentally infusing herself with muscular or perhaps psychical power. When she was finished she raised her arms straight in the air and lowering them slowly, crossing them over her small upturned breasts, she bowed to her audience. Next she quickly jumped to the floor and with the speed and agility of a cheetah positioned herself under the table. We heard a loud groan and to everyone's amazement the table began to move straight up in the air. GOD, that table had to weigh three hundred pounds! It was designed not to move. When the table reached the full length of Tarnisha's arms she carefully lowered it to the floor. She was laughing as she emerged from its cover and to everyone's utter relief she freely walked into the seclusion room. The door was quickly locked.

The institution was rife with Tarnisha stories. In one of them, it was said that she broke down the four inch thick bolted door of the seclusion room at the exact date and time she promised. In another, she fractured several ribs of two male attendants who were attempting to restrain her. Once she was installed in seclusion, she remained there until the curse lifted. This could take several days, even weeks.

She would be allowed to leave, during calm periods, to visit the bathroom. It was an unofficial union rule and enunciated very clearly by Ed Connolly, a pleasant faced solidly built attendant from H-4, that at least three attendants and preferably four would accompany her during these instances. Once in a while the call would go out to the H Building for assistance. The unlucky attendants who lost the coin flip would don their jock straps before traveling to the B Building. Tarnisha could be one bad bitch! But, there was something I liked about her. She was unique and one very good performer.

I was notified in October of my final hurdle - the time and place of the police department physical. I viewed this with the same amount of apprehension as every other point of the process. It was a pretty strict physical; the candidate had to be in optimum condition with almost perfect vision. It was also necessary to hear the sound of the whispered voice at twenty feet.

The one thing that I fretted about was my blood pressure. When I joined the Marine Corps my first reading was so high that the Doctor required me to sit down for a few minutes until it subsided. I suffered from 'white coat hypertension.' Just seeing someone with a white coat and a blood pressure cuff coming at me would precipitate a rise in my blood pressure. I could envision it happening again; my police career could be extinguished somewhere between two bleeps on a sphygmomanometer, a name I could hardly pronounce.

I was so preoccupied with this morbid possibility that I slipped into a depressive state on the day of the exam. My worst fear materialized when the doctor, after having twice performed a reading, asked me to step aside and wait a few minutes to be re-tested. He explained that my blood pressure reading was abnormally low. I was ecstatic! I knew that this unexpected condition was temporary. Anyway, I passed on the third hit and to my delight passed the entire physical. Now, assuming they called for a list, I had a job. I left the Cambridge Y and lit up a Lucky - the world looked good to me that day.

On November 22, 1963, President John F Kennedy was fatally shot in the head by rifle fire while riding in an open vehicle through the streets of Dallas. Vice President Lyndon Johnson was sworn in, almost immediately, to succeed him. Lee Harvey Oswald, a communist loving, off the wall former Marine was apprehended and charged with murder. Jack Ruby, a sleazebag of the first order, gunned down Oswald. The nation lost its innocence and a small ripple moved away from an obscure tiny country named Vietnam in Southeast Asia.

Eight

Almost a year would pass before I would be sworn in as a Boston Police Patrolman. The eligibility list was finally established, but it would remain inactive for months. To ensure my continuity as a police candidate I undertook another exam initiating the process all over again, a backup in the event the standing list followed its two year cycle and lapsed into oblivion. My casual approach to this second test cost me a few points but I still ended up with a respectable score. I fell back into the easy rhythm of an existence tempered with the promise of success.

Nevertheless, there were some major developments. For one, Michael Weinberg convinced me to move off the grounds. I was not a hard sell for I knew that I could not remain in the Male Home once I was called for the police department. Mike was never comfortable living on the grounds. I sensed that this prolonged immersion into a sea of insanity offended his deeply held belief in the infinite malleability of the human essence. Michael was a powerful environmentalist. He refused to acknowledge that organic influences of any kind could alter or limit human psychological development. He believed that environment alone accounted for human potential and was totally responsible for variations among individual personality styles. Michael argued that the key to change derived from a recognition of this notion and a conscious effort to limit the effects of negative conditioning.

For example, a person suffering from chronic depression needed only to work his way out of it, through mental imagery and self-discipline.

Confronted on a daily basis with a population of suffering people permanently twisted into irreversible psychosis presented an affront to Michael's core values and consequently precipitated some personal depression accounting for his wish to move. At least that's the way I read it. Michael was unconventional. His tall lanky stature and soft brown eyes masked an unyielding spirit. He resisted the conformity imposed on him by the transparencies of an organized world. He heard a different drummer and stepped to his own music. I liked Mike. He was 'beat'.

I coaxed Ed Jesser into the deal. He was also ready. His Queensbury Street apartment, located near Boston State College where he attended class, was breaking up. Unless he wished to move back to East Cottage Street in Dorchester where he had grown up he had little choice. The Male Home was not a valid option, he had always considered it an extension of the Ward.

He was not altogether wrong about this. Some of the residents were not hitting on all six cylinders, a few were peculiar and there were others who were downright crazy. One attendant, assigned to the eleven to seven shift in the I Building, would regularly report aerial bomb attacks to the hospital operator minutes after arriving for work. I witnessed two separate incidents of psychotic episodes among hospital personnel. One of them smeared shaving cream all over himself and the bathroom walls on the second floor. When he ran out of shaving cream he used spray paint. The other guy lapsed into a prolonged hallucinatory state. The voices just kept on coming, driving him into a frenzied condition. Both of these individuals were forcibly removed from the building by psychiatric aides from the Mass. Mental, a nearby hospital facility.

No administrative level was immune to this strange phenomena. It was almost as though mental illness was catchy, but a more educated guess might suggest that 'some' people attracted to the world of the mentally ill might be carrying their own psychological baggage. Once submerged in an environment where extremes of behavior are tolerated, even encouraged, mimicking may well result. The clinical term used at the time referred to this variety of behavior as, 'adaptive reactions'

Forgive me if I sound pretentious, but this thing can work in reverse. One day I ran into a patient in a Friendly's Restaurant, located in the American Legion Highway shopping mall, not far from the hospital. He was sitting at the counter sipping on a cup of coffee. Aside from the unpressed appearance of his clothes he looked like any other customer, but I knew this man to be a patient at the State Hospital. How could I not? He constantly hallucinated outside my window every Saturday morning - nonstop.

"David," I asked, "Why aren't you speaking to the voices now? You do it all the time at the Hospital?"

"Because, at the Hospital they know I'm crazy, and here they don't, and what's more, I don't want them to!" he replied. Good answer, I thought.

John Eckles, a friend of Michael's, would come in as the fourth addition to the apartment. John was an ordained minister and a former Marine Corps Drill Instructor. He was a square jawed, heavily muscled man, a few years older than we were and in a word, the most resourceful person I had ever encountered. One of his favorite paintings depicted a man standing on a mountain gazing upwards toward the heavens. John said that the subject of the work reminded him of himself, a man alone in his own thoughts, carving out his relationship with God and his place in the world. He eventually became the Pastor of an old historic Boston Church. We four were an unlikely combination. "NUTBAGS," Jesser would conclude many years later.

We moved into a second floor furnished flat in a four-family brick building at 11 Follen Street in the South End, a neighborhood that had seen its best days and whose re-emergence was more than twenty years away. The entire apartment was painted in one color, an off gray. We believed that the woman on the fourth floor was a prostitute. She slept most of the day. Sometimes we baby-sat for her four year old daughter.

Occasionally we were visited by roaches, but continual spraying kept them under control. We got along fine, at least at the beginning. Responsibilities and household chores were divided equally among us, as was the sixty-five dollars a month rent and other living expenses. Our modest food budget required us to shop in Haymarket Square, a large partly outdoor market section in the North End, a flourishing Italian neighborhood near the center of the city. Here there was an outlet to accommodate every budget. One day Mike and I purchased five pounds of bacon for a buck and a quarter in an underground bargain basement meat store on Blackstone Street. When we attempted to fry it on Sunday morning it turned completely to fat in the pan. What could you expect for the price?

Apartment living provided us a grant of freedom that was non-existent in the Male Home - parties, parties and more parties. Sometimes they spilled over into the next day. This was not permitted on the grounds of the State Hospital. The hospital rules were occasionally flaunted of course, but if discovered, the violator was immediately evicted. Not so on Follen Street. Life was sweet there. Apartment living was fun. Expenses were low. Work was simple. School was manageable. My social life was humming and the future seemed rosy. Everything was under control.

It is often the simplest event that precipitates the most profound change. The assassination of Archduke Ferdinand of Austria in 1914 set forth a chain of events that loosened a war on the world. In retrospect, that singular action was a cataclysmic event. The 'mini-clysmic' event in my life that foreshadowed radical alterations in my lifestyle is traceable to the day I first saw a framed high school graduation picture of Michael's cousin Beverly on top of his bureau. Beverly was radiant, blue eyed and blonde. I was at once struck by her beauty and awed by the angelic expression in her eyes as she gazed upwards.

"Mike, she is beautiful! Who is she?" I asked.

"She's my cousin," he answered.

"I would like to meet her, Mike," I uttered, standing there with a feigned comic look on my face.

Suddenly his expression contorted, reminding me of Norman Bates, the central character in the movie *Psycho*, moments before someone was on the verge of discovering his mother - stuffed in the attic.

"Phil, you can go out with any cousin I have, but not her," he stammered. "It's just, it's just not a good combination," and he left it at that. This naturally piqued my interest.

Several weeks passed and Michael invited Beverly to dinner. He cooked pork chops. Michael loved pork chops; he ate them all the time. It was part of his Jewish rebellion. She was gorgeous - blonde, beautiful and flashy.

Michael told me that it had been only a few years since she was declared the runner up in the Miss Massachusetts Beauty Pageant. He said she should have come in first but the winner beat her on height. Beverly was only five feet two. She weighed about one hundred and twelve pounds that day and came across as aloof. Michael no sooner served dinner when, without warning, she bolted straight up and instructed Michael to drive her to her Brookline apartment. Perhaps she saw a roach, I later suggested.

"No" Michael said, "That's just the way she is." She never even touched her dinner. Michael didn't seem to mind, but I thought she was rude. I told Mike what I thought and assured him that I had no interest in his cousin after that demonstration. And I didn't.

Time passed and Beverly visited the apartment more frequently. She complained that she was coming off a divorce and didn't like being alone in her one bedroom Brookline apartment. I wondered what might have happened to cause the split. I avoided her initially. The pork chop deal still bugged me. She met most of our friends, including our dates. In my case that was Maria, a thin wispy platinum blonde with a cute face and a laid back sense of humor. Just being near her would push me into a fit of laughter. Then there was Crystal, a bleached blonde hairdresser from Blue Hill Avenue, a few years older than me and with a bulging chest and a New York City accent, and Bee Bee, a long legged, pouty-faced and sexy graduate nurse from Connecticut. There were also a couple of others in between.

Beverly was always cordial, greeting them with a "Hello" and frequently engaging them in light conversation, but more often than not she remained at arm's length and kept herself busy. I recall her crocheting a lot, though I never hung around the apartment long enough to see the finished product. She threw a verbal slide-ball at me one day. She walked past the couch where I was relaxing and out of the clear blue she whipped it at me. "I like your girlfriends. They seem nice, but not one of them is a real blonde." Beverly had pizzazz. That was for sure.

My sleep was interrupted one morning by the shrill ring of the telephone. It was Warren Brown, the soft spoken, chocolate skinned President of the State Hospital's Employees Union. He informed me that two popular attendants had been fired for alleged brutality against a patient in the I Building. As I was an organizer in the Union it fell upon me to investigate this incident. Brown said I would have to prepare a defense for the two attendants if I came to believe there were no grounds to the complaint or if they were being dealt with unfairly by the administration.

The fired employees were accused of sitting a naked patient on a hot radiator during the eleven to seven shift on I-3 because he refused to go to bed. Apparently a seriously psychotic patient (that described all of them in the I Building) reported the employees to the head nurse the next day. The staff conducted a cursory investigation and the two attendants were summarily fired.

I had accepted the position as a union organizer because it permitted me to earn two bucks a head for every new attendant I got to join the union. I didn't like the accompanying responsibility that came with the position. I was highly uncomfortable with the prospect of the upcoming investigation. A few days had elapsed since the firings and Brown commented that "A growing number of attendants believed the guys were being screwed." In fact, the dismissal of the attendants was quickly taking on the dimensions of a 'cause célèbre' among union members. Brown had just handed me a hot potato and I knew it. I cursed the day that I took on the job of union organizer. I didn't go back to bed. Instead, I had two cups of coffee, smoked a cigarette, showered, got into my car and drove to Morton Street. I stopped briefly at the Administration Building, explaining my mission to Doctor Greenblatt's hospital assistant and received permission to interview the victim/patient and any possible witnesses, one way or the other. He stipulated that the head nurse had to be present during the session.

I headed straight to the I Building and entered I-3. The I Building was the State Hospital's equivalent to the bottom level of Dante's Inferno, except here the condemned were all innocent. The wards housed the most severe of the institutions chronically ill. They imaged a carnival replete with tragic human figures - a place for polite society to deposit its strangest anomalies, one-way down the chute and onto the most rudimentary and least ornate of its carousels. It was a merry-go-round that featured the most extreme specimens of human maladjustment; the most withdrawn, the most apathetic, the most blunted, the most incoherent and the most delirious. Bolted down and secured in an autistic world, their circular ride was endlessly repetitious and always ended up where they were before.

Their day passed in measured intervals of eating, drinking, physical release and sleep. Rational conversation was all but lost and the environment suffered from a continual barrage of incessant rambling, eccentric phraseology, salad talk, bizarre behavior, rigidified physical positioning and grotesque facial expressions. The I Building was home to the original fecal pin, a foot long shit stick shaped in the form of a bowling pin, molded secretly over a period of several months by a patient who was ultimately discovered eating and salivating over it. The floors on the ward were of a synthetic marble texture - deliberately installed to facilitate the frequent hosings that were necessary to remove the human waste that stuck to them. Many of the patients messed themselves and had to be washed down the same way. The stench on I-3 saturated the ward like a cloudless vapor.

It was no wonder the head nurse, a petite little bundle of nervous energy who introduced herself as Ginny, smoked six packages of Pall Malls a day. To accomplish this, she explained, it was necessary to smoke one cigarette after another continuously throughout the waking day and evening, relying on only four hours of sleep, itself punctuated by incidents of waking up to smoke. I was not surprised to learn years later that she died from cancer of the lungs, but at this point in time I was relieved to make contact with an intelligent mind and a warm disposition.

Ginny didn't waste any time and immediately guided me to the abused patient. His name was Ronald. He was a very severely brain damaged thirty-four year old white male, a ninety-five pound waif, unable to speak or communicate. He had lived his entire life in institutions. He refused to wear clothes and spent most of the time scampering around the ward on the balls of his feet. That is most likely what he was doing the night he refused to go to bed, ricocheting from one place to another. This activity most likely intensified when he became agitated.

"Look, look at his butt," Ginny said, "see what those bastards did to him, he looks like a zebra." She continued, "A patient saw the whole thing. Ronald kept on getting out of bed; he refused to stay put so they sat him on a hot radiator to punish him."

It was clear to me that he suffered from brownish red burn marks vertically impressed across his buttocks. "Who is this patient?" I asked.

Ginny invited me into a small makeshift kitchen just off the central corridor that ran between the recreation room and the dormitory area. On the way in she instructed the attendant to bring John into the kitchen. She offered me a cup of coffee and I reached into my left shirt pocket for a cigarette to go with it but the package was empty. I crinkled up the pack and threw it into a nearby wastebasket.

Ginny slid her king size jobs across the table where she was sitting, "Go ahead have one," she said, "A Pall Mall is just a Lucky with a hard-on."

I cracked up. I never heard a head nurse talk like that. Most of them, especially the younger ones, were kind of snooty. I liked Ginny right away; she had a worn down honest look about her. Her face was somewhere in transition. She was one of those people that could have been as young as thirty or as old as forty; it was hard to tell. I had the sense that she was always struggling against the tide. She was clearly upset about what had happened. She commented further that she suspected the same two guys of abusive behavior in the past. "But never anything like this," she added.

The kitchen door opened and the attendant escorted the patient/witness in. I was astonished to see John Hendrix standing before me looking rational and calm. I recalled him as a patient in the H Building, one of the younger ones and the most gravely ill. He was a light complexioned, red-headed guy about forty-five years old. For the first few months on the ward he sat ramrod still with his hands clenched in front of him. He wore a vacant expression and appeared unaware of his surroundings. He had to be spoon-fed and remained in a stuporous condition. He came out of this state almost overnight but quickly slid to the opposite end of the continuum becoming highly excitable and verbally incoherent. Although he could walk he remained fixed in his oversized vinyl chair and angrily glared at his extended fingers, all the while issuing a stream of incessant, rageful and disconnected speech at them as if they were real people. In a naive effort to embarrass him into normalcy I had penned in small faces on the tips of each of his fingers to illustrate the utter ludicrousness of his behavior, but he just kept on rambling away. John Hendrix was one of the sickest people in the hospital and here he was standing in front of me looking like the epitome of reason.

I stood up and extended my hand to him. He grasped my outright palm with both of his hands and said "Hello." His hands trembled slightly and his speech was halting.

I introduced myself but he remembered me from the H-Building. He said that he liked the night attendants and thought the red-headed kid with the whiffle (Jesser) was funny. I explained my role to him and promised that I would be as brief as possible. I asked him what happened the night Ronald was forced to sit on the radiator.

He looked straight at me and with all the hesitation removed from his voice said, "They grilled him Mr. Vitti; they grilled him on the radiator because he wouldn't go to bed." Hendrix witnessed it because he had gotten up to alert the attendants that a patient had fallen out of bed.

I questioned him for about five more minutes. He named and described the two fired attendants. I was convinced of their guilt. I thanked him and he returned to the population on the ward.

The seeming recovery of Mr. Hendrix knocked me for a loop. I could hardly believe the transformation. He was a diagnosed catatonic schizophrenic, the most serious of all categories of mental illness. I learned that such patients may remain in a condition of supposed lethargy for months, even years, sitting in the same position and unwilling to communicate in any manner. Suddenly a convulsive change may occur, projecting the patient into a state of extreme protracted excitability, followed, sometimes by a period of lucidity.

Apparently that is where I caught Mr. Hendrix, in a lucid state. His was the most dramatic change I had ever witnessed. But I knew it wouldn't last forever; it never does. The fear would eventually grip him again; the tension would inevitably mount pushing him into a state of dread panic. His hands would clench, his eyes would close and his body would stiffen - and there he would remain - locked inside of himself in a tight little psychological bundle until the horror passed. Contrary to the withdrawn appearance of the catatonic patient, he is supersensitive and mentally alert. Doctor Goldberg said it was similar to the heightened state of anxiety experienced by a child playing tag when his secret place is threatened by the closing presence of an opponent. Holding still and tight the child waits, frozen in place, until the menace leaves and the fear of detection is over. Somewhere down the line this paralyzing anxiety would once again envelop Mr. Hendrix, but for the moment he was an excellent witness.

Ginny escorted me to the door, chatting all the way across the ward. I remember thinking that she was the only beam of light in this dark place. I thanked her and headed back to the Administration Building.

I was accompanied into the front office by a secretary. Doctor Greenblatt's administrative assistant peered at me over his dark horned rimmed glasses. I sensed that he was ready to do battle, but I disarmed him quickly enough with my next comment.

"The union will not contest this," I said. I shook his hand and walked to the door. I was amused by the stunned look on his face. "In fact" I concluded, "I think the administration should seek criminal charges. They're two no-good bastards to do what they did." Actually, I knew from my college criminal investigation course that the hospital didn't have a good case, not with the only witness being psychotic. I decided that the next day I would call Brown and quit my union position. I knew that I would take a lot of heat from certain elements of the union for my unwillingness to defend the fired attendants. The job wasn't worth the aggravation.

I got a bite at the G & G and returned to my apartment late in the afternoon. I was comically surprised to see Beverly down on her hands and knees cleaning the space between the front threshold and the linoleum with a toothbrush. She was doing a lot of housework for us even though she didn't live there - but this was amazing. I didn't expect that such a beautiful female could also be so domestic. It was obvious to me that Beverly was fastidious.

I was also driven by this perfectionist need to order my environment. Jesser knew this and delighted in rearranging my room during my absences - especially my precisely lined up shoes. Seriously, its true - cleanliness and orderliness have always been paramount with me - especially as a young guy right out of the Marine Corps. Call it an interlocking neurosis - whatever - but on that day I began to engage Beverly on a different level. My feelings surrounding the pork chop incident subsided and the seeds of a romance began to bloom.

My first date with Beverly was a walk through the nearby Northeastern University campus. Beverly liked guys who wore white sneakers and button down shirts. She wished for the finer things in life and talked a lot about shopping at the Andover Shop in her home town and Bonwit Teller, an exclusive women's store in the Back Bay. In reality, she spent a lot of time in

Filenes' Bargain Basement on Washington Street in Boston. "Good quality clothes cheap," she said. She explained to me the status difference between a Mercedes Benz and a Caddie suggesting that the Mercedes was the choice car of people after they tired of a Cadillac.

As far as my own car was concerned, it was beginning to show signs of wear. I was putting twenty-four thousand miles a year on it not going particularly anywhere. Most of it was city driving. It was approaching sixty thousand miles and would require about three hundred dollars to pass the annual inspection. It was 1964 and the Ford Mustang had just made its debut. It came on the market with a lot of fanfare. I drove across town to Commonwealth Avenue to look at one.

As I neared my destination my car began to experience engine trouble. It began to cough and sputter. I nervously turned right onto a ramp that ejected into the lower level of the car dealership. I didn't have to turn the ignition off - the car just died. I rolled it into a parking spot and immediately began to negotiate a trade for the sleek new Mustang that was displayed so impressively tantalizing on the elevated platform in the middle of the floor. I can't recall what the salesman was willing to give me but I figured that any amount would have been better than nothing. I lucked out and the salesman excitedly informed me that a prospective buyer had just canceled and that I would be able to pick up the ordered car in just a couple of weeks, as long as I wasn't fussy about the color. Normally there was a long waiting period for delivery, he said. I signed the necessary paperwork. It was contingent on my getting financing and I believed that I had gotten a real good deal. I was rid of a broken down car that wouldn't even start and in exchange I would end up with a brand new Mustang. The down side of it was that I would inherit a bill. I think it was about twenty-five hundred dollars after a small down payment, in addition to the trade in, and I got a little shaky when I thought about it. I didn't like the idea of owing money for the first time in my life.

Beverly didn't like the idea either and by this time our relationship was heating up. "Why not keep it in the family?" she asked, and suggested that I buy her Volkswagen and avoid finance payments.

This sounded like a pretty good idea and we agreed on a selling price of eleven hundred dollars. It exceeded the book value and was a fair price and besides, I had just about that much money in the bank. She agreed to replace the cracked front windshield and repair the radio - that was a must. Meanwhile, Beverly allowed me to borrow the car for transportation to work, in exchange for driving her back and forth from her Brookline apartment to Boylston Street where she was employed as a dental technician. She complained of getting parking tickets every day. In fact, that is the reason she wanted to sell it, she explained. We both benefited from the deal and the arrangement worked smoothly in the beginning.

I lacked the control in my relationship with Beverly that I had with the others, but I increasingly came to enjoy the time I spent with her. The more I saw her, of course, the less I would see anyone else. After a while Beverly was the only girl I was taking out. She maintained her apartment in Brookline but continued to visit Follen Street after work. She was not the only female spending a lot of time visiting. By this time Jesser was getting really tight with Dell and the two women became friendly. Even on her days off Beverly would come to the apartment and help us clean. She was never satisfied with the sanitary level of the place and was given to ordering my roommates to perform housekeeping tasks.

That is what she was doing the day the place blew up - ordering Eckles to empty a wastebasket. He didn't like being told what to do and rightfully retaliated with a few comments of his own. I didn't like what he said and in response I flew off the kitchen counter and came nose to nose with Eckles who was standing resolutely in the middle of the kitchen. Jesser said it would have been the battle of the Titans (At 5'8" and one hundred and seventy pounds I was hardly a Titan, but no doubt it would have been one hell of a fight). The situation became white hot and Jesser and Mike were getting more nervous by the second. My heart was racing and I was seriously pissed; so was Eckles. Somehow good sense prevailed and no one struck the first blow

My anger slowly diffused but my spirit was dissipated in the process. I was disappointed and embarrassed; things now wouldn't be the same in that apartment. The bonds of camaraderie were broken and in the aftermath I decided to move out and back into the Male Home. And that is what I did. I packed up my belongings and returned to my second floor room - exhausted.

At about this time Beverly and her car, for some strange reason, seemed to disappear off the face of the earth. She left me flat and without an explanation. I can't recall who called whom, but when we finally talked over the phone, she told me that she had gone back with her old boyfriend. All I knew about him was that he was Jewish and an engineer. I guessed that he had more to offer than me.

Beverly still wanted to sell me the car and I still needed one. I felt especially bad about not being able to pick up Mrs. Hambleton. The old lady cushioned me and said she understood but I knew that she was spending a lot on cabs. I withdrew eleven hundred dollars from the bank in the form of a cashier's check and each day, for about a dozen days, I would drag myself out of bed early, borrow a car from another attendant, a different one each time, pay the guy two bucks for gas and drive to the intersection of Boylston and Dartmouth Streets in the Back Bay to pick up the Volkswagen. The mutually agreed upon exit strategy required that Beverly would drive the car to the Male Home in Mattapan and in return I would transport her back to work.

Beverly was usually there, although sometimes I would have to retrieve her at the office, but she never had the car. She predictably apologized for the car not being ready and always blamed the repair shop. It was getting warmer, the summer was coming on strong and the lack of sleep was rubbing my patience thin. I met Beverly once again and offered her the money but she informed me, without the slightest hesitation, that on the advice of her boyfriend she decided to raise the price by one hundred and fifty dollars. And she still didn't have the car!

That was the straw that broke the camel's back! I lost my friggin' mind right in the middle of Boylston Street! I let go with a barrage of obscenities in full view of the public, and all of them directed at Beverly. Looking back at the whole thing, I must have appeared insane - running back and forth and up and down Boylston Street, flailing my arms while pushing the middle finger of each hand straight up to the heavens and spewing vitriol at this innocent looking baby doll. To this day I can say that I was never so angry in my life. Beverly just gazed at me with a mildly perplexed expression on her face throughout the entire episode.

I am convinced even now that she never understood the core of my anger. I returned to the Male Home and vowed never to see Beverly again. I felt completely stripped. I ended up losing an apartment, a friend, two good roommates, a car, a few girl friends and the summer session at Northeastern. I had registered and purchased my books, but had never attended class because Beverly wished to have more time together. I felt like a real sucker.

I rested a few days, getting myself back together again. I bought an old Chevy for two hundred bucks that lasted only two days before I had to junk it, followed by a reliable ancient Plymouth that cost me thirty-five bucks and got me around pretty well. I joined with two other attendants, both of whom were former Marines, and rented an apartment in a wooden triple decker at 5 Balsam Street, just around the corner from the G & G. I still needed an off-grounds residence once I got the call from the police department. I left firm instructions with my friends at the hospital not to disclose my location to anyone, particularly Beverly, in the event that she came looking for me.

I got along well with my two roommates. John MacNeil, a husky, energetic happy faced guy was almost never there (I never knew where he went). The more intense Harry Whittier, with whom I was stationed while in the Marines, spent most of his time with his girlfriend Vivian, a thin, delicate, loving companion with a pretty face, black bangs and adoring eyes - all reserved for Harry.

The divorced woman upstairs was a fiery red-head with a passionate sense of justice and a couple of well mannered, nice looking kids. The family downstairs were a ne'er do well, jerk off the system type - but pleasantly disposed none the less. I regained my footing and things began to go well again.

Nine

T hings slowed down to about 33 RPM that summer. Neither Harry nor John were party guys and I deliberately kept things cool. This was a family neighborhood and there was no point in blowing the police department job after having gone this far. I remained on my best behavior with only one small lapse. Ed Jesser and I, together with two other attendants, emptied out a party on Marlborough Street that was full of Boston College assholes after we learned that some of them were lifting money from the girls' pocketbooks that were lying on the bed. I pulled the plug on the stereo and the four of us, standing together in the living room, demanded that the students leave. To my surprise they filed out sheepishly through the front door and down the stairs. We ended up having to drive the female's home. Some of them were crying.

It would have been a good time to resume the Museum trips with Leo but he had been discharged from the hospital. I wouldn't catch up with him for a few more years. I still worked with Jesser. Sometimes after work, in the mornings, we would drive to Uphams Corner in Dorchester, a busy urban square located right down the street from where Jesser had grown up and just hang around rapping and taking in the scene. Even then Ed was storing the cerebral rods that would someday fuel the future political and social insights for which he would become known.

I was burned pretty badly one more time that summer, but it was the result of a ten hour stay on Nantasket Beach. It was the first, worst and last sunburn I ever had.

Beverly reappeared on the scene sometime in July. We were painting the apartment and the bell rang. John answered the door and showed Beverly in. Somebody had ratted me out. I had mixed feelings about seeing her. I put the brush down and took Beverly to the G & G. Beverly's mother was Jewish, but this was the first time Beverly had ever witnessed poor city Jews. They were colorful to me - outlandish to her.

She apologized for what had happened. She said she went back with her old boyfriend because she felt sorry for him. "He had only one lung," she lamented.

It was his idea to raise the price of the VW, not hers. Perhaps he was jealous, I thought.

"You can just have the car," she implored.

"I don't want it anymore," I chuckled. "My Plymouth is just fine, Beverly, just fine. Let's go for a ride." We ended up at Houghton's Pond.

Things were happening. Sometime, just before the first semester began, a Boston Police Sergeant talked with some of my neighbors about me. I knew this was part of the department's background check. Vinny said that was a good sign.

Between August 2 and August 4, 1964, two U.S. Naval Destroyers, the *Maddox* and *Turner Joy*, reported aggressive action by Vietnamese Torpedo Boats in the Gulf of Tonkin. President Johnson authorized retaliatory action.

On August 29 1964, the *Boston Strangler* struck once again. An elderly woman was found murdered in her house in Roxbury; a nylon stocking was wrapped around her neck. Lieutenant John Donovan of the Homicide Unit accepted jurisdiction of the investigation.

On Wednesday September 23 1964, I opened a letter from the City of Boston Police Department, Office of the Police Commissioner. I knew what the contents would reveal. I re-read it several times.

The Passage

September 22, 1964

To: Phillip M. Vitti

Sir,

I am directed by the Police Commissioner to notify you to report to the line-up room, Boston Police Headquarters, 154 Berkeley Street, Boston, at 9:30 AM, Wednesday, September 30, 1964, to be sworn in as a patrolman in this department.

You will begin your three months course of Recruit Training on that day and should have with you a fountain or ball point pen. Please dress in a business suit, wearing a shirt and tie.

Bring with you two copies of your birth certificate, two copies of your discharge from the U.S. Military Service, if any, and three letters of recommendation from persons with personal knowledge of your character and reputation.

Please sign and mail to this office as soon as possible, the enclosed acceptance form.

For the Police Commissioner:
William J. Taylor Deputy Superintendent
Chief, of Bureau of Personal & Training

So this is what it all boiled down to, a terse and impersonal letter, devoid of even a congratulatory note, ordering me to undertake the initial process of police induction. My sojourn through the clinical world of the mentally ill was drawing to a close and would be replaced by a longer journey - one that would take me into a more immense world where the patients lived without walls, drove cars and carried guns. The lessons of the State Hospital would not be lost - they would provide me with the analytical detachment necessary to maintain the edge in volatile situations. This would work for me throughout my career.

I felt good - it was an achievement, like graduating high school, or surviving boot camp in the Marine Corps. I first shared the news with my aunt over the telephone.

"I knew you could do it," she said. "I'm proud of you. Your mother would

75

be too. I can't wait to tell Jeanette. But please, Phillip, be careful, police work is dangerous." (It certainly was. In the two years that I had worked at the State Hospital two Boston Police Officers had been killed in the line of duty. Officer John Gallagher died on May 25, 1962, shot by a burglar in a bank robbery and James O'Leary died on August 23 of the next year as a result of gunshot wounds sustained in the pursuit of a dangerous criminal). Dangerous? Yes, but that possibility did not preoccupy me.

My biggest concern at the time was not forgetting my pen on Wednesday. Later that afternoon I officially notified the Boston State Hospital of my intention to resign. Sunday would be my last day.

Ten

I fell into an uneasy sleep the night before the swearing in ceremony. It was early in the AM before I finally dozed off. I dreamed that night. I dreamed --- -a very long dream.

In it, I sat in a movie theater. It was dark but I knew that it was the Broadway Show, located in Somerville, right across the street from the house where I grew up.

I was still a boy and I sat in the middle of the theater, about half way up the aisle. I was completely alone and the darkness felt good. I didn't want anyone to see me crying. I was racked by inconsolable grief and pain. I felt abandoned and vulnerable. I wished to remain there forever. I couldn't hear a sound around me. There was no movement - not even the usher or the light of his flashlight could be detected.

Suddenly the blank screen exploded in a spectrum of vivid colors and animated imagery! I rose from my chair, mesmerized by the expanding cartoon that danced across the stage. The exaggerated lines portrayed rolling green hills against a background of a soft blue sky. A yellow ball was fixed high in the heavens. I stepped up to the front stage and walked carefully across its surface. I became increasingly more transfixed by the sight of a bean-stalk growing out of the earth in front of me. Its branches stretched above the clouds. I reached out and touched the giant screen. I pushed the left side of my body into the action, first my leg and then my arm. In just moments I was absorbed into the other side. There I stood, a living part of a bizarre caricature of an artist's fantasy.

When I regained my equilibrium I was able to make out the animated forms of two young women. They summoned me with their hands to the area of the beanstalk. I began to approach them. As I got closer I could plainly see they were pretty and both enjoyed beautiful expressive brown eyes. They were identical in every respect. They looked like Cinderella split into two. They wore wooden clogs and their gray frocks were tattered and torn. The only difference between them was their expression: one had a happy face and the other was sad.

I walked close to them. The sad faced one reached out and held my hand. Her hand was firm and reassuring. My anxiety passed and was replaced by a sense of purpose. She placed my hand in the warm palm of the happy faced one who smiled down at me and led me to the bottom tendril of the beanstalk. I was implicitly aware that they both expected me to climb it. I did not wish to leave these women but I knew what I must do.

I placed my hand around a green shoot protruding from the plant and dug my foot into the stem. It felt solid and cool to the touch. I pushed up hard and my body lifted. I began the climb. In the beginning it was difficult and I lost my footing several times. I was overweight and I was puffing really hard. As I climbed higher I had the sensation that my weight was coming off and my body was getting longer and more muscular.

Just as I began to feel more in control I was joined on the vine by a middle-aged man with a crooked nose. I knew this man and I knew that he was evil. I was frightened of his intentions. I looked fearfully into his eyes and to my horror, his face began to contort. It moved and twitched and twisted and turned. His teeth grew longer and sharper and his face became covered with hair. In a brief terror filled time he underwent a total metamorphosis and when the change was completed he reached a clawed hand to my right arm and tried to pull me off the vine.

I looked down to the ground and begged for help but only one of the women was present and she was powerless. I wrenched my arm away and almost immediately experienced a surge of strength. I began to fight this beast with increasing confidence and renewed vigor. I struck a hard and direct blow to the left side of his face and then another and another. He lost his grip and fell backwards. I was amazed at how easily he plummeted to the ground. When he hit the surface he was quickly swallowed up by a temporary fiery opening in the earth. He was finished. I was the victor! I would never fear this evil again! It was as though I were relieved of a great weight.

The remainder of the ascent was almost effortless. Eventually I pushed up through a cloud cover and rested on a flat puffy plateau. I looked around in astonishment and that is when I saw her - the ethereal form of a woman that could only be Andrianna Tranquillo. She stood upright on a shifting cloud, looking very real and more beautiful than I had ever imagined that she could. She was wearing a white satin gown that clung loosely to the curves of her body. Her jet-black hair and deep brown eyes contrasted perfectly with her soft white skin and lush red lips. She smiled and beckoned to me. There was an aura all around her and her position seemed to shift slightly with the wind. I slowly approached her and when the distance between us narrowed I could plainly see a blue door off to the left. She pointed to it and in a soft melodic voice instructed me to "Open it."

I placed my hand on the large golden knob and twisted it to the right. The door opened and Andrianna handed me a pair of 3-D glasses. I put them on and peered inside. I saw a long dimly lit tunnel that seemed to stretch endlessly into infinity - a breathing, pulsating passageway that rose and fell and twisted and turned through the dark. Flashing lights punctuated the darkness and human shapes were silhouetted against the walls. I stepped behind the door and my ears were immediately pierced by the increasing intensity of a shrill sound.

I finally woke up. The alarm clock was ringing. The big day had arrived!

TWO

By doing our duty, we learn to do it.
----------E. B. Pusey

Eleven

We numbered thirty-three. It was said to be the smallest class in the department's recent memory - thirty white males - solid core Irish with an impressive scattering of Italians, nine to be exact, and three black guys, one of whom (Prescott Thompson) had worked at the Boston State Hospital, although I only vaguely knew him. Working class stiffs from blue-collar families - the final products that fell through the strainer, standing together, inwardly proud behind masks of impassivity. Most of us were military veterans but only the Korean War guys received preference on the eligibility list.

Our surroundings were uninspiring - a drab, singular colored, partitioned off area adjacent to the line up room, buried in the basement of Police Headquarters. Beginning at 8:00 AM prisoners from across the city's districts would be paraded behind a large rectangular section of opaque glass and intermittently displayed for criminal identification purposes. Detectives, some of them garishly dressed, wearing suits and sporting green felt hats, stood with crime victims on the opposite side - a recurring part of an early morning drama. When the line-up was over the detectives who didn't make a case, or were not busy in court, broke out the Dominoes and three or four games would be simultaneously played out until mid-morning. Chess, Checkers and Dominoes were the only games authorized by the

1950s rules and regulations to be played in a police facility. We didn't know it then but we were screwing up the routine that day.

Deputy Superintendent Bill Taylor administered the oath. A distinguished looking man with a square jaw and a pleasant smile, he was destined to become the first Superintendent in Chief of the Boston Police Department and one of its grand patriarchs. I raised my right hand and swore allegiance to the Department, the City, the State and the Constitution - the whole 'shla...meel"

I flashed back to Officer Napoleon and wondered if he had taken a similar oath. Other memories competed for my attention. *One of the most poignant transported me back to January 31 1958, to a men's room no less, in the Nation's capital. I found myself in charge of fourteen Marine recruits destined for Paris Island in South Carolina. I had won this awesome responsibility because I was a P.F.C. in the Marine Corps Reserve before I joined the regulars, and so it automatically fell to me to take charge. My Aunt Mary and my best friend Brian had accompanied me to South Station to say good-bye. It was a good thing they did, because I didn't know how to get there.*

I met up with the group, identified myself, explained my orders, said my good-byes and boarded the train. We went as far as Washington D.C. where they enjoyed a three-hour layover before they would finish their trip to Yamasee. I should emphasize that they enjoyed this layover, this one last fling at freedom, not I, who was literally sick to the pit of my stomach with fretting about the possibility of losing even one individual before I arrived at the training base. This failure, I knew, would result in an automatic discharge; I would be washed out before I had had the opportunity of proving myself. The Marine Corps was tough about those things. I knew that if one of these guys got drunk, or lost, or whatever, and failed to make the connection, my ass would be grass.

I was standing in front of a sink washing my hands, engulfed in multiple mental possibilities of this depressing scenario, when my thoughts were interrupted by a guy drying his hands at a nearby washbowl.

"Where ya heading, kid?" he asked.

I was initially suspicious of his intentions but I answered him anyway, "I joined the Marine Corps and I am on my way to Paris Island."

My suspicions quickly dissolved once I got a better look at him. He was casually dressed and was wearing a black soft felt hat. He had a kind of street look about him that reminded me of a hundred tough guys I knew in the city.

"How long will you be in?" he asked.

"Four years," I responded.

"That's a long time," he said.

We walked out onto the terminal. He looked at me very pointedly and paused for a moment. "Yeah, that's a long time," he repeated, "but look at it this way. Think of your life as a book and the Marine Corps as a chapter of that book. If you keep your nose clean and get an honorable discharge, that chapter of your life will read well. But if you end up with a dishonorable discharge you will either have to eliminate that chapter or leave it in. In that case, the book of your life will not read well."

I was completely thunderstruck! I gazed back at him and managed to get off a garbled "Thanks for the advice," and suddenly he was gone. He seemed to disappear as quickly as he had appeared, but he left me with a whole new perspective. The gig was up and I knew it. I needed to get serious and leave my juvenile ways behind, particularly my irresponsible attitude, a reckless attitude that had resulted in an overall C-minus average to show for four years of high school, and that included several disciplinary actions, an expulsion from one school and a suspension from another, firings from two jobs, countless fist fights and threats of a court-martial from the Marine Reserves for my failure to attend meetings. Yeah, it was all over. Things were changing and I had to get with the program! This chance encounter with a stranger had jolted me into an upper realm: it was a pivotal point in my life and it fortified me for the pounding that would begin in less than twenty-four hours.

I was being bumped up once again, to a higher level of personal responsibility, but this time the gush would have to sustain me far beyond a four year hitch. I looked around at the expressionless faces in the room and I quickly became aware that my two and a half year flirtation with intellectual and personal spontaneity was coming to an end. The conditioning process had already begun.

After the oath was completed we were given directions to the Police Academy and released. A showcase cop was standing outside Police Headquarters directing traffic at the intersection of Berkeley and Stuart Streets. I figured they had put him there to impress us. I learned later that his name was Bernie McGarry. Bernie wore a white hat and gloves, the uniform of the Traffic Division; his impeccable appearance was further enhanced by his soft spoken ways and polite demeanor. No doubt he did service to the image of Boston's Finest, unlike a few of the others that I would meet.

The Police Academy was located on the third floor of District 4, a dingy red brick building on Warren Avenue in the South End of the city about a block away from the heart of Dover Street, Boston's counterpart to New York's Bowery District or Chicago's West Madison Street. Every city had a skid row, but the close proximity of Dover Street provided District 4 with the dubious distinction of having the highest DK (drunk) arrest rate in the country. I learned that the cops kept a few unfinished bottles of whiskey around to treat the DTs - a simple act of compassion, I supposed. In any event, we reported there to begin our training the following Monday.

The program was designed to last thirteen weeks. It was crammed full of police subject matter. Some of it was fluff. The most important material dealt with the right of arrest. Captain Bill Hogan was the subject matter expert in this area, although that term was not used at the time. He was a mild mannered man with a keen mind, a sincere disposition and a wooden leg - the result of an amputation that stemmed from an on-duty injury. I heard he had fallen through a roof earlier in his career. I vividly recall him standing before the classroom directing his pointer at a large training aid that depicted the palm side of a human hand with the thumb and fingers separated and extended straight out. Each appendage represented a distinct right of arrest. Starting with the inscribed thumb and moving across the four fingers from left to right, he would repetitively drill us that a police officer had a right to arrest for any felony committed in his presence, or for reasonable suspicion of a felony committed outside of his presence, or for any misdemeanor (a crime punishable by less than three years in a house of correction) for which he is granted a right of arrest by statute, or misdemeanors that amount to a breach of the peace, and/or finally, as the result of any warrant.

"That's it," he would say. "It's all here; learn this and you've got it all."

Of course there was a little more to it than that. One had to acquire a knowledge of which offenses were classified as felonies versus misdemeanors, and which particular misdemeanors were arrestable, or what kind of behavior amounted to a breach of the peace, but it was a neat graphic compression of a huge complex area of criminal law.

Sergeant Francis (Barney) Schroeder, a tall, seemingly strict man, covered the history of the Boston Police Department and the Rules and Regulations. No one could possibly learn them all, including the 'brass,' but what we already knew was that this huge compendium of restrictive measures, some of it bordering on nonsensical minutiae, could be dragged out at any time and applied if 'they' wanted to screw someone. I heard reverberations of the 'keep your nose clean theme.' Barney was a conscientious guy and somewhat pensive. Perhaps, even then, he was vaguely aware of the double tragedy that lay in wait for him.

Detective Bernie Hurley taught report writing, case preparation, evidence collection and court procedure. Bernie was a slight guy who liked sporty jackets and bow ties. His large glasses gave him a kind of Mr. Peepers look. He was both technical and sensitive. He wrote a poem to the recruit class before we graduated and they thought it was funny. Years later I bumped into him in front of Police Headquarters. He was retiring and was on his way up the front stairs to the Personnel Division on the fifth floor. He wanted to present the staff with a cover letter to add to his personnel folder acknowledging his gratitude to the Boston Police Department for a satisfying career. Bernie was a different kind of cop.

For my money, Lieutenant 'Billy' Burke was the most memorable. Glassy-eyed and prematurely gray, he resonated like a wise old sage with an ability to balance the practical with the philosophical and the interests of the public with the welfare of the officers. He made it all sound simple.

"Use common sense," he would say. "That's ninety percent of the job. Cops can make a real difference in a person's life. Go that little bit of extra and make a friend for the police department - God knows we need them!" Billy Burke knew it too!

It wasn't all fun and games out there, and that's where 'Bo Bo' Olsen came in. Bo Bo was a big, ruddy faced guy who was more comfortable in a fight than a classroom. He taught weapons training and self-defense. He was not big on the PR but he was one hell of a guy to have around if you got into a jam. Like the others, his concern for the safety and welfare of the recruits was overriding - that, in fact, was the common thread that wove these different men together.

Captain Arthur Cadigan was the Commander of the Police Academy. He was a tall, large framed, impressive looking man with a distinctive military bearing, including a Ted Williams' whiffle. He was also a lawyer. The only time I ever spoke to him was to request that he not send me to the Traffic Division for a permanent assignment. He assured me that he wouldn't.

"We've spent too much money training you to do that," he concluded.

Actually, Traffic was a sought-after job. It was clean and there was plenty of time between breaks - enough to take in a movie - free of course, like a lot of other things were back then, but I wasn't ready to retire.

It took a couple of weeks for us to relax and begin to identify as a group. Along about this time we converted from civilian clothes to khakis. My classmates were amazingly ordinary. They were like a lot of guys I grew up with - at least the ones who stayed out of trouble. Ethnic kids from across the city's neighborhoods; they had hung on corners, played sports, drank on the weekends, graduated from high school, did a stint in the Service (the ones that weren't drafted had joined up), got out, looked for a job, got married and raised a family.

The police department offered them instant middle-class status, recognition, a steady paycheck and an eventual pension. Most of the recruits would complain, or perhaps 'boast' is more like it, that they took a pay-cut for the cop's job. I couldn't say the same thing. It was an increase in money for me. My last paycheck at the State Hospital amounted to $72.60. My first paycheck on the police department was for $101.14. After taxes I was clearing twenty-five bucks more - Not bad.

Ordinary guys, yes, but by no means unremarkable. I took an instant liking to Mike Giardiello; he was a mix between a gentleman farmer and a dilettante. He often referred to his boyhood summer experiences on a small farm. He reiterated the simple rewards of the rustic life. He also entertained a healthy appreciation of the fine arts, especially the theater. He spent a good part of his days off wandering around the theater section of town taking in the earlier and less expensive afternoon performances. He was very different from the standard recruit in this respect. He kind of reminded me of Perry Como. Affable and easy going, educated and urbane, his plate was always full. Mike was pleasantly amused by the form in which the class was congealing. He once pointed out to me the natural attraction of physical size in a macho bravado setting.

"Look at them," he said. "They all want to hang around with the two biggest guys in the class."

It was true. Kenny Hegner and Bob Guiney shared twelve and a half feet and close to five hundred pounds between them. They were popular with their classmates. In fact they, along with ten of our classmates, volunteered for the newly formed Tactical Patrol Force (TPF) upon graduation from the Academy. The TPF was employed in the toughest neighborhoods in the City, particularly the infamous 'Combat Zone,' a seedy, violence-prone four block area of honky-tonk joints, servicemen, sailor-bait chicks, prostitutes, cop fighters, extortionists, leg breakers and stone cold killers. These men were destined to become a pervasive presence in these mean streets. I, for one, had learned the perils of volunteering while in the crotch - so had the other two Marines in our class.

Frankie Graham, one of the shortest guys in the class, became our class president. I could never recall there being a vote. Twenty-five years later I would verify that there never had been an election. He had nominated himself and Al 'the Fed' Charbonnier seconded the nomination. A little more investigation would establish the link - Frankie, at the time, lived at 423 Bunker Hill Street and Al lived around the corner at 85 Pearl Street in Charlestown. It was a scam, but most of our classmates would go to the end of their careers believing that they were in the men's room when the vote was taken. But that's what those 'Townies' were like! I finally confronted Frankie with the truth and he laughed it off. On a more serious note, Graham would become renowned for his honesty - down the line.

One of the other Marines was Ronny Conway from Dorchester. We shared many similarities. About the same age, weight and height, we had spent the same four years in the Marine Corps and, of course, we were called for the job on the same day. We experienced a parallel rise through the ranks and a similar academic background, except for one degree that is. Ronny would go on to earn his Doctorate. The 'Doctor,' as he later became known, had one abiding adage. Looking straight out and screwing his cheeks up slightly, he would declare,

"It's nice to be important, but it's more important to be nice."

It might have sounded corny, but Ronny was genuine. Moreover, he took this belief to the end of his career.

Not everyone appeared so pleasantly disposed. There was one guy who snarled and ground his teeth a lot. Many of us got the impression that he didn't like cops. If he didn't, he had a good reason. His brother had been shot and killed by a State Trooper in a case of mistaken identification. The academy staff was said to have questioned him about this and he had convinced them that he was fine. Some of us wondered, however. Apparently he adjusted well enough once he got into a permanent assignment; I never heard any beefs.

Twelve

We received our badges on Friday afternoon of the third week. My number was 2079. There is a mystical quality about a police badge, no doubt about it. The awarding of badges is the most extraordinary collective event in the career of a police officer. Cops often refer to the badge as a Shield - an ancient connotation. It is the most distinctive and visible piece of equipment that sets the police officer apart from the civilian population. It is an enduring symbol of power and the only piece of equipment that a Boston Police Officer is required to carry off duty. The awarding of the badges is the day when police candidates became cops! It is also the day when an ego can rise faster than a helium balloon. Lieutenant Burke was well aware of this effect, and together with Barney Schroeder, spent a good amount of time admonishing us not to use the power just yet. Barney explained that we still did not know how to back up the badge with the proper force, if it became necessary.

"Yes," Lieutenant Burke interjected, "keep the badge in your pocket. Wait until you are properly trained to back up your authority before displaying it, otherwise you may end up embarrassed when somebody tells you what you can do with it."

We were dismissed early that day. When I returned to my Balsam Street apartment Beverly called to say that she was on her way over. I was seeing her almost every night. I had just gotten off the telephone when I heard a knock on the door. It was the ne'er-do-well guy on the first floor. I invited him in.

"Is everything all right?" I asked.

"Yeah, not bad," he replied, "but I'm having a problem with the guy in the corner Deli. He keeps on parking at the fire hydrant. I have two kids here. What would happen if we had a fire? I keep on asking him to move but he refuses to. I asked him again today, but he told me to mind my own business. I told him there was a cop who lived on the second floor and he said that it was none of his business either."

"Is he down there now?" I asked.

"Yeah. I just talked to him; he's in the store. I think he owns it."

My neighbor sucked me right in. I should have gotten on the hook and dialed DE-8-1212, the police emergency number, or called the district station directly. It was only around the corner on Morton Street, but against the good advice I had received just hours before I decided to handle the problem myself. I didn't like the guy's remarks about it not being any of my business. After all, I was a resident cop. Who did he think he was anyway?

"Don't worry about it. I'll handle it," I remarked as I walked downstairs into the street.

I saw the car parked at the hydrant and made my way into the corner Deli. I approached the little roly-poly guy behind the counter. I had seen him around before and I knew that he owned the business. The store was empty of customers.

"Pardon me sir, but do you own that blue Ford parked in front of the hydrant?"

"Yes, as a matter of fact I do. Who are you?" he asked.

I displayed my badge. "I'm a police officer and I live next door," I responded.

"So what?" he sneered.

"So I'm asking you to remove your car from the hydrant!"

"What are you, some kind of a rookie?" he retorted. A sarcastic look of amusement crossed his face. "Are they giving kids badges now?" he added.

This guy was starting to get to me, but the last thing I wanted to do was to create an incident. I was still assigned to the Police Academy and just starting my six months' probation. Back in Somerville anyone who spoke to me that way wouldn't have been still standing, but things were different now. This guy knew he had me over a barrel.

"Look pal, just move your car," I said, my voice noticeably strained with anger.

He looked down at my badge, which I still held in the palm of my hand. He looked back up at me and placed his hands over the rolls of fat that hung from his side and said, "Take that badge and shove it!"

To make matters worse, a customer walked into the store and overheard his last remark. I was flushed and unsure of what to do next. I certainly didn't want to call the police. That would have been too embarrassing. Besides, he acted like he had a big 'in' at the station, probably knew the Captain, I thought.

"Okay, have it your way," I muttered.

As I made my way out the door, I turned toward him one last time and promised that he would be hearing from me.

It dawned on me that Vinny Lopez might be working that night. He would help me, and I was meaning to see him anyway. When I returned to my apartment Beverly was there waiting for me. She could see that I was upset.

"What happened?" she asked.

I assured her that I would explain, but first I called the station. I spoke with the police officer on the desk. He said that he knew Vinny, but I was too late. He had just retired. Vinny was a "great guy" the cop said. I agreed and politely hung up the phone. "Too bad," I lamented. I lost a police friend and my problem was still not solved.

I escorted Beverly to the G & G for dinner. On the way I passed the violated fire hydrant and I was markedly relieved to see that the car was gone.

The next day I shared my embarrassment with Bobby Trotter. Bobby was a non- critical sort of guy whose face always beamed with a perpetual smile. He chuckled. We both agreed that I should have heeded Lieutenant Burke's advice and kept my badge in my pocket - better there than up my ass.

Around the mid-point of the training period we were assigned for one week to the firearms range on Moon Island, a narrow spit of land extending into the Boston Harbor and connected by a bridge to the city of Quincy. We were issued six shot, 38-caliber, four-inch barrel revolvers. The first morning was devoted mainly to learning the nomenclature, care and maintenance of the weapon. That afternoon kicked off a week of shooting with Friday reserved as qualification day. My closest competitor was another Marine, a big-feeling guy who always made me feel uncomfortable. Only one or two points separated us at the end of each day. The lead would bounce back and forth between us. On Friday it bounced in my direction and that was the only day that counted. I could see that he was burnt up about this. "Too friggin' bad", I thought.

We were issued our uniforms around the end of October. During the first week of November we were assigned to one of the various police districts for one week of training. I drew Station 16, an archaic red brick front building located in the city's fashionable Back Bay. Station 16 was also the location of the horse stables - home to the department's police horses. The place stunk.

On the first day I was assigned to Wagon 1600 with Officers Molano and O'Brien. The wagon was generally used to transport prisoners and sick persons. It wasn't my idea of an action car. I spent most of the day riding around the district with either one or both of the two officers.

I carefully wrote the proper information, including a description of the calls for service and the weather conditions in my small blue paper bound pocket filler. At 1:55 PM on November 2, 1964, we responded to a sick assist call at the corner of Massachusetts Avenue and Newbury Street. No one was in the vicinity. At 3:15 PM Officers Molano, O'Brien and Vitti, responded to a radio call to the intersection of Dartmouth and Boylston Streets to pick up Isador Rotman and transport him to the Boston City Hospital - possible heart attack. And that was it. At 5:45 PM we were relieved.

The next day I worked with Officer Molano in a two-man car. The calls were mostly routine and of a service nature. What I recall best of all was Henry's advice. I can hear him now as though it were yesterday.

"Always keep cool, kid. Keep your wits about you. Think of what you're gonna do as you're approaching the call. Never speed recklessly through the streets. You don't want to kill a pedestrian on the way to a phony incident or one that is cleared up before you get there. Never run to break up a fight 'cuz you'll tire yourself out and end up getting your own ass kicked."

I listened intently.

The next day I rode with a boring guy who failed to make much of an impression on me. I could see that he didn't enjoy the 'job' the same way Henry did. He was more interested in getting through the day without any major incidents than with sharing advice with a rookie. He bailed out of the car on Newbury Street about fifteen minutes before the end of the tour, trusting me to drive the cruiser back to the station in time to be relieved.

"So long," he said. "You know your way back to the house (the station) don't you?"

"Yeah, take it easy," I assured him as he stepped into his car.

I lied! I had no idea where I was, but I was unwilling to admit it. Apparently the wearing of the blue uniform was unable to remedy a lifelong deficient sense of direction. Neither was my street directory, which provided me with the names of intersecting streets that I had never heard of. Actually I was right around the block from the station, but I could have been in Cambridge, the next town over, for all I knew. I became increasingly fearful that I would return late and get my partner into trouble for leaving me in the street, not to mention the chagrin that I was bound to feel when the Sergeant questioned me. There I was, a lost cop, sitting for the first time behind the wheel of a police cruiser.

The time was getting shorter. I had less than ten minutes to make it back and that is when I decided to --- **to ask a pedestrian where the police station was!** He was crossing Newbury Street about 100 feet from where I had let my partner off. I was still in the area, still looking for a familiar landmark or sign that would orient me. Failing to do so, I rolled the fully marked police cruiser to a stop, blocking the path of my unknowing mark. He looked like a businessman, blue suit, glasses, brief case, the whole bit.

"Pardon me sir, but could you give me directions to Station Sixteen?"

Once the initial shock wore off he moved two steps backward and gazed at the cruiser. His expression changed from contemplative to incredulous. He riveted his eyes on me.

"I don't know if you're putting me on or not," he uttered. "It's hard to believe that a cop doesn't know where the police station is."

I abashedly agreed, offering him the feeble explanation that I was a new cop, unfamiliar with the neighborhood.

"It's straight up Hereford Street," he said, pointing diagonally across the street from where we were positioned, "but that's one way going in the other direction, so you'll have to go around the block."

I felt like a real dope. I could almost have landed a stone on the roof. But better to be embarrassed by a guy who I probably would never meet again than one of the 'bosses' on the department who would be evaluating me during my probationary process. I smiled and thanked him. I sneaked a backward glance at him in the rear view mirror as I pulled away. He looked perplexed.

The progression of years would eventually raise this incident to a level of hilarity. But even time would not dull the debilitating effects of the second incident that occurred one hour later. Just minutes after stepping off a Massachusetts Transit Authority (MTA) bus on Blue Hill Avenue on my way home, I was confronted by a six foot, solidly built, Jewish looking guy who pleaded with me to arrange transportation for him to the Mass. Mental Hospital, just off Huntington Avenue in Roxbury and about fifteen minutes from where we were standing. He looked seriously agitated and he rocked back and forth as he spoke.

He explained that he was a former mental patient who from time to time required re-hospitalization due to relapses. He stated that he was about to have another one. He could feel it coming, and I could see it coming! He needed to be confined, he said, because when he 'flipped' he wanted to physically harm his father.

I didn't ask any further questions. I immediately entered a sub shop, popped a dime in the telephone and called the emergency police number. I requested a wagon for a 'sick assist.' About seven long minutes later a police ambulette (station wagon) arrived on the scene. A black cop was driving and a white cop was sitting in the passenger seat, riding shotgun. The station wagon eased up to where I was standing with the former patient. I looked at the passenger seat guy and a foul attitude floated out the window. I knew right away this was not going to go down easy.

The white cop peered up at me through the partially opened passenger window. He didn't have the courtesy to roll it all the way down. He was wearing what looked to be a two day growth of beard and the top of his uniform hat was ringed with dirt. He looked mean and shabby.

"Who are you?" he gruffly asked, apparently more interested in my identity than my problem. The fact that I was wearing the uniform of a Boston Police Officer didn't faze him - he was more concerned with just who it was that was invading his district than providing a police service.

"My name is Phil Vitti," I retorted. "I live in the neighborhood and I was on my way home when this man stopped me and requested a ride to the Mass. Mental. He's in the initial stages of a breakdown and wants to be confined to avoid injuring his father. Would you mind giving him a ride?" I calmly asked.

The shabby cop just sat there, fingering his beard and looking out the window. After almost a minute passed he snarled,

"What the fuck do you think we are, a baby-sitting service?"

It was a stinging rebuke to everything I believed a police officer stood for. I was knocked off balance momentarily and the mentally ill guy looked stunned. He began to cry. Before I could stop him, he ran off. Although I was furious, I tried to keep my cool. I was still a rookie and didn't need a major incident with a veteran cop.

"If anything happens to that guy or his father, it's your fault," I said. "I did everything I could do."

"Nothing is going to happen," he commented, as a smirk slowly moved across his face.

"How do you know that?" I asked.

"Because I've been dealing with these fucking nuts for eighteen years; that's how I know."

That was my opening and I made good use of it. "I've been dealing with them too, for eight hours a day for the past two and a half years. I worked at the State Hospital before I came on this job." (The cop behind the wheel had also worked there- I remembered seeing him around, but he remained silent.)

I continued, "I know for a fact that some patients experience an 'aura' just before they crack. So if anything happens with this guy, it's on your conscience, not mine."

I felt satisfied that I had said my piece, and having said it, I abruptly turned and walked away. I never looked back at either of the two cops. I didn't care what they thought. They sucked - especially the guy in the passenger seat.

I heard the car drive away. I spent about fifteen minutes looking for the 'complainant' but he had disappeared into the early evening. "Probably looking for his old man," I feared. I saw him in the street several months later and I apologized to him for the offensive conduct of the shabby cop.

"Ya know," he said, "I stood in the rain for hours campaigning for Question #8. What a lousy way to get treated."

No shit! Question #8 was a ballot question designed to provide a series of small step raises to the police. The police had won a very narrow victory, thanks to the senior citizens in the nursing homes who put us over the top and to guys like him.

There was a lot of talk getting swapped around once we returned to the Academy. The 'war stories' had already begun. Every recruit had his own experiences - some of them were good and others were not. First impressions are lasting and my episode with the outrageous cop had singed my conscious memory. It was disheartening, and I was bitterly disappointed. I began to think that perhaps Jesser was right when he said,

"Why would anyone go to college to become a fucking cop?"

This police officer had done more harm than good. He had failed to help the guy, exposed his old man to danger, and put me down in the process. He was a piss-poor example of a cop. I bristled whenever I thought about him but I had to push the experience to the back of my mind. I had other things to worry about - like Beverly being pregnant!

I didn't think I heard it right either, but yes, it was true. She wasn't feeling well and she went to the Doctor for a check-up. He did a test and the rest was history. When she told me, my first reaction was stunned silence - followed by a stream of unintelligible verbiage. I sure didn't strike the image of Sir Galahad. I was letting Beverly down and I knew it. She stood facing the wall. She bowed her head slightly and with her left hand covering her eyes, she quietly sobbed.

Once I got a hold of myself, I apologized.

"I'm sorry, Bev. It takes two to tango. I'm in this thing too, and I won't let you down. It's a good excuse to marry you - that is if you'll have me."

When I thought about it, marriage didn't seem like a bad idea. Beverly was a prize catch - a real head turner - an accomplished ballet dancer and a bit of an entrepreneur. She had earned a hundred and fifty bucks a week clear during high school by teaching dance. That was a phenomenal sum for a teenage girl in the Fifties! Not to mention that I had always secretly nursed an ambition to marry and have a family in the future. My solitary orphaned childhood status nourished this fantasy. I wished to emulate my older cousin, Dick Cash. I had a deep and abiding respect for him. A handsome and athletic guy, he had married one of the most beautiful women in the town of Plymouth, a blonde, blue-eyed Italian-American. He and Mary had settled down and raised a family in a storybook country house with the traditional white picket fence, small garden and chickens that laid eggs. A simple life style - there was nothing wrong with that. To this day, they have enjoyed a long, loving and stable union.

"Yeah," I figured, "Why not? Go for it!"

I reassured Beverly of my support. She stopped crying and settled down. I held her in my arms and gently rocked her back and forth. On December 12, 1964, we were married with the immediate family present at a simple candle light ceremony in a small Unitarian Church on Washington Street in Dorchester. The wedding had been quickly arranged by Beverly's sister Thelma and her husband Joe - they knew the minister. My roommate, Harry Whittier, was my best man. (I was disappointed that I was unable to marry in the Catholic Church but Beverly's prior marriage had precluded that). I was three months short of my twenty-sixth birthday that night - the night that G.I. Joe and Barbie were wed.

December also witnessed the Department engage in its time-honored tradition of supplementing the Traffic Division, in preparation for the holiday shopping rush, with whatever recruit class that was in training. Back into the streets, but this time for the purpose of traffic control and parking enforcement.

Superintendent James (Bukie) Buchanan's generous award of a few C-days, strung on to my scheduled days off, permitted Beverly and me to enjoy a brief escape into the technological world of the future at the World's Fair in New York City. I was mesmerized by an exhibit that portrayed the progression of the human family through time. Spectators were transported in a tracked vehicle through a dark tunnel, pausing at appropriate points to view amazingly life-like robotic displays of animated figures, featuring the evolution of the nuclear family. In 1964 we arrived at a homey scene depicting a relaxed male head of the family sitting with his slippers on, in an easy chair smoking his pipe, looking proudly at his loving wife and his obedient children sitting affectionately at his feet. The eventual dismantling of the display foreshadowed the actual dissolution of much of the American family in the coming decades of the Seventies, Eighties and Nineties. Parts of the display were shipped to Disney World in Florida where it was reassembled. (I viewed that 1960s scene once again, years later, but it didn't look real anymore).

Shortly after our return from New York we moved into a one-bedroom basement apartment in Roslindale, a sort of suburbanized section of the city. Cops were required to live in the city and 'Rozzy' was popular with many of them. West Roxbury was even more appealing, but it was also more expensive. It marked the beginning of a new phase in my life.

By the time I returned to duty the class was entering into its downward cycle. There were about two weeks remaining in our Traffic Division assignment. Once the holidays were over, it would be just another couple of weeks back at the academy and presto, we would, as Jesser might comment, achieve full-fledged 'cop-hood.' It was an absorbing time and the streets of downtown Boston were teeming with Christmas shoppers. Washington Street was brightly decorated and the big stores like Jordan's and Filenes displayed animated window exhibits that competed for the attention of passers-by. Christmas music was piped into the streets. All was well in my world!

I took a little good-natured ribbing from my classmates when they learned that I was married. Billy Quinlan, a tall, lanky, amusingly sarcastic guy made it pretty clear that marriage would diminish my sex life.

"You'll get less now than what you got before," he laughed. "After you get married you need an appointment".

Billy was the class philosopher. He, like most of my classmates, was married!

My most striking recollection of this initial period of street duty was the enormous and persuasive power of the uniform. Its magnetic attraction was inescapable. One could not hide in it, or from it. A small upward movement of my right hand could cause a car to come to a screeching stop. In fact, I took advantage of this a couple of times when, against my better judgment, I hitchhiked to work. Women smiled, flirted and gestured. Even boorish men benefited from the effect of the uniform - they became instant coffee shop celebrities. It provided free transportation on the transit system and cars automatically stopped when I crossed the street. Some people said, "Hello" while others shied away, but almost always there was some sort of reaction.

However, the uniform could also be a double edged sword. Once it got me a front row seat in Matthews Arena on St. Botolph Street in the South End to view a sparring match featuring Cassius Clay, the newly crowned 'United States Heavyweight Champion;' but I was almost trampled on the way out while attempting to protect him from his frenzied fans. When the match was over he gave me the 'nod,' signaling me that he was ready to leave. Apparently he believed that I was assigned there, and he certainly couldn't be expected to realize that I was off the district, 'sneaking a peak.' That was one private detail I never was paid for.

The uniform could get pretty heavy and cumbersome too, particularly in cold, foul New England weather. Long-johns secreted under the uniform pants and shirt; gun belt paraphernalia covered by a jacket and thick woolen overcoat topped off by a raincoat, a white rubberized hat, a reflectorized traffic belt and a whistle suspended by a silver chain draped over the left breast pocket - it hardly made for a good foot chase!

The last week or so at the Academy was a real drag. We were on the edge, anticipating graduation and our new assignments. They filled in with a lot of guest lecturers. One in particular sparks my memory. He was a middle aged, medium built police detective whose supposed expertise was 'Sex Offenses.' He delivered a lecture during which he clearly stated, without cracking a smile, that oral sex, even when practiced between married men and women in the privacy of their own homes, was a perverse act that amounted to an arrestable offense. This was an archaic belief, even in the Mid-Sixties, so I raised my hand and objected to this crap.

"Sir," I began, "what you are saying counters the mass of psychological evidence that is available. Oral sex is not a perversion and in fact it is widely practiced." (I was careful to note that it was not my preference.) The class fell silent, but nevertheless I stoutly continued, "It's regarded as normal, providing both parties agree to it."

The class quietly awaited the speaker's reaction, but it never came. I had made my point, and I could sense that my classmates were allayed that I had put this garbage away. Lieutenant Burke was standing in the rear of the classroom with his head down and his hand covering his face. I thought I saw him snicker. Again, seemingly innocuous incidents can wind up making the most profound differences. The future would reveal that this was one of those occasions.

On Friday January 15, 1965, thirty-three trainees graduated from the Boston Police Academy. The ceremony took place at the Police Post on Morton Street, not far from the State Hospital. Captain Cadigan handed out the certificates while Deputy Superintendent Taylor sat to the rear of the podium shuffling papers and Lieutenant Burke sat two chairs away, to his left.

Beverly attended the ceremony with my aunt and my sister Jeanette. I received the 'shooting award' and an honorable mention for the second spot, academically. There was only a fraction of a point separating Walter Tower and me. It was just as well. Walter didn't smile much, and coming in first was important to him. I was given a cigarette lighter with the Boston Police Department logo emblazoned on the cover.

Arthur Cinelli and I were reassigned to District 3, the North Dorchester-Mattapan section of the city, home to the State Hospital and one very nasty cop. As I have said before, the core of our class was transferred to the newly formed Tactical Patrol Force. The rest of the crew was spread around the city's districts. Even the Traffic Division got a couple of guys, one of whom was Ronny Conway. Nobody went to Division 16. That was considered the 'Bon-Ton' division and you needed connections to get there.

That evening we celebrated our graduation with a dinner at the Police Post. We all shared a feeling of accomplishment. I felt that I had reached another rung in life. Walter Tower showed up carrying his handcuffs. He was raring to go.

Thirteen

District 3, the most non-descript of the city's dozen or so police stations, was dangerously situated on the blind side of a rise on Morton Street, a heavily traveled thoroughfare that extended across the northern boundary of Mattapan. This, combined with its austere checkered yellow brick facade, worked to place the casual visitor in a discomforting setting. The cranky expressions worn by the police clerks behind the front desk reinforced the sense of uneasiness.

Mattapan itself was uneasy, due to the demographic changes working across the district. Blacks, many of whom were from down South, were gradually replacing the Jewish population. Real estate values suffered a temporary decline and unscrupulous real estate 'blockbusters' and profiteering bankers had a field day. The Mason-Dixon Line that separated the races was said to be Woodrow and Blue Hill Avenue. This turned out to be a transparent barricade. Eventually the poorer and less educated blacks would entirely displace the worrisome Jews. In the beginning most of them rented; the ones who did own often lacked the finances to keep up with the repairs. Greedy landlords sucked their properties dry, the neighborhood went down and crime rose concomitantly. This was about a decade away, but for the time being the largest population of Blacks resided between Washington Street on one side and Blue Hill Avenue and Talbot on the other. This was the 3-2 sector and during its busiest period in the evenings it was serviced by a rotund black cop named Winkie and his partner Michael Roach - the stuff of my nightmare on Blue Hill Avenue.

I was chewed out the first day I reported for duty. I entered the station and as was customary, saluted the front desk. A Sergeant told me to report to the Captain. I readily complied, but I was wearing my police hat when I entered his office. I had consciously decided that I should be 'covered' while on official business and in the presence of the District Captain. That's how it was done in the Marine Corps, but I was soon to learn that the police department was different. Captain Corkery, a rakish, good looking man with light brown curly hair took one look at me, sat back in his chair and in a voice steeped with anger, very succinctly ordered me to remove my hat. That, he said, was the first thing a Patrolman did when he entered the Captain's office!

I was thoroughly shook up, but his ire managed to heighten my receptiveness for the rest of his message, which amounted to the standard drill concerning the department's expectations of me. That was the last time I ever spoke to him. Captains were some kind of demi-gods, and I had no wish to test this man's will. I kept out of his way - like everyone else!

I was assigned to the day shift for the first two weeks. Vinny Calarese was my Training Officer. Vinny's respectful demeanor wasted the shallow caricature that cops were power hungry and oppressive. He enjoyed his job, respected people and was genuinely concerned about my training. Each time he taught me something new he would look at me very intently, squinting his eyes slightly while searching for some physical or vocal sign of affirmation. I felt completely at ease with him. He gave me a lot of good tips.

The day shift was a ten hour tour. Even with a two hour lunch, it dragged on. There weren't many calls, so most of the time we just rode around waiting for something to happen. We ran some errands for the station and were busy after school was let out doing school crossings. There was generally just a trickle of incidents each day. Everything required a report. I carried three by five inch cards in my uniform jacket, complete with notations reminding me of the necessary information I would need for any possible situation. Motor vehicle accidents, armed robberies, disturbances, warrant arrests, fire alarms, auto thefts, missing persons, breaking and enterings, dog bites and lost handbags were the most common incidents.

The biggest nightmare, for the cops as well as the victim, was a homicide. There were seventy-seven separate items and categories of information that had to be included in the initial report of a homicide. Everything from the time and date the officers received the call through to the ultimate removal of the deceased's body had to be recorded, such as a description of the premises, including how the victim was lying, the names of each officer and detective on the scene, the Medical Examiner and the time he responded, notification of the relatives and of course, most importantly, the identification of the deceased. The information required for most ordinary incidents could be included on a standard report form referred to as a '48'. The front of the card mandated basic 'fill in' information. The 'story' or 'narrative' was reserved for the rear. A homicide, because of its sheer volume, necessitated a 'special'.

Once the initial 48 was complete, the officer would approach the front desk and hand it to the Duty Supervisor, usually a Lieutenant, for his review. If it passed inspection the officer would be released and resume patrol. If it failed it was returned without explanation. It was left up to the officer to discover his mistake(s). Sometimes it would be something as innocent as a punctuation mark. This, of course, took time. Time was more bountiful in the middle Sixties.

I was reassigned to the night shift sometime around the beginning of the third week. Nights consisted of rotating shifts: 12:30 AM to 7:45 AM one night, followed by 5:45 PM to 12:30 AM the next. They were referred to as first and last-halves. The late shift was also called a midnight watch. It had the effect of working fourteen hours in one twenty-four hour period, followed by a day off. It was difficult getting used to, but in spite of this, some cops actually preferred it. I didn't.

In the next few months I became fully immersed into both my job and the police culture. Because of a tight financial situation I had dropped out of school for a while, and as a result had few distractions. Most of the cops had partners, but I became what was known as a 'bouncer' - filling in, in a wagon or car whenever there was a vacancy. Sometimes I landed a walking beat; I enjoyed that most of all. Occasionally I was assigned a one-man car, unofficially referred to as a 2089. I didn't mind that either. It afforded less opportunity for getting into trouble. That is, the kind of trouble generated by a partner.

There were a lot of drunks on the police department in those days and it was rumored that District 3 was a dumping grounds for a good many of them. There were eighteen licensed premises in the district. The booze was free; there was one cop that made it a point to hit every one of the joints on a nightly basis. A slightly chubby guy with a cherubim grin, Johnson would began the tour sober and end up smashed. Nobody wanted to work with him. Johnson was like a bad penny; they tried spreading him around but being a powerless rookie meant my turn kept on coming up. One evening we were assigned to the wagon, a police vehicle designed to transport prisoners. Toward the end of the tour Johnson initiated a drunk arrest. As we were escorting the guy into the rear of the wagon the prisoner turned to me and remarked,

"Your partner is stiffer than I am."

Unfortunately, it was true. Johnson loved being a cop, especially when he was looped. I got really pissed at him one night. I was assigned a walking beat and discovered the front window of a liquor store broken as the result of a breaking and entering (B & E). I called in on the 'box', a direct street phone to the station, for assistance and Johnson showed up. He surveyed the break and suspecting that one or two of the display bottles were full, started to reach in the window to pull one out. I saw my career going up in smoke! I was still on probation and had worked too hard to get to where I was to allow this to happen. I took out my stick and stepped between Johnson and the broken window. I warned him in very clear language,

"If you put your hand through that window I'll break it!"

He flashed a sheepish smile at me and withdrew his arm, and at that moment we came to an understanding. Whenever we worked together after that, and he was DK, I insisted that he stay glued to the back seat and leave the police work up to me. That arrangement worked better.

It's too bad it had to come to that, but there was no other way to handle the problem. Complaining to a Superior Officer about Johnson was unthinkable. Cops didn't squeal on other cops - that was simply the way it was. That philosophy resulted from a long tradition of police officers working together in close and dangerous situations. Cops needed each other to survive. The guy you burned today might be performing a rescue operation on you tomorrow. I understood that, and I wasn't looking to make any enemies. Nor did I wish to be branded a 'rat' so early in my career. The widespread problem of cops drinking on duty would fade away in the future. Heightened levels of danger, increased workload and greater liability mandated more responsible behavior. Simply put, it became more unacceptable. Johnson too, would cease his drinking, but the damage would have already been done. He died prematurely of a diseased liver.

Johnson wasn't the only drinker. I was picking up my paycheck one day and bumped into Arthur Cinelli. He was a scrappy little guy, older than most of the other recruits. I didn't see him much anymore because he worked on 'the other side of the house'. The two platoons assigned to the night shift worked interchangeably with each other.

"How's it going Arthur?" I asked.

"Better now, I'm finally working with a guy that doesn't drink." Arthur grumbled that most of the guys he was required to work with prior to his new partner were boozers.

Then he went on to complain that he wasn't getting any details. Arthur was married with a family before he got on the job. He lived in a housing project in East Boston. He was looking for a better 'shot', but he needed more money than his weekly salary. Private details helped. Cops were paid by local businessmen for their services on construction sites, supermarkets and bars, but you had to be in with the clerks to get a good job. Rookies got the 'blood details' in the joints, or the ones that nobody else wanted - and there weren't many of those.

"Don't you think it's odd that they sent two Italians to this district?" Arthur asked, implying that ethnic prejudice might have played a role in determining the assignments.

"Probably just a coincidence," I answered, which seemed to satisfy him.

"Anyway, I'm trying to get over to District 9 (Roxbury). There are plenty of details there," he said.

"It's a tough district, Arthur, the toughest in the city. It shouldn't be hard to get,"

"Yeah, Phil, you're right. Take it easy." He shook my hand.

"So long, Arthur, and good luck."

Arthur eventually got his transfer and he did a lot of details, but his luck didn't hold out.

Arthur developed heart disease; he retired on a medical disability in 1973 and died less than two years later. Getting back to the station, the ordinary cop assigned to the district was a pretty decent guy. However, due to our rookie status, Arthur and I kept on drawing the guys whom nobody wanted to work with, because they were drunks, or do-nothings or foul-tempered. We kept on coming up with the same stiffs.

I looked forward to working with Charlie Anastasia whenever his partner was out. He was a well-built, good-looking guy who took pride in his appearance. He complained a lot, but he did his job. He once remarked to me that the public was our enemy. Perhaps he was resorting to some hyperbole, but most of the cops held to some variation of that theme. Contact with the public usually meant complaints or trouble. Cops were dammed if they did, and dammed if they didn't.

The most common complaint that I heard, over and over again, centered on the Department's failure to back up the cop in the street, even when he was doing the job they wanted him to do.

"You're on your own out there," Charlie would say.

He echoed another clear sentiment when he admonished me to be leery of a Department that was unwilling to correct a situation they knew about, like Johnson's drinking, until it was too late.

"Whatever happens, one way or the other, they'll leave you hanging in the end," he lamented. Charlie was bitter, like most of the others.

Dan Sweeney was an energetic, compact and tough, little red-headed guy. I enjoyed working the wagon with him because he chattered and drove throughout the entire tour. Even on a last half he never 'pulled up' in the cemetery or behind Franklin Field to nap during the early morning hours when things got slow. He shared a fiery and passionate sense of justice with his sister Jean, who coincidentally, had lived upstairs from me on Balsam Street. Sweeney was bitter about having been transferred from another district because, he explained, he had tagged a protected bookie. He didn't like the idea that the bosses could 'fix tickets' over the heads of the Patrolmen who issued them.

"The only one who ends up paying the fine is the poor slob with the oldest car, who doesn't know anyone," he said.

A couple of years later he converted his rancor to action and was elected Vice President, and then President, of the newly established Boston Police Patrolman's Association which was fated to be labeled the most militant police union in the country. Dan was the second President, following Dick Mac Eachern, the radical founder.

An old-timer named Lindsey left me with the most lasting impression however. He delighted in going slightly off the district to his bantam sized white colonial house, situated on a picturesque side street off of Morton Street, near the Galivan Public Housing Development in Dorchester. Similar houses sold for about twenty thousand dollars at the time. While circling around his property he would invariably tell me about his life as a child and about his current family. He had little going for him as a kid. He was an orphan, and he knew that I was too. But he was happy and fulfilled now, and he wanted me to know that.

Lindsey looked more like a weathered construction worker than a cop. He was built like an ox - thick and heavily muscled. Once he laid a hand on someone in an arrest situation, it was all over. The guy went wherever Lindsey wanted him to go.

"My family is in that house," he would say. "My job is to protect them in every way I can. I will never do anything to hurt them, or to break my family up." And then came the message. "The things on this job that can screw you up are booze, broads, and bribes. There's plenty of it if you want it, but in the end you will hurt yourself and your family."

Lindsey worked hard for his family. Like a lot of other cops he also worked another job. It might have been in a warehouse, I'm not sure. I have never forgotten what he said, or the sincerity in which he said it. He conjured up the image of a medieval knight, suited in his most shining armor - strong, powerful and faithful - standing before the moat of his castle, ready to do battle with whatever evil may dare to intrude.

Booze, broads and bribes - the three Bs. I knew about the booze. It had already affected a conservative twenty percent of the station. It had devastated Johnson. Broads were dangerous, that was for sure. I had worked a couple of details at the Sportsman, a blood joint on the district, and had been propositioned several times. Another time I was sitting in an elevated train in uniform, lost in my thoughts, when a well dressed, good looking chick wearing high heels tapped her way in my direction and just as the door opened she handed me a scrap of paper. Before I could acknowledge her, she was off the train. When I unfolded the paper, her name, address and phone number was scrawled across the front.

But the bribes, I wasn't so sure about the bribes. Most cops didn't like paying the full price for anything - that was obvious from the get-go. There was a shared expectation that they should get the discounted price on whatever they purchased in the district. Those who went for the jugular didn't pay for anything. Haircuts, newspapers, coffee, donuts, lunch - they just walked out before the bill came. I enjoyed getting the reduced price myself. I felt like I was getting a deal, but the real gougers made me nauseous. They were an embarrassment.

I can recall one of the Lieutenants on the desk sending me out to Simcoes, a late night hamburger stand on Blue Hill Avenue, to pick up the 'inside station' order. It involved almost a dozen hot dogs, hamburgers, frappes and tonics. When the order was ready the waiter handed it over to me.

"How much?" I asked.

"No charge," he answered

"Look, I'm serious," I said. "I want to know how much this is."

He hesitated. I repeated myself, "I want to know." The firm tone of my voice left him scant wiggle room.

He looked at me like I had three heads, but nevertheless began to add up the bill on a piece of paper.

"Seventeen bucks," he said.

I pulled ten dollars out of my wallet and gave it to him.

"I'm sorry," I apologized. "I only have a sawbuck; they owe you the rest."

His last comment was, "Don't worry about it."

I picked up the order and left.

But I did worry about it. I worried a lot! I worried all the way back to the station. I had a wife and a kid on the way, and I couldn't keep on dropping tens all over the place. Besides, the whole situation was humiliating. It cheapened the uniform and violated my standards. By the time I walked into the 'house' with the order it was evident, by the curious look on the Lieutenant's face, that Simcoes had called to inform him that I had insisted on paying the bill. I handed him the order, swallowed hard and in as temperate a voice as I was able to summons, I explained to him that I didn't mind running errands for the station, but in the future would he mind giving me the money first? He failed to return my ten bucks, but he never called me in again either.

The following night I told my story to another cop at the district, believing that he would understand my dilemma and perhaps even support my 'pay for what you order' philosophy.

"What are you worrying about?" he said. "If we tagged for angle parking in front of Simcoes they'd be out of business. They're only too happy to take care of us."

"Yeah, sure," I replied.

I stopped pressing him on the subject. Maybe they would have him go the next time. Still in all, that's not what Lindsey was referring to. Where was this big bribe money? It didn't look like ordinary patrolmen were getting rich. If they were, why did they scramble to do details and take second jobs?

Fourteen

These men had a hard edge. Though their temperaments differed, and their personalities ran the gamut, they shared a common bent toward suspicion and cynicism. Part of this was simply the armor of a good cop, consciously donned to increase efficiency. Cops couldn't afford to be naive. They operated in a world rife with deceit and subterfuge. Getting conned was a major embarrassment in front of their peers. A damaged ego was only one possible price for naïveté. Physical injury, even death, could also result. Admittedly, some of this hard-nosed stuff, especially among the rookies, was a thin veneer to gain acceptance by the more seasoned veterans. But, in spite of this, the mistrust was real. There was no mistaking it. It hung over these men like a dark shroud. It came from down deep inside their gut.

The years would reveal that it was shaped by the incongruities of a system permeated with politics, prejudice, personal favoritism and self- interest, played out in an ever changing social system that places its guardians in an arena and infuses them with a prolonged exposure to the rancid side of human nature while demanding that they face personal danger on a continual basis, in a game without winners, where the rules of engagement may change in the middle of a tactic.

An old timer put it to me this way.

"The job isn't on the level, kid. It never was and it never will be. Forget about all that crap you learned in the academy. This is where you'll learn the job, right out here in the street. And the first rule is, don't trust anyone! I'm not just talking about the bad guys. I'm talking about businessmen, the so-called pillars of the community, who are receivers of stolen goods, druggists that sell dope to junkies and teachers that diddle kids. Everybody's got an angle, or they're doing some kind of a swerve. That includes the Department too - the bosses, the brass, right up to the Commissioner. They say they want you to do the job, but when it starts to get hot they'll stick it up your ass. Don't go out on a limb, cuz they'll cut it down when you get too far. All we've got is each other, make no mistake about that! The most important thing you can do is to go home to your family in one piece, so don't be afraid to shoot if you have too - better to be judged wrong, than dead right."

A small part of this message was driven home to me one evening, about two hours into the shift. I was assigned a one man car. As soon as roll call was finished, I jumped in the cruiser and proceeded to the intersection of Blue Hill Avenue and Talbot for the purpose of placing a Metropolitan District Commission Community Facility under surveillance. A twelve year old kid had broken into the place the night before and was drowned after falling into the pool. The incident was read off by the Lieutenant at roll call and we were advised to keep an eye on the place to prevent further occurrences.

I nestled the marked cruiser into a spot on the other side of the intersection, between a car and a large truck that provided some limited cover. Boredom had almost propelled me to leave when bingo, I hit pay gold. Two white teenage boys climbed over the fence and entered the pool area. After requesting a back-up over the car radio I exited the cruiser and casually walked across the street. I quickly scaled the fence and came down on the other side. And there they were - both of them, standing together at the side of the pool. Perhaps they were debating if they should try the water. It was still early in the spring and cool outside. The pool was just being tested. It had not officially opened. I caught them by surprise. They gaped at me momentarily, but quickly overcame their paralysis and ran off in different directions. I caught up with the slowest one (that's the way it usually is) and ordered him to stop. He complied. I did it! I made my first breaking and entering pinch! It wasn't too heavy but I was proud, nonetheless, that I had accomplished what the Lieutenant had asked. The arrest would send a message to other potential offenders and perhaps save a life. When my back-up arrived I instructed the kid to climb back over the fence and into the officer's outstretched arms. As I transported my prisoner to the district I enjoyed that great feeling of satisfaction that every rookie experiences with his first arrest.

I was not ready for the loud vulgar statement of the Duty Supervisor behind the booking desk, a big balding Irishman who sat there glaring down at me as I stood alongside my prisoner and explained the circumstances of the arrest.

"What kind of shit are you bringing in this station?" he bellowed. "Get out of here and don't ever come back in here with anything like this again!"

I was mortified and had difficulty believing that a Superior Officer (above the rank of Patrolman) would embarrass me this way in front of a young kid and every cop within hearing distance. Had he refused to book the offender in order to avoid the consequences of a juvenile record, I would have understood. I was having second thoughts about that myself. I would have been satisfied to bring the kid home and simply notify his parents. He didn't seem like a bad kid, just mischievous. But for me to be the object of such disdain for having done my job was both puzzling and humiliating. I felt pretty bad. I ended up taking the kid home anyway. He lived in the Franklin Hill projects. His father was a retired cop, off on a disability pension. At least he thanked me for my time.

I cleared up the puzzling aspect of this unsettling experience years later. Apparently the big bald Irishman resented Italians. Boston was an Irish city and the police department belonged to them. The trend began with the early waves of Irish immigrants who flocked to the city in the middle and latter part of the nineteenth century. Most of them were attempting to escape the misery and death caused by the potato famine in their homeland. They wrestled with the Yankee Blue Bloods over power and influence through the years. Discrimination against the Irish, at its high point, was so blatant and cutting that signs admonishing prospective employees that "Irish need not apply" were hung out in front of Yankee establishments. The expanding immigrant population became an increasing threat and in 1885 the power to appoint the Police Commissioner was taken away from the Mayor and transferred by statute to a three-man board appointed by the Governor. This was a translucent effort to retain Yankee control on Beacon Hill, home to the State House and all that was Blue Blood and proper in Boston.

The power to appoint the Police Commissioner had been returned to the Mayor just two years before I got on the job. Mayor John Collins, an unpopular Mayor with the cops and regarded by them as a major 'skinflint', appointed Edmund J. McNamara, a former FBI Agent, as Police Commissioner. Meanwhile Boston had become a multi-ethnic city with the Irish clearly at the helm. Increasing amounts of Italians, and to a lesser degree, 'Negroes' were entering the police department. This was seen as a threat to a few individuals who were disquieted by the changes. Lieutenant Brendan Callahan was a manifest symbol of this resistance. It was a white Irish man's job to this guy. He made it difficult for the newcomers. In the years to come his son would become a renowned New York based FBI agent - and an expert on Italian Organized Crime. Was it any wonder?

To get back to the point, I was stung by this Lieutenant's rebuke but mine was not a unique experience. Cops believed they were always getting rebuked - by the bosses, the newspapers, the courts and the public. The cumulative effect of this steady hammering intensified their isolation from society and produced what I came to understand as the 'cynical view'. It's a shared perspective on most features of the human condition and it is almost always different from the mainstream.

I learned a little more about why the job wasn't 'on the level' just after midnight on a last half shift. The streets were barren and the few stores in the neighborhood had long since shut their doors. I was assigned a foot-beat. I thoroughly enjoyed 'walking assignments.' They provided a grant of freedom that radio-equipped, motorized patrol cars failed to offer. There were no portable radios in those days, hence, an absence of radio-transmitted assignments.

The officer was assigned to a specific route and required to patrol it. He was expected to maintain visibility and detect 'breaks' with regard to commercial establishments and small businesses by checking for open doors and broken glass. If a 'break' went undetected until the next shift the officer would have a lot of explaining to do. (He would be in the shit.) He was also required to call in every forty minutes on the Signal Box, a silver colored metallic chest topped with a blue light that flashed when the station wished to communicate with the Patrolman. The box contained a street telephone linked directly to the district. It was manned on the other end by a cop who sat at the 'Signal Desk.' An old-timer named John generally was assigned this task when I was working. He was the last of a breed that were permitted to retire at age seventy. There were twenty-eight of these police boxes in the district and it was important to learn all of their locations.

A few guys would abuse the system, of course, by giving the guy on the signal desk a telephone number where they could be reached if necessary. The Signal Desk Officer would automatically punch them in at the designated time. Meanwhile they could be home installing a linoleum floor, or off with their 'hugger' somewhere. When the tour was almost over the officer would make one quick check of his route, scanning it for any obvious problems. Occasionally the Patrol Supervisor, normally a Sergeant, would check the officer on the beat to determine if he was 'out there.' Sometimes he would make an agreement in advance to meet with the officer at a specified location at a predetermined time. The Sergeant would enter the name of the officer, his location and time of meeting in his log book. Usually he wouldn't check the guy again, so the cop could head for his 'dugout' (the rear of a store, gas station, etc.) where he could relax. That's the way the game was played. Officers who were assigned a permanent walking beat (like Vinny Lopez) could be generally counted on to take a more intense interest than Officers who were assigned temporarily on a fill-in basis.

On this particular night I saw a couple of white guys entering the basement door of an old abandoned movie theater near the intersection of Blue Hill Avenue and Columbia Road - pretty odd for that time. I didn't know the attraction but I doubted it was legitimate. I waited in the shadows until both of them were inside, and with the aid of my flashlight, picked my way down a set of cement stairs littered with debris and broken glass that led to a thick wooden door. I opened the door and stepped onto the floor on the other side.

A large rectangular, dimly lighted room gradually came into view. After my eyes adjusted to the thick layer of tobacco smoke that hung over the place like a transparent pall, I was able to make out the images of a few dozen guys playing cards around several wooden tables unevenly spaced around the room. The middle table was long and flat and several men were huddled around it. I could clearly hear the cascading sound of dice as they skittered across the surface.

A medium built, savvy looking black guy was talking to one of the men who was standing over the table. It sounded as if they were having an argument. He was so intently engaged with the man that at first he didn't see me standing there. When he eventually became aware of my presence, his body seemed to undergo an involuntary jerking reaction. He quickly regained his composure and began to resolutely walk in my direction. Apparently he was the doorman in what was obviously a large illegal gambling operation. His strained expression revealed his frustration with my intrusion.

Having reached me, he gingerly grabbed me under my right arm and attempted to turn me around in the direction of the door. "Come on kid," he said. "You're gonna get in trouble in here."

I couldn't believe this guy! I felt like I was getting arrested!

"Wait a minute" I angrily responded. "I think you're a little mixed up. You're the guy who's in trouble, not me. Now take your hands off me or I'm going to take you in." He removed his hand from me but otherwise seemed un-fazed by the rest of the message, continuing to insist that I leave.

I was alone and there was nothing to be gained from remaining there. I wasn't even sure if I had a right of arrest. The sensible thing to do would be to call for a Patrol Supervisor. There was a box located near the corner.

"Okay Buddy, have it your way." And with that, I stepped into the night air and headed in that direction. Curiously enough, I was about half way to my destination when I spotted the Sergeant on the other side of the street. I waved to him and he came to a stop and waited for me to cross. He was a big round faced guy. I had never seen him before.

"I'm glad I ran into you, Sarge. I was just getting ready to call you."

"What have you got?"

"I have a gambling operation, Sarge. I followed a couple of guys in there - right across the street - in the basement of that old movie theater and the doorman is real arrogant. He's acting like I'm some kind of trespasser. Do you wanna take a look?"

117

Even the darkness could not conceal the bright smile that slowly expanded across his features turning his face into a Halloween pumpkin.

"No, it's all right", he answered. Let's go back to the house and you can write out a report. That's what you're supposed to do. The Detectives will handle it."

I complied, of course, but somehow I knew that nothing would ever happen. I never bothered the joint again. It was no use. I figured that was an example of the third B (the bribes).

Danger was a constant! It could strike any time at any place. That was simply a fact of a cop's life. They didn't talk about it much, but not for a moment were they unaware that life could unexpectedly take a turn for the worse. It happened to me about 4:00 one morning. I was assigned to a one-man car and answered a routine call for 'loud voices' in a three story yellow brick apartment building at 229 Washington Street in the 3-2 sector. It was a slow night and I welcomed the interruption. The last time that I answered a similar call it turned out to be a loud radio.

I figured that it didn't take two men to turn down a radio, so I never mentioned to the dispatcher that I was a 2089, (a one-man car). I parked the cruiser across from the address, locked the doors, walked across the street and entered the hallway of the building. I stood in the inner hallway and listened carefully. It was quiet. I was almost ready to leave when I heard what sounded like a loud argument coming from upstairs. I climbed up two flights of creaky wooden stairs to the suspected apartment. I knocked loudly on the hollow core door with my nightstick.

"Open up - Police!" I shouted in the most commanding voice I could muster.

The door opened a crack. I grasped the knob and gave it an extra push. A slender, dark skinned woman was standing on the other side sobbing pitifully. The dim light given off by a single bulb in the far corner of the room glanced off her badly bruised and bloodied face to produce a horribly distended and surreal effect. Her torn nightgown slid up and down over her heaving breasts.

"Where is he?" I asked.

"In there," she said, pointing to a closed room off the kitchen.

"Who is he?"

"My son," she sobbed.

"Did he do this to you?"

"Yes, yes," she cried out. "Be careful, he's crazy!"

I had no idea of what was on the other side of that door. Working against my own fear, I demanded that he step out into the room where I could see him.

"Come on out, I want to talk to you," I commanded. I repeated this twice - followed by more silence - followed by more fear!

I was in a tough spot. I figured the most tactical way I could handle this situation was to take the mother downstairs to sit in the cruiser, allowing me the time to call for an assist. Good idea, but the situation deteriorated more quickly than I could coax the mother out of the apartment. She was still crying and looking for her coat when the door opened and out he came.

He stood there for a moment in the faded light. He appeared to be slightly overweight for his five foot nine inch frame. I couldn't make out his features or expression, but I knew he was maniacal. He issued a string of obscenities at his mother, the first of which was "bitch," and before I could stop him he leaped across the floor in what seemed like a single motion and belted his mother across the face with a clenched fist. She fell to the floor and began coughing up blood. Gurgling badly, she begged for her son to stop. "O Lord, O Lord, please don't hit me again," she cried. I cursed myself for having failed to block the attack. It wouldn't happen again!

The fight was on and it was one hell of a knock down drag out! I pulled him away from the woman. At this point he directed his wrath against me and caught me with a straight shot to the chin. Now I was really pissed! After that it was no holds barred. I hit him with my fists, as hard and as fast and as many times as I could. He returned the fusillade, but strangely enough I could hardly feel him connect. I didn't like this mother beating piece of shit and I was determined to subdue him. I forced him out into the hallway and down to the second level, punching and kneeing him all the way down the stairs. One more flight and at least we would be in the street. Even if he escaped, his mother would be safe.

She stood at the top of the flight of stairs, crying and begging him to stop fighting. His reaction to this was an attempt to unsnap my holster. This guy wanted to kill me with my own gun! For one instant I experienced a feeling of complete abandonment. There was nobody here to help me. At the State Hospital I would have had some help by this time, even if it was just a patient, but here I was alone and vulnerable. My firearm was an impediment to me and an advantage to him. I pushed his hand away from my holster and with one final surge of strength I pummeled, pulled and yanked him down to the first landing. To my profound relief, once having reached the bottom hallway, he gave up!

"Okay, okay, motherfucker, that's enough!" he gasped.

But I still had one more thing to do. I kicked his legs out from underneath him and he hit the floor with a thud! Almost simultaneously I rolled him over onto his stomach and placed my knee strategically into the small of his back. I was out of breath and barely able to squeeze out the command,

"You're under arrest; put your hands behind your back!"

He complied with my order, offering me minimal resistance - just enough to complain that I was hurting him. I unsnapped my cuff case, removed the contents and clicked the metal restraints down into the locked position - first on his right wrist and then on his left. I can't tell you how much I valued this small mechanical contrivance. These restraints were my only support.

I rested momentarily. Actually, we both rested. But my job was far from over. I needed to transport this prisoner back to the station. I fished my pockets but was unable to find the key to the cruiser. I must have lost it during the struggle. I had no other choice but to drag this guy to the nearest call box which was located about two blocks away at the corner of Washington Street and Erie.

I pulled him to his feet and searched his clothing for a weapon. He was clean. I tried unsuccessfully to console his mother. I began my walk to the box, pushing and pulling the prisoner the full distance. When I finally reached the welcome device I inserted my brass key into the oversized keyhole and opened the door. The knuckles on my right hand were scraped and bleeding. I spoke directly into the receiver just as we had been instructed to do in the Police Academy.

"Yeah, what's up?" the voice on the other side asked.

"This is the 3-1 car. I have an arrest. Could you send me a wagon to Wash and Erie?"

"Right away," the old timer crooned.

Within just a few minutes of each other, a wagon and two cars arrived, their dome lights and sirens fully activated.

"What have you got?" one of the Officers asked.

"A real asshole," I responded. "It's good to see you".

By the time I had completed the investigation and did the paperwork the day shift was coming in. I appeared that morning in the Dorchester District Court for the arraignment at 9:00 AM. One of the complaints was for an 'Assault and Battery against a Police Officer.' The case was continued for two weeks. Enough time for my knuckles to heal. The defendant defaulted, and the mother never showed up for either hearing. I earned a total of six dollars in court fees - payment for two appearances. It would take another couple of months for my front teeth to tighten up.

There are a slew of other memories that compete for attention when I think back about those early times, not the least of which was the rapidly escalating rumors that were engendered when the number designation of the district was converted from 19 to 3. This occurred just prior to my arrival. Some officers saw the change as simply a reordering of the districts while others insisted that it foreshadowed wholesale district closings. Cops are rumormongers by nature. They are information sensitive to begin with and this tendency is further enhanced by the close physical proximity they share over time and place.

I vividly recall witnessing my first unintentional homicide. A sixteen year old girl was thrown to her death about two blocks away from me. The speeding motorcycle she was being transported on careened out of control and struck the median strip in the center of Blue Hill Avenue. This ejected her about twenty feet into the air, twisting her body into a half somersault and cruelly crashing her straight to the ground on her head. I bolted to the scene but she was dead when I got there. Her long flowing hair was so matted with blood that her head resembled a giant oozing blood clot.

The operator, himself about sixteen, was unlicensed and drunk. He suffered only minor injuries. He was taken to the Boston City Hospital for treatment. One of the nurses told me that they had to order his friends out of his room two days later for being boisterous and having drunken parties. He apparently was enjoying himself.

The saddest event was pulling a dead five year old boy out of a construction pit into which he fell and drowned. I knew his mother. She was a friend of one of my past neighbors on Balsam Street. She was a conscientious good mother. I knew the kid, too. I recognized him as soon as I saw him, his face frozen in death, his tiny body lifeless. He was playing with his older brother right outside the house just after a drenching rain. He fell out of sight for a few minutes. By the time his brother spotted him, face down in the water at the bottom of a ten-foot hole, it was already too late. Make no mistake about this: cops never get hardened to dead kids. It is always a soul wrenching experience. It chips away at the narrowing pool of faith that gets them to the next tour.

One early morning, about 6:00 AM, the dispatcher ordered us to an apartment on Stratton Street in the Franklin Field Housing Development for a sick assist. We were late, about eight hours late, to be exact. The victim, a seventy-six year old Jewish male, was sitting on the hopper. He was slouched over forward; his eyes and mouth were open, but his heart was still.

"How long has he been like this ma'am?"

"He's been like this since last night at ten o'clock," the old lady who had answered the door replied. "I've been sitting here with him all night waiting for him to come out of it, but he hasn't moved. We've been married for fifty-one years. The kids are grown. It's just the two of us. Is he dead?"

The old lady stood there, slightly bowed. Her long bony hands were clasped together in a prayerful position in front of her mouth. She looked wistfully up at us. She wanted an answer to what she already knew. He was dead all right. So dead that rigor mortis was setting in. The old lady knew too, but she needed the police to tell her. It had to be official and that is where I made a mistake that I would soon regret.

"I don't know ma'am," I said. "I am going to call the Doctor. He will examine him and let you know."

I should have just told her the truth. She was prepared, but the rules clearly stated that only a medical doctor could make that determination, and rookies didn't question the rules. I felt pretty badly for the old lady. It was a tough way to end up - not much to look forward to.

About twenty minutes later the Police Doctor arrived. He was a short 'fella', somewhere between Adolph Hitler and Charlie Chaplan. He earned a small sum for every sudden death he responded to. I don't think he missed many calls for service, no matter what time of day or night. It was rumored that the Medical School he graduated from was not accredited in the state of Massachusetts, hence he was unable to be affiliated with any of its hospitals. He was notorious for his insensitivity toward the surviving family members. He was also known for opening up the refrigerator of the victim and eating leftover food. I had heard that he was a real 'pissa' and I was about ready to find this out first hand.

I greeted him at the door and as succinctly as his brusque manner would permit, I quietly, in a voice just an octave above a whisper, explained the circumstances.

"Good morning Doctor. We got this call about a half an hour ago. We have an elderly dead male sitting on the hopper. The woman in the bathroom is his wife. She waited eight hours before she called the police. She said she was waiting for him to come out of it. They've been married over fifty years and she's having a hard time coming to terms with this. She asked me if he was dead, but I couldn't tell her. I told her that you would examine him and let her know. You'll have to be careful with her."

I don't think he liked my advice. He looked at me and didn't bother to respond. He walked straight into the bathroom and looked down on the patient. He placed two fingers over the dead man's wrist, turned toward the wife, and in an indifferent monotone voice asked,

"Who do you want for your undertaker?"

He made no other comment, not even a condolence.

It was official now. She began to softly cry. She cried for a long time. She had lived with this man for a long time.

"We didn't have much," she uttered in between sobs, "just two kids that live in other states. He was a good man; he worked hard."

When the old women didn't respond to his question, Doctor Greer called a funeral director of his own choice. Procedure required that the police wait for the body to be removed. It could sometimes take a long time, especially when a grieving spouse or family members remained in the house. Sudden deaths are still among the most disliked of police calls for assistance. My partner and I remained with the body until the undertaker arrived, and the Doctor went on to another sudden death. We both expressed our sympathy to the lady. In her grief she failed to recognize the callousness of this Police Doctor.

On the way back to the station I commented to my partner that it was hard to believe that a medical doctor could be so insensitive.

He agreed and added, "The son of a bitch probably gets a cut from the undertaker for any business he drums up."

Sometimes incidents have a happy ending, like the evening that Charlie Anastasia and I transported a cardiac case to the Boston City Hospital. When we placed the guy on the stretcher in the rear of the wagon he was completely without vital signs. This was verified by an emergency medical technician on the Fire Department who also responded to the call.

"Is he dead?" the victim's wife asked somberly.

"We don't know," Charlie replied.

Not taking any chances, I jumped behind the wheel and Charlie entered the rear of the wagon with the dead guy. It was a brand new vehicle and I reached a top speed of eighty miles an hour as we raced down Blue Hill Avenue to the City Hospital. The cars directly in front of me, in the left lane, automatically peeled off to the right at the sound of the siren as it penetrated the quiet of the early evening. All except for one person that is, who panicked and stopped her car abruptly in front of the speeding wagon. To avoid hitting her directly in the rear I jerked the wheel to the right, causing the wagon to almost tip over on two wheels. As luck would have it, the right lane was absent of any traffic allowing me sufficient time to regain control. The deceased man was thrown from the stretcher onto the floor amidst audible cries by Charlie that I was trying to kill him, too.

Suddenly Charlie began to bang on the metal wall behind the driver's seat.

"No shit, Vitti, you ain't gonna believe this - get to the hospital, this guy is breathing!"

Apparently the fall from the stretcher and the jarring motion of the out of control vehicle had stimulated the patient's heart; at least that's the way the Emergency Room Doctor explained it to us. We couldn't wait to inform his wife of the good news. She was ecstatic to learn that the lease on her husband's life had been extended. She literally was stifled with joy. As for Charlie and me, we felt pretty good about being cops that night.

I got hit with my first lesson on welfare abuse when Dan Sweeney and I responded in the 300 Wagon to 160 Norfolk Street relative to a sick assist. Our official written report stated:

> Upon arrival we met Clarisa Harris, an 18 year old unmarried colored female, of said address who complained of flu-like symptoms and requested to be transported to the Boston City Hospital. The officers observed five young siblings in the apartment, ranging in age from one to five years old, sleeping together in one bed. There was an absence of any other furniture and the apartment was unheated. The only source of warmth was a lighted gas jet located next to a broken window. Miss Harris stated that the she was the mother of the children and had been forced to sell the furniture to supplement her welfare check. The officers refused to transport Miss Harris under these conditions. These officers advise that the Welfare Department be notified.

What was not included in the report was any mention of the complainant's obstinate nature or her insistence that she should be taken to the hospital regardless of the children's safety. Sweeney clearly explained to the woman that she would have to obtain a reliable baby sitter before she could be transported to the hospital. She got really angry and stomped her feet. We received a second call on this later in the evening after she managed to get a male friend from a nearby 'party' to remain with the children. As we were walking out of the house she threatened him, "You better do the right thing or I'll punch your teeth out."

Her babysitter retorted, in a deliberately feigned baritone voice, "Not my gold one, honey."

The guy had a sense of humor, but I wondered aloud if he would remain there until she returned. Dan didn't think so, but promised that we would check later. On the way to the hospital I asked the girl how it was possible to make the same mistake five times. She had spent her entire teen-age years pregnant and without the benefit of a single husband. She was a good looking chick. Her attractiveness was obviously causing her problems but at some point she should've put the plug in?

She answered, "Because God gave me all of these children and I love every one of them."

To the uninitiated that explanation might have sounded like a pathetically sincere response, but not to the cops who were dealing in the real world. Having five kids and remaining unmarried amounted to a thinly designed effort to increase the Welfare payments. Each additional child resulted in an incremental step raise. The system generated increased dependence. It just didn't work, and the cops knew it.

We were ready to leave the hospital and go back on the air when, surprisingly, I bumped into Cindy, my old State Hospital girlfriend. She was standing in a corner of the emergency room shaking down a thermometer when I saw her. She was an RN assigned to emergency. She looked up and our eyes met. She had never seen me in uniform before. There we were, both fully attired servants of the public, one in blue and the other in white, at the beginning edge of our careers. The professional aspirations that we once shared were now a reality.

She peered at me rather skittishly. She seemed unsure of what to say or do. I was pretty stunned myself! She looked as soft and pretty as ever. She was wearing a sack dress type uniform, a Sixties fashion that draped straight down her figure concealing her natural curves. It was the first one I had ever seen and I confused it with a maternity dress.

Perhaps Cindy had married and was pregnant, I reasoned. If that were the case it meant that we both were expecting a child. How ironical! I wanted to share this with her. I wanted to tell her what a great girl she was and how much I had enjoyed her, and that I still appreciated what she had done for me, especially helping me with the State Hospital theatrical performance. I wanted to apologize for hurting her, though I was still not sure of exactly what I had done or had failed to do.

"Cindy, are you pregnant?" I asked.

It was a sincere question but Cindy didn't interpret it that way. Two wives and three daughters later I have come to understand the gender nuances of language. Cindy heard it differently. Perhaps she thought I meant,

"Cindy, you look fat."

Her expression became pained. Her eyes filled with tears and reminiscent of the night of her graduation, she abruptly turned away from me and disappeared. This time, forever.

And yes, I said two wives, but I don't want to get ahead of my story.

Fifteen

District 3 was moving along pretty well. Although I didn't like working last-halfs (the midnight shift) I was more than satisfied with my progress. I was adjusting all right and my confidence was growing every day. I had reached the stage where I was beginning to relax. I was even getting around my disabling sense of direction. Charlie reduced my anxiety even further when he pointed out that most streets were off a main street, or a street off of a main street, and that the numbering system generally began closest to the center of the city and increased as it moved outbound. The most important things to learn were the main arteries, boulevards and intersecting ways. They were the spine and skeletal network of the district. I confess that I sometimes drove around the area in my own car with a map, on my days off to get it down. Getting lost and being unable to reach a call for assistance was my most nagging fear. "Never forget your street directory." Charlie admonished.

And I never did. In fact, I taped a three by five inch card about eye level in a metal military type locker that contained my uniforms in our apartment, reminding me of what equipment I was required to have. I glanced at it and checked off the items before each tour of duty.

       BADGE

       (1) Gun belt

(2) Revolver, a--loaded, b--extra rounds

(3) pad and pen

(4) club

(5) box key

(6) whistle

(7) street directory

BAD WEATHER GEAR

Rain-coat, hat, boots, gloves

Traffic-belt

I liked the police department and enjoyed going to work. It was a whole new world. No two tours of duty were the same. Being a police officer was becoming an intricate part of my personal identity and was contributing substantially to a new and emerging professional self-image. It fit in well with my gregarious nature and permitted me to peer into the personal and intimate lives of others, admittedly a life-long preoccupation. It was like having a front row seat to the greatest show on earth.

However, there were some negatives. The hours were long and the pay was short. There was no compensation for court or overtime and the average cop made about two-thirds of what a skilled laborer earned.

A cop's job didn't stack up too well against the limitless opportunities of the Sixties; hence it was not a position hotly coveted by the educated elite and was regarded as an object of derision by some. Cops were portrayed in the media as arrogant and bumbling. Even Police Sergeant Joe Friday, the star of Dragnet with his clipped dialogue and technical professionalism, failed to rescue the police from this negative stereotyping.

I took a lot of kidding from friends and associates - even a couple of family members. One of them demeaned the low pay while the other chided me for the overweight condition of some of the officers. A marked effect of the job was the inability to go anywhere in a social situation: parties, family get-togethers, functions, etc. without encountering some wise guy mouthing off about the insensitive, stupid and mixed up priorities of the police department, or the outrageous behavior of an individual cop or more likely some cop who had given him a ticket.

This incessant police bashing takes place everywhere - from the hick towns of New Hampshire to the smog filled cities of California. I am still convinced that this punishing commentary is the single most outstanding reason that pushes cops into exclusive relationships and close internal associations. It fosters a sense of 'we against them,' a shared perception that only a cop can understand what another cop is up against. This was even more highly prevalent in the Sixties and early Seventies and led to the 'thin blue line' mentality.

Improved salaries, greater education and slightly more positive media perception as the years have gone on has slightly softened this public lashing, but it has not changed the fundamental premise that cops attract criticism wherever they go and whenever they get there.

Sometime around the beginning of June I reported to work for a first half shift. I expected to fill in the wagon with Bammer Rowell, a well-conditioned, no nonsense athlete, or George Tarantino, a steady guy with a sardonic sense of humor, depending on which of the officers were on a day off. They were both pretty good guys. Instead I was enjoined in the 3-2 Car with the nefarious Michael Roach, the prophetic realization of a dread fear hatched the very night of our first encounter, that someday I would be forced to work with this man.

I was a 'bouncer,' a powerless rookie bouncer at that, still on probation. My assignment in the 3-2 Car was inevitable. His partner, Winkie, had suffered a heart attack and was going out on a disability pension. Roach himself had been on injured leave since before I was assigned to the district, the result of a broken right arm received in a forcible on-duty arrest. But on this evening he was back. He needed a partner and I was assigned the ordeal. The next few weeks were among the most difficult that I have ever put in on the police department.

There is no ingredient more important to the morale of a police officer than a good working relationship with a compatible and reliable partner. Roach was reliable all right. Indeed, he was well respected among his peers. He was tough and he knew his stuff - a great guy to have with you if you were in trouble. He was tenacious and always got his man - the hunter cop - once he got you in his sights, the rest was history. He never missed. He had an uncanny ability to strike fear into the hearts of even the most hardened criminals. He was also able to affect control at the most chaotic and violent disorders. The fear he generated in people far exceeded what might be expected from a middle aged, medium built, five foot eight inch man.

I never learned where his power originated or where it resided, but it made me as uncomfortable as it did the bad guys. Just being near Roach was like being in the presence of a dark specter.

When roll call was finished I picked up the cruiser keys. Anxious to win Roach's approval, I asked him if he wanted me to drive. He nodded his head, yes. Once in the cruiser I asked him,

"Are you still sore about the difference we had on Blue Hill Avenue with the guy who wanted to hurt his father?"

"No," he curtly answered.

I even tried to downplay its significance, explaining that "Maybe I over-reacted because of my State Hospital experience." (I didn't believe that.)

"It's water under the bridge," he said, and never said another word to me for the remainder of the night.

We hardly spoke, even when we responded to calls, and that's how it went, night after night, shift after shift. This guy wouldn't talk to me. Last halfs were the most difficult. I drove all night while Roach would just sit there, a vacant expression on his face, gazing out the partially opened passenger window. Occasionally, just after sunrise on a last half, when most ordinary patrolmen would be tired and quietly awaiting the end of the tour, Roach would start talking. I recall him commenting that he hated to work with drunks, but it was like I wasn't there when he said it.

I believed he was giving me the silent treatment because he disliked me. I still felt that it was due to our earlier encounter. Once again I asked him if he was ticked off because of the Blue Hill Avenue incident.

"Mike, are you still pissed because of the beef we had – is that why you won't talk to me?

"No," he said, and without the slightest change in his expression he matter of factly added, "I don't like you because you're a rookie. I don't know your reactions. You're not time tested."

I didn't agree with him, naturally, but at least he had said something! I constantly strove to impress him after that. I picked up the slack whenever I could. I handled as much of any assignment by myself as possible. I single-handedly disarmed a man with a knife on Morton Street who was attempting to harm himself. (I vividly recall the night because the man threatened that he was memorizing my features so that he could someday hunt me down and kill me.)

I did everything I could to loosen Roach up, but he was the most hermetically sealed man I had ever encountered. He was cold and cynical, thick skinned and combative. He lacked an inner core of human warmth and came across as totally insensitive. He didn't care who he offended. He adhered to his own rigid code of morality and seemed resentful that its underpinnings were being corroded. He was a psychological recluse, capable of functioning only when he was called into service. I sensed that he cultivated his energy between assignments. Perhaps it was the sudden discharge of this built up power that so intimidated people. The police department mattered to him and young up-starts like me were a threat to the status quo.

I wished that I had never mentioned that I intended to finish college. This was an indelible blemish on me as far as Roach (and some of the others) was concerned. What did college boys know? What was their understanding of a world full of liars, cheaters, frauds and con-men? Roach detested applying book learning to police work. He recognized the value of an education, but it wasn't for cops.

One night followed the other with Roach. Things got worse instead of better. I dreaded going to work. The cold treatment had begun to weigh on me. The silence was oppressive. It came to a boiling point early one morning on a last half tour. It was about 2:00 AM and the radio cracked the heavy silence.

"3-2 Car"

"Answering"

"Get over to 46 Epping Street for a women screaming."

"On the way," I responded."

I switched on the outside dome light, reached over to the panel and popped the siren button into the ready position. The streets were quiet but I wanted to be prepared.

I asked Roach "Where is Epping Street?"

"Look it up!" he snarled.

He refused to help me locate the address. Time was of the essence. A speedy arrival could make the difference that could save a life! Why, at a time like this, would he insist that I lose time by searching through a street directory? But, he did and he wouldn't renege.

The lighting in the cruiser was poor and the inside light was broken. I stopped under a street lamp and removed my street directory from the inside left breast pocket of my uniform jacket. I opened it and began to nervously fumble through the pages. It took time for my eyes to adjust to the subdued lighting. There it was - Epping Street - about half-way down the page. It ran from 615 Wash. to 22 Norfolk. Thanks to Charlie, I knew how to get there. I stepped on the gas, unwilling to suffer any further delays.

Upon arrival we spoke to a woman who pushed her head out the second floor window. She appeared to be about forty years old and it was obvious that she was tanked. She hollered to us that he was gone, but she'd call us again.

"If the son of a bitch comes back."

"Use the telephone the next time," Roach shouted back.

I couldn't understand Roach's reaction. Initially I attempted to rationalize it - maybe this was one of those calls that came in all the time - a phony and Roach knew it. Perhaps the woman was nuts and got like this every time the moon was full. However, my mental gymnastics didn't help. I was getting more irked at Roach by the minute!

We were on our way back to the station to write our report when I laid it on him.

"Mike, why wouldn't you direct me to that call?" I asked. "Why the fuck did you make me use my street directory?"

"Because that's the only way you'll learn."

"Did that call ever come in before? Did you know something about that woman?"

He refused to answer. Silence enveloped the car. I could feel myself slipping down into a darker region of consciousness, one that precipitated painful memories of an earlier time when I experienced the same cold indifference and careless treatment by a cruel adult. Then I was an orphaned child thrown into a dependent and inextricable relationship over which I had no control. Now I was a mature adult, a rookie regardless, working with a seasoned cop. But the intervening years had stiffened my resistance to this calculated tyranny. In short, I had no intention of absorbing personal abuse. I was still on probation and didn't wish to call attention to myself, but Roach had it coming!

"Mike, I've had enough of you. I don't want to work with you anymore. You're a ball buster! You should have given me directions to that location. That was no time for me to learn how to use my street directory. When the tour is over I'm going to speak to the Sergeant and request to be reassigned. I'm not going to tell him what happened - just that I want out - a personality clash, that's what I'll tell him."

Roach did not comment. He just sat there peering out the window as if nothing had been said.

When the tour was over I hesitatingly approached Sergeant Murphy, a snowy haired man with an easygoing disposition. I looked at him, sincerely summoning up all the heartfelt courage I could draw and made my plea.

"Sergeant Murphy, I would like to request to be taken out of the 3-2 Car with Roach. We have a personality clash. I'm not able to get along with him. I've never complained about anyone in my life - a teacher, a boss, an Officer in the Marine Corps - no one! But I can't work with this guy."

I sensed that he empathized with me. He turned around and walked up the stairs into the station and disappeared inside. (I believe he talked with one of the clerks.) In a couple of minutes he returned and motioned me to join him on the top step.

"It's done," he said. "You're all set."

"Thanks, Sarge. I really appreciate what you've done."

I experienced ecstatic relief, as though a great weight had been suddenly lifted from my chest. "It's done." The words sounded like music to my ears.

Unfortunately, it was only done for the next tour of duty. After returning to work from two days off I almost became ill to learn that I was back in the same car with Roach. It was like I had never left. Three calls and two assists (backing up other cops on assignments) punctuated the stony silence helping me to get through the shift.

I complained to the same Sergeant once again, and once again I was removed from the car for one night and then reassigned with Roach on the following tour. It was painfully clear to me that this was a deliberate game with the chief clerk making the moves.

The chief clerk has always been a basic patrolman. And patrolmen (patrol officers as they are now called) occupy the lowest rung on the police hierarchy. Back in those days, however, the chief clerk wielded an enormous amount of power in the station. Assignments, details, squad changes and most personnel moves went through him. Most of them abused their power. It was widely believed by the district cops that they 'took care' of the favored few.

The chief clerk at District 3 was no different. What he lacked in size he made up for in bravado. Big feeling beyond his small stature, he carried himself like the 'cock of the walk.' I learned through the grapevine that this guy didn't like the idea of rookie patrolman calling the shots. I suppose he believed that only he or the Captain had the right to make car assignments. Consequently, he disregarded the Sergeant's recommendation (and my request) and assigned me as he wished.

There was no point in pressing the issue. I would end up being regarded as a cry-baby. My fate was sealed for the time being. I had no choice but to work with Roach. I asked myself, if he were such a great cop, how come they were forcing me to work with him? Generally good cops had no problem finding partners, but nobody was fighting to be assigned to the 3-2 Car. I wanted a walking beat and here I was bound to a car with a partner with whom I shared a mutual revulsion. All this time Vinny's walking route was being covered by bouncers - most of whom would have preferred to have been assigned to cruisers. None of it made any sense and nobody gave a damn, except for the chief clerk who, for whatever twist of ego, had consigned me to hell. But I was determined to stay the course. I relied on the sense of discipline that I had developed in the Marine Corps to sustain me.

There was a baby coming and I awaited this event with great anticipation. Beverly was well on the way and was due some time around the middle of July. She seemed encouraged that in spite of the late date she was still hardly showing. We lived in a comfortable one bedroom basement apartment in the rear of a traditional brick house at 56 Cornell Street in Roslindale. The kitchen was large and the apartment backed up to a well kept garden surrounded by an expansive green lawn which was already hinting of its lush potential. I was content there; I felt that the apartment was an appendage of the natural world.

Beverly had quit her job as a dental assistant by this time and was devoting her full time energy to homemaking. The sparsely furnished apartment gleamed like a polished jewel. The budget was tight but good things were on the way and I had no intention of allowing my frustration at work to spill over into my home life, although it was inevitable that some of it would creep in. Going to work was becoming an increasing chore. My mood swung from anger to depression and finally - resignation.

Sleep was an escape valve. That is what I was doing - sleeping, when Beverly awakened me to take a call from the station. She handed the phone to me - it was the clerk's office. I figured it would be the offer of a detail (that no one else wanted, of course) but instead the clerk instructed me to call the Intelligence Division at Police Headquarters and ask to speak with a Deputy Superintendent Edward Blake.

"For what?" I nervously asked.

"I don't know, he just wanted me to give you the message."

Man, that was some kind of message! I instantly went into full-scale alert. Deputy Superintendents were Command Staff personnel, like Generals in the military. What could he possibly want with me? There must be some kind of mistake in my personnel folder.

I didn't waste any time dialing the number. The phone rang once on the other end and was picked up.

"Intelligence Division, Officer Mike Flammia. Can I help you?"

I identified myself and explained that I had been instructed to call and speak with a Deputy Superintendent Edward Blake.

He asked me to repeat my name. "Officer Phillip Vitti," I answered.

"Okay, Phil. Hang on for a minute."

"Deputy, I have an Officer Vitti on the phone. Do you want to pick it up in your office?"

There was silence. The next two minutes passed interminably. I could hear the heightened rhythmic beating of my heart. I had no inkling of what to expect. If I was in trouble, I didn't know for what. It occurred to me that it was a good thing that I had admitted to my court record in North

Carolina. I was at a loss to explain what else it could be. The quiet was finally terminated.

"Hello, this is Deputy Blake."

"This is Officer Vitti, sir. I was instructed to call you on the phone."

"How are you?" he asked.

He sounded business-like, but pleasant. I began to feel more relaxed, but I was still leery.

"Fine," I answered.

"I'd like to meet with you," he said "How about tomorrow?"

"Yes Sir," I responded.

We agreed to meet at eleven in the morning. I knew, however, that I could not bear the wait. I did not want to appear impudent but I summoned the courage and asked,

"Sir, may I respectfully request, what this is in regard to? I mean, am I in trouble or something?"

I could hear him chuckle. "No," he said, "you're fine. This is about a job."

He said no more - he didn't have to. I was stupefied! I crisply thanked him for his consideration, exchanged good-byes and hung up the phone.

That was the end of any more sleep. I couldn't wait to share the news with Beverly, but she didn't seem awed or even particularly impressed. I don't think she understood its significance. This was a Deputy Superintendent at Headquarters who wanted to interview me for who knows what. I had no idea of how he knew me. My biggest connection on the police department was a Sergeant who had been confined at several different times to the Boston State Hospital. Everybody knew that you needed connections to work out of Headquarters, and I didn't have any.

I was a little disappointed by Beverly's indifferent attitude, but then again, how could she be expected to know? I didn't tell her much about my job, preferring to keep it separate from my personal life. According to one of the instructors at the Police Academy (I don't recall whom) that was the best way to do it, and I agreed. When it came right down to it, Beverly was not a receptive audience anyway. She had grown up differently than me, not richer, just differently.

Her father, a strict Scotsman with a strong moral code, was a skilled laborer. He worked at the General Electric plant in Lynn, the same as my uncle. She was raised in an old rambling house, badly in need of repairs, in Ballardvale, the poorer section of Andover, one of the state's most affluent towns. She was popular in high school by virtue of her good looks. Her grades were fair. She was a skilled ballet dancer and teacher; her boudoir consisted of an unheated bedroom on the second floor. Nevertheless Beverly, thought her means were modest, living on the edge of a world permeated with the symbols of materialism - she was well acquainted with power, prestige and money. Beverly was an ordinary working class girl by most measures, the granddaughter of a retired reserve police officer known as the 'Constable of Ballardvale', and lived in an un-ordinary world for she was the Prima Ballerina of her mother's eyes. Beverly intimated that it had been her mother who had pushed her into a failed marriage with her high school boyfriend, the son of the president of a mid-sized steel company and the sire of one of Andover's most prominent families. None of this contributed to an understanding of a cop's world.

By the time I reported to work that evening the word was all over the place. A couple of the guys jostled me good-naturedly.

"Hey Vitti, got any more big dimes?" That sort of thing.

I couldn't convince them that the call from the Headquarters' Deputy had come from out of the blue. I never talked with Roach about it. He didn't talk.

I tagged a car parked at a fire hydrant near the intersection of Balsam Street and Blue Hill Avenue. That was the last ticket I would ever write on District 3.

Sixteen

The Intelligence Division was tucked into the far left corner of the second floor of Police Headquarters, an architecturally unappealing seven story stone building set on the periphery of the city's South End. The Commissioner and a couple of the 'brass' had offices on the sixth floor and the Operations Division, the heart of the department's emergency response network, occupied the seventh.

I was standing in the lobby apprehensively mulling over possible responses to questions the Deputy might ask when one of the two elevators that serviced the building came to a stop and released its passengers. One of them was a woman about my age whose peppery good looks momentarily distracted me - actually, stunned is a better word. A delicately framed, finely dressed full bosomed female, she would have stood out in any surroundings, but in the wholly masculine world of the 1960s police department this unexpected intrusion of choice femininity had a derailing effect on me. Not a bad place to work, I thought. Looking straight ahead, she quickly passed me. I don't think she noticed me standing there. The elevator door clanged to a close.

I boarded the next one. "What a beautiful chick," I mused. She reminded me of Liz Taylor. A few years later I learned that her name was Pat Fay. She was a keypunch operator in the Personnel Division.

Officer Mike Flammia was at his desk, typing a report, in the Intelligence Division office when I entered. He stood up and with a slight smile shook my hand. Mike was a soft-spoken guy with a slight stoop to his gait. He was the Deputy's clerk, and while he was not exactly beaming, he was still a welcome contrast to the sour faced clerks at District 3. The 'office,' as we came to call it, was one large room with a few messy desks scattered around.

The Deputy occupied a small glassed in cubicle across from the door. It was plainly marked, 'Deputy Superintendent Edward Blake, Commanding Officer, Intelligence Division.' I introduced myself to Mike. He smiled again, did an about face and walked into the boss's office.

I stood by for about a minute, mesmerized by a wall chart displaying mug shots of various hoods around the city. I was surprised at how many there were. Many of them were Xed out as the result of a gang war that had raged out of control for several years.

The way I heard it (later accounts of this incident differed), the trouble began on Salisbury Beach, a stretch of sand near the New Hampshire border, the result of a fight between James 'Buddy' McLean, a Somerville guy and one of the toughest kids I had ever known and Edward 'Punchy' McLaughlin, a Charlestown hood and former McLean associate. It was rumored to have started over an attack on an overly stacked female - a dishonored girl with a squeezed boob, attacked by Punchy while walking by him. A bruised ego, a failed apology and a beaten up boyfriend (who had attempted to avenge her) completed the ingredients for an escalation of this incident into a seven-year war that ended with more than forty casualties.

As rumor would have it, Buddy entered into the affray on the side of the girl and her boyfriend and subsequently handed out a serious beating to Punchy McLaughlin, as he did to all his foes. I clearly recall him growing up. He was a few years older than I was but even then he had a searing reputation as someone not to mess with. It was said that he was a gentleman - unless triggered. Once his anger was ignited, it was all over. He beat everybody he ever fought, one way or the other. There was no sense in beating him anyway. He was a sore loser so he'd even the score at some point - whatever way he had to do it. After the beach incident McLean survived an attempt to dynamite his car.

Bernie McLaughlin, who was one of Punchy's two brothers, was not so lucky however. He was shot-gunned into eternity at high noon in City Square in front of two hundred witnesses, all of whom failed to see anything. I'm a little ahead of my story, but McLean was eventually gunned down while crossing Broadway in the Winter Hill section of Somerville, a few blocks from where I grew up. There was enough going on at the time to hold my fascination. It looked like these Intelligence cops were heavy hitters.

The heaviest hitter of all was Deputy Blake himself. He stepped out of his office and motioned for me to come in. He was a rugged looking man about six feet tall with a strong chin and receding gray wavy hair. I could plainly see that he was a war torn veteran of the police department with his best years behind him. The deep lines in his face added to his seasoned good looks. I was awed by this man. After shaking hands I sat across from him on one side of a beaten up desk. He lit a cigarette, removed his glasses and stared intently at me. I had the strange feeling that he was looking into my soul. This guy couldn't be conned. Oddly enough, I felt assured in his presence. He got right to the point.

"We're looking for someone with a new face to work undercover. The Police Academy recommended you. You could work nights or days. If you want the job you'll still be assigned to District 3 but detailed here. You could go back there at any time. You may not like us, or we may not like you. It's a temporary assignment which could last for a couple of weeks or a couple of years, there's no way of telling." Then he asked,

"Do you have any relatives in the North End?"

"No Sir, I'm originally from Somerville."

"That's good, because you may have to hang around the North End in a T-shirt."

I think he was probing to see my reaction to working in an Italian neighborhood. "Are you interested?"

(*He has to be kidding*, I thought). "Yes Sir, I am."

"Good," he smiled and offered to show me around.

He introduced me to Bill McGrann, a wizened old-timer who was close to retirement, and to Bob Howland, a ruddy faced guy who, I learned later, was the brother of Superintendent John Howland, one of the heavies on the sixth floor. Both of them were clerks and they had just entered the office.

He continued his orientation, impressing me with a cursory introduction to the record system. I had never been comfortable around paper but this system provided easy access to information and stood as testimony to the Deputy's competence - nicknames, crime classifications, known criminals, associates, descriptions, photographs, addresses, gangs, La Cosa Nostra, the whole panorama - stored, categorized and neatly filed. He made it clear that the clerks maintained the system and provided the only access. If I needed anything I would be required to ask one of them.

"This is the Intelligence Division," he explained. "We collect and disseminate information. It goes to the appropriate agency or unit for action. We stay out of the picture. Avoid making arrests unless something serious happens in front of you and there's no other choice or you'll blow your cover, especially when you appear in court and every two bit hood trips over each other to get a look at you."

He escorted me across the office to the door. Before we got there he crushed his cigarette in a nearby ashtray and lit another. He continued talking.

"You're not going to be coming in here much anyway. We're gonna keep you under wraps. Be sure not to talk about what you're doing, even to your family. There are no heroes here and you'll never get credit for what you do. And don't trust anyone, especially cops. Okay?"

"Yes Sir. When do you want me to report for work?"

"Take the weekend off and give me a buzz about eleven Monday morning."

He said that he would take care of everything at the district. That meant three days off. He shook my hand once again, this time with an even firmer and more deliberate grip. He wished me well and returned to his office. It was that fast. This guy was all business.

I could hardly believe my good fortune - imagine, an undercover assignment, just six months out of the academy! I had experienced an oracular sense about the whole thing, especially when I was being interviewed by Deputy Blake - a vague inner awareness that the event was occurring and that somehow deep in my unconscious I knew that it would. It was as though a prophetic external intelligence had fingered me for some untapped talent, but more realistically for it to be happening this early in my career was mind-boggling! Destiny was knocking at my door and I was more than willing to open it.

The undercover offer had blown my mind! Things would never be the same after that. This singular journey would span an entire decade. It was like being scooped up by an updraft and deposited into a universal time funnel and then set out on a solitary flight from which I would eventually alight into a changed world and a mutated police department.

Getting back to June 1965, my ties with Roach were over, and that too accounted for part of the elation I was feeling. Except my fascination for this man would never end. He was an enigma. Somewhere buried inside me I knew that he was a good cop, not my kind of cop for sure, but a good one just the same. More than twenty years would pass before a failed religious retreat furnished me with some insight into what made him tick.

I wasn't looking in either direction when I crossed Columbus Avenue on the way to Beverly's Volkswagen and my return trip home. I was startled back into reality by a close brush with a passing police cruiser.

"Hey you," the cop behind the wheel hollered, "What are you trying do, get yourself killed?"

I dropped by the State Hospital on the way back to Roslindale. It was getting warmer and that was a sure sign that some of the guys would be sitting on the benches outside the Male Home batting the breeze. I hoped to see Paul Memos, but curiously enough the benches were vacant. I plunked myself down on one of them and waited. The penetrating rays of the June sun felt good. Life was simple here, I thought.

I missed the secure feeling of a shared existence that provided for one's elemental needs. I missed the fun, the spontaneity, the diverse personalities and the intellectual stimulation that existed here. I missed Paul Memos, Kevin Murphy, Ed Jesser, Mike Weinberg and a score of others - even the wildly proselytizing Wilbur Beer. They added color, contrast, depth and occasionally 'social disaffection' to an otherwise melancholy environment. I missed the buoyancy and the hope and the zeal of young guys who were just passing through the place on their way to bigger and better things. Here they dared to be themselves. I missed the patients too, whose personal brands of psychosis placed them at odds with society's push toward conformity.

I didn't miss the low salaries, the lack of professional growth, the dead-end nature of the job and the low opinion people generally held for Psychiatric Aides or the demeaning manner in which they were sometimes treated by the professional staff.

Out of the blue a patient ambled down the walkway and rested on a bench directly across from me. I tensed up as soon as I recognized him. He was the nut who had attempted to stab himself on Morton Street, the guy who said he was memorizing my features - "guinea features" were his last words on the subject. He smiled at me and waved hello. It didn't take long for me to realize that he didn't have an inkling that I was the cop whom he had sworn to track down and kill! (So much for that worry.) Cops don't look the same out of uniform. This lesson would be reinforced many times throughout my career.

He looked serene - probably on Thorazine I figured. It was a powerful remedy for violent behavior.

I remembered when I had worked in the Reception Building, having accidentally drunk a whole pitcher of orange juice that one of the nurses had secretly spiked with this potent sedative for the purpose of it being slipped to uncooperative patients who refused to take their medication. It happened about twenty minutes before the end of the shift. I began to feel groggy and after my relief arrived I stumbled down the stairs to my car that was parked in the driveway just outside the building. I pulled myself into the front seat and before I was able to turn on the ignition I passed out. I didn't come to for eight hours. I was awakened from my deep sleep by a third shift attendant who had spotted me slumped behind the wheel with my head down. He pounded on the windshield until I opened my eyes.

Thorazine, and its companion medication Stellazine, acted as chemical restraints for distraught patients whose behavior didn't warrant seclusion. These drugs had replaced the balls and chains of medieval times and were quickly substituting for the vanishing straight jacket of the twentieth century. It was certainly working on this guy. He was no longer hell bent on destroying himself, or me. He seemed blissful. We made small talk for a couple of minutes and then he drifted off.

Following that, two young employees descended the front stairs of the Male Home and sat down on separate benches. From the crisp white appearance of their hospital uniforms I could plainly see that they were recent hires. Apparently college students, they were wrapped up in a political conversation. They were intently discussing Vietnam, a small country in Southeast Asia. A reference to the Marines snagged my attention.

Sometime around the first week in March 1965, President Johnson, who had been recently elected to the Presidency by a landslide victory over Barry Goldwater, dispatched two battalions of Marines to DaNang and authorized them to engage in 'Search and Destroy Missions.' The next month he doubled the overall military strength raising it to eighty thousand troops. One of the attendants believed that the situation looked ominous. "There's been a series of escalations," he commented, "starting with Kennedy who increased the so called advisors from six hundred to sixteen thousand. A wider war is imminent," he concluded.

The other one disagreed. "It will stop the advance of the communists and stabilize Vietnam," he countered. "They're only a piss-pot of a country to begin with, how much can they take?"

I sat silently by and listened. I tended to agree with the second guy. That amount of military personnel should have been able to stem the tide. Besides, everyone agreed that the Communists had to be stopped. In retrospect, it didn't take long for Johnson to raise the ante in Southeast Asia. In his January 'State of the Union Address,' he called the nation to his vision of a great society. He said something about wiping out every vestige of poverty. (The cops thought this would amount only to a big giveaway program.)

Johnson devoted very few words to Vietnam, stating that the military advisors were there simply to "help against Communist aggression" but by the end of the second week in February he had authorized air attacks over this little country. Two weeks later Ed Jesser, after having taken a semester break from college, was swept up in the Gulf of Tonkin draft. He ended up in Vietnam assigned to an Army Intelligence Unit. Two years would pass before I'd see him again. Neither one of us realized that the air offensive was tantamount to a Declaration of War! I don't think I would have believed that by the time the war had ended these air attacks would have dropped more tons of explosives over Viet Nam than the entire ensemble of bombers and fighter planes of World War 2. But who was a fortune teller?

There were many other extraordinary events still waiting in the wings. Things were getting ready to pop! The Beatles were pushing the envelope and the first public draft card burning took place. It was downplayed because a few of the participants were mental patients and most of the cards were photocopies. The 'free speech movement' was beginning to affect campuses beyond Berkeley.

Nineteen sixty-five also witnessed the end of segregation in public accommodations. This struggle had been brewing since 1956 when a gutsy black woman with tired feet, named Rosa Parks, refused to sit in the rear of a bus in Montgomery, Alabama. Unfortunately, its fruition had come a little too late for me and the 'T' (Al Stroman) to enjoy a night of liberty in Jay-Ville.

In addition, in the Watts Ghetto of Los Angeles there was a serious racial riot which had started over the issuance of a traffic ticket. Ignited is more apropos. The black rioters were derided for looting, lighting fires and destroying their own property. Several people were killed. The disorder gave birth to the slogan, *Burn Baby, Burn!* But that occurred on the other side of the country and anything could happen in California.

Before the year was out two young war protesters would burn themselves to death. Things were happening all right! The seeds of disruption were germinating; a new and more violent generation of black leaders was emerging; the illusion of Camelot was dead and the idealism of Johnson's Great Society was already beginning to crumble. In a few more years it would be ready for the scrap heap. The complacency of the Fifties with its white middle-class sanitized *Father Knows Best* ethos was coming to an end - but the nation, as a whole, had yet to pick up on it.

The two attendants left for the cafeteria. I went home. Later that evening I celebrated my new job over pizza and a couple of beers with Beverly and the couple next door at the Pleasant Cafe, a neighborhood bar and restaurant on Washington Street in Roslindale. They had had a baby recently. The woman, in plain language, vividly recounted for Beverly the effects of her 'water bag,' as she referred to it, breaking. Beverly reacted squeamishly. In the privacy of our apartment she described the woman as crude. I never mentioned my 'undercover deal' - only that I would be going into plain-clothes for a while.

THREE

The ultimate tendency of civilization
is towards barbarism.

----------Hare

Seventeen

At precisely 11:00 AM Monday, June 15, 1965, I nervously lifted the telephone out of its cradle and dialed the private number that I knew would connect me to Deputy Superintendent Ed Blake. He picked it up on the second ring and that set the pattern for the next two and one-half years. This was the beginning of a long and memorable telephonic relationship with a high-level Police Commander who, from his desk, would mold my development as an undercover police operative.

Once beyond the exchange of preliminarily civilities, he went right to the point and issued me a uniquely simple assignment.

"Go out tonight and see what you can find."

"Anything in particular, Sir?"

"No, just see what you can dig up and give me a call tomorrow about the same time."

"OK Sir. Thank you. I'll call tomorrow."

And that was it! I waited till I heard him click the phone down on the other end and hung up. I wasn't looking for a fully laid-out Marine Corps type operational plan but I had hoped to get a little more direction accompanying this vague assignment. His intention, nevertheless, was entirely clear. I knew fully well that this was a major test. I had better come up with something or I'd be miserable and back in the 3-2 Car with Roach.

This fear diminished over time, but until I was made 'permanent' almost three years later, it never ceased to act as a negative incentive to produce

I was a non-rated Special Police Officer, temporarily assigned to the Intelligence Unit, Bureau of Inspectional Services, Police Headquarters. That was the department's method of keeping the pressure on. Either the officer performed satisfactorily or he was sent back to his original division. It made sense, but it didn't take me long to learn that the standards were unevenly applied. Politically connected guys were permanently assigned from the start, or at least they didn't have too long a wait. The really plugged-in cops made detective. That was the ultimate hope of these plain-clothes assignments - but that didn't enter my mind at the time. I simply wished to survive 'opening night.'

So I did what any enterprising cop would do. I verified some continuing criminal activity that I already knew about and reported it to the Deputy the next morning. The focus of my attention was an eight story yellow brick fleabag hotel that sat like an up-ended shoebox on the corner of Berkeley and Chandler Streets. It was a well-known place of prostitution and a source of embarrassment (and, I suspected, payoffs) for the police department, particularly because of its location - halfway between headquarters and District 4. Although there had been a number of prostitution arrests made on the premises the Licensing Board refused to shut the place down permanently, preferring to suspend its license a day or two, on Christmas Eve or some similar period of depressed business activity. I recall asking the nattily dressed and flamboyant Dapper O'Neil, Commissioner of the Licensing Board, who appeared as a guest lecturer at the Police Academy, why the members of the board seemed so adamant to not end this disgrace. His long-winded and somewhat rambling disconnected reply made no sense to me at all. I can only recall his concluding remark.

He said that, "The waitresses would end up out of work and they could least afford it."

Even the most naive recruit enjoyed a chuckle over that explanation. Anyway, this was my chance to get a shot at the place and I took full advantage of it.

I knew a little about the "Dip" from a girl that I had dated back in 1957, just before I went into the Corps. I met her at the Liberty Mutual Insurance

Company which was located on Berkeley Street, diagonally across from Police Headquarters. We both worked there; I was an elevator operator and she was a file clerk. The year 1957 was a recession year so that was the best job I could land, despite my being a high school graduate. I was employed as a custodian at the Sheraton building on Atlantic Avenue before that, but I was fired for shooting my mouth off at the building superintendent. Anyway --

Mary was a 'good kid' from a traditional Lebanese family who lived on Appleton Street in the South End. The Diplomat Hotel was a center of ignominy in this otherwise stable, working class, multi-ethnic neighborhood. She often complained about the place when we passed it on our way to her apartment. She pointed out a cabby to me one evening, commenting,

"He's out there every night, shuttling guys back and forth from the place. Everyone knows about it, especially the police, but they don't do anything."

I could only recall that he was slightly bald. Apparently things hadn't changed much after my discharge - just his hairline.

At 8:35 PM that evening, about one-half hour into my surveillance of the Diplomat Hotel, I observed a red and black 1964 Chevrolet Checker cab, license number 703, registration 893, pull up to the intersection of Chandler and Berkeley Streets and release a male passenger who entered the front door of the hotel. The driver was an exceedingly thin middle-aged guy with a receding hairline, gray at the temples, about 5 foot 8 inches tall, 140 pounds. He wore glasses and was casually dressed in gray chino pants and a green jacket.

The passenger remained on the premises for about one-half an hour. About ten minutes after he entered I peered inside and observed him sitting at the bar with an approximately twenty-six year old, good-looking and well-dressed blonde Caucasian female. Twenty minutes later he exited the club and entered the rear door of the hotel on Chandler Street. The blonde female entered the same door about five minutes later. At 9:46 PM the man returned to the street and entered the same Checker cab that had been parked on the corner and was transported away from the scene. The blonde female emerged from the rear door and entered the nightclub, resuming her place at the bar, where I later witnessed her sitting with another man.

The Checker cab returned three more times before 1:00 AM, each time releasing male passengers who performed similarly to the first 'trick' of the evening. Except for one guy, who staggered away after declining an offer of a return ride. Before the place closed I witnessed half a dozen females in fancy attire and about the same number of men entering and leaving through the rear door. They were usually separated by about three to five minutes going into the hotel - only on one occasion were they together. It took them between thirty to forty-five minutes to do their business. About three minutes punctuated their individual arrivals back in the street. The guy normally blew the scene and the female usually re-entered the club to kick the process back in motion.

I would repeat this sort of an evening many times in the beginning of my undercover years. At some point it occurred to me that, despite their well-groomed exteriors, these women functioned as basic receptacles for male deposit. They were repetitively used throughout the night by one guy after another. How much could they screw? And how clean could they be? It had to be a tough way to make a living!

I called Deputy Blake the following morning, feeling reasonably assured that I had something to give him. At least I hadn't walked aimlessly around the streets all night coming up with nothing. I had placed a hotel under surveillance - a place of ongoing criminal activity - and was able to document it. I had identified a specific cabby involved in what I suspected was soliciting business for prostitutes. I'd bet the Deputy hadn't known about him. A few apprehensive moments passed. I swallowed down a final gulp of coffee. The smoldering ash of my second cigarette was still burning in the delicate undersized ashtray on the coffee table. The rather pleasant, but matter-of-fact voice of Deputy Blake intruded into the morning silence and vitalized my senses into a fully heightened state.

"Deputy."

"Good morning Sir. It's Phil Vitti."

"Hi Phil, what have you got?"

I referred to the first page of my newly acquired nine by six inch stenographers' notebook that contained the rewritten notes of the prior night's car surveillance of the Diplomat Hotel. I provided a full chronology of events, including descriptions and what I was most proud of, specific information on the suspected cabby procurer and his vehicle. It wouldn't be too difficult to identify this guy since Hackney Carriage, a designated unit of the police department and charged with the responsibility of regulating the cab industry, was located on the first floor of Police Headquarters.

I realized that the goings on at the Diplomat Hotel were nothing new. The place was notorious as the closest thing the City had to a brothel - but serving up the 'hack' might have been a new piece of information. And it was! I could tell by the tone of the Deputy's voice that I passed my first major hurdle. No matter what, I had demonstrated that I possessed the discipline to conduct a lengthy surveillance and provide an objective account of unfolding events.

"That's fine, Phil - do the same thing tonight."

On this second day he expanded on his instructions, suggesting that I begin work at about 8:00 PM and check out the joints until they closed at 1:00 AM

"Check for hustlers and B-Girls," he said.

"Peek in the door and if it looks active sit down and have a drink." He promised to reimburse me up to eleven bucks a week for expenses. Drinks ranged from seventy-five cents to a dollar-ten, plus a tip. That wouldn't go too far.

He distinguished between prostitutes and B-Girls explaining that prostitutes were usually overly dressed and came in from the outside. They generally sat alone and waited to be joined by a male patron. Once they struck a deal with a 'trick' they would leave the premises at separate times and meet at a predetermined location. If there was no action they moved on to another club.

B-Girls, on the other hand, were generally more lightly dressed and stayed in the joint, moving from patron to patron soliciting drinks. The girls more than likely consumed low-alcoholic drinks or colored water. They received a percentage of each drink from the bar. The bartender would keep an account of each drink he served on a 'tally sheet,' or would provide the girls with a specific type plastic mixer to be exchanged for cash at closing time. The Deputy advised me to watch the bartender in order to determine what method he used.

"Check the strippers," he added. "They work the bar too, and when they're performing they are not allowed to expose their pubic area or nipples. They are required to wear 'pasties' over the nipple area and it's a licensing violation to pull them down, even for a second."

In each instance that I noted a violation of any kind I was required to make a mental note of all pertinent information, such as the name of the club, the identity of the offender, the time of the offense, the specific activity, the presence of the manager, the method of operation and any other relevant facts. He advised me to reduce the information to writing at my earliest convenience, so I wouldn't forget. The following morning I was expected to provide the Deputy with a full account of my activities over the private line. (The shortened tour of duty, watching the strippers and the absence of written reports were excellent features of the job).

And that's how it went - a late morning telephone call - two rings and a pick up, followed by an explicit time-documented account of my prior evening's activities. Occasionally the boss gave me a change of assignment, with additional explanatory information, but generally I worked the vice end of the unit.

Deputy Blake, although a man of few words, would eventually guide me through the labyrinths of a mostly nocturnal world of glitzy nightclubs, hard-core pimps, overworked whores, loan sharks, shakedown guys, pornographers, bamboozlers, bookies and bad guys. This was a seamy underworld to be sure - full of scoundrels, replete with intrigue, violence, and occasionally even humor!

Initially my job was simple enough. I acted as the eyes and ears of the police department within the parameters of an enlarged four block area in the heart of Downtown Boston (which would become known as the Combat Zone), extending about one-half block in each direction of an interlocking grid - comprised of Boylston, Essex, Stuart, and Tremont Streets and its resonant center, the very heart of the Zone itself - a small section of lower Washington Street.

As I mentioned earlier, it was patrolled by the Tactical Patrol Force, the bulk of whose personnel were from my academy class. They generally patrolled in three-man cars - tough guys for mean streets! I painstakingly avoided anyone I knew for fear that they would inadvertently acknowledge my presence and blow my cover.

However, only one of my classmates had ever burned me, and it wasn't inadvertent. I had been sitting in a downtown nightspot on Boylston Street one evening when the bartender approached me and asked if I were a cop. I broke up, and laughingly answered,

"No one ever accused me of that before!"

He said that a cop had told him that he had graduated the Police Academy with me. It wasn't hard to figure out who the Judas was since I had witnessed them speaking to each other just minutes before. I called the cop on it the next day and he vehemently denied that he had said anything. Had he told me that it was a mistake and that he was just fat-mouthing I might have believed him, but he buried himself as far as I was concerned with that bullshit denial, which made him forever guilty in my eyes. But that would happen in the future.

At the present time I was still struggling with the dilemmas posed by my new job. Being identified would curtail my usefulness - my short-lived undercover career would be over. I'd end up back in the heap. Undercover work put a crimp in my life style. It was a good job - but it came with a price tag.

When I did the Downtown Lounge that night it was like a rendezvous with my past. The biggest club in the Zone, it had been around for a long time and had changed names several times over the years. In the early Fifties it was known as the Silver Dollar Bar; however, it was the Palace when I first encountered it as a teenager.

Back then, the front door entered into a large dim room, dominated by a really long semi-circular bar with tables and walkways on both sides that emptied onto a small dance floor that was crammed with people - either slow dancing or jitterbugging. Johnny Pretzi, a tough-guy boxer with a mercurial temper, was one of the bouncers. Fights, which most of the time were over women, could be expected to break out at any time. A remark, a pat on the behind, a bump on the dance floor, jealousy - any number of things could trigger a jam - and it was Pretzi's job to end it. I can tell you, he was nobody to mess with. He went five rounds in a boxing match with Rocky Marciano in Providence, Rhode Island in 1949. That was quite a feat, even though he lost the fight by a knockout. He was also a weight lifter and it was rumored that he had posed for the 'Shawmut Indian' - the bronze bust of a Native American that symbolized the Shawmut Bank of Boston.

I was in the Palace one night when Pretzi slapped a girl named Ann O'Connor across the face. I didn't know what had precipitated the argument but Ann blew up and amidst a barrage of vulgarities she struck him back. He was getting ready to slap her again. Against my better judgment, I haltingly moved in their direction to intercede. I fervently hoped that the altercation would be broken up before I got there. I knew that I'd get the shit whaled out of me, but there was no other alternative. I lacked a real choice. I knew Ann's brother, Timmy; we had gone to grammar school together. I figured it was better to take a beating than to gain the reputation back in the neighborhood of being a coward by allowing a buddy's sister to get slapped around.

I was about two feet away when Ann invoked the name of Rocco Bellero, the most feared member of a large Italian family of six brothers - Joe, Frank, Bruno, Rosario and Salvatore Bellero — tough guys with reputations (whose names I would learn later). They frequented the nightspots in the North End and on Lower Washington Street. Joe Bellero had an interest in the New Yorker Bar near the corner of Washington and Boylston Streets and Rocco hung around there. Pretzi immediately ended the assault, his right hand frozen in mid-air. He looked worried to me - he apparently had no wish to engage Rocco.

A couple of the patrons hustled Ann outside. I don't know how the beef was straightened out but I was relieved to be out of it. The years worked their strange irony - Rocco went to the can for the shooting death of a mother and her kid - believed by many to have been an unintentional act - the result of a blind rage. And Johnny Pretzi was murdered, shot to death by a terrified off-duty Boston Housing Authority cop outside a South Boston bar room following a heated argument.

I was thinking about those old days when I landed a stool at the bar. The place really hadn't changed much, but now there was a stage in the middle of both sides of the bar set up for striptease acts.

I bought a beer and Delilah came on. The music blared and she danced across the polished wooden surface, her body moving to the primal rhythmic beating of the drums, obedient to an ancient choreography crafted to titillate the layered realms of male sexual fantasy. She stopped about three-quarters of the way down the floor, just in front of where I was sitting, and with her legs perfectly straight, seemingly fastened to the stage by spiked high heels, she abruptly bent her tall curvaceous body from the waist down and with her hands on her hips she pushed her face directly into my line of vision. She stared at me for a brief moment, offering the men on the opposite side of the stage a full rear view of her finely molded derriere. Her dark eyes, made all the more luminous by a thick layer of mascara, mirrored a keen intelligence.

She reminded me of Cheryl. God knows how I loved that girl! I had known Cheryl since she was a kid. She lived on the next block. I was about a year and a half older than she was. I had never paid much attention to her until she hit fifteen when, seemingly overnight, she blossomed into a women. She was my first flame and the fire died hard.

Cheryl was cursed with a rebellious spirit, suffused with intellectual and physical maturity well beyond her years. She was amorously referred to by the boys in Somerville High as 'Sheena' (Queen of the Jungle) - a mythical pop hero of the pre-feminist Fifties admired for her physical vitality, adventurous spirit and voluptuous body. I was infatuated with Cheryl - that's why I promised her mother that I would find her after she had run away from home. That promise precipitated my introduction to the fated Combat Zone!

I put two small facts together and decided to check out some of the downtown clubs. Cheryl had told me, at length, about a twenty-nine year old Coastguardsman off a weather ship docked in the Boston Navy Yard that she used to go out with, and with whom she was trying to get over. She commented that his name was "Duke" and that he was a part time musician who played the bass in a downtown nightspot.

Coincidentally, Cheryl's buxom friend Pat Champney, a slightly older attractive strawberry blonde with a reputation of going out with sailors, was also missing from home and was believed to have run away. It didn't take a Sherlock Holmes to suspect that they were together.

Cheryl and I had been dating for a while before she took off. I had hoped that she would redirect her affection from 'the Duke' to me, but it wasn't in the cards. I was seventeen years young and still in high school; I couldn't compete with this man of the sea. A bruised ego aside, I swore to myself that I'd find her.

It took three days to track her down. I physically checked every swabbie joint from South Station and Charlestown to Downtown Boston looking for anyone who knew Duke. Finally, when I was in the Novelty Bar on Washington Street, the last place I intended to check that day, I found a bartender who not only knew the Duke but also recognized a snapshot of Cheryl. He commented that Cheryl hung around with a "big nice looking broad," who, from his description, could only have been Pat. He told me that Duke's band, the "Krazy Kats," was scheduled to perform at the Novelty at 8:00 that evening. That would give me time to go home and take a shower. I was hot and sweaty from hitting the pavement. That's when I made my first mistake. In my exuberance, I shared this information with Melissa, Cheryl's brainy sister. She was already in college following two double promotions in high school. Most of the time I avoided her - she made me feel like a donkey - and why not? I was still striving to get through the General Course at Somerville High, having been dumped from Christopher Columbus (a good parochial high school in the North End) for poor grades and fighting. That sort of notoriety was plus behavior in Cheryl's eyes. I wore it like a badge of honor, but Melissa was a different type altogether - she was a goody-two-shoes and clearly didn't approve of me. Perhaps, in addition to concern for Cheryl's safety, Melissa was secretly envious of her sister for the daring and exciting life she led and that drove her to insist that she come along. A hidden urge, maybe, but before the night was over I would regret having caved into her.

We took the elevated train from Sullivan Square Station into town. We arrived at the Novelty about fifteen minutes early. On the way over Melissa hatched a plan that would have me standing outside the club while she went inside to negotiate with the Duke for the return of her sister. I didn't like the idea of her going in alone but she convinced me that 'turning on the tears' would soften him up, rather than 'riling him up' as I would more than likely do. She was wrong! I was still standing in front of the place when Melissa ran back outside crying. She was beside herself. Between sobs, she blubbered,

"I asked him please, please, tell me where my sister is - and he told me to go fuck myself!"

I couldn't believe I heard her say that - Melissa never swore! She had to be really broken up. I tried, but I was unable to calm her. Then the whole thing hit me right in the gut and I felt myself going off. This guy was way out of line. Cheryl was still a kid, even though she possessed the body of a woman. Most guys that age would have regarded her as 'jail bait.' He was hurting Cheryl and causing heartache to her family, not to mention how badly I felt about her. And to add insult to injury, he had just finished insulting Melissa and made her cry. This guy had to be a real jerk.

I felt flushed and my hands began to shake. Ordering Melissa to wait for me, I angrily yanked open the front door and quickly walked inside. The place was already crowded. I moved around the patrons and approached the elevated stage where the band was assembled. The members were talking casually and tuning up their instruments - getting ready for show time. I stood there at the edge of the platform fuming, looking up at the musician with the bass. He rendered a rough facsimile to Jimmy Dean - except his face was twisted up into a perpetual snarl.

"Is your name Duke?" I asked.

"Yeah! What's it to you?"

"I don't like guys who swear at girls and make them cry," I responded.

"So what are you gonna do about it, asshole?"

With that, I reached up to his instrument and violently ripped the strings from the tailpiece. He tried to kick me in the face but I caught his foot in midair and pulled him off the stage. He came crashing down with his instrument, both falling to the floor. I caught him with one good shot to the left side of his jaw but before I could do any more damage the bouncers were all over me.

Once the situation was calmed down Duke agreed to talk with me about Cheryl. He asked me to meet him in five minutes outside the rear door, explaining that he wanted to wash his face first. In my haste to locate Cheryl I stupidly agreed. I figured that he knew I meant business and wouldn't dare try anything.

That was another miscalculation - I met him outside all right! The blackened rear door opened up into a small filthy back alley. That's where I was standing, on schedule, ready to talk to the Duke about Cheryl. But he wasn't alone when he came out as I naively believed that he would be -the entire band of Krazy Kats were with him! I didn't have a chance. They performed their opening number on me. They spent the next minute kicking and punching at any exposed surface of my body that was within striking distance. My attempts to defend myself were futile; nevertheless I was swinging wildly and still on my feet when it ended as suddenly as it had started. They just regrouped and went back inside - it was over and I was hurting.

I staggered to the front door of the nightspot and met up with Melissa, who was still waiting for me. She didn't know what had happened. The right side of my face was bruised and beginning to swell. A trickle of blood ran down my chin. Melissa tried to comfort me as she wiped my face with a Kleenex. I was explaining what happened when all of a sudden who should appear bigger than hell - Cheryl and Pat strutting down Washington Street like they owned it! They were dressed alike - two hard looking, underage runaways wearing pedal pushers and revealing tight sweaters - their faces painted with bright red lipstick, caked-on rouge and blue mascara. They looked shocked to see us.

I approached Cheryl as gingerly as possible, knowing full well that at the slightest provocation she would bolt. I reached out and touched her hand reassuringly.

"Please Cheryl, come home. Your family is heartsick. I am too. Your mother is sorry about the argument and she misses you. She begged me to find you."

I let loose a steady stream of persuasive prattle and I sensed that I was making headway when her sister sort of moseyed over and joined us. Melissa asked to speak with her sister privately. Cheryl consented and they moved about twenty feet up Washington Street while I stood by and made small talk with Pat.

Apparently, from what I could piece together later that night, Melissa feigned indifference toward Cheryl, mistakenly believing that would be the appropriate response to what Cheryl was doing. It was a cold, ineffectual intellectual reaction, typical of Melissa, but not appropriate for winning over her sister. Cheryl took it as a sanction.

Without warning both sisters turned and ran from each other in opposite directions on Washington Street.

Cheryl cried, "You couldn't care less, I'm never going home!"

Melissa retorted, "I'm not either."

They were both crying and I was stunned. How was I ever going to explain this to their mother? I took one daughter into town to recover another and ended up losing them both!

Pat and I both chased Cheryl. I was counting on the greater sensibility of Melissa to ultimately prevail. Cheryl turned right on Essex Street and I caught up with her just passed the Golden Nugget Bar – a loud scuzzy joint similar to the Novelty. It was also referred to as 'Izzyotts,' the name of the owner who was a colorful little guy with a soft hat and a big ego who doubled as an occasional light columnist for a local rag. The band was banging out an Elvis tune. The door was wide open and the melody resonated in the street. I pleaded with her to return home - initially to no avail.

The Passage

As part of the persuasion process I treated her and her increasingly alienated buddy Pat to a full meal at the Essex Deli on the corner of Essex and Wash. The place was full of an unimaginable array of characters - late night shoppers, passers-by, sailors, guys on motorcycles, young chicks, cops, wise guys and drunks - and no doubt we blended in with the decor. Me, with my swollen and bloodied face and they, two cheaply dressed, overly built, sassy looking teenage knockouts

Throughout this whole ordeal I concentrated on Cheryl, never once alluding to Pat. In fact, I probably inwardly blamed her for Cheryl's intransigence. After all, she was the older of the two and should have had better sense. And that was my final mistake of the evening. I clearly witnessed the bitter reaction of a young girl disregarded and ignored. To my sublime relief Cheryl agreed to return to her family and Pat began to wail, lamenting that,

"No-one gives a dammed about me and I'm never going home."

That was the side of the equation that I hadn't considered. They were both in this thing together and Pat felt abandoned.

By this time we were out in the street, heading toward a cab, when Cheryl abruptly changed her mind once again. She blubbered to Pat, "If you're not going home, I'm not either."

At that point I was out of patience. My head throbbed and my right eye was almost closed. There would be no more sweet talk! I motioned to a cabby for a ride. As he opened the door I grabbed Pat by the upper arm and shoved her in. I reached up, held on to Cheryl's ponytail, and pulled her in behind us. I knew that I was acting violently but it seemed that I had no choice. Besides, I was so worn down by the physical and emotional pain of the evening that I didn't give a damn. I wasn't about to lose my hard earned bounty. When the three of us were secure in the rear seat I instructed the cabby to take us to Somerville.

"Not in this cab," he shouted, "no one who treats girls like that will ride with me."

"Look pal," I angrily responded, "I'll treat you worse than this if I have to. These girls are runaways. I'm just trying to get them home. You can speak to their parents once we get there if you'd like. So let's go!"

There was no mistaking my serious intent. The cabby shifted the car into first gear. He understood the urgency and finality of my message. Without further protest he transported us back to Somerville. The taxi cost me a buck and a half.

He waited while I took Pat to the door. Her mother, her voice shaking, thanked me and allowed her daughter in. I booted it out into the street - I didn't want to hear anything.

I escorted Cheryl to her second-floor apartment on George Street. Her mother greeted her with open arms. They both cried while holding on to each other tightly. To my relief, Melissa had returned. She cried too. So did Jeanny, Cheryl's fraternal twin sister, a mirror opposite of her birth partner and one of the sweetest girls in the neighborhood. (Jeanny had taught me how to dance - well enough for us to have won first prize at a local record hop). Cheryl's mother promised that she would never forget me - still she did. Cheryl continued to go out with sailors, but to the best of my knowledge never returned to the downtown night scene. Conversely, I couldn't get enough of it. I was compelled to return - again and again.

Undaunted by my painfully distressing introduction to the downtown nightlife, I was irresistibly attracted by the vibrant magnetism of the place. I liked the way it beat. I liked the music, the action and the chicks. I was drawn to the dangerously titillating entertainment power that emanated from its source. It held a heightened appeal to the young - especially the angry, the disaffected, the rebellious and the curious. I was all of those things. It was a forbidden place where dark shadows concealed the baser motivations, plots, plans, schemes and wrongful deeds of its denizens. Its only attribute was its unique quality to strike an uneasy and occasionally violated cord among discordant groups of sleazeballs, gangsters, motorcycle gangs, thieves, revelers, homosexuals and most of all, sailors and the female bait that hooked them. My ticket to this world was a thin yellowish paper, a temporarily issued Marine Corps Reserve I.D. card, documenting the fact that I had served two weeks on active duty at Camp Lejeune, North Carolina between June 23, 1956 and July 7, 1956. On a blank line underneath the name of my outfit - H & S Company, 2nd Battalion, I had a friend type in the date - March 18, 1935 making me 21 years old, old enough to drink. This was my pass to the wicked world of Boston's nightlife - until I enlisted in the regular Marines in January 1958.

Had any doorman carefully examined the I.D. card he would have easily detected the sham. It was obvious that the fabricated date bore no relationship to an authorized space for a date of birth, but no one really cared. They were only looking for a paper document, anything to cover their asses.

At least once, sometimes twice on a weekend, I would hit the night spots beginning with a cheap meal at Hays and Bickfords Restaurant on Boylston Street which was guarded by the outside presence of two menacing looking stone-cut Lion sculptures. I invariably ambled down to the lower Washington Street section of Downtown Boston in search of excitement, a dance floor and a date. I didn't find many dates but I did a whole lot of dancing. I moved easily among the large assortment of bars such as the Palace, my favorite with its two dance floors - the rear one was for romantic encounters, and the Novelty where I never did see the 'Krazy Kats' again. Apparently a group of Somerville kids stormed the place one night and kicked their asses right in the middle of what ultimately became their last performance; the Golden Nugget on Essex Street; the New Yorker with its cozy downstairs dance floor and lounge; Ed's Western Playhouse on Lagrange Street (a sleazeball joint) and a score of lesser known places scattered around the area. I usually ended up at the Hillbilly Ranch (another double dance floor joint, pulsating at the edge of the South Cove). Country and Western music, particularly Hank Williams' melodies such as 'Honky Tonkin,' 'Rambling Man,' 'Alone and Forsaken,' and 'Long Gone Lonesome Blues' flooded into the streets whenever the front door opened. Mostly I just danced. A limited amount of cash prevented me from drinking a lot or making a move on a chick before closing time. Needless to say, the girls knew that game too. I didn't score too much.

Occasionally Peter Gallo, a neighborhood buddy, joined me in these weekend forays. As skinny as he was, Pete was one of the toughest kids on the block and he was fearless. He was doubtless also victimized by my overt hostility towards sailors, a deep bitterness rationalized in part by a pseudo allegiance to the rivalry that had traditionally existed between the Marine Corps and the Navy, but mostly fueled by the lingering sour effects of losing my girlfriend to a swabbie and the beating I was handed out in the back alley of the Novelty when I tried to retrieve her.

I recall going into town with him one Easter Sunday; we were all decked out! I was wearing fourteen inch pegged pants with white saddle stitch down the side and a white-on-white roll collar shirt and snap-jack shoes. A blue velvet jacket with a five-way collar completed the effect. Peter was dressed similarly but with a twelve-inch peg and a pink-on-pink dress shirt, leopard-skin pants and an oversized blue cashmere topcoat. We were cool!

I don't know what we were expecting to happen on an Easter Sunday, but the place was dead. We ended up taking in a thirty-five cent movie at the Stuart Theater, an old dilapidated show house on Washington Street. We had miscalculated. Easter is a religious holy day in Catholic Boston, a singular and quiet day; nighttimes, especially on the raucous weekends, was another story.

We frequently ended up in fist fights with sailors (and civilians) which were sparked by the slightest provocation - a callous remark toward a waitress, a dirty look, an intentional nudge, a confiscated seat after returning from the dance floor - just about anything could trigger a jam. A couple of times we wound up running through the streets just ahead of the bouncers and the cops who were chasing us. We always managed to elude them. One time we even went back for seconds.

That was the late 1950s version of the area predestined to become the Combat Zone: Honky-tonk joints, rock and roll, country and western music, bar roving sailors, painted women on the make, broken love affairs and episodic violence.

A lot of criminal conspiracies were hatched there and I knew it even then. I clearly recall sitting in the Palace one evening, just across from where I was presently seated. I had a 'buzz' on and the solid drumbeat of the music intensified my sense of intrigue with the place. I fantasized how exciting it would be to work as an undercover cop in a joint like this. It would be the best of both worlds - an attractive compromise that would permit me to remain in this electric place as a responsible agent.

That was in 1958, just a week before I enlisted in the Regulars, and here it was seven years later and that is precisely what I had become - an undercover cop in the Combat Zone!

Delilah finished her number and came down from the stage. She fell out of sight for a minute and the next thing I knew she had perched herself on the barstool next to me. She asked if I would like to buy her a drink. Perhaps, I thought, that was the way she set up her marks - first by staring at them during her performance, and then sitting with them after she descended the stage. I politely declined, explaining that I was getting ready to leave. She flashed a petulant look at me and moved on to another patron. I made a mental note of her name, description, language and the time of the request. It would become a part of my next day's report to Deputy Blake.

Reflecting back over my career, I have often wished that I had been able to shed the discipline of my superimposed role for just enough time to have enjoyed a drink with Delilah because, without question, she was the best stripper that the Zone had ever featured. She raised her performance to the level of an art form and did it with poise and dignity.

Over the next few years I was spectator and observer to countless striptease acts. There were about nine joints in and around the Zone that featured exotic dancers. I would learn the identities of almost one hundred women, whose names were more exotic than their dance. Some of the more memorable ones were Mona Flores, Hesa, and Senorita Carrita in the Vagabond; Gi Gi, Anjalla, and Felicia in the Showbar's Zeigfried Lounge; Amber Mist in the Pickidilli; Ramona, Sonya, and Misty Doll in the Four Corners; Maureen Marsh and Joanne Henry in the 123 Club; Melody Jay, Manuella DeMar and Tony Rose in the Garden of Eden; Antoinette and Kita in the Carrib; Anita Cari, who was the lewdest of them all, in Peter and Harry's Piano Bar; Lisa in the Guilded Cage; Tempo Ray, Chinsey, Maria Valeri and most notably, Tanya Rienza of the LaSalle Lounge on Warrenton Avenue. Tanya was a hot number who possessed a peculiar talent that enabled her to rotate her boobs singularly, or together, to the right or left, or synchronously in opposite directions without causing the tassels to become entangled.

The strippers often removed their 'pasties' to fully expose their breasts. In fewer instances, they yanked at their 'G strings,' providing a momentary glance at a tuft of pubic hair. Occasionally they danced completely in the nude. They bumped and grinded and writhed, and stretched. Some were better than others. A few were deplorable and a couple were remarkable, but not one of them demonstrated the seductive quality, movement and grace of Delilah.

I have often wondered about her. Who was she? Where did she come from? What was her background? Why did she choose to disrobe in front of strangers? There was more behind Delilah than a well-shaped derriere. Although I never saw her again, her mystery would be ensconced in time.

The strip joints were a Sixties addition to the Zone. They began to creep in while I was away in the service and were in full sway by the time I started on the police department. There were other changes too, and there were several more clubs. I closely monitored more than sixty joints in all. Pornography, in the form of movies and shops, was seeping in and prostitutes were becoming increasingly numerous.

I wasn't out on the street ten minutes when I ran into Popeye who was standing at the corner of Wash. and Lagrange eating a cheap hot dog. Apparently he didn't like the changes. At least that's the impression I had when I talked to him. I had known Popeye back in the Fifties. He was a little guy, perfectly proportioned, but only a couple of inches taller than a midget. His biggest feature was his large brown eyes - they sort of bulged and drooped at the same time. He struck me as a miniature version of Peter Lorre, a famous character actor of my youth.

Popeye liked hot dogs back then too, back when I first met him in Joe and Nemo's on Washington Street. One of a string of hot-dog joints, it was originally started by two barbers who, back in 1909, sold steamed hotdogs from their shop. They were delicious and the price was right. Popeye was standing next to me at the counter back then, munching on a bag of chips. On a hunch that he was hungry I ordered him a hot-dog and a coke. He thanked me and we got into a conversation. As it turned out, Popeye was a pretty bright guy and a character in his own right. He knew a lot about the downtown action. He described lower Washington Street as "Scollay Square moved up."

Scollay Square had been Boston's sin center back in the war days. It was said that Navel ships passing each other at sea would often use semaphore to flash messages back and forth posing the question, "Have you been to Scollay Square?" Like the Zone, it was play-land to the sailors of the Boston Navy Yard. It was filled with barrooms, cheap restaurants, strip joints, tattoo parlors, penny arcades and a church. I had some memory of the area because that was where, at the age of seventeen, I got my first tattoo - the name 'Phil,' set off by two greenish-blue stars on my upper left arm. That was at Professor Oscar's, a small over-crowded room on the second floor of a dingy building overlooking Cambridge Street. I can still conjure up the fading vaudevillian and burlesque houses - the Old Howard and the Casino. It was a rite of passage for every virile male high school student to hook school at least once to attend a performance. I did so myself, once, but the great bombshell burlesque queens - Sally Keith, Ann Corio and the legendary Tempest Storm were fading memories by then.

Other than that I didn't know much about Scollay Square and by the time I was discharged from the service it had become a flatland, victim to the wrecking machines and bulldozers of urban renewal. Government Center would slowly rise in its place - an impressive complex of municipal, state and federal buildings intermixed with fancy clothing stores, restaurants and myriad establishments that would service the thousands of people who would work, pass through or conduct business there.

Popeye enchanted me with story after story of Scollay Square people - their relationships, their misdeeds, their hopes, aspirations and business ventures. In fact, that was the place of the first Joe and Nemo's.

"They began on Stoddard Street," he said, "and ended up with twenty-one branches, as far away as Florida. There was something there for everybody," he reminisced. Some of his commentary was biting and crude, but nevertheless he was an astute observer of the scene.

In the late Fifties he had told me tales about the downtown doings. He was literally in a position to know as he lived in a cheap flophouse over a joint in the plangent center of the fated Zone. The site was marked by a little known, but historically important stone carving of the Liberty Tree, registering the past location of a real tree where the early colonists had gathered on their way to revolution.

A decade later Popeye was still a fixture in town - a resident and a hanger-around who earned his dough by doing errands for people, sweeping floors and performing odd jobs. He once commented that "The lower Washington Street section of Boston was like the bowels of the city - an asshole, where all the crap flowed, every city needs one."

That's what he meant by his remarks referring to the downtown section as "Scollay Square moved up" - a place where people were allowed to seek gratification for their baser desires, his inference being sex, booze, drugs and money. Popeye knew his stuff! That's why my ears perked up, after meeting him so soon into my new life, when he commented that "The place is taking on a new twist. A lot of people that used to come here are gone. The place is changing. Even the sailors are pretty much out of here. They were getting their asses kicked by the motorcyclers and there aren't as many dance floors to cut up on anymore. The Guineas are 'shaken' the place and the whores are making their 'sugar-daddies' rich. Nobody gets laid for nothing anymore, and if you do find a broad you'll probably end up with the clap. It ain't romance, it's the old do-re-me."

"Look," he grumbled, as he pointed to an attractive black streetwalker as she made the turn from Lagrange Street onto Wash, "the stovepipes are moving in. It'll cost ya fifteen bucks to change your luck. The place is gone!"

Popeye never asked me what I was doing; he never asked me in the Fifties either. We just talked. I was uncomfortable remaining on the street in an open view for too long. I didn't want to be over-exposed so when he started to get redundant, I broke it off.

"So long pal, I'll see you again." And I was off.

At about 9:10 PM that night I checked out the Darbury Room It was a notch classier then the rest of the dives in the area. I stood by the cigarette machine pretending to fumble around in my pockets for change. I walked in and out a couple of times.

At 9:45 PM a tall thin white singer named Irene, dressed in a black evening gown, came down from the stage and hustled a couple of drinks from two different men who were sitting at the bar. Shortly after, I left the premises.

At 10:30 PM I arrived at the Chantilly Lounge. It looked quiet, so I left after fifteen minutes.

At 11:00 PM I positioned my car up the street from the Diplomat Hotel. The same cab that I had reported the night before was parked outside. On my way to the men's room I observed the driver inside talking to the bartender. There were a couple of females sitting by themselves at the bar. On the way out I heard one of them refer to the cab driver as "Jimbo".

At 11: 15 PM I entered the Lasalle and ordered a beer at the bar where I overheard a conversation to the effect that a guy named Henry was selling Desoxin, a brand name amphetamine, over-the-counter at the Gordon Rexall drug store on Commonwealth Avenue in Brookline, an affluent suburb bordering on Boston.

At 11:45 PM I observed a singer, Pat Rainy, finish her performance and then sit with a patron who ordered her a drink.

At 12: 30 AM I observed Brian Dyer, a reputed Somerville bad guy, enter the premises. Brian was a feared criminal. He was the kid I grew up with who was eventually imprisoned for killing four people in Sammy White's Bowling Alley in Brighton. (He ended up tattooing their names on his chest.) I left the premises.

I returned to the Diplomat and remained outside until 1:15 AM, at which time I ended the surveillance for the night. I again carefully recorded my observations in my notebook and that is how I reported them to the Deputy on the following morning, in a precise and detailed fashion. The whole night cost me $1.85, for two beers.

Wednesday evening was pretty much a repeat of the night before; The Inner Circle Lounge at 8:30 PM (no action), the Diplomat at 9:25 PM (no action). It was so slow that I began to think I must have run into some kind of stag party at the Diplomat on the previous Monday. Finally, I hit the Lasalle Lounge at 10:30 PM where things started to pop.

At 10:45 PM a short, approximately twenty-five year old white exotic dancer named Ecstasy got up on the stage. About two minutes into her performance, I overheard a patron remark to the bartender,

"She's real nice."

"Yeah, but she would cost you an awful lot," the bartender replied.

"How much?"

"Probably an arm and a leg."

"Well tell me - how much," the patron asked again.

"I don't know, but I can find out for you."

At 10:50 PM the bartender approached the man and whispered something in his ear. The customer exited the lounge and waited in the lobby. I followed him and observed him paying the guy behind the front desk for what I suspected was an upstairs room. When I returned to the lounge Ecstasy was no longer present. This observation, together with what I had overheard, was evidence that the hotel clerk, the club dancer and the bartender were tied in together with the prostitution action.

The Darbury Room was quiet at midnight, so I tried the Chantilly where I did observe Joe the bartender, a six foot, approximately forty year old white male, serve two people after hours - at 1:07 AM and 1:15 AM respectively. (It cost me $2:45 for two beers.)

The first of literally scores of times that I was 'cruised' (solicited for sex) occurred in the Big M, a mammoth club with an elliptical bar, situated about three quarters of the way down Massachusetts Avenue between Huntington and Columbus.

The Big M and the 411 Club on Columbus Avenue were frequented almost exclusively by black hookers and the white male patrons they serviced. The Big M, by far the more active of the two, was a classic example of urban commercialized assembly-line sex. It was managed by an outrageous six foot, two hundred and fifteen pound, gruff-talking former bouncer nicknamed 'the Dog' who was as colorful a character as anything Boston's underside had ever had produced. I once overheard him remark that he preferred to make one buck illegitimately rather than two honest ones. His mind naturally gravitated toward beating the system and I believed he was good at it.

Both of these clubs were located in black neighborhoods outside the parameters of the Zone. Deputy Blake suggested that I "put the peep on them" following Thursday's report. The lingering apprehension that I was experiencing associated with my undercover role was greatly intensified as a result of this new assignment. This was a 'colored' neighborhood, and I was an unarmed white cop. (Carrying a weapon increased the risk of exposure. Hookers frequently rubbed up against the men they solicited to determine if they were carrying guns.) Eventually the exaggerated aspects of this fear subsided when I realized there was no basis to it.

The truth was that whites, much to the indignation of neighborhood residents, had dropped in on these neighborhoods for years to have sex or to buy drugs. Racism was not a factor on Columbus Avenue. The races were fused together in this illicit street activity. The organized criminal element who influenced the street action worked to keep things cool. It was in their financial interest to do so. The 'Ghetto Riots' that were destined to soon rack the nation would also affect Boston and spell the end to white solicited street-level prostitution in black neighborhoods. The practice of 'forced busing' would further isolate neighborhoods and cap the practice.

But this was 1965 and business was booming. The action at the big M was fast and furious! The hookers came in from the street and searchingly moved around the bar surveying the white patrons for business. They were careful to give a wide berth to anyone that 'smelled' like a cop. Soliciting a police officer meant getting pinched (arrested) which resulted in court time and legal fees. Moreover, the 'third pinch' could end up with a stretch in the

Framingham House of Correction for Women. Cops were an anathema and were to be painstakingly avoided.

The Vice Squad would occasionally put someone in a bar to snare a hooker. Their standard operating procedure required the undercover operative to sit silently at the bar and wait to be solicited. That normally involved a hooker approaching the supposed patron and asking if he wanted to "go out."

The response of the arresting police officer was clearly delineated under the law. He would be permitted to ask questions, but only ones calculated to substantiate the unsolicited offer of sex in exchange for money. Under no circumstances could he plant the seed of an offer in the female's mind for that would be considered 'entrapment' by the court and would constitute grounds for dismissal.

What it boiled down to was this: after the standard, "Do you want to go out?" the officer was permitted to ask "How much?" Assuming that the prostitute offered him a price, say fifteen dollars, he was permitted to ask what he could expect for that price. Once she described specific sexual activity - normally sexual intercourse, oral sex or both, she was primed to be arrested. She'd then be escorted from the bar to the cruiser. The girls were almost always cooperative and willingly complied with the officer's instructions. Don't forget, they had to go back to work the next night and face the same cops again. Better to keep good relations with the vice guys. In short, it had to be a clear unsolicited offer on the part of the offender and the language needed to be specific. It was usually in the vernacular.

I had a little more latitude than ordinary undercover cops did because my job, at least in the beginning, was to gather intelligence and not to make arrests, but I chose to follow the rules anyway. It felt better that way. A few cops didn't see things my way - they cut corners and put words in prostitutes' mouths and eventually the cops' reputations suffered.

My first actual solicitation occurred early Thursday evening, June 17, 1965, at the Big M - and oddly enough it was by the only white hooker in the joint. (It was unusual to find a white hooker in a black joint.) Her name was Melinda, a plump blonde with unsightly black roots. She sat next to me and asked me three questions,

"Do you ever go out?"

"Are you looking to go out?"

"Would you like to go out?"

I answered each question with a smile. She acted like I was a 'dud' and left. I was proud to describe the event to the Deputy the next day. He urged me to ask more questions the next time, like "How much?" and "What kind of sex?"

It was a little embarrassing in the beginning. I mean, let's face it, in spite of the hard street-wise image I entertained of myself, I was still the product of a largely Catholic parochial education taught by nuns and priests and a family that taught me respect for women. I felt awkward discussing raw sex as though it were a marketable commodity. I was about ready to further my education.

This is how the solicitation went down the following evening in the Big M. About 8:40 PM Friday, June 18, I was approached by Denise, an approximately twenty-five year old 'colored' female, thin and wearing a blonde wig, who asked,

"Do you want to go out?"

"How much?"

"Twenty dollars."

"That's kind of high."

"I'll stay with you a half an hour."

I begged off, commenting that I was kind of tired. "I had a tough week." I flashed a weary grin and went back to my beer. Denise left and moved on to another patron. He bought her a drink and after a few minutes of conversation he headed out to the street. She followed him about a minute later. She returned in less than ten minutes. I heard another female at the bar ask,

"Didn't that trick come off?"

"You know what happens, sometimes they get to the corner and chicken out."

The most distinct and unambiguous offer was delivered at 9:14 PM the following Monday. This time it was Gloria, a tall and medium-built black female about twenty-five years old, who asked me,

"Do you want to go out?"

"I don't know honey. How much will it cost?"

"Fifteen dollars."

"That's kind of expensive."

"What do you want? I'll suck you and fuck you."

"Where do we go?"

She answered, "To my place. I ain't got no place around here. Besides it's getting hot around here anyway."

As long as she was talking, I continued to pump her.

"How do I get to your place?" I asked.

She instructed me to go down to Mass. and Columbus and hop a cab, then to go two blocks beyond the 411 Club where she would meet me in another cab and then follow her.

"Do I have to pay for both cabs?" I asked.

"Yeah, honey, but I'll make it worth your while."

I offered the excuse that I was looking for something a little closer. I assured her that she was good looking and that I was tempted but that I didn't like the two cab part. She looked straight at me with her large misty brown eyes and smiling weakly, she broke it off with a,

"Yeah, baby, I know all about that shit."

She made it with the next guy though, after sitting with him for less than five minutes. He got up from the bar and left. I followed him to Mass. and Columbus where he hopped into a waiting cab and headed down Columbus Avenue in the direction of Park Square and the 411 Club.

About two minutes later Gloria exited the Big M, entered the next available cab and rode off in the same direction. Now I had just a little more to report on the following morning. I was confident that I was getting the operation down and moreover, demonstrating my knowledge of it to the boss.

I would be cruised a number of times at the Big M before the month was out. I reported each encounter in detail to the boss on the following morning. Most of the other incidents were just variations of the ones I have described. There was a spectrum of opening remarks. One girl began her conversation with me by suggesting that we had gone to bed before. Another one remarked that I looked lonely sitting there by myself and would I enjoy a little company? Although the approach was sometimes different, they invariably got around to the same question, "Do you want to go out?"

followed by an agreement on the price and the type of sex. It was generally fifteen dollars plus cab fare, and three to five dollars for a room (referred to as a trick pad) which was generally a dirty and unkempt rented apartment. The sex act itself could be either sexual intercourse or oral sex or both. The cost generally increased with the service.

The 411 Club was a smaller and less intense version of the Big M. Similar to Morley's (the Big M), most of the bartenders were white, but at the 411 Club they seemed to enjoy a friendlier and more relaxed relationship with the hookers, in contrast to the other place that viewed the women as mere economic units. For example, I was sitting in the Big M one evening when I overheard 'the Dog' order the bartender to "Go over and get her."

"She's all right," the bartender responded. "She always lays it down as soon as she comes in." It didn't take a genius to figure out just what she laid down besides herself.

Before the month was out I was solicited three times in the 411 Club. The first girl asked for twenty bucks but was willing to drop to fifteen. "Go right across the street to 410 Columbus and I'll meet you," she promised. As an added incentive, she added, "Ain't no cab fare, honey."

I declined, but I ended up with another scrap of information to prove my worth as an undercover cop - I was able to identify another trick pad location.

Carol, who was the most memorable of the 'pros,' broke me up. Tall, dark and starry-eyed, she asked for twenty dollars, plus one for the cab, while assuring me that I would be pleased with her.

"There's no bitch in here that can do 'frenchies' like me," she moaned enticingly.

"How much time will I have?" I asked her.

She looked at me, laughingly feigning impatience, and clearly replied, "I don't have no clock on my ass."

A couple of nights later she was good-naturedly ragging another black hooker for having a blacker ass than she had. Carol was delightfully spontaneous and seemed at ease with herself. She acted as though selling her body was just another way to make a buck. So why not have a laugh doing it?

As time went on I came to entertain the impression that black hookers,

174

on the whole, were more resigned to their fate than were their white counterparts, who generally struck me as more emotionally turbulent under the surface. I theorized that white females, having more doors open to them to begin with, had to travel a greater psychological distance to cross over into the realm of prostitution. Black prostitutes were more likely to view 'hustling' as a way out from behind the eight ball. Was it prejudice or pop psychology that brought me to that conclusion? I'm not sure to this day - but it makes a lot of sense.

One other difference was price. The bottom line for blacks was fifteen bucks while whites wanted twenty. This probably had to do with supply and demand, together with lower operating costs exacted by the bar owners for the price of doing business in black neighborhoods. The downtown joints were generally more expensive to work than joints in the ghetto neighborhoods. But no matter where - up town or cross town, everybody had a piece of the action - the pimps, the joints, the cabbies, the apartments, the hotels, the bail bondsmen and the lawyers. The smallest piece went to the hooker - white or black she was at the bottom end of the food chain.

Toward the end of the month I learned that the Big M was operating 'after hours' (beyond the time allowed by their liquor license). It was 1:50 AM and the place was going hot and heavy downstairs. There was drinking, women and a lot of noise. I took a bunch of car registrations and relayed the information to Deputy Blake over the phone on the following morning.

"That's good Phil, we'll take care of it."

I figured the place was hit, or the word got to the manager, because on Monday, July 12, at 1:06 AM, just after 'last call' at the Big M, I overheard 'the Dog' complain to a guy standing outside, "I don't give a fuck about the deputies, the police department or anything. I'm surprised at them - first they knock off the whores, now they want to knock off the drinking. If they want to pinch me, why don't they just come in here and pinch me?"

I wondered about that too.

The Peppermint Lounge at 117 Tremont Street was the biggest action joint in the Combat Zone. It later became known as the 'Living Room' and was managed by a half-assed sharpie named Peter Fumari. The prostitution action was pretty heavy and the wise guys were shaking the place down. The way Joe (the Animal) Barbosa, a Portuguese fighter out of New Bedford,

Mass. eventually told the story was that he demanded two hundred and fifty dollars a week, or ten thousand up front as a one-time payment for the price of doing business. The manager forked it over, but only after Joe and his friends tore the place up.

Barbosa was a hit man referred to as the 'biggest killer in the Commonwealth' by a local newspaper. Without a doubt he was the most feared criminal in all of New England. He was sitting in the Intermission Lounge the first time I saw him. He was a darker and more heavily muscled version of Rocco Bellero. He wore a light mohair suit and was wearing sunglasses even though the place was dimly lit. He looked menacing. There was no mistaking who he was or the deadly violence that he was capable of inflicting. He was precisely the kind of stooge that the 'Office,' the local term for the Mafia, was looking for, a not to be fucked with extortion man. They called it 'protection money'.

Barbosa wasn't alone in this effort and the Peppermint Lounge wasn't the only place getting squeezed. The whole area was up for grabs. Another guy that I saw walking in and out of the joints was Jack Scampa, a big six foot five inch, fired Boston cop, suspected to be an enforcer for the Office. Jack actually was pretty pleasant looking and he was known for backing up a cop in a jam but his large bulk spoke for itself. Guys like Barbosa and Scampa were the ominous developments in the 1960's Zone that Popeye breezily touched on.

I didn't start hitting the Peppermint Lounge until the first of July. Although most of the whores were white, the joint didn't discriminate. The first action I witnessed involved an expensive looking black hooker who was sitting at the bar with a white guy. The deal apparently having been consummated, she left and he followed. She remained in the lead with the trick about twenty feet behind. I tailed them to the Elliot Street Garage where they drove away together in a 1965 Cadillac with blue plates. I couldn't get close enough to identify the State but I thought it was Connecticut Registration VF413. I considered obtaining a registration number a small success because it documented my efforts and demonstrated that I wasn't goofing off.

The next night I was sitting at the bar sipping on a beer (beer was a possible giveaway for an undercover cop, but with the expenses they allowed me, I didn't have much choice) when I was approached by a well-dressed baby-faced blonde with a bouffant hairdo. She introduced herself as Monique and asked me if I wanted to go out. After I strung her along for a while she dropped the price from twenty-five to twenty dollars.

"I'll give you an around-the-world or half-and-half the French way, or any way you want it."

When I asked her where we would go, she instructed me.

"Go to the Lasalle Hotel and pay the guy at the desk eight dollars for a room and I'll meet you there."

When I reported the following morning the Deputy recognized her name immediately, commenting that she was known for "turning more tricks in a night than any other whore in the Combat Zone."

"She's good for three or four hundred bucks a night," he laughed.

Before the month was out the *Record American* reported that four women and two men had been arrested by Vice Squad Detectives in connection with raids on three Combat Zone night-spots (one of which was the Peppermint Lounge) and charged with, among other things, 'Immoral solicitation.' Included among them was "Monique Larkin, 26 years old of May Street in Cambridge."

I believed that these arrests were a product of my surveillance efforts, but I never knew for sure. The Deputy never confided in me how he handled the information I provided him - and I rarely asked.

One of the other girls who had been arrested was Barbara Knight, a twenty-one year old shapely red-head with a beehive hairdo. She was also arrested in the Peppermint Lounge; however I had never seen her before. She was probably just starting out, in which case she had about seven productive years left as a prostitute. Blake once commented that after twenty-eight years old these women were over the hill. They burnt out fast!

The next time I was in the Diplomat I noted that their method of operation had changed from the slower pace that I had observed on the first night that I had put the bug on it. There were about eight prostitutes in the combined bar and lounge area. Between 8:35 PM and 10:32 PM I observed four specific instances of hookers connecting with tricks. In every instance the female left first, followed by the male. Each time, with the female leading the way, they went directly upstairs from the lobby. In one case I overheard the trick ask if they could go somewhere else but the hooker refused, explaining that she was not able to do that.

The guy sitting next to me at the bar commented, "Maxie keeps them moving."

As it turned out, Barbosa was strong-arming the Diplomat to the tune of twenty five hundred big ones a week. At least that's what he said when he spilled his guts to the Feds a few years down the line. With that kind of dough Maxie had to 'keep them moving'.

At 11:52 PM I observed the bartender, a white male nicknamed 'Speedy,' slip some bills to an unknown hooker-type sitting at the bar.

"Are you making any money?" he asked.

"Not a cent," she replied.

That was it for the Dip for a while. I had the action pinned down pretty good. And once more I felt confident that the boss knew it. I would soon go on to something else. Things were happening. They were happening on the home front also.

My otherwise tranquil civilian existence was about to be tempered by a new ingredient. Beverly's due date was drawing closer!

Eighteen

I **nervously awaited the first indication** that Beverly would be starting into labor, readying myself to be off like a shot at the first symptom. I had been planning the transport for three weeks. I had assembled a list of phone numbers that she could call in the event that an emergency arose while I was working. I included the phone numbers of nearby cab companies, private ambulances and of course, in the event of a dire crisis - the police department.

I physically measured the varying distances of the possible responding units with my car odometer and carefully calculated their estimated times of arrival. I set aside a sufficient amount of cab fare if my wife used a taxi. I personally contacted the night dispatchers of the closest transport companies to ensure a speedy response and was careful to keep the young couple next door fully apprised of Beverly's condition. I repetitively drove over the route to the hospital in the event that it was me who drove her - down Cornell Street, right on Washington, left on the Arborway continuing straight through to the Jamaicaway, right at Huntington Avenue and left onto Longwood. The Boston Lying-In Hospital was located on Longwood Avenue about halfway down from the intersection. There would be no time for getting lost!

This hyper-vigilant preoccupation with crisis and emergency was a collective product of my Marine Corps training, State Hospital employment and most of all, the calamitous nature of my new job. Police work alone will produce this affect. Eventually time and training work in concert to provide the embryo cop with the maturity to place this sense of impending disaster in perspective, but there still remains a lingering effect. It is one of a number of lasting and unifying traits shared by the police that differentiate cops from other professionals.

So when she experienced her first contraction that Monday afternoon I was off in a shot. I quickly ushered Beverly into the Volkswagen and tossed her overnight bag onto the rear seat. We were proceeding down the well-rehearsed route to the hospital when, to my utter frustration, I overshot the exit leading to the Huntington Avenue cutoff! I ended up somewhere behind the targeted hospital in the Fenway area. Man, I was unnerved.

At that point Beverly got behind the wheel and drove herself. As I've already pointed out, I have always suffered from a disabling sense of direction; time and practice have somewhat mitigated the problem but it will never cease to be a burden. Successive promotions have further reduced my anxiety by increasing the distance between my role and that of primary responder - a factor that motivated me to study for promotional exams in the first place.

Ultimately that small error didn't matter anyway. We arrived at the hospital in plenty of time. I stayed with Beverly throughout the afternoon, leaving her side only to go to work at about 8:00 PM. I returned by 2:00 AM and then remained in a small enclosure set aside for expectant fathers until one of the nurses gave me the bum's rush just after breakfast.

"There's no sense hanging around here," she ordered in a benignly authoritative manner. "Your wife is nowhere near ready. Go home and go to bed. We'll call you when the time comes - it could be tonight."

Her manner indicated that there was no room for argumentation. I left the phone number where I could be reached and headed to my uncle's house in Brighton. I'd wait it out there, I reasoned; perhaps I could get a little shut-eye while my Aunt Rita listened for the phone.

I fell into a restive sleep until sometime late in the afternoon when I was gently prodded into awakening by my aunt. My sister Jeanette had called the hospital and was now on the phone with the news that Beverly had given birth.

I nervously picked up the receiver and stammered incorrectly into the phone.

"Am I a father or a daughter?" I asked.

Jeanette laughingly replied, "Beverly's given birth to a healthy baby girl. She had a tough labor, but the baby was born without complications."

At 2:39 PM Tuesday my first child was born, a six pound, five ounce whaling little infant who would alter my life irrevocably. I was elated, so elated in fact, that I forgot to get pissed at the hospital for failing to notify me of the birth of my daughter as the maternity nurse had promised. I thanked my sister for the backup. Jeanette seemed to always know when things were about ready to happen.

A half-hour later I was sitting next to Beverly. She looked peacefully drained. She smiled and lapsed back and forth into a peaceful sleep. I walked down to the newborn nursery and peered through the window. I saw a lot of little balls of pinkish-white and tan flesh behind the display glass but 'Baby Girl Vitti' was the only one who was crying.

I spent the afternoon at the hospital with Beverly. That night I flew around the Zone, hardly conscious of my surroundings. My feet were light and my heart was bursting with joy - a special kind of joy reserved only for orphans, one that conferred upon me the opportunity to be that which I myself had never experienced - a father. Kimberly Jean was the first of my three daughters, and the only one with a severe case of colic.

Kim was colicky all right. Her tiny body was consumed by abdominal pain! We learned that soon after she had arrived home. She would begin to cry at about 6:00 AM and carry on non-stop until 1:00 AM, allowing us less than four hours of sleep. We tried everything: Doctor's visits, changing formulas and moving her into different positions in the crib. Mostly, Beverly or I just walked her around. The only thing that seemed to help was late night car rides. For some unexplained reason the movement of the vehicle produced a soothing effect on the baby.

Beverly treated the baby with compassion and patience, never once losing her cool. I could not help but reflect on this in later years, when as a remedy for child abuse, social service agencies offered courses on techniques to employ to avoid beating crying babies.

In a couple of months Kim's ceaseless wailing brought us into conflict with Mrs. Malici, the childless and widowed landlady upstairs, who repetitively banged on the wall next to the kitchen admonishing us to "Give her water."

She was a cold woman and struck me as a double for the 'Wicked Witch of the West' in the 1939 classic *The Wizard of Oz*. The neighbors told me that her demanding and perfectionist nature had driven her husband to a premature death due to heart failure. An old stone mason, she worked him until he dropped.

She hit us with an unexpected thirty-dollar rent increase, payable the first of the month. She failed to give us the required one-month notice so I countered with my own unlawful two-week notice to move. But I didn't know where. She panicked and offered to retract the increase, almost begging me to stay. And why wouldn't she? We were a quiet couple and Beverly was a meticulous housekeeper. The rent was always paid on time and I shoveled snow in the winter and mowed the lawn in the summer. However, I was outraged and remained unwavering in my refusal to bend, despite her pleas.

As fate would have it, an old woman who lived one street away was wandering the streets in the neighborhood looking for a tenant to rent the second floor of her two-family house. We were introduced to the women by our next door neighbor who knew of our plight and shared our antagonism toward Mrs. Malici. I didn't know at the time that this old woman was suffering from advanced senility (probably Alzheimer's disease) and had escaped confinement to her house. She offered us one more bedroom for ten fewer dollars rent. It came to one hundred and fifteen bucks a month. Good deals don't last forever, so I snapped it up.

After a conversation with her son, who lived with his family next door, I learned that they hadn't intended to rent the apartment upstairs from his parents because of his mother's condition. Apparently she imagined that the previous tenants deliberately banged on the overhead floor to annoy her. However, he agreed to abide by our agreement and that is how we ended up moving from a cool basement apartment on Cornell Street to a hot attic apartment on Glendower Road. Kimberly continued to cry, but the old Lebanese couple downstairs didn't seem to mind. At least they never complained.

As for Mrs. Malici, she eventually rented her apartment to a good-looking chick, suspected by the neighbors of being a high-class hooker, whose complaint of a code violation to the city forced the landlady to provide her tenant with a second exit door.

Kimberly suffered from colic for the next few months, her tiny body wracked in pain. Even now I am convinced that this forging in fire helped mold her into the strong and independent women she was destined to become.

Nineteen

I was hit with another change of pace on the Monday following Kim's birth. The Deputy asked me to work days for the next month or so. I'd be chasing bookmakers this time and the whole city would be my domain.

I didn't feel threatened by this assignment because I already knew a little bit about how bookies operated from growing up in Somerville. Playing the numbers had been a daily pastime in the neighborhood.

The number was calculated by a complex formula of para-mutual wagering at the racetrack based on the placement of the horse, the odds and the amount of money bet. I have never fully understood exactly how it was determined, but the result was published every day in code form in a Boston Daily Newspaper. I had a pretty good idea of the horses and dogs, at least the win, place and show part of it.

The boss explained that he was interested in learning the locations of any gambling operations that I could dig up. This included numbers, horses, sporting events, dogs, crap games or whatever. He was especially interested in tracking down bookies. He suggested that I begin work at around eleven o'clock in the morning and work until about six in the evening.

"Start off outside some variety store or smoke shop and watch for a customer who purchases the *Armstrong*," he said, "and then tail him to wherever he goes to make a bet." The *Armstrong* was a gambling publication listing scheduled east coast horse races complete with the odds, past performances, weights, times and other quips of information that might aid the bettor in making a winning selection.

"Find out as much about the bookie as you can," he continued, "his name, description, car registration and the location of where he is booking. Note the time of the action, his method of operation, and most of all, his 'hide,' the place where he secretes the betting slips."

I soon realized that locating the hide was the most difficult part. It could be anywhere: the hollowed out leg of a chair, a scrimpy compartment embedded in the floor, a special place in the ceiling, a false container - the possibilities were limited only by one's imagination.

The most ingenious hide was the human mind itself. I learned that lesson on the very first day that I worked. The Deputy suggested that I begin poking around for bookies in the Brighton section of the city. In the first half-hour I tailed a guy with a newly purchased *Armstrong* to an outside market at the intersection of Faneuil and Market Streets. He talked briefly to an older white male in his sixties and walked away. Over the course of the next hour several other men, some of whom were carrying *Armstrongs*, spoke to the old timer. None of them made any purchases and in no instance did I see the old timer write anything down. Twice during the same hour I observed the old timer use a nearby pay phone. I was close enough to the guy on the second call to hear him call over some numbers and a couple of races. The old timer apparently had committed the betting information to memory and didn't have to write anything down. I was amazed. Even if he unknowingly accepted a bet from an undercover cop there would be no physical evidence to prove it.

I recounted my efforts with the Deputy the following day. He knew by my description and other information just who the guy was.

"His name is Frank Summers," he knowingly remarked. "He has a photographic mind." That was something Blake would know – he had one too.

I hit the Wonder Bar after that, but it was quiet.

At 2:25 PM I checked out the Shamrock on Washington Street in Brighton Center and then the Bright Spot down the street at 3:30 PM. I performed another outside surveillance of the Faneuil Market between

4:35 and 5:00 PM that afternoon but came up dry (no action). I ran into a card game with money on the table at Pat and Jerry's between 5:10 and 6:30 PM and called it a day. This joint was rumored to be jointly owned by a high-level Boston politician - but that wouldn't have stopped Blake from croaking the place if I came up with good observations.

The next morning I asked a guy standing at the corner of Brighton and Harvard Avenues where I could 'put a number in' or 'play the ponies,' and he directed me to a poolroom down the street. "See a young guy named Mike," he said. "He has reddish-blonde hair and takes horses. An old guy named Jerry does the numbers."

The place was located at 20 Harvard Avenue. I went inside and got into a game of 'eight ball' with one of the locals. The guy was good - he ran every billiard on the table after a successful break. On the last shot he accidentally sunk the eight ball and blew it. He wasn't too happy. He asked me to play another game but I politely declined. By this time I had spotted Mike getting ready to walk out the door. Just before he stepped outside I observed him accept money from a customer and write something down on a pad of paper.

I sprang for the game anyway, it was cheap enough. I wasn't anxious to get in a jam with the guy I had just played pool with and he looked like he was getting ready to throw the cue ball at me. I walked out the door right behind Mike and followed him to the Wonder Bar. I didn't want to get too close to him the first day so I broke off the surveillance. I had enough for starters.

After that it was back to the Faneuil Market, The 19th Hole, The Irish Village, Tony's Cyprus and the Crossroads Tavern. Things were pretty quiet until I went into Riley's Men's Bar at 3:15 PM. As I sat at the bar and ordered a draft beer, I heard a lot of 'horse talk' and noticed several *Armstrongs* lying around. I overheard a patron ask the bartender, an approximately 32 year old, 6 foot 1 inch, 185 pound dirty blonde referred to as Jack,

"Did we win?"

"Yeah, she came in for nineteen bucks - you'll get four."

Before I finished my beer another patron handed a folded paper over to Jack. He put it in his right pant pocket.

A fat guy came in off the street and furtively passed Jack an unknown object, which I presumed was a betting slip. Jack whispered something in return and the fat guy left about 3:45 PM. I followed him to a luncheonette located at 170 Brighton Avenue. He remained inside for ten minutes, after which he emerged and got into a 1963 blue Olds, Mass. Registration, 656419 and drove away. He took a right on Pleasant Avenue and returned to the luncheonette at 5:15 PM. I was sitting inside drinking a cup of coffee when he showed up. I observed a black guy approach the fat guy and give him money. The fat guy wrote something on a pad of paper and remarked,

"We're not cooking today."

At 6:00 PM, I returned to the poolroom and attempted to play a number with Jerry for the next day.

He asked, "Who do you know?"

"No one here at the moment.

He apologized for refusing to take the number explaining, "You have to know somebody; things aren't like they used to be."

Perhaps the police were cracking down, I thought. Maybe they were cleaning up their act. I hoped they were because it was a known fact that the bookies paid bribe money to the police and courts. That's what the boss was alluding to when he admonished me not to trust cops. I was amazed to learn the full extent of it. I learned later that the police were not cleaning up their act - just playing an old game. I would eventually come to the realization that 'bookie money' was the primary source of police corruption, but it wasn't the ordinary cop who was deriving the most benefit from these payoffs. However, I still had a ways to go before getting the system down.

The next day I dropped into a poolroom at 345 Washington Street, still in the Brighton area. I spotted the bookie right away. I overheard that his name was Charlie. He was a tall medium built white guy, about 32 years old. He was standing at the pay phone when I walked in, verifying numbers that someone was apparently giving him on the other end and writing them down on a small pad of paper.

When the phone conversation was finished several men approached Charlie, some of whom were carrying *Armstrongs*, and in plain view he accepted money from each of them, one at a time. In each instance, after he accepted the cash, he made a notation on his pad. From what I could hear they were making horse selections. Once he had collected a few slips he'd pass them to the cashier who would stuff them somewhere underneath the booth where he was sitting.

It didn't take long for me to get the routine down. I moved around the city, each day choosing a different neighborhood. In the North End most of the action was confined to the inside of small private clubs that lined the crooked streets of the neighborhood. It was almost impossible to get into one of them unless they knew who you were, but I noted the addresses of any club in which I observed men carrying *Armstrongs*. I followed patrons from the Blue Front Restaurant at 422 Hanover Street and the nearby Genoa Restaurant where a lot of bettors hung around.

In Hyde Park it was the Fireside Tavern that housed the hottest action. Charlie was the name of the bookie. A few years later the place became infamous when the District Attorney's Office raided it and came up with a list referred to as 'the Vitello List' (named after the bookie). The list included the names of police officers, some of them high ranking and suspected to be on the take.'

In Roxbury it was the Baby Tiger School of Boxing at 1783 Washington Street. There, a mixed crowd of bettors kept the place raucously busy, but it was booking, not boxing that interested the majority of the customers.

Southie hosted Vets Inc. at Emerson and Broadway. The action was so fast and furious that no one seemed to notice me (a stranger) standing there taking the whole thing in. It was my impression that I could have been wearing my uniform and they still wouldn't have cared.

There was no place immune from the presence of a bookie: barrooms, barbershops, street vendors, restaurants, diners, hot dog stands, poolrooms, bowling alleys, private clubs, fraternal associations, social organizations, civic associations, shoe stores, dry cleaners, florist shops, spas, meat markets, pharmacies, small businesses and even a dentist's office. I eventually uncovered a moving gambling operation conducted from a post office truck, another being operated out of the supply room of the John Hancock Company and another on the loading dock of the *Boston Globe*. Any place where people could meet and talk was ripe for gaming. By the time I ended these occasionally assigned gambling investigations, three years later, I would have uncovered almost one hundred and fifty locations that accepted bets throughout the city. They ranged from hit and run part time joints to hot and heavy full-time concentrated action.

I didn't learn the extent of this gambling network during the first month. Nor did I comprehend the sophisticated nature of its techniques and interrelationships amongst runners, writers, bookies, layoff men, odds makers, offices, etc. or the raking nature of the business itself. I still hadn't pieced together the nebulous links between the lower members of the enterprise and the organized criminal elements for whom they worked. Still and all, what became increasingly evident was the enormous amount of grease money that had to be spread around for this underground business to function as efficiently as it did.

Don't misunderstand - raids were occasionally conducted and arrests were made. Partly, it was my job to identify and describe the illegitimate operations and the errant offenders associated with them for subsequent enforcement action. The ordinary bookie took precautions, ranging from clever to ingenious, to shield himself from getting pinched while others appeared to operate as though they enjoyed immunity. For the few who did get arrested and convicted, the punishment was usually minor. Most of the time it was a small money fine not exceeding fifty dollars. It was obvious to me that a significant percentage of court personnel, cops and bookies were in bed together. I had a lot more to learn.

The next time I entered the Fireside Tavern Charlie was in the men's room, sitting fully clothed in a stall. In just a brief amount of time fourteen guys 'made play' with him. I witnessed Charlie writing, accepting money and making change. The bartender even brought him a drink. I also overheard Charlie comment to the bartender that,

"O'Toole was picked up by the police, but he wasn't McGlaughlin's trigger man."

I wasn't sure what hit he was referring to, but even a small piece of information like that, in spite of it being a scrap of casual conversation picked up from a bookie, could be helpful to the detectives investigating the case. Not only was it a possibly useful tidbit of intelligence but it also demonstrated that I was doing the job.

Big Jim's Shanty on Washington Street was the last and final joint that I hit before going back on nights. That's where I learned just how dangerous this new job could be. As soon as I went through the door it was obvious that the place was jumping. It was noontime and there was a long line of blue-collar workers waiting their turn to make bets with the bookie who was sitting at the end of the bar. The bookie hardly looked up from his pad and made no effort to conceal himself from view. He was as busy as a bank teller on Friday afternoon.

I sat at the bar and ordered a draft beer. When I finished it I ordered another one. The clientele was racially mixed but I couldn't help but notice a big prematurely bald black guy with a head as big as a melon sitting at the bar across from the front door - putting the peep on me. I didn't know what this guy's game was but he sure made me feel uncomfortable.

I got up to go in the men's room - a tactic that would enable me to walk past the bookie and get a closer description of him. From my position he looked like a marshmallow with a pencil stuck into his right side. The big guy got up and followed me into the men's room. He was a giant of a man - easily six foot, six inches tall. He was all brawn and looked to weigh in the vicinity of two hundred and seventy five pounds. I stood behind a guy and waited for my turn at the urinal. 'Goliath' was standing third in line behind me. I could hear him breathing.

Suddenly I felt a huge hand lock onto the upper rear portion of my right leg. He firmly, but gently nevertheless, cupped the back of my neck with his other hand. Strangely enough, I sensed that he didn't intend to harm me, hence, I failed to resist even when I experienced my body beginning to rise in the air. I went along with the game. He pushed me straight up to the ceiling. I was utterly and completely at his mercy. He could have crushed my testicles or thrown me savagely to the sawdust strewn marble floor. I heard a deep throaty laugh emerge from his giant head and after about fifteen seconds of feeling pathetically vulnerable he carefully lowered me to the ground. I shot him a sideways smile, cryptically acknowledging that I knew it was a joke all along. He was still laughing when he left the men's room. A guy who witnessed the whole thing remarked,

"If you didn't piss your pants on that one, you don't hafta go."

The following day I related the story to Deputy Blake. He theorized that the big guy was probably working for the bookie whom he suspected was Bill Maffi, the brother of Jazz Maffi, one of the original Brink's robbers.

"He was trying to throw a scare into you," he said,

"He did that," I laughed.

"Be careful," he warned me in no uncertain tone, "sometimes they can get rough. They've been known to send in a stooge to pick a fight with a guy they suspect is a cop and then deny that they had anything to do with it. They even help to break it up and call the cops to boot."

He didn't have to tell me twice!

I was happy to learn that I would be reassigned to the first-half shift at the beginning of the next week. I had had a pretty good first dose of the bookies. It wasn't that the job was difficult; locating bookies was like shooting fish in a barrel. Nor was it un-challenging - getting down their M.O. (modus operandi) took a little more time and required a modicum of investigative skills, but it was the afternoon drinking that turned me off, or perhaps I should say turned me on.

It was necessary to have at least one beer in every joint I checked. At twenty five cents a draft, eleven bucks went a long way. By late afternoon I'd sometimes end up half biffed. I pretty much worked it off, considering the huge amount of physical distance I walked just about every day - but the residual effect of the alcohol, nevertheless, left me with a slightly spent feeling by early evening. Besides, it was fattening and I have always struggled with the pounds. I enjoyed drinking a few beers but I preferred to limit it to Saturday nights.

My final day assignment involved a covert surveillance of a South End residence located at 85 Dartmouth Street, just a few blocks from Police Headquarters. Originally a townhouse, this three story brick bowfront had long since been converted into an apartment building. One of the apartments was being rented by a slick pimp named John Crawley who lived there with his girlfriend. Deputy Blake had been tipped off that the pimp intended to move at the end of the month so the Deputy wanted to know where Crawley would be relocating. My job was to tail him to his new residence.

I didn't want to blow this simple assignment. In spite of the fact that most of the people I dealt with never rolled out of bed until late morning or early afternoon I showed up outside this address at about 7:00 AM. I wedged my Volkswagen into a strategic position between two parked cars on the opposite side of the street, about thirty feet down from the intersection of Appleton Street and Dartmouth. A Volkswagen Beetle was an ideal surveillance vehicle because it fit into small places and was easier to conceal than conventional vehicles. Its comedic look removed it from the popular conception of a police car. Usually plain-clothes cops were expected to rely more on panel trucks or Fords and Chevys to do their business. Finally, what the 'Bug' lacked in speed it made up for in maneuverability.

I moved into the back seat of the car and began the surveillance. The first few hours passed by quietly. A portable radio helped me deal with the boredom. I kept my eyes riveted on the heavy wooden door leading to the front stairs. This game was more difficult than I had realized. Even a slight distraction could result in my failure to see the subject emerge from the building. Most of the Hollywood type surveillances were conducted by two men in the front seat. At least that would break up the monotony I thought, but it also would increase the risk of detection.

After about three hours two things happened: I became restless and the interior of the small vehicle became uncomfortably hot. It was warm outside to begin with and the slightly elliptical glass windows acted as a magnifying glass, directing the concentrated rays of the sun into the small car's interior, causing it to heat up. Opening the windows made it only slightly more bearable.

By noontime I was forced to leave the boiling hot vehicle and continue the surveillance from the outside. I moved endlessly around the neighborhood in an irregular pattern, frequently changing positions to avoid detection, from the sidewalk to a cement set of stairs, back to the curb and ending up at the farthest point out, a store front on the next corner but still within striking distance of the car. I needed to be ready to move as soon as my subject walked out the front door.

Also, around noon I experienced my first hunger pain. Unfortunately I never thought to bring a sandwich. An hour later I developed a more serious problem. I needed to go - to the bathroom, that is. At first I experienced mild discomfort, nothing that I couldn't live with, but as the hour wore on I felt increasingly strained.

The closest bar was almost two blocks away and I didn't want to chance being absent, especially during mid-afternoon, a likely time for my guy to make his bird. Each minute that went by brought me closer to prime time. I cursed myself for not having had taken a chance and left earlier. By the time 3:30 PM rolled around my bladder ached and the need for relief consumed me. Pissing was all I could think about. I looked around for a wooded lot with a big tree but the street was thickly settled with close-by apartment buildings and lacked any real open space.

Finally I couldn't wait any longer. I had no choice but to take a shot and head for the nearest public restroom, which I knew to be in the Regent Bar on Columbus Avenue, across the street from the 411 Club. It was the worst of all possible times. The whole trip would take me no longer than ten minutes but I knew that was more than enough time to blow the assignment.

When I arrived back on location the sun had peaked in the sky and was beginning its westward journey. The air had begun to cool. I resumed my surveillance, this time from the passenger seat of the car. I opened both side windows and patiently waited.

Now it was the mounting hunger pains that I had to contend with - I wanted to end the ordeal and head home! I considered what time I might break off this surveillance. I rationalized that Crawley probably had already left, or maybe the Deputy's information was wrong to begin with. I could not help but wonder what Beverly would have for supper. I hoped it was not another casserole.

At five minutes after five the front door opened and a sharp looking black female, carrying a suitcase, walked down the front stairs and entered an older Lincoln Continental parked across from the building. This was it I conjectured, she had to be Crawley's woman!

She was all dolled up, adorned in a blonde wig and skin-tight black satin slacks, set off at the ankle by bright red four-inch high heels. Her heavily sequined sweater revealed momentary glimpses of her bare midriff. She definitely fit the physical profile of an up-front hooker, I mused. More than likely she was heading to Crawley's new address. I speedily moved up and over the stick shift to get behind the wheel. I reached over and quickly turned the oversized key in the ignition and the car started. About two anxious minutes later the female bombshell moved her car out into the street.

I allowed two cars to get ahead of me and then carefully maneuvered my vehicle behind the second one. The Lincoln, taking advantage of the remaining green signal, moved through the intersection crossing Columbus Avenue and continuing on through to Dartmouth Street in the direction of Copley Square. The light turned yellow as she made her way into the rush hour traffic. The car in front of me stopped for the signal and that one event spelled the end to my first moving surveillance. There I sat, stuck in my VW on Dartmouth Street, like a helpless bug glued to fly paper.

I was red hot mad, and forgetting for a moment that I was a cop, I mentally cursed the driver for obeying the law and not continuing through the light. The light still hadn't changed over to red - he could have continued driving through the intersection like so many other drivers had always done in Boston. I considered moving around the obstructing vehicle and going through the light that, by this time, had converted to steady red, but the heavy traffic on Columbus Avenue further sealed my advance. I was dead in the water! After nine hours of boredom, punctuated by periods of extreme discomfort and pain, a consequence of my failure to calculate for the effects of time, weather and physiology on an extended surveillance, I had lost my subject. At least the next time I would know enough to bring along lunch and an empty plastic container, much like the ones they used in the H Building. But none of that was helping me at the moment.

Angry, frustrated and more than a little embarrassed, I nervously anticipated telling the Deputy about it the next morning. As it turned out, Blake was amused by my story. Mike Flammia told me later that my doggedness and candor had impressed the Deputy.

"You'll get another shot at him, Phil," he remarked in a thinly concealed effort to comfort me. "You have plenty of time."

He was right. A couple of months later I pinned Crawley himself, going into 248 Seaver Street in Roxbury. I picked him up in traffic. He was driving a souped-up hot pink Caddie and I tailed him there. I recognized him from a picture that I had obtained in Headquarters on one of my rare visits.

Pimps were easy to spot. Most of them drove flashy cars, which cops referred to as 'Pimp-mobiles.' They were generally late model Cadillacs or Lincoln Continentals, customized with additions such as coach lamps mounted on the roof over the side windows and continental kits (displaying a chrome encased spare tires) taking up the rear. Pimps in the Sixties had a flair for the ostentatious - black pimps especially. They draped themselves in bold colors, wore iridescent suits with patent leather shoes and displayed a preference for processed hair.

There were exceptions of course. I knew one who rode a bicycle but that wasn't until the early Seventies, subsequent to the Black Nationalist movement which created a powerful stirring throughout the nation and emphasized 'black pride.' The movement curtailed the excessively outrageous flamboyant behavior of most pimps which had always been a source of embarrassment to working class black people.

White or black, overt or covert, ostentatious or subdued, I believe that pimps are human scum - in my book they're only one step up from child molesters. Even in the criminal world they're positioned at the lower end of the status hierarchy. They're in the business of human exploitation and will stop at nothing to gain their ends, which are always unearned profits gleaned from illicit sex and the degradation of women. They have always resorted to a repository of techniques that range from human charm to physical abuse and torture to exact their bounty.

It didn't take me long to learn that the pimps controlled the street trade in the city. There was no way for a female to work the streets without a pimp. Having a pimp was her union card. Independents would inevitably be reported by other streetwalkers and forced into being a part of some enterprising pimp's 'stable' - generally between four and a dozen women.

Pimps were usually good-looking and persuasive and almost always charming, at least in the beginning. They sought runaways hanging around bus stations or girls who were otherwise estranged from their families. Some of them were so young that the pimps were, indeed, child molesters. Many of these young girls had drug problems, or if they didn't at the start they developed one - usually induced by their man to foster greater dependence on him. Once under his control the charm invariably dissipated and was replaced by calculated cruelty. The girl moved along a continuum from 'indulged female' to a 'possessed bitch.' Curiously enough, many of them remained under the spell of their oppressor in some mocking variation of the 'Stockholm Syndrome.' They appeared willing to accept intense degradation for the slightest attention.

Convicting a pimp for 'deriving support from a prostitute' was a three-year felony. Hence, it was an arrestable offense and a highly sought after pinch for a vice cop. However, without a victim willing to testify that she had been forced to hand over money earned from prostitution to her man, it was almost impossible to gain a conviction once the case went to court. Occasionally a distraught female would come to the police following a severe beating and request to make a complaint, but by the time she had to testify in open court she would almost always back down.

Most of the time she would be sweet-talked back into the fold. Often it was fear that dissuaded her and why not? She could be killed - that happened frequently enough. I had been peripherally involved with a case of a serial-killing pimp who was convicted of murder for stabbing and shooting to death a woman who had resisted him. She wasn't his only victim but she was the one whose bruised and beaten body police found plastered behind the rear wall of a closet in a Seaver Street apartment.

One evening, a couple of months after I went back on nights, I was stopped at a light at Mass. and Columbus and I was 'cruised' by a young black male (supposedly) about eighteen years old. At some point during the transaction I asked him if he thought that I was a queer.

"No," he said. "I'm a girl, but I don't want anyone to know it. I don't want no man coming on to me. I'm putting my ass out here on the street and nobody's gonna get my money but me."

She explained that as long as the other prostitutes thought she was a boy, she wouldn't be hassled. If they knew she was a girl, she'd be up for grabs and at some point she would have been forced to work for a man.

She guaranteed me satisfaction once she removed her clothing, promising, "You'll see what I got." She would have been willing to go for ten bucks. Even as I drove away she continued to reassure me of her gender and a good time.

At ten bucks she would have earned a better profit than the other hookers who were required to fork their money over to their man. In exchange for their earnings the women received free rent, food, drugs, clothing and a small allowance for personal things, plus legal protection if they were arrested. Each girl in the pimp's stable would be assessed an estimated level of earning power by her man based on her age and looks. She would be expected to earn at least that amount of money every night with very few nights off. Small modifications would be made if the girl was not feeling well or if she was menstruating, but generally she was expected to turn over at least that amount of cash. If the girl consistently made less than the expected amount she would be punished for holding back. The penalty could range from a physical beating or the withholding of drugs on through to the most severe forms of punishment, usually reserved for renegade or breakaway women, such as the insertion of a stove-fired, heated clothes hanger into her vagina - or like the women buried behind the plastered wall - death!

Over the course of the next few years I developed information on a number of men whom I had suspected were in the business of 'deriving support.' I got to know some of them very well - but they didn't know me. I picked them up in joints, on the street, in traffic, at the barbershop and with their women. I observed them, tailed them on foot and followed them through traffic. I listened in on their conversations whenever I could get close enough and even risked an indirect question in my undercover persona now and again.

They normally began their day in late afternoon. After leaving their apartments they drove to various locations around the city, but curiously enough, never very far from their neighborhood - and when they did it was rarely for long. It was as if they derived their sense of mastery from familiar surroundings. I learned that it was a common characteristic of organized crime types to remain close to the bone. There were a lot of reasons for this - phone calls, planning, exchanges of information, interaction with friends and business associates, personal protection, safeguarding of money, and not the least of which, the elevated feeling of security one got from dealing on one's own turf. This would change gradually as the decades wore on, mostly due to the proliferation and enhancement of listening devices and greater reliance on electronic surveillance by the authorities. But in spite of a few notable exceptions, that's the way it was back in the Sixties.

Pimps checked on their women, transacted business, picked up drugs, gambled, socialized, drank booze, bought clothes and had their hair cut frequently. They did just about anything but work, preferring to earn their profits from the dank underbelly of street level prostitution.

It was pretty frustrating for me. About all I could do was simply compile general intelligence information on their movements. I reasoned that with every additional piece of information I obtained they would 'possibly' be brought one step closer to prosecution, but I knew in my heart that this was just a rationalization. In reality, for the reasons I have explained, it was almost impossible to nail them.

That's why I became only guardedly enthused some time later when the investigative division of the Internal Revenue Service expressed an interest in making tax evasion cases against the ten top pimps in the City. That was how this agency had put the invincible Al Capone in the can. It was a basically a matter of Internal Revenue Agents tailing these guys around in order to develop a financial profile. If the pimps were unable to show an income that would justify their life style they could be tried for income tax evasion. There was more than one way to skin a cat.

"Would he cooperate?" the Government asked, referring to me.

The boss laughed. "You don't have to ask him twice."

The 'Government' turned out to be a wispy-looking red-headed guy with freckles, fresh out of college. He seemed a little nervous, but determined nevertheless. I gave him what he wanted - the top ten suspected pimps in the city:

John Crawley, 248 Seaver Street; Wayne Stanford, 44 Parker Hill Avenue; Nathaniel Stewart, 832 Beacon Street; Jim Haley, 1575 Tremont Street; Sammy Seaton, 1360 Boylston Street; Fred Keith, 35 Whales Street; Nat Roberts, 399 Mass. Avenue; Jesse Bryant, 11 Parker Hill Avenue; Nelson Parker, 50 Columbia Road; and Pretty Boy Pete Jefferson, of 181 Forest Hill Park.

I had put together a hand printed folder on each of them compiling all the fragmented information that I had developed over time - photographs, identifying physical characteristics, description of motor vehicles, registrations, personal associations, business associates, hangouts, habits, haunts, girlfriends, general lifestyle data, just about anything that was pertinent. I personally identified eight of the ten targeted individuals at their places of residence or some other location they frequented. They were fairly spread out across the regions of Roxbury, Dorchester and the Fenway.

When we both agreed that the agent had enough information, I dropped out of the investigation. I stopped following these guys, even if I spotted one of them on the street or in a joint. I even stopped going into the Sugar Shack on Boylston Street where a lot of pimps hung around strutting their stuff. I didn't want to 'tip' this intensive federal investigation. Tax evasion was a serious charge; even if the Feds nailed just one of these scumbags, the bum could do some serious time.

The weeks and months went by but I never heard from the agent again. A year later I attempted to call him, only to learn that he had been transferred. He had never bothered to contact me as he had promised. I left a message for him at his new office in Manhattan but he never returned the call. So much for that guy! The pimps continued to operate and the Boston Police Department lost a lot of good intelligence. I have been convinced over the years that what the Internal Revenue does best is the hammering of working people into compliance with income tax laws, policies, rules and regulations. Bureaucracy is their game - organized crime control is not. A lot of years have gone by since Al Capone and their last big caper.

Several years later I would get my first pimp - more than one in fact. But he wasn't black; he was an Italian guy with an Irish name. His co-conspirator was a light-complexioned black female. He got two years and a five thousand dollar fine. It had taken me almost an entire summer working in a full undercover capacity to make the case. He died before serving one day of time, but that's the way pimps are - slippery. Back to my story.

Twenty

By **the time I returned** to the night shift several of the downtown clubs had been granted a two o'clock license. As a result, I had to tack another hour onto my tour of duty. It didn't bother me though - I was having fun and I enjoyed the freedom that went along with my un-supervised status. With no exaggeration, I made an intense effort to perform in a trustworthy manner. I had no idea how ordinary cops worked under these conditions and being almost fresh out of the Police Academy I hadn't had time to build up any bad habits. I'm sure that was part of the Deputy's calculations in his decision to use a recruit to begin with. I believed that the best way to protect my job was to do it as honestly as possible. I was in the business of observing, documenting and reporting human/criminal behavior. It was all new to me, but old hat to the boss. It would have been foolish for me to have embellished a story or to have attempted to work a con on Blake - this guy was sharp and could smell a rat from a long way off. I didn't have to be told that my destiny was linked to his level of satisfaction with my work. That was obvious.

Some nights passed quietly with few incidents to report - others were so packed with action that I had trouble summarizing them. Expectedly, the tempo quickened as the weekends approached. Tuesdays, for some quirky reason, seemed the slowest. It was as if on Mondays a few spillover people were still hanging onto the weekend in a last ditch effort to keep the party going. By the time Tuesday rolled around they weren't looking for another headache - it was time to repair. That's the way it impressed me, anyway - Tuesdays were generally dead and the work night lagged.

Just as soon as I figured I had the job down the Deputy would prod me into doing a little more. For example, after having provided him with a full account of the specifics regarding prostitution activity in a licensed premise or in the street, including names, times, and registration numbers, he would urge me to use my car to follow the subjects to their destinations. His appetite was insatiable. He wanted every detail of information that I could possibly scrape up.

I can still reach down through the years and experience the quiet sense of satisfaction I felt after locating my first 'trick pad' at 52 Columbia Road. I had followed two cabs - one containing a hooker and the other her customer, from The Office (a comparatively plush nightclub in the Back Bay section of Boylston Street) across town to a multi-family brick apartment building in Roxbury. It was a tricky maneuver.

I had observed the action from the start. I was sitting at the bar, close to boredom, when a black prostitute named Jequita came in from the street. I knew her name because she had cruised me the night before out in the street. Cocoa-colored, tall, slender and busty, it didn't take her long to snag a patron. She accepted his offer of a drink and before she was finished I could plainly see by the pleading expression on his face that this guy was primed and eager to leave. I slipped outside and got into my car, which I had deliberately parked across the street in the ready position. About ten minutes later both subjects singularly left the club and entered separate cabs parked at a nearby cab stand. The hooker's cab took up the lead and her prize trailed behind her. Once they arrived at their destination, Jequita slipped into the apartment building from the Columbia Road side, while the trick, after settling with both cabbies, entered through the Seaver Street entrance. I stayed put across the street.

This guy could get rolled or murdered, I pondered. More than likely he has no idea where he is. A recurring question crossed my mind and puzzled me for a long while. How desperate for sex does a man have to become before he is willing to risk getting beaten and robbed going into a strange place with a Combat Zone whore? Blake's explanation that the pimps protected their action because of adverse effects that violence would have on profits never completely satisfied me. I eventually came to believe that these assholes were either plain dumb or so horny that they were willing to throw caution to the wind for a brief sexual encounter with a stranger. Perhaps some of them were even attracted by the very danger they invited - the real flaky ones.

About forty-five minutes later another cab pulled up to the main door and waited a short time. Jequita and her John walked out to the sidewalk and entered the cab together. I stayed glued to them through the city streets, eventually breaking off the surveillance back in town outside the 123 Club. Jequita never even waved good-bye to the guy that (I presumed) she just had sex with. She just got out of the cab and went back into the club. The trick continued into the night.

The next morning, at the end of my recitation, the Deputy remarked, "That must have cost him a couple of bucks."

Fifty two Columbia Road and 410 Columbus Avenue were two of the first trick pads that I had discovered during my early undercover career, but they certainly weren't my last. Before it was over I would identify one hundred and eighty-eight other locations, not counting 'gay sex pads' which added another dozen. I pinned forty-one on Columbus Avenue alone, twelve from Seaver Street, eleven from Tremont, nine from Massachusetts Avenue, three from Parker Hill Avenue and several more from Symphony Road. They were spread out from Commonwealth Avenue in the Back Bay to Emerson Place in the West End; from Chandler Street in the South End to Whales Street in Dorchester; Seaver Street in Roxbury to Hyde Park Avenue in Jamaica Plain. Anywhere that large and unfamiliar concentrations of people existed side by side offered cover for this illicit business.

Two-twenty-two West Newton Street in the South End was by far the most active trick pad in the city. A three-story wooden-frame house sitting between Columbus and Huntington Avenues (two main thoroughfares), it was ideally located for some fast paced hustler action. In the space of a couple of hours on a Friday night I counted ten hookers of various races using the place. Some of the women accompanied the tricks inside after alighting from cabs and private vehicles, while others walked to the location.

Moreover, I was reasonably assured that there were other hookers stashed inside.

Once, during a routine surveillance of the place, I was taken back to see a casual acquaintance of mine walk out the front door. His name was Andy and he worked in the cafeteria at the Boston State Hospital. He acted real jittery and was spinning around on the front porch looking in all directions as though he feared that he would be detected in his secret life. Andy was a sad case. You see, he was mentally retarded, but not sufficiently so that he was unaware of his handicap. He lived in a world full of pain, rejection and humiliation, his ego battered beyond repair by the irreconcilable frustration he experienced from his own personal awareness of his limitations, exacerbated by the debilitating effects of a lifetime of confinement at sordid institutions such as the Fernald Center for the Mentally Handicapped in Waltham (the institution that was responsible for placing him in his first real job at the Boston State Hospital).

I liked Andy - he wasn't a bad guy. I had never engaged him as a mentally retarded person but he made me nervous just the same. It was as if he were always defending himself. His attitude struck me as being in a perpetual state of flux between apologetic and testy. He frequently acted like he had a chip on his shoulder, daring someone, anyone, to knock it off. He often accused people of laughing at him. He was small but wiry, and he rocked back and forth when he spoke. I experienced, more than once, the uneasy feeling that he was ready to choke someone at the slightest provocation. I also recall him telling me that I was wasting my time going out with nurses. "They were snobby", he said, sneeringly remarking that he had 'a real nice girl' in the South End - but he never mentioned that she charged him about fifteen bucks for twenty minutes! That's about how long he was in there the next time I saw him. I remember thinking that Andy would have been better off if he had been more severely brain damaged - at least that way he would be less aware of his limitations.

So I was surprised and a little disturbed to see him coming out of 222 West Newton. I became even more worried once I realized that he was a steady customer. Andy didn't earn much and he was dropping his whole paycheck in a whorehouse. That bothered me but I didn't know what to do about it. I considered coming up behind him in the street and throwing a scare into him - especially with my being a cop and all - that would have cured him, I thought. Andy feared authority figures, and that included me, but I came to the wise judgment that it wasn't a good idea to scare the hell out of the guy like that. It would have amounted to just another assault on his self-esteem and I'd probably blow my cover over it.

Ultimately the Vice Squad unwittingly took care of the problem. They raided the place twice in one month, arresting a couple of hustlers and the woman that allowed the premises to be used for prostitution. The proprietor was so huge that the detectives had trouble stuffing her into the unmarked car. The whore action moved to another location and that was the end of Andy on West Newton Street. I saw him only once after that, at the Male Home, during one of my pop-in visits with Paul. I never let on that I knew anything and it was a good thing that I didn't - Andy would have shit a brick. He was edgier than ever with me since I had become a cop. And let's face it, when it came right down to it, what else did Andy have - cold and indifferent flesh? Although not a true romantic encounter it was better than nothing.

In the wash of many years I have come to believe that prostitution was a good thing for Andy. It was a source of sexual relief and protection from the callous indifference of a world unsympathetic to the personal anguish that certainly must have resulted from the strain of his being forced to live in the penumbra of awareness between clouded measures of clinical retardation and dull normal intelligence.

If he were lucky he wouldn't end up with the clap. Gonorrhea and syphilis, two highly infectious venereal diseases, were possible by-products of sex with a prostitute but five straight shots of penicillin would usually take care of it. This was the Sixties and Aids was still a far way off. Rubbers had yet to become a prerequisite of commercialized sex.

I passed my final hurdle with Blake a couple of weeks after I went back on nights. He ordered me to check out an apartment building at 845 Boylston Street for prostitution activity. It was a seven-story brick complex.

"The action could be coming out of any number of apartments," he said.

The whole scenario is still crystal clear in my mind. I parked opposite the place sometime around 7:00 PM. It was an unusually warm September evening. I walked across Boylston Street to the front door of the building and absent a clear strategy I began to look over the outside registry of names. I don't know what I expected to jump out at me - prostitutes didn't advertise - but that's when I got lucky. The front door opened and a tall shapely white female about twenty years old stepped outside. She was wearing a clingy velvet dress without any outer apparel. Spiked high heels added about two inches to her height, making her about five feet eight inches tall. I glanced at her and our eyes locked.

"Who are you looking for?" she asked.

She caught me off guard. I hastily scanned my memory bank and curiously enough came up with the name of a girl from my grammar school days who I hadn't seen for years.

"Dorothy Hutchinson," I answered.

Dorothy was an 'A' student. Cute and perfectly obedient, she was heading straight for the convent. She sat in front of me in the seventh grade and wore her hair in a long blonde braid that I was always trying to stick into my inkwell, but it never quite reached. She never complained, even when the nun asked if I were bothering her.

The girl in the velvet dress asked me to describe Dorothy so I made up a description:

"A short well stacked blonde," I said.

"Oh, I know her," she remarked. "I think she moved."

Now I was convinced that this chick was action. "That's too bad. I liked her," I mumbled as I waited for the hustle to begin.

"Will anybody else do?" she asked

I couldn't believe my luck - I was ready to score!

"Yeah, you'll do."

She asked me my name.

"Uh, Mike, Mike Russo," I answered somewhat haltingly.

That was the first time that I had used my full undercover moniker and it felt odd using a phony name. I borrowed that too, from my childhood, from a kid who had lived in my neighborhood. He was a tough, but polite, Italian teenager a few years older than me. He possessed rugged good looks and was one a hell of athlete. He was what every kid on my block wanted to be. I liked him because he said hello whenever he saw me, unlike most of his friends who acted as if my age group didn't exist.

Mike Russo was born in that very instant. I named him without giving much preliminary thought about who he was or who he would eventually become. He would remain my companion for the next several years, evolving from a flat uni-dimensional monosyllabic character to a fully developed multi-faceted personality with a distinctive bearing and lifestyle. He was as much a fantasy creation as a product of my work. He has hung with me well beyond his operational life which came to an end on July 2, 1975 - the day that I was promoted to the rank of Sergeant. We have never completely separated and even now I can feel his presence.

It didn't take me long to realize that I should have used my true first name in the event that I bumped into somebody who knew me and who might have addressed me as Phil (which happened) or even worse, an adversary could have noticed the variance between who I said I was (Mike) and the name tattooed on my left arm (Phil). That also happened. Unfortunately, there was no such place as an undercover school that taught the techniques of subterfuge. Consequently, I was forced to learn the game as I went along.

Though it might sound paradoxical and puzzling to the uninitiated, despite my many years as an undercover operative I have always held close to the enduring simple values of honesty and forthrightness in human exchange (it's too complicated to do otherwise). A good undercover cop must stay as close to his inner-core that his assumed role will allow. I seldom experienced dissonance as a product of my dual roles. It happened only once, and that was still a long way off.

The chick standing in the doorway introduced herself as Sandy. Hookers were like undercover cops - they lied about their names, even at the booking desk following their arrest. She was gushing and I could see that she was eager to get my business so I continued to ask questions, both as a delaying tactic and as a means of eliciting additional information.

"How old are you?" I asked.

"Twenty-four", she answered.

"Do you have a girlfriend?"

"Yeah, she's upstairs," she responded.

"Do you mind if I get a look at her?" I asked. "My friend's enjoying a drink at The Office, the club on the corner. He's quite a bit older than me but he's a great guy. Whenever we go out I line up the chicks and he pays for the action. His main concern is that the girls are good looking and show him a good time." I dropped the hint that he was loaded. Her eyes got big and then narrowed.

She agreed to give me a preview, so I followed her onto the elevator, getting off at the fourth floor. She invited me into apartment 403 where she introduced me to her roommate Pat, who, like Sandy, was in her early twenties. Unlike Sandy, whose good looks were accentuated with a hard edge that cheapened her, Pat still had the dollish look of an innocent adolescent. She was seated in front of a large mirror combing her long black hair, clad in a sheer nightgown that barely concealed her cute figure.

She turned around and chimed, "Hello."

"You're both beautiful," I remarked to Sandy. "How much?"

"Thirty five each."

"Is that the total charge?" I asked.

"It is for you honey. But that don't stop you from tipping for a good time."

"Yeah, the price sounds right. What will we get for that?" I asked, feigning embarrassment.

"Whatever you're into - one on one, two on one - as long as it don't hurt."

"You're on as far I'm concerned," I assured them. "But I still have to check with the old timer; he's carrying the bread. Do you mind if I use your phone to call The Office? Maybe he can meet us up here." Sandy pointed to the phone in an obvious gesture of approval.

I dialed information, supposedly to obtain the phone number of The Office, but of course the phone was busy. All the while I was memorizing Pat and Sandy's phone number. My mission was complete! I begged off, explaining that I would have to look for him in the joint and we'd return when I found him.

"You better hurry or we'll be busy," Pat replied.

"Catch ya soon" I promised, and I made my flight. I never saw them again. I don't know what the women thought when I failed to return.

Perhaps they figured that I couldn't find the guy or that he didn't want to go. It didn't make any difference - I had more information than Blake could reasonably expect me to acquire and it didn't cost the department a dime.

I looked forward to sharing my success with him the following morning. Moments after he answered the phone, I laid it on him.

"You're right about there being whores working out of 845 Boylston Street. I talked to two of them last night," I reported.

I ran through the whole chronology, recapping the essential information at the end. "They're white, in their early twenties; their names are Pat and Sandy and they operate out of apartment 403. Their telephone number is CO 6-0474 and they go for thirty-five bucks apiece."

Now Blake would have something to put his teeth into and report to the Vice Squad, who in turn would call the number and attempt to make a date. The detective on the Vice Squad would probably explain to either of the hookers that an old customer had passed the number along. If the women bit then the detectives would have a 'double pinch' coming up.

I was heading for a caffeine high and waiting for an "at-a-boy" but it never came. Instead, after I had finished the rest of my report, he instructed me to return to 845 Boylston Street and see what else I could come up with.

"There are other whores in the building," Blake explained. "See if you can pin their apartments."

I sensed that he was impressed with my information but he never once let on. Instead, he was asking me to duplicate what had begun with a lucky break and more than likely would not happen again. I was mildly irritated by the escalation of this assignment. What did he expect? For me to get cruised again in the lobby?

Masking any tone that would hint of anything less than a professional response to his order, I asked, "Deputy, how would you suggest that I do that without being in the building itself?" He bowled me over with his reply.

"Get into the building by ringing a bell - anyone's bell." He paused and then added, almost as an afterthought, "Hide in the broom closet once you're in."

I have returned to that memory many times throughout my career, especially whenever I have addressed 'crime watch' groups, admonishing them to never buzz anyone into a building unless the person's identity has been established - but there is always someone who will, and I found that someone, night after night at 845 Boylston Street.

It didn't take long - I was admitted on my second ring that evening. However, disappointingly enough, once I was in I discovered that there was an absence of broom closets on most of the floors. I feared that if I explained this to Blake he would consider it a cop out so I decided that I had better come up with a plan!

I surveyed the interior of the building; it was rectangular shaped and consisted of seven floors. There were two elevators, one on each side of the building, which released passengers onto each floor. There were also two stairwells which allowed people to walk up and down between levels. I needed a vantage point from which to view the prostitutes and their customers without exposing myself as they entered, first the building and then into their apartments.

I developed an uncomplicated strategy, but first I would need a piece of equipment. I left the apartment complex and visited a nearby beauty shop where I purchased a two-sided makeup mirror, about six inches in diameter. One side consisted of an ordinary mirror while the opposite side produced a magnified effect.

'Anybody' re-admitted me into the front lobby. My plan required that I place the mirror in an upright position against the rear wall on the landing between floors to reflect the image of anyone getting off the elevator and/or walking down the corridor where the apartments were located. Next, I reached into my pocket and pulled out a matchbook. I carefully removed a sufficient number of matches and placed them in an upright position against each apartment door in the specific hallway under scrutiny.

Simple! Now I would hang out on the stairwell between floors, just above the mirror, and wait until I heard the familiar ding of the approaching elevator, a clear signal that its passengers would be released momentarily. I would quickly look into the mirror to sneak a peek at whoever got off. If it were a prostitute and her trick I'd wait until they'd had a sufficient amount of time to enter her apartment, after which I would determine just which door match had been knocked down.

By this time I had developed an eye for recognizing prostitutes and their customers. Styles of dress, behavior, age differences and demeanor were the predominant differentiating characteristics. The most obvious tip-off was a flashily dressed young female with a casually attired older male, especially if the female were black and the male white, although on rare occasions it would be the other way around. A lot of the guys wore furtive expressions and some of them were just plain dopey looking. Frequently, only money could account for the relationship and, of course, there were hookers that I had gotten to know from being around town.

Beginning on this first night, and continuing for the better part of a month, I spent three to five hours a night moving silently around the building. I set up my 'mirror and match' game in almost a dozen locations. It was the most boring, difficult and painstaking of any of the undercover investigations that I had conducted during those early years. My legs strained under the pressure of having to assume a crouched position for such extended periods in order to peer into the mirror. I lived constantly with the fear of detection, especially by those residents who chose to use the stairs instead of the elevator. To avoid such a confrontation while I was hovering between floors necessitated keeping my ears peeled for the slightest sound of approaching footsteps while simultaneously readying myself to bolt up or down the stairs or across the hallway at the earliest warning. Often two or more matches would be knocked down in a row by legitimate residents, either entering or leaving their apartments or perhaps by just walking by, causing me to have to surreptitiously set up the sulfur-helmeted sentries repeatedly.

A felled match alone was not a conclusive indication that a hustler had caused it to fall. Final proof required me to physically identify her in the apartment. This involved my having to knock on the door, usually during the day, under some false pretense such as miss-identifying the apartment, or asking to borrow sugar, or carrying a clipboard and requesting survey information. The latter was a great technique that I would perfect as time went on.

When the investigation was over I had successfully pinned five trick pads - apartment's number 204, 401, 403, 404, and 502, complete with names. In two instances I was even able to obtain phone numbers by asking to borrow the telephone.

"Good work," Ed Blake said.

I sighed after I hung up the phone. I felt good. I knew that I had proven myself. I was solid - I wouldn't be going back with Roach anytime in the near future. Mike Flammia confided to me a couple of days later that the Deputy had referred to me as a 'digger' in a conversation with his boss, Superintendent John Howland, Chief of the Bureau of Inspectional Services. Coming from Blake that was no small tribute!

I came to regard obtaining personal information on hookers, without having to lay out any dough, as a kind of specialty. There was a certain challenge to it. Before three years had passed I had amassed information on about three dozen locations - complete with names, prices, descriptions and most importantly, phone numbers. Most of these women never worked the streets, confining their activities to nightclubs. They were a notch up from the common streetwalker.

There were some that worked principally out of their apartments and avoided clubs. They were referred to as 'call girls' and charged more for their services - over a hundred dollars a night was about average. They were better looking, more refined, more personal, provided good sex and avoided drugs. Some of them didn't even have pimps. I met one who was working on her Master's Degree at Boston University, in Psychology no less.

The higher up the prostitution hierarchy they were, the more difficult it was to develop the information. I fed their names to the boss as soon as I got them. The calls girls were also spread around town: Waunita, 69 Park Drive, Suite 10; Carol and Tracy, 12 Sonoma Street, Apartment 1; Demita, 426 Marlborough Street, Basement; Winnie, 511 Beacon Street; Tanya, 62 Chandler Street, Apartment Two; Sandra, 1575 Huntington Avenue, Apartment 703; and Michelle and Cindy, 226 Parker Hill Avenue were among the most memorable. The suspected queen of the Madams herself was Mrs. Fox who resided at 566 Commonwealth Avenue, Apartment 802. I believed that she was a contact woman for any number of high-class hookers.

Midway through the 845 Boylston Street investigation, the monotony of this tedious assignment and the growing sense of complacency that I had begun to experience were violently disrupted by an off-duty incident. At 10:15 PM Thursday, September 9, 1965, I was attacked by five punks, two of whom attempted to stab me, at the Cornell Drug Store on Washington

Street in Roslindale, just a couple of blocks up from where I lived in a generally quiet neighborhood.

I had worked a day shift 'pinning apartments' and I was enjoying a night off as a result. I happened to be in the drug store buying an ice cream for Beverly when two raggedy-assed looking kids entered the store and approached the counter. They began to ask the proprietor, a tough old bird named John Capone, a lot of loose and unrelated questions like "What do you put in a black and white frappe?" or pointing to some cookies on the rack they inquired, "Do those cookies crumble?" Pretty foolish stuff.

It was obvious to me that these wise guys were just stalling for time, probably just waiting for me to leave so they could tip the place over. The druggist suspected the same thing. He looked at me with knowing eyes, a silent communication imploring me not to leave. Capone was nobody's fool. He deduced that he was about to get robbed, and knowing that I was a cop he didn't want me strolling out the door.

The situation was getting more ominous by the minute! Shortly after the first two punks came in two more approached the front door. They remained outside but within hearing distance of their companions. The drug store was situated on a main drag and as I assessed the situation, it was evident to me that the two youths in front of the store were taking up guard positions outside the front door for the purpose of surveying the surrounding neighborhood. A fifth youth sat in a car with the motor running near the intersection of Washington and Cornell Streets. I suspected this was the get-away car. The only other person in the store was the soda jerk, a tall Italian kid behind the counter.

It was a perfect setup! Even the most naive rookie would have suspected that an armed robbery was getting ready to go down, and there I was, off-duty, absent my firearm. My only weapon was the dripping ice cream cone that I was holding. To make matters worse, a big hand-written sign hung outside the old wooden phone booth warning people that the phone was out of order and thus preventing me from calling the police! I was screwed!

I needed to stop this thing before it started. Perhaps I wouldn't be making a heavy armed robbery pinch, but no one would be getting hurt either. My idea was to forewarn the culprits in some way that the guy standing at the counter with the ice cream cone was a cop. Thoughts raced through my mind! Hopefully, they'd call the thing off. There was no point to taking the place down with a cop standing there - unless they intended to kill him and that wouldn't be worth it - everyone knew that killing a cop was bad news. Cop-killer manhunts never ended. I sure wished I was carrying my gun - but who would have figured this - and in my own neighborhood!

I informed the first two grubs that I was a cop and ordered them to leave the store because they were acting boisterous (they weren't - but I had to say something). They took offense at this and demanded that I show them my badge. I reached in my right rear pant pocket to fish out my tin, confidant that once they saw it they'd be gone. Suddenly, without warning, I was punched on the head from behind by one of the lookouts. I later heard through the grapevine that he had claimed that he had never heard me identify myself as a cop, so he had presumed that I was getting ready to knuckle one of his pals and decided to take some preventive action. The next few minutes were among the worst that I would ever experience throughout my entire career! I chased the little bastard out onto the street and then the shit hit the fan!

I caught up with my assailant and was holding him by the back of his jersey. He struggled violently, kicking and punching in a futile attempt to free himself. Next, the get-away car kid jumped out of the vehicle and came at me with his arms swinging. I pushed him over the roof of the car but by the time he hit the street I was being pummeled by the other four kids. They were on me like stink on shit! The driver quickly rebounded, ran around the car and joined the others in their circle of destruction.

In the beginning I was doing all right - I beat them off me like rag dolls! They were lightweights. Not one of these punks weighed more than one hundred and forty pounds soaking wet, nor did any of them reach five foot six inches in height. I was working out with weights at the time and the effects of the training were evident. Only as soon as I banged one punk out another would take his place.

One of them attacked me with a ten-inch screwdriver. Fortunately I was able to disarm him and throw the weapon over the fence behind me. Another assaulted me with a hunting knife, slicing open the skin on my right shoulder. I repeated the same tactic except this time the little bastard's arm almost went with the knife.

I suppose I could have used either of the two weapons against any one of them but I preferred flinging them beyond their reach. The final report would be easier to write that way. It would get hairy if someone were killed or seriously injured with a non-issue weapon, even if the casualty was a bad guy. A cop learns early on to think of the report that he will be required to write from the very beginning of the incident. Whatever happens will have to be justified at some point in the future. A cop rarely has the luxury of time when making a decision. He must go on his gut with whatever he (or she) has now, unlike the extended periods of time a jurist sitting in review may have to pontificate on the issues. Some things never change.

The collective battering administered by ten arms and ten legs was beginning to work its toll. I kept on yelling to Capone to call the cops. I knew that he had a phone somewhere in the back room, so I felt a tinge of hope when I saw him go inside without being obstructed. The soda jerk kid tried to help me but quickly turned away as soon as one of the punks lunged at him with a knife. I didn't blame him, actually. He wasn't getting paid to put his life on the line (like cops).

The unremitting barrage of fists and feet continued to deplete my strength. I realized that I was tiring more quickly. That's when I decided to invoke the 'law of the street,' a fundamental belief shared by most cops that, in the event of a multiple assault and battery on a lone officer it's necessary, no matter what, to arrest somebody - anybody.

"It doesn't make any difference who," Charlie Anastasia would say. "Hold on to one of them until help arrives."

I picked the kid with the striped shirt because he was the closest one to me. I knocked him to the ground and threw myself on top of him. He struggled in vain to wrest himself free but I rode him like a bucking bronco. Unfortunately this action set me up for a combined offensive strike by the others and there wasn't a whole lot I could do about it. I was figuratively a sitting duck - sitting on top of a little scumbag on a public street, a block from my house, unable to use my hands and feet to protect myself. The scumbag's accomplices lined up on the other side of Cornell Street, four deep, and took turns repetitively kicking me in the head. My face began to heat up as blood rushed to the injuries. I could feel my head begin to swell and my eyes begin to close. I was in this for my life!

I don't know how many times they connected but each time I lost more strength. I prayed to God not to pass out. That was precisely what they wanted - for me to lose my grip on their friend so that he could escape. The more they kicked me, the more determined I became that someone had to be arrested for this, and that someone was the kid I was locked onto.

I heard one of my attackers yell, "Where's my gun?" I never saw one materialize and I was almost too tired to care. As a final resort I grabbed my prisoner's oily hair and threatened to kill him. Gasping for breath between utterances, I blurted, "The next one who kicks me - I'll kill this motherfucker! I'll smash his head in! I swear to fucking God!"

I cupped his bleeding head between my hands and forcibly positioned it a few inches above the street, ready to crack it against the curb if they continued the attack on me.

The street was covered with blood - his blood, my blood and their blood. My hostage and I had both suffered head and facial wounds and we were bleeding profusely. The kid feared that I was getting ready to kill him.

"Leave him alone. He means it - he'll kill me!" My prisoner begged the violent little band to end the assault. "Leave him alone - fuck the whole thing."

At about the same time the kid was pleading for his gang to back off the druggist returned to the street. Despite the fact that John was in his sixties he was fiercely spirited and in pretty good shape for his age. He was holding a broomstick that he picked up from inside the store. He stood in the street, waving the stick menacingly, and in a loud voice he warned, "The cops are on the way."

To my sublime relief, when my attackers realized that I wasn't about to let go and that the cops would be arriving momentarily, they jumped in the old junk car and peeled out, laying down some rubber on the street. My bloodied eyes, compounded with the evening's darkness, obscured my vision and prevented me from getting the registration number of the fleeing vehicle. One of the culprits exhibited some indecisiveness and hung back for just a brief moment. He bore a resemblance to the kid I was sitting on - the possibility that they were brothers passed through my mind. The entire fight lasted only a few minutes, but it seemed like an eternity!

Fearing a return visit, I dragged my unwilling captive into the drugstore.

I ordered the pharmacist to lock the door while we waited for the police, whom he assured me were on the way. John offered me the stick to use on my prisoner but he wasn't offering me any resistance at that point. He was docile and besides I was exhausted.

I still hadn't caught my breath when I heard the reassuring shrill of the responding sirens. They came from everywhere. One of the first guys to arrive was Officer Dick MacEacern (who was still two years away from fulfilling his destiny as the first elected president of the newly incorporated Boston Police Patrolman's Association). He jumped off his motorcycle and ran into the store. Tall and ruggedly good-looking, he emanated a kind of wildness that in the next couple of years would be converted into a singularity of purpose. He was a real police officer who predated the 1970's Clint Eastwood version of the roguish hero-cop.

The prisoner was bagged and transported to the station in the 5-2 car where he was identified as William Butts Junior, 19 years old, of 84 Appleton Street in Wollaston. Meanwhile, a neighborhood woman had called the Boston Police emergency line to report "suspicious behavior." She stated that she had observed the teenage occupants of an older Chevy convertible, Massachusetts registration N17-359, throw a bag into the bushes only to retrieve it five minutes later. This could have been the gun that I never actually saw.

The dispatcher checked the listing, determined that the car belonged to Butts, and put it out over the air. MacEacern and I heard the transmission while we were at the corner of Washington and Cornell Streets looking for my wallet that had been thrown from my pocket during the fight. Almost immediately MacEacern spotted the suspect vehicle passing by the intersection, occupied by a white male driver and a female passenger. MacEacern reported his observations to the dispatcher, hopped on his bike and chased the car down Washington Street where he was eventually able to pull it over.

After I fingered the driver as one of my assailants he was arrested and transported to the police station, where he was subsequently identified as John A. Wiley, 19 years old, of 16 Johnson Terrace, Dorchester. I later learned that the other kids had jumped ship but the driver had returned to the scene of the crime with his girlfriend to find Butts. I don't think to this day that he believed I was a cop.

Wiley and Butts were booked, fingerprinted, photographed and placed in a cell to await court action. I charged Wiley with assault and battery, a relatively minor crime and classified as a misdemeanor. Butts, on the other hand, was charged with aggravated assault and battery with a dangerous weapon, to wit a shod foot, because he had shoes on when he kicked me.

I never hung the knife or the screwdriver on either one of them because I didn't know who had actually possessed it - it could have been one of the kids who had escaped. I played it straight. Moreover, I ensured that once they returned to the station they were treated properly and did not become subjects of the street justice that was almost always employed against cop fighters back in those days. Butts even thanked me for that.

I spent the better part of the early morning at the Boston City Hospital where I was diagnosed as suffering from multiple bruises and trauma and released after being x-rayed. I was present for the arraignment of the two youths at the West Roxbury District Court where Judge Casey found 'probable cause' and bumped the case up to Superior Court for trial. He ordered the prisoners held on twenty-five hundred dollars bail. I wrote a 'special' (report) that day for my office and worked a full tour that evening, during which I continued to experience a lot of pain. However, my physical pain was nothing compared to the psychological pain that I would experience once the case was tried in Superior Court on November 29!

Judge Rosen was assigned to hear the case. The Assistant District Attorney assigned to the court was a young guy who looked to be fresh out of law school or college named Robert McDonnell. I figured he hadn't been in too many real jams in his life so I was relieved to learn that Detective John Curren, who had handled the case in the District Court, would continue to assist the government at the Superior Court level. John, a jug-eared guy with a pleasant disposition, was a skilled police prosecutor.

I was standing in the rear of the courtroom before the first session got underway, wondering when my case would be called. McDonnell sought me out and asked what I might regard as a suitable punishment. I quickly reviewed the facts, accentuating that these kids were part of a group who had attempted to kill me on a street corner. I explained that I suspected that they had intended to perpetrate an armed robbery of the drug store, though they were prevented from having committed an overt act in that direction. I also pointed out that I didn't charge them with the possession of the knife or screwdriver because I honestly could not identify who it was that had attacked me with these weapons. I added that I had treated them fairly and had never used excessive force at any time, although both of these kids had struck and kicked me during the fight. I reminded him that both of the culprits had extensive juvenile records that included a wide variety of offenses. I then answered his original question, recommending that the offenders be imprisoned for what they had done, and if that were not possible, that at the very least they should be placed on probation which would require them to account for their time to the court.

"I want justice - simple justice. What do you think?" I asked.

He tightened up a little and looked at me rather haughtily and answered, "It's not what I think, it's what the jurist thinks that counts, and he thinks that you were a wise-guy young cop looking for trouble and found it."

At that moment the whole system fell out from underneath me. I was shocked and mortified by McDonnell's response. This was not the way Judge Adlow had said it would be when he addressed my recruit class from the bench three weeks into the Police Academy.

In spite of being off duty at the time, I had almost lost my life on a street corner while trying to prevent what I believed would have been an armed robbery with life-threatening consequences. I was administered a serious beating by five punks with weapons who had tried to kill me. I was injured, spent part of the night in the hospital and never delivered the ice cream to Beverly (who, by the way, never got too shook up by what had happened). After all this, a pompous-assed Superior Court Judge, no doubt a product of privilege, had the unmitigated gall to suggest to this school boy sycophant, who I suspected got his job through political pull, that I was a "wise-guy cop looking for trouble."

Did it ever occur to him that I would have to be a real stupid cop to pick a fight with five kids with weapons? Or was he judging me by my youthful appearance or my Marine Corps whiffle? Or did the case get mitigated because the judge knew the father of one of the kids as another cop suggested?

I didn't know the answer then - and I still don't, but this much is clear - my faith in the judicial system was undermined that day and my memory cells were permanently singed by the injustice of this judges remarks. I was deeply disenchanted on that November morning and this petty court official knew it. Perhaps it was unfair of me, but I accused him of believing the same thing about me that the judge did and he never denied it.

It was all downhill after that. In spite of the fact that one of the defendants defaulted, the judge found them both guilty and fined them each one hundred dollars. Judge Rosen apologetically explained to the father of Butts, the defendant who was present, that if he couldn't afford to pay the fine, he would be permitted to pay it over time (sort of a court installment plan). The judge smiled at the defendant and his father - he never once looked at me. Case Closed!

Oh, by the way, in the years to follow, the aging proprietor of the Cornell Drug Store would shoot and kill two youthful offenders and wound a third in two separate armed robbery attempts at his pharmacy. The shootings were ruled self-defense. The defendants never went to Judge Rosen's court.

My next project involved extensive surveillance of a joint called Leonardi's, located on the first floor of the former Paramount Hotel, close to the intersection of Washington Street and Boylston. This hotel was a sleazy eleven-story domicile whose final days were numbered.

My interest in the place was sparked initially by an incident which had occurred in the street right outside the club. I witnessed a thin bleach-blonde streetwalker stick a lighted cigarette directly into the left eye of a guy whom she was arguing with while he was being restrained by two cops. I couldn't blame the cops though, because the guy was getting ready to backhand her when they intervened. Each officer grabbed an arm. He stood by helplessly on the sidewalk, pinned against a parked car by the two TPF Officers, while she deliberately twisted the cigarette out in his eye. It happened so quickly that the cops were unable to stop her. He let out an infuriating scream and struggled to free himself from the officers' grasp, swearing and kicking at them in the process. He ended up getting arrested and while the officers stood there in the street with their prisoner, waiting for a transport, she quietly slipped into the bar.

It was a while before I would learn her name. I referred to her in my recitations with the boss as 'Skinny Legs.' Ordinarily I would make up my own nicknames in the instances when I was unaware of an individual's identity. (This happened frequently - as an undercover operative, it was of course impossible for me to establish an individual's name by officially questioning him. Whatever information I came up with, I had to acquire from chewing around the edges).

About two weeks into the Leonardi investigation I learned that the prostitute's first name was Eva and that she lived in an apartment at 832 Beacon Street on the Kenmore Square side of the 'New Back Bay' (as it was sometimes referred to in an effort to distinguish it from Boston's traditional Back Bay, which included everything to the north, between the Public Gardens and Massachusetts Avenue). One evening I observed her in a cab and tailed her there. Coincidentally, the boss had passed that address on to me as being the residence of a black hooker named Carol Cannon, who supposedly resided in suite three, on the first floor in the rear. I suspected that they lived together although I was never able to establish that fact by observation. It was a hard place to observe.

Eva ended up in the middle of a lot of downtown action. She was well known to everybody - from the wise guys to the cops. She was one wild Combat Zone bitch! I doubted that she took any crap from anyone, including her man.

Leonardi's was a small, dimly lit, raunchy joint permanently drenched with the pungent odor of stale beer and whose days as an entertainment filled cabaret had long since passed. A square shaped bar occupied the center of the room and on any given night about a dozen whores worked the place. I was amazed at the brazenness and rapidity of the action.

The first women who cruised me introduced herself as Cherise. She was a cute looking white female with a small heart shaped beauty mark penciled underneath her right eye. A beret covered her shortly cut, layered hair. She socked me with the standard solicitation rap, finally appealing to me that I wouldn't have far to go to meet up with her. I would only have to go to the nearby Plymouth Hotel which, she said, "was right next door." She promised that she would join me after I paid the clerk for a room. The total cost would amount to forty bucks.

"Not much for a good time," she said.

It turned out that Cherise Linehan, also known as Mary Jo Casserly, was a regular in the place and was well known to the Vice Squad. Unknown to the Vice Squad however, was that Cherise and most of the other women who frequented Leonardi's were using the Plymouth Hotel, a smaller version of the Paramount, on a regular basis in furtherance of their trade, suggesting a conspiracy between the two businesses.

I checked the place out every night and let me tell you, the joint was really jumping. Over the next few weeks I learned the identities, on at least a first name basis, and the 'Modus Operandi' of most of the prostitutes. Eventually the girls stopped cruising me but they continued to operate openly in my presence.

The Deputy explained, "They figure you're safe because they've never been pinched when you're around."

That advantageous result was a product of long-term undercover work (which would provide multiple benefits over time).

At some point, early in the Leonardi investigation, Blake instructed me to meet two other officers from the Intelligence Division at a specific location for photographing the movement of prostitutes and their tricks between the bar and the hotel. I met with Peter Ryan and Tommy Mitchell at 8:00 PM on the second floor of a Boylston Street shop, directly across from Leonardi's and the Plymouth Hotel. The designated meeting place was a millinery (a business that made women's clothes and hats) whose workers had quit for the day. Blake had made a deal with the owner to allow the police to use the place for surveillance purposes.

This was the first time I'd had the opportunity of working with other investigators assigned to the same unit. I liked them both immediately. Peter, a skilled technical man, went about setting up the tripod-mounted 35-millimeter camera at a vantage point overlooking the two points of interest. Peter was a pleasant guy with a cherubic grin. He smiled and laughed a lot. He was very Irish and coming from West Roxbury, an affluent part of the city, I figured that he was connected because he appeared to be a 'skootch' shorter than the strict five foot eight inch height requirement necessary for acceptance onto the police department. (Years later he confided in me that during his physical he had done a 'tippy-toe' when the old examining physician looked away for a moment, which caused the light on the end of the measuring rod to illuminate).

Peter was a man who was deserving of respect. He told me that he had been assigned to the Intelligence Division since its establishment in 1961. He also told me that he was a Lieutenant Detective. That wasn't true of course, although I believed him at the time. He was just a Patrolman like me, but someone had to stay overnight in the shop to hand the key over to the owner in the morning, and Peter was already lining me up for the job. (I have forgiven him these many years later for this ruse, for as it turned out, Peter was exceedingly honest and came through for me on more than one occasion.)

The other guy was Tommy Mitchell, an astute investigator and pleasant guy who struck me as an Irish version of Frank Sinatra. Roughly equivalent in height and body build, he exuded that same aloof charm and self-confidence that characterized Sinatra. He even moved with a tantamount hint of a swagger and possessed a similar bad temper, once triggered. He was fated to become known for twice beating the hell out of 'Benny the Bomb', a petty North End based wise guy given to bouts of braggadocio. I don't know what Benny said or did, but it was a mistake both times.

Once the camera was set up in the window Peter vigilantly peered outside, ready to start flicking the action, but nothing was happening. Women were walking into the place but no one was walking out, much less entering the Plymouth Hotel. One hour went by and then another. There should have been ample opportunities for photographs, but still nothing. I was embarrassed and I knew that my credibility was at stake. This was the first objective test of the reliability of my information, and it seemed doomed to failure. I insisted that someone must have spotted the camera in the window, but Peter disagreed.

"The outside window is too dirty to see through, especially at this height," he argued.

"I'll prove it." I haltingly said.

There was no way I could be sure unless I checked the bar itself. I walked down the stairs and surreptitiously slid out the front door, made my way around the block and approached Leonardi's from the opposite direction. Before entering I shot a quick glance up to the second floor of the shop and I was barely able to make out the outline of the camera behind the window. I was relieved to have verified my suspicion but I wasn't sure if an unsuspecting person would have seen the same thing.

Once inside, I noted six of the regular prostitutes talking to men at the bar. I patiently waited until I observed a solicitation go down. It was business as usual, except for one thing - once the deal was made, the female, followed by the male, descended a dark set of stairs in the rear of the joint. I suspected that the stairs led to an underground passageway which connected Leonardi's to the Plymouth Hotel. My suspicions were confirmed a half-hour later when the same women, using the same set of stairs, returned and joined another man at the bar. I never saw the guy return but I suspected that he had left through the front door of the hotel. I was ecstatic and couldn't wait to brief Peter and Tom by phone as to what was happening.

Using an outside public pay phone, I carefully dialed the number of the second floor business (which I had previously jotted down). After three rings Tommy answered (I recognized his voice).

"Hello."

"Hi Tom, it's me Phil. Look, this place is really moving, but like I figured they must have spotted us in the window because none of the action is going out the front door. You won't believe it but they're using an underground tunnel which I think connects with the hotel."

"Well, I'll be dammed," he muttered in quiet amazement.

"Look! Do me a favor," I asked. "Drop in the joint yourself to confirm what I have seen. I don't want Headquarters to think I'm nuts."

I mentioned that I would reimburse him expense money - not that reimbursement would have been necessary, Tommy would have sprung. He had his own expense account.

He kindly agreed to my request which bolstered my hope. He followed my circuitous route around the block, dropped into the joint and sat across from me at the bar. After less than half an hour he was able to confirm the existence of the intense prostitution activity, which I had been reporting consistently. Most importantly, I was personally vindicated by this confirmation!

I rejoined him back in the shop a little before midnight. Tommy reported our observations to Peter, whom I still believed was a Lieutenant Detective.

Peter busied himself taking shots of men leaving the hotel. Even without the women he said it supported my observations.

If there were any doubt that we had been spotted in the window it was dissolved a half-hour later when two hookers, flashing short pants and high heels, walked down Boylston Street from the direction of Tremont. When they reached the front of Leonardi's they stopped and looked up at us (we were looking down from behind the dirty window) and both of them waved. So there it was - my suspicions were conclusively confirmed! Peter smiled, an obvious sign of acquiescence, and I settled down for the first time that evening.

The only thing that remained now was the sleepover and, being the junior G-man, it fell to me to perform this duty. There were a lot of rats in and around the place (I feared the two-legged ones most of all) so Peter generously loaned me his firearm for protection. I promised to return it first thing in the morning. Peter and Tom left, sneaking the equipment out with them, and I set up for the night.

I called home for the second time and wished Beverly a "good night." I continued my surveillance of the front door of the hotel through a different window, which provided a more angular view. The downtown hookers continued to use the place. The giant neon Budweiser advertisement, which vertically embraced the Paramount marquee, bathed the millinery in an eerie red glow. The dark shapes of people moving around their rooms, some of them preparing for bed and others having sex, were silhouetted against the drawn shades. At about 2:00 AM the lights were extinguished. The show was over.

I placed my light-sensitive binoculars down and attempted to sleep. I laid flat on an elevated cutting board which extended about three feet into the air. The black night descended on the zone silencing its sounds.

I took off my sneakers, rested on the wooden board and closed my eyes. As I reflected on the events of the evening my mood was pleasantly lifted by my good luck. What if I hadn't had the presence of mind to double-check Leonardi's? I would have looked pretty bad, I thought. Perhaps, Blake would have suspected that I had exaggerated my previous reports, or worse yet he could have forever doubted me. It could have affected my longevity in the unit. Who would have ever known that Leonardi's and the Plymouth Hotel were connected underground? (More than likely they shared a common cellar as many old building do in Boston.) I learned something that night - never assume, and never leave anything to chance.

As the morning wore on I was jolted from my cataleptic sleep by the sound of what seemed like a thousand scurrying feet. Something had set the rats in motion. I guessed that it was the beastly feline that the owner had left behind. It was the biggest cat that I had ever seen. I could have sworn one of the rodents sided against my foot. I jumped up and turned on the light - everything looked normal. By this time the rats were well hidden, and the cat was nowhere to be seen.

I put my sneakers back on and placed a large piece of brown wrapping paper underneath me, overlapping the board about six inches in each direction. This was designed to provide me with an early warning signal should a rat be getting ready to join me in my makeshift bed. It furnished me with a little insulation.

I questioned what kind of a businessman would possess only one key to his livelihood. I wondered how the workers would have gotten in if the owner failed to show up. I met the owner in the morning, though I can't recall what he looked like. I thanked him for his cooperation and hurriedly walked back to Headquarters where both Peter and my car were waiting. By this time I knew that Peter was not a Lieutenant Detective, but it didn't make any difference. I was still a rookie and I did what rookies were expected to do. I accepted the police department's pecking order. I was the low man on the totem pole. I had learned that brand of officially imposed modesty in the Marines. I thanked Peter for the loan of his gun and briefed the Deputy in person (he got a kick out of the whole thing) and went home.

I would continue to monitor Leonardi's, but that phase of the investigation was finished. There was only one small piece of the puzzle remaining. That concerned the status of a fairly ordinary looking white woman about thirty-five whom I had observed sitting at the bar night after night staring mindlessly into her drink. I had never witnessed her cruise anyone. She seemed kind of old for a hooker. Nor did she dress stylishly, preferring knee-length woolen skirts, brown nylon stockings and loafers. Her best feature was her long and wavy, flaxen like hair that fell to the center of her back.

She reminded me of a leftover from the Fifties, an out of sync be-bopper, possibly an alcoholic who had never gotten the message that the downtown scene had changed. Maybe she was still waiting for her number one sailor man to walk in the door and sweep her off her feet, or maybe she was suffering from a broken heart. Maybe a lot of things - and maybe she was selling her ass. Once I saw her leave with a man, but he had approached her - it could have been just a pick-up.

She was a riddle and I was both humanly and professionally curious to learn where she was coming from. The opportunity presented itself one Friday morning when the place was emptying out. She, uncharacteristically, asked me for a ride home. I jumped at the chance. Somehow I knew that it would pose no risk to my identity that I had forgotten my magnetized phony registration plate. She wouldn't be looking for my number. I escorted her to my car, which was parked nearby on Tremont Street. We chatted as we drove across town. She told me that her name was Irene and directed me to a long narrow street off of Dorchester Avenue near Fields Corner, where she lived, presumably alone, on the second floor of a standard three-family house.

We climbed the rickety front stairs and continued up to the second floor. She searched in her bag for a key, opened the door and stumbling ever so slightly over the threshold, apologized and invited me in. She repeated that her name was Irene and asked me mine.

"Mike," I answered.

She excused herself and went into the bedroom. I waited for her in the kitchen. I was still perplexed; she still hadn't mentioned anything about money. What was I going to say if she was just looking for a one-night stand? That's where self-discipline would have to come in. I was married and my job was at risk. I had no wish to test fate.

About two minutes later Irene returned to the kitchen where I was still waiting. She had removed her outer clothing and shoes. She was wearing a sheer pink slip. She stood about two feet away from me, presenting me with an open opportunity to view her. Actually, she wasn't bad looking. She had a nice figure, curvy and well proportioned - the poor lighting further enhanced her attractiveness.

She narrowed the gap between us and placed her arms around my waist, pressing herself against me. I placed my hands on her bare shoulders, readying myself to disentangle and beg off. This had gone far enough. I thought about the consequences to my marriage and job if I allowed this seduction to continue. It was a tough spot to be in.

Suddenly she looked up at me rather coquettishly and whispered, "Twenty dollars."

I was relieved that she did. I demurred, explaining that I had a girlfriend and didn't want to start "cutting up this early into the relationship."

She seemed to accept that explanation. Pulling away, she thanked me for the ride and wished me a good night. I was satisfied that I had completed the final piece of the puzzle.

I related the story to Blake the next day, describing her as a part-time whore and a full-time drunk. She hustled for drinks - that was about it. That explanation satisfied my curiosity as to why she sat at the bar all night and didn't leave with a man until late in the evening. She was a pathetic case, a loser, a plain ordinary looser. Blake agreed, and I moved ever so much closer to becoming a street-hardened cop.

At 5:17 PM, Tuesday, November 10, 1965, the power went out in Massachusetts, Rhode Island, Connecticut, New Hampshire, Vermont, New York, New Jersey, Pennsylvania and parts of Canada, plunging the whole Northeast section of the country into total darkness in what came to be known as 'The Great Blackout'. The problem was believed to be located somewhere in Canada. It was an awesome demonstration of the interconnectedness and fragility of the continent and it raised the frightening specter of sabotage.

As a consequence, I was notified to report to District 3 for reassignment for the remainder of the crisis. An old-timer cautioned me to stay on the main street. He said, "Stay on the main drag, that way you'll stay out of the shit." I thought that was strange advice and was unwilling to follow it. Getting in trouble was a natural consequence of the job. I wondered, would he have given me the same advice if the neighborhood were white? I wasn't sure. There was more crime in black neighborhoods. That was true, but didn't that spell the need for a greater police presence because there was also more victims?

Some panic and violence were reported in other areas of the affected region but surprisingly enough, in District 3 the evening passed without incident. By contrast, I witnessed neighbors helping each other and college students volunteering to direct traffic at blacked out intersections. In hindsight, this was an early example of the burgeoning sense of social consciousness among college students that would turn to shock the country in the years ahead.

I worried about Beverly and Kimberly back at the home front. On the plus side, they had enough candles and it was a warm night. On the negative side, no one knew how long this blackout would last.

Cops handle emergencies - the public takes that for granted. That's what they're paid for. It's a downer for the cop though, because while a civilian is home tending to his family during natural crises such as storms, hurricanes, blizzards, tornadoes, earthquakes, floods and the like, the cop must leave his or her family and respond to the needs of the larger community. Each time that I have had to leave my family throughout the years for such emergencies, I have consoled myself with the fantasy that once retired I would watch the first New England blizzard of the season through my living room window and not worry about anything - not even the snow piling up.

The lights came back on in Boston at 9:06 PM. Less than four hours had passed and the feared crisis was over. I was still in one piece despite the fact that I spent a goodly amount of time patrolling the back streets.

I was detailed back to Headquarters to continue my plainclothes assignment for what I assumed would be another extended period of time. However, at 7:45 AM Thursday, December 9, 1965, I received the disturbing news that I was reassigned to the Traffic Division for duty until further orders.

This was to be a temporary assignment, to assist the traffic division until the end of the Christmas rush. I was positively frustrated at this bureaucratic bumbling. After everything I had done to protect my identity and enhance my undercover role (I had even refused to take paid details), it was unimaginable that the police brass would be so careless with my life that they would stick me in the middle of a traffic post, risking me to full exposure.

Blake tried to get me out of it but he was unable to squash the transfer.

"Priorities," Blake was told by a senior command staff member - some unnamed Superintendent. "It was just a matter of priorities," he said. "The department had to deal with the increased traffic flow generated by the holidays." That's how Blake explained it to me.

I didn't buy this explanation. Why was I the only 'priority' who was being reassigned? There were a number of other detailed cops sprinkled around Headquarters. What about them? How did they get to stay? Or, were they the 'connected priorities?' Of course I kept my mouth shut and did what I was told to do. In a few more weeks I'd be back anyway, I rationalized. I figured that Tommy Mitchell was assuaging me when he commented that I could get closer to the wise guys in uniform.

"They don't pay any attention to a uniformed cop," he said, "They only sweat the guys in plainclothes."

It turned out he was right, especially when it came to bookie and loanshark operations. I picked up some pretty good information concerning both organized crime activities outside the Iron Horse, a landmark North Station Bar. I discovered that I was able to get closer to the action while in uniform than in civilian clothes. Bookies paid no mind to uniformed cops and uniformed cops didn't hassle bookies. It was just that way.

Investigations involving gaming operations belonged to the detectives. For one thing, it took more time to perform a gaming investigation. In order to make an arrest, a cop would have to make play with the bookie. That was the good reason why the department relegated these kinds of investigations to the detectives. The bad reason was that an overzealous cop could tip over the apple cart and interfere with the envelope that was heading up the ladder.

As I eventually came to piece it together, graft money, protection money or whatever one wished to call it, moved from the street bookie to a designated individual in the District Station, usually but not always, a Sergeant Detective, who functioned as a 'bag man' for the senior commanding officer - who more than likely was a Captain. At the Detective Supervisor's level the money was ordinarily broken up according to rank and delivered to the bosses and the detectives who were willing to accept it. (Not everyone did). The Patrolman usually got zilch, other than maybe a sawbuck at Christmas time if the operation was on his beat.

Department wide systemic money corruption would eventually end due to the efforts of a reform Police Commissioner and generally better working conditions, but back then bookie money was considered by many to be a natural supplement to an inadequate wage. Gambling was a victimless crime - there was no way to get rid of it - so why not make a buck? That was the justification, however muddled. And there were a lot of bucks to go around - right up to headquarters, where I suspected that certain Superintendents and Deputy Superintendents (Blake excluded) were getting fat.

Eventually some of the money reached the judges (and the politicians in the form of campaign donations) who in turn influenced the appointment of selected Command Staff personnel. It was one big greasy game. None of this was done in the open of course, but it was happening and everyone knew about it. And there wasn't a damned thing anyone could do to end it because payoffs were endemic to the system. A great many of the key personnel considered the extra cash to be part of their benefits.

However, it is also true that even back then, when graft money was indigenous to the job, there were cops on every level who were unwilling to accept it. Moreover, many of these cops, detectives included, did their job in spite of the obstacles put in front of them.

Captain John Slattery, the former Commanding Officer of the old 'Flying Squad' back in the late Fifties and early Sixties, was a notable example. A seriously dedicated and entirely honest former State Trooper, he rode rough shod over bookies and after-hour joints. Tommy Mitchell said that Slattery "wouldn't pull back." The trouble was that there were more dishonest bookmakers than there were honest police officials.

Bookies had power and ordinary patrolmen couldn't do much about them. The resentment spawned from this condition added force to the rising tide of police unionism.

That explanation probably contains more information than I actually understood at the time, but it is still skeletal in content. The subject of police corruption is both fascinating and complex. As the years rolled on I would learn more about it, and become increasingly riled by its ugliness.

Incidentally, this principle of 'blue camouflage,' which held that cops in uniform were insulated from identification because, supposedly, people did not see past the uniform to view the officer as an individual, didn't work so well when it came to the Catholic Order of the Sisters of Saint Joseph's. One day I was standing at the corner of Causeway and Friend Streets surveying the traffic situation, dressed in my full winter gear, which included a heavy woolen uniform coat, a scarf and a hat. To avoid detection I was also wearing dark sunglasses and heavy earmuffs. In spite of all this, a nun in full habit walked by and greeted me by name.

"Hello Phillip," she said. "How have you been?"

It was Sister Tablia, my third grade teacher, a kind and charismatic women and one of my great childhood influences whom I hadn't seen for many years. She had spotted me right away underneath that mountain of deception. I was dumbfounded and for a moment struck speechless.

The years had left her with the same beautiful countenance that she had possessed in my youth. She was a little shorter than how I recalled her but her mental acumen and physical alacrity were unchanged

When I regained my composure I returned her greeting and asked, "How are you doing, Sister?" She nodded. I wasn't sure what she meant.

"As you can see, Sister, I've become a cop. Would you ever have believed it?"

"Sure, I would," she answered. "I always had faith in you - you were a good boy."

That was a white lie but I loved her for saying it. And with that she moved on alone, unlike most nuns in those days who ordinarily walked in pairs. Sister Tablia was different - she always had been.

After the holidays I was reassigned back to Headquarters to resume my undercover investigations. I continued to focus my attention on prostitution, especially in the downtown area.

At about 6:40 PM Friday January 28, 1966, a series of four gas explosions tore out half a block in downtown Boston. It was a five-bagger. The first alarm came in at 6:41 PM. The next day, the *Boston Globe* reported in a front page spread

"Blasts Rip Hub Night Life Center -- 9 Die... Four Explosions, Fires Wreck Two Hotels, Cabarets, and Shops ... 30 More Bodies May Be in Debris."

The Paramount Hotel, the Plymouth Hotel, the Gilded Cage and Leonardi's were demolished by the force of the blast. According to a *Globe* reporter, "Eyewitnesses said that at least 30 patrons at Leonardi's bar on the first floor of the Paramount Hotel plunged to the basement when a section of the floor collapsed."

Bill Brett, a cub photographer for the *Boston Globe*, had just left an awards ceremony at the Masonic Hall at the corner of Tremont and Boylston Street, so his camera was in the ready. It was his picture that appeared on the front page of the newspaper the next day. He alerted his office immediately. In his eyewitness account he stated that he heard a massive earth-shaking explosion, followed by a cloud of billowing black smoke that moved down Boylston Street. People were fighting and clawing at each other to get out of the hotel. On the police end of things, the Tactical Patrol Force had to be mobilized to deal with the small-scale looting which had broken out.

The Fire Department worked tirelessly for the next twenty-four hours performing many rescues. Despite the heroic efforts of the emergency response agencies, the final toll amounted to ten people killed. Irene's limp and lifeless body was one of the last to be pulled out of the wreckage.

I had been conducting a surveillance outside 832 Beacon Street when I heard the first report of this downtown explosion. I was waiting to tail Skinny Legs to Leonardi's, which had become an almost nightly exercise. Around 6:30 in the evening she would generally leave her apartment and be transported by cab to this nightspot where she would begin to hustle and, I believed, sell drugs. I was most of all interested in uncovering her supplier. I suspected that he was a major pimp named Leon Stewart whom I regularly saw entering her building - more than likely he lived with her. I would have liked to have had observed him passing her some dope.

Skinny Legs was so predictable that about half the time I waited for her in Leonardi's instead of tailing her from her Beacon Street residence. It was bitterly cold on this particular evening, providing me with all the more justification to wait for her inside the bar. But, for some strange reason I had decided, at the last minute, to tail her from her apartment instead of waiting for her in the warmth of the bar. Perhaps I was listening to an interesting talk show on the car radio - I did a lot of that. Or possibly I wanted to test the heater in my new Bel Air Chevrolet. I can't recall. In any event, I was sitting outside 832 Beacon Street that night - the night when 'hell' opened up downtown. Old Lady Luck was with Skinny Legs and me that evening, but she had abandoned Irene.

I have returned to the memory of that unfortunate woman many times throughout the years. Where did she exist? What was she thinking when she crashed into the fiery rubble below? Back then I had been more than willing to dismiss her as a 'part-time hooker and a full-time drunk.' That intemperate remark had contributed to my image as a street-wise cop, but it had done little to reveal the truth about who Irene was and how she ended up buried in Leonardi's basement.

1961 -U.S Marines Corp, Vieques Island off coast of Puerto Rico

Phil - Boston Police Academy recruit - 1964

May 1939-Phil, at 2 months, and his father, Dominic Vitti,
at 28 years old; four months before he would die

Graduation from Boston Police Academy - Phil and his Aunt Mary Volante Morvan - 1964

One Of The GREATEST!

A sketch of Deputy Superintendent Blake at his retirement party - 1967

Detective Ralph Ryan escorting handcuffed
Mike Russo to a jail cell at District 4 South End

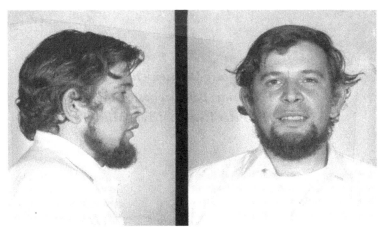

Mike Russo's 'mug shots' from undercover gun case

Boston Police Intelligence Division - Jim Lynch, Gerry O'Roarke, Pat Brady, Bob Dapkas, Jim Cox, Jack Schroeder, Peter Ryan and Tom Mitchell

Retired and loving it!

Twenty-One

The prolonged solitude of the job eventually produced an anomic effect. I came to feel like a warped version of Emerson's eyeball floating through space. But, where his communed with nature, mine moved principally through the glitzy world of the Combat Zone. Where his followed an unencumbered path, mine was connected to Police Headquarters by a telephone line. Where his experienced the sublime sensation of free flight, mine was required to ingest, process and report criminal information data - a veritable floating intelligence system so to speak - stopping, starting, pausing, hovering and moving once again in an endless and ever widening probe of the city's masked environs.

As time went on I provided the boss with increasing amounts of information on persons and places associated with prostitution, gaming, licensed premises, extortion, loan-sharking, drugs and booze in a continually expanding matrix that provided an insight into the inner workings of street-level organized crime. These included prostitution action in the Regent, the Bradford Lounge, Enricoe's, the Bostonian, and the Broadway Hotel where the clerks; Jacky, Louie, Manny, Sonny, Homer, Donald and Happy, all white guys and one Asian were sharing in the proceeds; loan-sharking action in Kerry's Village and the Four Corners, heavy organized crime guys hanging around Jay's, their black counterparts, Tootsie Bennet, (Vanity

Plate-'Toots-1') the king of late night entertainment, who operated between Roxbury and East Boston, the bad-assed Patterson brothers, a Roxbury based duo of fear who were plugged into the white mob, after-hours activity in Mingchow's Chinese Restaurant on Saratoga Street in East Boston, Ollie's Barbecue in Roxbury, Frank's on Ninth Street in South Boston, big time after-hours alcohol sales in the Mafia-connected Coliseum on North Street in the North End, Black Jack card games after 5:00 PM on the second floor of 1360 Boylston Street near the Fenway, also in the Nucerne Annex and Depot Cafe in the North Station, connected games at 467 Hanover Street in the North End and behind the green store front at 41 Charter - 335 and 351 Tremont Street and 449 Blue Hill Avenue in Roxbury (run by the Dominoe brothers), suspected gambling sites in Chinatown, 61 and 62 Beech Streets, 12, 15, and 27 Tyler and 28A Oxford, and a deliberately constructed, almost windowless apartment building, intended to be used for gambling on Porter Street in East Boston.

The longer that I was at it, the more I had to add and the easier my job became. My confidence increased with each new item of information that I was able to supply and Blake's trust in me grew proportionately. Eventually he would issue me fewer and fewer assignments, content with permitting me to develop my own leads. I would come to view organized crime as if it was a puzzle and I would experience satisfaction with each new piece of acquired information that added to its clarity.

One of my early obsessions centered on street-level prostitution and the precise level of organization which supported it. I agreed pretty much with the prevailing police opinion that, for the most part, it was a freewheeling, pimp driven, capitalistic venture; a dark and dangerous trade based on raw physical competition which was played out on the city's streets, Columbus Avenue in particular.

Columbus Avenue is a major thoroughfare in the city that connects Park Square, at the edge of Boston's downtown section, with Walnut Avenue in Roxbury. It was designed in 1868 along the lines of a Parisian boulevard. It has undergone many changes throughout the years but back in the early Sixties and Seventies it was populated mainly by low-income Blacks.

It was a Ghetto area and its residents suffered the standard host of indignities that attached to marginal urban life including substandard housing, dirty streets, broken homes, crime, delinquency and intense prostitution once the moon came out. Its convenient location and many exit points attracted 'white hunters' that prowled the streets in search of forbidden sex. The transient nature of the population and the powerlessness of the residents, fused with these factors, set the stage for some really quick-paced, wild-assed hustling which began as soon as the street lights came on and continued unabated until early morning.

Most of the serious action took place in an eleven-block area between the intersecting streets of Massachusetts Avenue and Clarendon Streets. The Big M and the 411 Club were located on opposite ends of this torrid one-half mile stretch and fanned the movement of females, mostly black and a few white, who promenaded up and down the avenue soliciting men in cars and on foot for sex. They were gaudily dressed, well built, often times good-looking women wearing tight clothes and cheap jewelry, their honor lost and their safety imperiled, selling their wares to strangers in a nightly parade of female flesh. I watched the show for months. Initially I was dumbfounded that this prostitution trade could be so open and obvious.

I recalled a similar experience in Beirut, Lebanon in 1958, during the U.S. occupation, when I was temporarily assigned to M.P. duty in the red-light district of the city for the purpose of keeping the American military personnel out of the area (which turned out to be an impossible task). The prostitution houses seemed endless. In fact, Beirut held the unofficial title of the 'whore-house capital of the world.' I'm not sure if the title was deserved, but in any event, the brothels stretched for blocks. In spite of the fact that prostitution was legal there the women stayed in or directly outside the houses, while here in the U.S. they were walking up and down the streets, cruising motorists and stopping cars like there was no tomorrow. They caused frequent traffic jams.

Of course prostitutes were arrested sporadically by cops in unmarked cars posing as white hunters, or by the Vice Squad for being common night-walkers, an offense which required the officer to note three or more occasions of street walkers stopping cars and soliciting the operators. The police effort was too futile to stem the tide and the lure of making a fast buck in exchange for a quick sex made the risks worthwhile.

What struck me as curious about the whole thing was the tendency of the hookers to stick in the same one or two block area, as if they were unwilling to cross over to a new block. At first I attributed this to habit, until I noted several instances of street walkers who were apparently unwilling to cruise pedestrians and parked motorists who were only thirty or forty feet away from them but on an adjacent block.

I constructed a hastily drawn map of the area, listing the eleven hot blocks that made up the strip between Mass. Avenue and Clarendon Streets. Then, for a couple of hours each evening, I placed specific sections of the network under surveillance (usually from my personal car).

I noted each instance that a hooker had crossed over from one block onto the other. After a few months the pattern was unmistakable - the ordinary hooker worked the same two-block area night after night with little variation. The only exceptions to the rule were the three streets comprising the first segment - Wellington Street, Claremont and Greenwich Park and that was likely because it was the smallest area to begin with.

It was apparent to me that the hooker action was being regulated by preconceived agreements. To test my theory I deliberately positioned myself, late one Friday night, on the corner of Braddock Park and Columbus Avenue. A curvaceous Mulatto prostitute with a voluptuous behind and a tiny waist was working the traffic as it passed by West Newton Street, about twenty feet from where I was standing. Her breasts jiggled as she walked and her body parts moved sensually as she sauntered up the street, spreading her sex appeal all over the block like a heavy perfume.

Her name was YaVette. I recognized her from the 411 Club. She noticed me standing there and I sensed that she wanted to come over so I broke the ice and made some dopey remark about the weather. She clearly appeared unwilling to cross the street.

"It's starting to get cold," I casually remarked.

"Yeah, honey, it is, but I can get you awful warm if you want to come over here."

I was reluctant to press it beyond that because I didn't want to make her suspicious. However, I was convinced that she was playing the game by some kind of rule and I suspected that once I moved into her territory she'd hit me with the full treatment. I begged off with some feeble excuse and cut out of the area.

The next time I saw YaVette she was dancing in Jerome's, a big time B-girl strip joint on Washington Street. Jerome's was managed by an obese, expressionless, middle-aged guy nicknamed Big Nick, a fringe character whose sagging facial features and jowls resembled a pile of melting wax. Nick was an indelible feature of the streets. He usually parked himself on the sidewalk in front of his joint. Popeye, in an unexpected stroke of metaphorical insight, once referred to him as an amorphous blob that absorbed money on one end and oozed out protection payments on the other.

Peculiarly enough, I would run into YaVette in the years to come. Whenever I did, it would trigger off my early memory of Blake's reaction to my theory that prostitution enjoyed a greater degree of organization than was commonly believed, which was precisely what I suggested to him on Monday morning.

I summarized my proof in a brief amount of time, offering him the benefit of my long-term calculations and waited for his rebuke. I sweated that he might remark:

"You're seeing things kid or maybe you're reading it wrong or whatever.

But it never came. Blake was a smart guy, the smartest guy I have ever known when it came to the workings of the underworld. But, unlike many of the tough talking and blustering know-it-all Police Commanders whom I would meet in the future, he kept an open mind.

That's not to say that he agreed with me - he didn't say anything. It's what he did that I recall. He assigned one additional investigator to work with me. That was the second time that I was to work with Tommy Mitchell.

I enjoyed the opportunity of working with someone else, even if it were only for a brief time. I was a young inexperienced police officer, cut off from the normal police network that converted young men into savvy street cops. I was alone and on my own out there, and sometimes I floundered. I had a multitude of questions about the department and no one to answer them. I wasn't about to ask the Deputy - he was too high up on the chain of command. Tommy was the perfect guy to work with - most plainclothes cops in those days wouldn't tell you if your coat was on fire, but Tommy didn't fit that mold. He was more than willing to help anyone. He was a 'good guy.'

During the next few months we became totally submerged in the world of prostitution. By the time Tommy was reassigned to higher-level organized crime investigations I would know eighty percent of the city's prostitutes on a first name basis, in addition to where they worked and lived, and Tommy would have taught me a great deal about physical and motor vehicle surveillances, emphasizing the contrasts among the various methods.

"If you have a pretty good idea of where someone might be heading, follow him in front of his vehicle," he would say, "especially if it's a long stretch and it's unlikely that he will be making a turn. Keep your car out of his rear view mirror as much as possible. No one expects to be tailed by a guy driving in front of him. If you're behind the subject, blow the horn at him - you'll avoid suspicion that way. Break up your image and wear a hat sometimes. Remember, it's real important to know when to break it off. Don't blow the investigation just 'cause you think you've been made'. A lot of hard-core criminals are tail shy. They're able to spot a tail and shake it off real fast. Most of all don't get careless out there," he emphasized. "Remember, most of the time you don't know who you are dealing with and he doesn't know you either. He could be a crackpot, or wanted for some serious shit, or maybe he's fresh off a new crime and he thinks you're onto him. You never know what a guy like that will do!"

For me, knowing when to break it off was the most difficult part of a tail. One evening we were conducting a two-car surveillance of a high-class blonde hooker. Blake was very interested in this woman for some reason which he never shared with us. He had a penchant for secretiveness.

Tommy called me at the house and left a message with Beverly for me to "follow the red-head." Beverly had no idea what I was doing and she thought the message was strange, though she never bothered to ask me about it.

I understood the message, of course, and I made a happy effort to comply with Tommy's instructions. I knew she operated out of the Chantilly Lounge, so I showed up there about eight o'clock in the evening and waited outside. I tailed her to two hotels where she turned a couple of tricks. I met up with Tommy later that night and he joined in on the surveillance and we double-tailed her to a couple of other locations.

It was almost 2:00 AM and we figured that she was wrapping it up for the evening. I was tired and ready to call it quits. She left the lounge and got into her car which was parked a couple of blocks away. I jotted down the Rhode Island registration number on a pad of paper that I kept on the passenger seat beside me. By this time I could write numbers, streets and other information in the dark without having to look down.

I followed her to Columbus Avenue and waited for further instructions from Tommy who was operating directly behind me. Suddenly he pulled up to the right side of my car and gave me the high sign. With his arm extended midway in the driver's side window he flicked his hand downward, signaling me to break off the surveillance and head for the rack.

In my youthful rookie exuberance I misinterpreted the communication, believing that he wanted me to continue the tail. And continue the tail I did - all the way to Lincoln, Rhode Island, a distance of more than sixty miles one way. I followed her right to her house, a tiny white bungalow surrounded by carefully manicured bushes. The lawn was littered with small plastic children's toys that were illuminated by an oversized full moon. She stooped down and picked up a couple of the toys before she disappeared through the front door.

Just another independent suburban divorcee whore, I said to myself. She could have even been married I guessed. I wondered anew why the boss was interested in her, but I never found out. I yawned and headed north. The registration number checked out to the same address - it wasn't worth the trip.

Blake was genuinely surprised that I had taken the surveillance that far. I didn't learn until I met up with Tommy the next night that I had misconstrued his signal. He laughed like hell when I told him. It's a story worth telling.

As the investigation continued we logged in hundreds of miles on surveillances and spent countless hours establishing the relationship between various pimps and their women. Even after Tommy was reassigned to other duties I continued the tedious task of putting together the details of the many stables that existed across the city.

My belief that prostitution was loosely organized continued to gain credence. I spotted pimps checking on their women out in the street and occasionally escorting them to court. I ascertained that women who were arrested two or three times, and thus threatened with jail time, were moved out of Boston and bussed to cities like New York and Hartford, Connecticut. They were replaced by a fresh bunch of girls moving in the opposite direction. I observed several instances of known pimps dropping off jail-endangered hookers and picking up new ones at the Greyhound Bus Station on Saint James Street, just around the corner from Police Headquarters.

I unearthed the final proof one day in late fall when I witnessed a large gathering of pimps at 410 Columbus Avenue, which served as a pimp's apartment in the daytime and a trick pad at night. At least a dozen of the major pimps from across the city showed up. I knew something about most of them. They pulled up to the front door in flashy cars, one after the other. To avoid police scrutiny a parking attendant utilized the surrounding streets to park their vehicles despite the fact that there were ample spaces out front. It was too early for a card game, so I theorized that they were having some sort of meeting.

I knew that the Vice Squad had stepped up their action against street level prostitution and had been really hammering the hookers. They were also surveilling the pimps and banging them with any offense they could hang on them, even Chapter 90 motor vehicle violations. As far as I was concerned, the pimps mainly had to be discussing one thing - the heat in the street!

I was ecstatic that I had stumbled onto this meeting. I mentally compared it to a mini-scale pimp version of the infamous 1957 Appalachian meeting in New York State, which was the first to have offered overwhelming evidence of the national existence of a crime syndicate known as the Mafia. It was a lucky break.

I just happened to be in the area on one of those rare day tour assignments. I was putting the peep on the Regent Café when I discovered the action. The Regent was located right next door to the suspected pimp's apartment building and I had been watching the place for a guy wanted by the City of New York for murder. I had a picture of the fugitive that Mike Flammia had sent me in the mail. It turned out to be a bonus day even though I never spotted him.

I laid the whole thing out to Blake that same day - complete with I.D.s, registration numbers, descriptions and the duration of the meeting which, incidentally, had lasted for more than four hours.

The way Blake eventually summed it up for the Brass, in an official presentation, was that street level prostitution was controlled by a loose confederation of agreements among pimps. That understanding was largely the result of my long bromidic work and I was delighted that Blake had taken my theory seriously - not only that, but it was good for a little more time in the outfit.

Sixty-six came and went - it wasn't a bad year. I had been able to pay my bills and save a little and Beverly had started working as a part-time dental assistant for a dentist in Brighton. I resumed college in January. Northeastern was still a bargain. They had recently converted from a semester to a quarter systems. The price of a quarter dropped to seventeen dollars a credit hour from the previous twenty-two dollars per semester credit level. The effect of this conversion increased the price of a full course by seven bucks. Although many of the students figured that this conversion was a back-door maneuver to pump up the tuition, the majority of them didn't complain too much.

Things had been changing with regard to criminal procedure since 1961 when the U.S. Supreme Court dropped a bombshell on the states with the 'Mapp vs Ohio' decision, which relied on the Due Process Clause of the Fourteenth Amendment to establish the same rights for all citizens of the United States as required by the Federal Government. The effect of this decision was to establish the 'Fruits of the Poison Tree Doctrine' which simply premised that illegally obtained evidence could not be used against an individual in court. Prior to this, other states, including Massachusetts, had allowed such evidence to be used. For example, if a cop illegally entered someone's house without a warrant and recovered stolen goods the goods could still have been used as evidence of the individual's guilt. The illegal entry could be dealt with in a civil action against the cop, but the evidence could be judged on its own merits in a criminal court proceeding. Now, following the Mapp decision, that same evidence would be considered poisoned and could not be used against the defendant because it had been gained as the result of an illegal warrantless entry.

The second Supreme Court bombshell was dropped in 1966 in the Miranda Case, which affirmed the right of an individual to be warned by the police of his right against self- incrimination. Briefly, the police would now be required to warn a suspect, whom they intended to question, that anything that he said could be used against him. The broad-based police opinion argued that this would nullify the use of admissions and confessions. The charge of 'handcuffing the police' was taken up across the country and leveled at the court.

Northeastern University, and other institutions which espoused professional law enforcement, had little choice but to support these judicial principles and attempt to clarify their meaning through their curriculum. The enlightened view held that eventually the application of these principles in day to day police work would result in a more effective and better educated police service. The argument was simple enough - the problems generated by these decisions would require not only better trained, but also better educated police officers.

The early Sixties had marked the beginning of the modern Police Professional Movement in the U.S. and these decisions jettisoned its growth. I didn't like these decisions but I bought into the professional development philosophy and gained a great deal of satisfaction from being a part of this early pioneering effort. That, of course, didn't make school any easier - it was still a real grind.

I generally carried a five-course load during the school year and attended school throughout the summer. The 6:00 PM classes fit in well with my work schedule at the Intelligence Unit. I enjoyed most of the law enforcement instructors, especially the Assistant Dean, Tim Moran, a tower of a man who would become one of the guiding forces in my life. I formed relationships over time with a small cadre of dedicated students, most of them cops who shared inquiring minds, and with whom I shared a common struggle to find the place where theory met practice - or in other words, where the rubber met the road. Speaking for myself, this professional struggle would obsess me throughout my career.

In 1966 the war in Vietnam intensified. Military personnel reached a level of 375,000 troops and the war was costing twenty-five billion dollars annually. The media carried stories charging that almost fifty percent of U.S. aid was being diverted into the black market. By late summer the U.S. had bombed the North Vietnamese capital city of Hanoi (and Haiphong) destroying two-thirds of the country's oil supply.

The North Vietnamese let go with an effective counter punch. Increasingly, Americans were turning against the war, and the beginnings of the anti-war movement made itself felt across the nation. By the end of the year slightly less than fifty percent of U.S. Citizens supported the war effort.

In March Watts exploded again. Massive rioting convulsed this section of Los Angeles. Property was destroyed and homes were burned leaving two people dead and fifteen persons injured.

In April the Collective Bargaining Law for the Police took effect. This historic first gave the police the right to bargain for better working conditions. This breakthrough was a significant step leading up to the birth of the Boston Police Patrolman's Association. It was the biggest ingredient in the stew which would eventually boil over and change the relationship between the bosses, the cops and the politicians. It meant that the police would no longer have to grovel before the public for a raise the way that Mayor Collins had forced them to do.

In May Stokely Carmichael, a young articulate black student activist was elected to the Student Non-Violent Coordinating Committee after campaigning on a platform of Black Power and physical retaliation. Increasingly, the peaceful tactics of Martin Luther King were being denounced by an ever expanding vocal minority, especially since the 1965 slaying of Malcolm X who was killed after breaking with the Black Muslim Movement. King and other black moderates who advocated non-violent change were referred to as Uncle Toms.

That month also set off the 'Summer of Urban Race Riots.' Blacks rioted in Chicago, Cleveland, Omaha, Jacksonville and Brooklyn. The National Guard was utilized to stop the street violence and fire bombing of property. Before the end of 1967 almost sixty cities across America would have exploded into riots. The most devastating disturbance occurred in Detroit where forty-two people were killed and three hundred and eighty-six were injured. The total, across the country, would amount to one hundred and forty-one dead and more than forty-five hundred people injured.

That summer also saw the introduction of LSD, mini-skirts and acid rock. Military boots, flowering skirts, scarves, mid-calf overcoats and long hair were in. The Beatles continued to hammer out their rebellion and MoTown was on the rise.

The Warren Commission, which conducted an inquest to determine the truth surrounding the assassination of President Kennedy, was set up in July. Before the investigation was finished they would document sixty different versions of the events that had led up to the murder.

The T-Bone (Al Stroman) and his wife Phyllis traveled to Massachusetts to visit with Beverly and me around that same time. Phyllis was a knock out, a racial composite of delicate and beautiful features. But even her pleasant countenance couldn't erase the unspoken question of race, a rat-maddening malady that drenched the air and hovered over us like a dark specter. Although we were out of the Service and away from the now defunct laws of segregation that had prevented us from enjoying a night in the town together, we still couldn't escape the implications of race. They were everywhere!

On November 15, 1966, Thomas De Prisco and Tashi Bratsos were killed in the Nite Life Cafe on Hanover Street in the North End while they were reportedly attempting to collect one hundred thousand dollars from the wise guys to put up as bail money to spring Joe Barbosa who had been arrested on a gun charge. Their bodies were dumped in South Boston and eighty-two thousand dollars in collected funds were stolen. The word from the street was that the 'Office' (the local branch of the La Cosa Nostra or Mafia) wanted to keep 'the animal' in the can. Barbosa had done their dirty work, killing and brutalizing numerous people, but now he was regarded as an out of control mad man. He was bringing bad publicity onto the mob. There was more than one way to cool a smoking gun.

Ironically, Tashi Bratso's brother was destined to become a Boston Cop, and one of the suspected killers of the two collectors would be the father of another. They were both pretty decent cops at that, and not an unusual phenomenon in the police department - brother and brother, father and son, same genes and similar environments, but opposing life styles. The academic cynics would perhaps refer to the element of force and the persuasive power of authority, common to both, that binds these relationships; but these smug explanations fall short of a full understanding of the phenomena.

On January 27, 1967, my childhood buddy, Brian Gill, was honorably discharged from the U.S. Navy where he had served for better than four years as a Commissioned Officer. I cannot recall when I first met Brian

- he has always been there. Our mothers had wheeled us side by side in carriages down Broadway in Somerville. We were inseparable as kids and had spent our early days playing in the back of an alley where the rear of my three-decker, four family house and the front of his two-family house were located.

Our imaginations knew no bounds - a wooden walkway leading to his house became a sleek ship of the sea. His younger curly haired brother, Frankie, often joined us as we set sail into the open ocean, the three of us taking turns as Front and Rear Admiral. The third guy would be the passenger. Small pieces of yellow clay found in the ground constituted proof of the devil's head and we summarily stomped the bits back into the black earth. A makeshift, 'for boy's only', wooden clubhouse was the place where we and the gang spun stories and made plans. We argued, fought, made up and played sports.

Guys like Ted Williams and Joe DiMaggio were our heroes. Brian taught me how to bat a baseball and I taught him the techniques of Indian hand wrestling. We got into mischief, occasionally provoking certain of the neighbors, whom we charged were old crabs. We went to confession on Saturday afternoon, Mass on Sunday and attended Novenas during the school year (being Parochial school kids we didn't have much choice). We shined shoes on Saturday night, delivered newspapers, sang songs, performed in school plays, enjoyed John Wayne movies and believed that we were destined for Hollywood.

We fell in love with the wholesome good looks of Doris Day and squabbled over which one of us she would prefer to date once we came of age. Most of all we dreamed - we dreamed about the way life would be someday. We dreamed of a picturesque home in the suburbs (should we decide to get married) with plenty of pets and a professional position with a stinking rich annual salary of ten thousand dollars.

Brian grew to be a darkly handsome, muscular and tough athletic kid, the product of a Greek mother with enduring values and a self-educated, intellectually astute Irish father whose depression-born cynicism and biting wit added a Spock-like (from Star Trek) dimension to Brian's keen intellect. He used it well, working his way through Tuft's University - partly by his earnings as a bartender in the New Deal Cafe in Scollay Square.

I was in the Marine Corps during that period and by the time I was out Brian was in the Navy. We maintained contact while on leave and through occasional letters, but eight years had passed since we had chummed around together and now, like me, he was married.

It was uncanny how I learned that he had been discharged. I called his mother Lulu, whom I always addressed as Mrs. Gill, to inquire about his exact discharge date. I was not aware that he had received a three-month early release. As fate would have it, the phone rang on the other end as Brian walked in the door. His mother was shocked.

"I'll get that," he said. "It's Phil." He picked up the phone and spoke into the receiver.

"Hi Phil."

"Hi Brian, it's good to hear from you."

I had the strange feeling that our brief conversation was predestined, a telepathic event, cast in time and waiting for this very moment to be played out. After some scant conversation, I asked him,

"Can you make it over here Saturday night?"

"I sure can, Phil."

"Get ready to tie one on, Brian," I warned him. "We've got a lot to catch up on - figure on staying for the weekend."

I gave him directions and that ended our conversation. Neither of us wanted to keep Lulu waiting.

Friday night arrived and Brian was right on time. He stepped through the door carrying a case of Bud. That was the first time I met his wife Naomi. She hailed from Brooklyn - her accent was not as pronounced as that of many New Yorkers whom I had met over the years. She was a good looking and well-stacked red-head. It didn't take me long to pick up her vibrations. She wasn't run of the mill - she was different. Tough, fiery, wild and restless, she pulsated with a nervous energy that I felt within just a few minutes of meeting her. She was savagely sensual and I could understand Brian's attraction to her. On the other hand, Beverly, a high-tension act herself, appeared sedate in contrast to Naomi.

We wasted little time with the introductions and the party began. We laughed, talked, reminisced and projected the future, finally passing out sometime around 4:00 AM. We had killed almost two cases of beer.

About ten o'clock the next morning I was startled out of an uncomfortable sleep by Naomi, who was kneeling over me with her hand in my back pocket, searching for my wallet. I learned that she was looking for money to buy coffee and donuts. Beverly was looking on, in the middle of a giggling fit, obviously amused by Naomi's assertiveness.

Once revived, Brian hung in for a couple of hours before they headed out. He didn't seem happy to me - there was something missing. Even the night before I'd had that feeling about him. He thanked us for a good time. I accompanied them both to the front door, reversing my directions to him as we walked down the stairs. I caught a brief unsettling glimpse of him just as he entered his car. Something wasn't right. He looked sad and let down - unfulfilled, perhaps. I sensed what he was feeling. It was almost as though I were looking back at myself through a broken mirror.

In the last month of the year, the Federal Bureau of Investigation issued a report on the La Cosa Nostra in the New England area. The organization totaled fifty members, twenty-five in Boston, thirteen in Providence, five in Worcester, four in Springfield and one in Portland, Maine. Joe Barbosa sat in his jail cell fuming, his mind riveted on revenge - and on how many of them he could take down.

Twenty-Two

The Gay bars were a part of the Boston nightlife. As far as I can recall there were about a half-dozen of them back in the Sixties. The most well known was the Punch Bowl, located at the edge of the Bay Village and across from the former Statler Hilton Hotel, an elegant old behemoth that occupied the entire block between Columbus Avenue and Arlington Street. Two others, Jacques and The Other Side were situated in Bay Village itself, which was a small enclave made up of five streets sandwiched in between the South End, the theater district and the Back Bay. Bay Village was an up-scale area that was increasingly becoming a magnet for both male and female street-level prostitution. Most cops referred to gay bars as 'fag joints.' I was required to monitor them like any other nightspot.

Henry Vara, an unsmiling medium built guy who wore large framed glasses, owned the Punchbowl and one or two of the others. He didn't seem like a bad guy or even a man with a cause, just a businessman who was trying to make a buck in a selective niche in the market. It was my impression that Henry was a man who was constantly at odds with the police and the Licensing Board for what he considered harassing and discriminatory treatment. He probably wasn't too far off the mark as gays were disliked, even hated, by a lot of straights, cops, and politicians.

There was a City Councilor who used his seat to whip up negative sentiment against gays, accusing them of using the city as a homosexual breeding grounds; the implication being that a vote for him would protect the citizens against this scourge. I never gave it much thought one way or the other, but from time to time I was required to check out the gay bars for any overt homosexual activity such as touching, caressing, hugging, fondling or diddling that might take place in or around the premises. I was expected to be especially vigilant on Halloween night because some gay males used that occasion to cross-dress and to perform wedding ceremonies.

At one time there was an enforced Boston City Ordinance prohibiting a person from disguising oneself which had been enacted specifically to prevent this behavior on that particular evening. There was enough of the Puritan ethic, fueled by ethnic prejudice and intolerance, remaining in the old city to sustain the enforcement of this ordinance well into the Fifties.

I was embarrassed the first few times I had to do these investigations. I was afraid that someone who knew me might see me going into a gay bar and think that I was 'queer'. My anxiety eventually eased as I became more adept at quickly casing a joint from the outside (and the inside) to see who was around. If I spotted anyone whom I even vaguely knew, especially cops, I'd be gone in a flash!

I stayed in the Punchbowl about an hour the first time. It was a large and tastefully decorated place and I sat at the bar nursing a beer for the whole time. I mentally reviewed the whole range of current psychological explanations purporting to explain the origins of homosexuality, from the 'arrested sexual development theory' on through to the 'dominant mother theme' but none were sufficiently convincing to enable me to comprehend same-sex attraction which seemed pretty far out to me.

As modern times have suggested many of these past clinical explanations amounted to psycho-babble anyway. Currently the clinical world is leaning more toward biological and genetic explanations as the basis of homosexuality, the implication being that it's just the way some people are wired up (so much for psychological accounts).

A couple of patrons sitting at the bar looked over at me but when I failed to acknowledge them in any way they just kept on drinking. I felt uneasy, but I was fascinated with the culture of the place. I was especially intrigued by a gentle looking silver-haired woman who moved freely among the patrons, engaging them in a mutual show of affection, and whom I overheard refer to herself as a 'fag hag,' an endearing slang term that is indicative of a straight women who dates gay males. It would take me thirty more years to understand the complex reasons why.

Gay bars, like the other joints, tended to attract different clientele. I learned over time that the Punchbowl had the standard assortment of, at the risk of committing an oxymoron, straight gays so to speak, who enjoyed the psychological support and the social and sexual opportunities provided by an inverted environment of like-minded and similarly sexually oriented men. A few of them even seemed embarrassed to be there.

Jacque's, conversely, catered to a younger and more flamboyant crowd that included a few drag queens and transvestites who, now and again, used the place for cover. The Other Side started off gay male, but gradually became more dominated by lesbians. The two groups seemed to remain aloof from one another.

I was intrigued by lesbians and had been since reading the *Well of Loneliness*, a classic of lesbian literature, which had been written by Radclyffe Hall back in 1928 and was still kicking around in the Fifties. It was a thoughtful treatment of a young woman's anguish coming to terms with her sexuality. It left me with a much better understanding of lesbianism. During my early undercover days I frequently checked out Cavana's on Tremont Street in the South End, a mixed place with a strong lesbian influence. I had been going in there since before I enlisted in the military. Perhaps I had been trying to unravel the family mystery surrounding my second cousin Veronica, a nice person whom I had always liked and whom I had suspected was a lesbian although the family never spoke of it.

I never had any answers either, but I witnessed a real jerk get the shit kicked out of him one night. The incident started inside the bar, the result of an argument between two women who were involved in a relationship. I didn't know what they were arguing about and failed to pay much attention as conflicts among the women were pretty common in this joint. My attention was more riveted on a guy whom I suspected was a drug dealer. One of the combatants, a seriously distraught young woman, ran out of the bar and stood out on the street quietly crying. (In those days the straight world divided lesbian women into 'femmes,' the more delicate variety and 'butch' or 'dykes,' the more mannish types). This young woman was clearly a femme. She was delicately built and strangely beautiful. Her hair was long and fine and fell gently into soft ringlets over her shoulders.

I left in a few minutes. My natural curiosity compelled me to hang out front for a while to see how this scene would be played out. A couple of minutes passed and two foul looking guys walked down Tremont Street from the direction of the Bradford Hotel. They were seriously unkempt and looked as though they had just crawled out of a sewer. Upon reaching Cavana's they stopped in front of the woman and rudely began to gawk at her.

The larger of the two guys easily reached 6 foot 2 inches and weighed more than two hundred pounds. He was a mean looking guy with a heavily scarred face, possibly the result of a knife fight. He asked the distraught woman why she was crying. She continued to cry, almost uncontrollably now, and between sobs she begged him to leave her alone. He refused to respect her wishes, this time demanding that she comply with his request. When she refused again he reached out and squeezed her breast, calling her a bitch. He ordered her, for the last time, to explain why she was crying.

I don't know what cued them, but almost simultaneously four big 'bull dykes' (a demeaning term reserved for the biggest and heaviest of dykes) came pouring out of the front door and were all over this guy, punching and kicking him in an unrelenting ferocious attack until he fell to the street - after which they commenced to dance all over his body turning him into a bloody pulp. He covered his face and head with his arms and rolled up into a huge ball on the pavement, pitifully reduced to a completely non-offensive and self-protective mode. His small, thin, ratty looking companion pulled out a knife and threatened one of his friend's assailants, but when she lunged at him he dropped the weapon and ran down Tremont Street leaving his pal on the sidewalk who continued to get wailed.

Although I was fully enjoying this small piece of street justice, I was uneasy with the prospect of this bloody transaction turning into a homicide. I was a cop and no matter what my role, undercover or not, there was an expectation that I must act to protect life - even this asshole. The nearest phone was a full block away. I had the options of notifying Operations directly or I could get physically involved and attempt to break it up. That

I knew would be sudden death and frankly, this guy just wasn't worth it. He was getting what he deserved. I'm not sure to this day which alternative I would have selected, but the women themselves ended the assault and scattered in every direction.

One of the bartenders, a guy name Fitzie, came out armed with a club for the finishing touches and at that point I intervened and persuaded him to go back inside. The beaten down goon slowly lifted himself from the sidewalk and painfully stumbled down the street. I have always wondered what he said once he caught up with his companion.

But to get on with it, Mario's, a couple of blocks away, attracted a more effeminate gay, while the nondescript Sporter's on Cambridge Street emanated with sadomasochistic themes, fierce looking guys wearing leather and draped in chains. Playland, on Essex Street in the Zone, was the original gay bar in town. It was a dark and perverse place where so called 'straight' men indulged their hidden needs. Conversely, Napoleon's on 52 Piedmont Street was strictly a classy place. They enforced a strict dress code requiring their patrons to wear a jacket and tie before being allowed to enter the front door. It was the most civil and well-behaved nightclub in town, and it survived into the late Nineties.

The most remarkable consistency about the gay bars, at least back then, was how well regulated they were. The bartenders were aware that the cops wouldn't cut them much slack and were quick to jump on behavior that might land the club in front of the Licensing Board. With the exception of overcrowding, the most chronic violation, especially in Sporter's, there was not a whole lot to report. But of course there are exceptions to everything, and I ran into one of them in a newly opened, unnamed, intended gay bar on the second floor of Kerry's Village, a derelict-type, street level joint in the South End. This bar was rumored to be owned by a suspected loan shark named Sammy Frachata, a squash headed, powerfully built mob-connected guy with a cynically depressing sense of humor.

I was banging around the South End one evening when I noticed a lot of people, mostly gay males, entering the side door of Kerry's Village. I followed them up the stairs and onto the second floor which opened up into a large room that contained a bar and several booths scattered around the perimeter. The place was packed, mostly with men, and the jukebox was blaring. Several same-sex couples were moving around the dance floor. This was the first time that I had ever witnessed men dancing together and I was appalled. This was a clear violation of Licensing Board rules at the time.

A huge blonde-haired drag queen, who called himself Silvia Sidney, was sacheting around the place, emitting a steady stream of lewd and offensive language. He featured himself as a comedian and was known to be really wild. He occasionally performed at The Other Side. At one point he approached a pear shaped women who was sitting at the bar. He gingerly removed one breast at a time from inside her low cut dress and placed each one of them on the bar. She possessed large pendulous boobs and didn't seem to mind them flopping around loose. Silvia began to roll them on the ash-strewn, beer-soaked bar and asked her what she liked best "fucking or sucking."

"Sucking," she answered. "Fucking is nice, but it don't beat sucking."

He then went on to something else but she continued to sit there in a stuporous condition with her boobs fully exposed while she engaged in a repetitive monologue, asserting over and over again the merits of oral sex over sexual intercourse.

I sat at the bar and ordered a beer. I was shocked to see men fondling one another on the dance floor, and that wasn't all. Another guy was getting a hand job in one of the rear booths while others still were sitting around talking and laughing like nothing was happening. When I had seen enough for a king-size report I got up, ready to leave.

A patron motioned for me to come over to where he was standing against the wall. When he thought I was ready to pass him, he abruptly moved in front of me, delaying my progress. He motioned with his head for me to look down, and that was the last shocker of the evening - he was holding his penis, an erect pencil-thin organ, in a white handkerchief displaying it for me as I brushed passed him. My years working at the State Hospital helped me to get past him and the incident, but I will never forget the stark and ugly reality of that evening.

I relayed the whole story to Blake the next morning. I clearly recall describing the place as a "den of iniquity." He got right on it and determined quickly that the operation was not licensed. Apparently the owner was relying on an extension of the downstairs bar for authorization to operate.

The word in the street, as I heard it that evening, was that Sammy figured there was money in gays and wanted to cut in on some of Vara's action.

The Vice Squad closed the place over the weekend, almost as quickly as it had opened. That was the end of the unnamed gay bar over Kerry's Village and it served as a demonstration to me of what the police could do when they really wanted to.

Male street-level prostitution was a relatively minor but growing problem in the city. Most of it was concentrated around the vicinity of the Greyhound Bus station, sometimes referred to as the 'Gayhound Station,' a block from Police Headquarters. It involved about a dozen players at any one time, mostly young boys, oftentimes minors, who exchanged sex for money, usually with older men. They lurked on corners and in doorways stretched out between the station and Bay Village. One of the biggest operators was a young and good-looking blonde-headed kid who lived with a female prostitute at 593 Park Street and referred to himself as Terry the Faggot. I struck up a casual conversation with him one evening and he told me a little about the business. His most memorable statement revolved around male hustlers. Terry said they started out straight but invariably ended up gay.

He explained, "They go from getting blow jobs to giving them. Eventually some of them end up paying for sex." Summing up his own feelings, he remarked, "I'm a hung-right faggot and I only got so much time to make some serious scratch, and I ain't wasting any of it." Like their female equivalents, male prostitutes too, were all finished in their late twenties.

Eventually, just from being around, I was able to identify about eight more male prostitutes, mostly between the ages of nineteen and twenty-five, but the Vice Squad didn't seem overly interested in going after them unless they received a complaint that one of them was a runaway. That made it simple. All the cops had to do then was to scoop the kid and have his parents pick him up. For whatever reason, male prostitutes operated in a greater envelope of security than the female variety. Perhaps the vice guys felt more uncomfortable getting cruised by males, or maybe it was more difficult putting them in (court) under the common nightwalker offense. In any event not too many of them ever got pinched.

I bumped along fairly easily in '67 - the job increasingly became second nature. I was more comfortable working the streets and more assured that, even on a slow night, I would be able to come up with something. There were enough people, places, bookies, pimps, wise guys and whores to keep me busy, even on Tuesday evenings. I enjoyed the freedom of the job, especially the lack of supervision. I didn't have to stand roll calls, respond to complaints, answer the radio, or work with guys like Roach and if I made a mistake there wasn't anyone around who would see it - and I made plenty of them.

One night, contrary to what Tommy Mitchell had taught me about motor vehicle surveillances, I hung a really tight tail on a guy who was driving a hooker in his own car. I followed them to the Jamaica Plain section of the city. He circled around a few blocks and began to drive down Peter Parley Road, a steep hill leading to Washington Street. I hung back for a while and just before he made the turn onto the main drag, I drove slowly down to the intersection.

Suddenly he backed his vehicle in front of mine, blocking me from making any further progress. He alighted from his car and approached me from the driver's side, angrily accusing me of following him. He sputtered that it was real obvious that I was tailing him and demanded an explanation. He told me that he was licensed to carry and threatened to put one through my head unless I explained what I was doing. All the while he was carrying on, the hooker, a tall well-stacked brunette with at least three inches on him, was standing in the street getting a good look at me. I managed to talk myself out of the jam; he was more nervous than I was. Although I think he was bluffing about the gun, the incident could well have ended up a tragedy. There were other such incidents but I don't want to bore you with the details. Suffice to say, I was the only one on the department who knew about them.

I was stopped any number of times by the police for 'Operation 16,' a program set up to snare young drivers in stolen cars by stopping youthful looking suspects and checking out their paperwork. Most of the stops were made by the Tactical Patrol Force who could come on pretty strong, especially one officer, whom I later learned was a former Marine named Harry Prefontaine, a big husky guy with intensive eyes, a sharp mind and a resounding voice whose very presence alone could be intimidating. Harry meant business.

I often wished that I could have just flashed my badge and been on my way, but that was one mistake I hardly ever made. I scrupulously adhered to Blake's advice not to reveal my job to anyone, especially cops. I was twenty-eight years old at the time, but that didn't preclude the cops from checking me out. A few nights I was pulled over more than once and each time I routinely went through the standard drill.

The first time that I broke the rule of silence occurred that same year in the dead of winter on the opposite side of 248 Seaver Street in Roxbury, next to the Franklin Park Zoo and close to the exact geographical center of the city. I was parked there one night, putting the bug on Crawley's apartment building. It was cold and a light wind had laid down a clean dusting of snow on the street's surface. The beams of oncoming headlights cascaded off the glaze covered cars that were parked along the street, producing an intermittent soft white glow effect. The engine was running and the car's heater was working overtime. It was a tough night and I felt pretty immune from any intrusion.

I had been sitting there for about twenty minutes, listening to the car radio, when I saw the familiar blue of a police cruiser slowly roll past me. It stopped about twenty feet up the street and a big strapping cop stepped out and lumbered over to where I was parked. I opened the driver's side window and he politely asked me for my license and registration. He was at least six foot three inches tall and he weighed every bit of two hundred and twenty pounds. He cut an idealized image of a police officer - tall, dignified and handsome. Strangely enough, he reminded me of Officer Phillips back in Somerville. I was impressed with the level of civility he maintained throughout the entire encounter. I thought he was, more than likely, checking for white hunters as they were becoming a hot button issue in black neighborhoods.

After carefully checking my registration and license, he handed them back to me and asked,

"Were you originally from Somerville?"

"Yes," I replied.

He continued quizzing me. "Was your father's name Dominic?"

Dominic! Was my father's name Dominic?

I was taken back by his question. My father had died in 1939. He was originally from Plymouth, Massachusetts and had lived in Somerville for less than three years after he married my mother. Most of his family had died before I could ever know them. His sister was my Cousin Dick's mother and she had passed away recently. I had always thirsted for even the scantiest piece of information about my father, a man who, by every account, was said to be loving and loyal to his wife, and proud of his infant son. I did know that he had wrestled professionally as a young guy, was a cook in the Conservation Camps, had a good sense of humor, liked music, enjoyed dancing and had bought a small delicatessen on Broadway in Somerville shortly after he married. It was during the depression - things were difficult and an early death had spared him from the ultimate failure of the business. He had kept a book of photographs of his newborn son and he had inscribed on the outside cover this note:

"Within this book contains the key to the treasure of my heart."

This was about all I knew about my father and here was a stranger, a police officer no less, standing outside of my car in a cold and stormy night who knew him.

"Yes," I anxiously answered. "His name was Dominic - he died when I was a baby." I asked him how he knew my father.

He went on to explain that Mickey (my father) and his older brother Buddy had been the best of friends. He introduced himself as Walter Warren and told me that he was originally from Somerville. He didn't have to explain any further. I knew the whole deal. I had heard about the Warrens throughout my childhood. My mother and aunt had spoken of them many times. They were a great family with a gargantuan reputation for doing good and Buddy Warren, particularly, was a ray of sunshine during an otherwise bleak time. He had tended the store when my mother was visiting my father in the hospital. He never asked to be compensated. He also baby-sat for me - Walter did too. I remember my aunt telling me that. "But just for a short amount of time," she would conclude, "because Walter was just a kid himself."

The infant and the kid had grown up, and here we were, facing off at each other on a desolate wintry night in Roxbury. I thought I detected a slight look of disappointment move across Walter's face. And why not? It was a hell of a way for Dominic's kid to wind up - a white hunter chasing whores on Seaver Street. I could not let the officer walk away believing that falsehood. I quickly made up mind to come clean and tell him the truth.

"It's not the way it looks, Walter," I said. "I'm a cop working out of Headquarters. I'm pinning some of the prostitution action on Seaver Street - that's why I'm here."

He seemed relieved once he saw my badge. The weather didn't permit us to chat for very long. He smiled, shook my hand and returned to his cruiser. I left right after that. There was no point to stretching things out - my cover was blown, at least for the night. But, hopefully, Walter wouldn't think that Dominic's son was a pervert.

Ed Jesser was discharged from the Army sometime in February. He returned to the family homestead on East Cottage Street in Dorchester and landed his old job back at the State Hospital where he remained until he finished college. I busted his ass for this, taunting him that he was going backwards. He seemed to have changed a little - his humor had taken on a more acerbic edge. He was less relaxed and more impatient. In a word, he was more serious.

By this time the anti-war movement was really puffing up and demonstrations and other kinds of actions were taking place across the country. I asked Ed what he thought about it all.

He hated them, he said. "I hate the Hawks and I hate the Doves" (metaphors that captured the sentiments of the pro and anti-war activists). "I hate the fifteen percent of motherfuckers on both sides of the issue."

Ed told me about his homecoming at Logan Airport after being discharged from the Army and having served in Vietnam. He was in full uniform for the final time of his life. He had disembarked the plane and had collected his luggage. He was still in the terminal, walking toward the exit, finished forever with the Army and planning his renewed life, when a disheveled looking young guy suddenly appeared in front of him and spat in his face.

"What did you do, Ed?" I asked.

"I clocked him - what the fuck else?" he responded.

Nineteen sixty-seven was a transitional year - the Boston Police Department would be shocked out of its apathy by the first of a series of tumultuous events that would challenge it to its very core. In April the Boston Police Patrolman's Association was incorporated. After the politicking was over and subsequent to the five to one vote in favor of the patrolmen forming their own distinctive union separate from the bosses, President Richard MacEachern and Vice President Dan Sweeney took over the leadership.

Sometime during this period, when spring had turned into summer, the city would experience its first racial riot. It started outside the Welfare Office in Roxbury's Grove Hall, the result of a planned arrest operation involving a group of belligerent black women who called themselves 'Mothers for Adequate Welfare.' None of these women were graduates of the school of social etiquette - some of them had chained themselves to the wall in protest of what they perceived as an inadequate level of welfare support.

The majority of these women were seriously overweight and stylistically offensive. They were looked upon with ridicule, especially from whites, and were generally thought of by the cops as social parasites. Like many others who would soon follow, who lacked a social constituency and possessed zero political power, they pressed their ends to the ultimate, refusing to move and moreover, fixing themselves to the Welfare Office in a trespass situation.

The black riots had taken their toll of the nation and the level of tension between the races had reached an unprecedented height. The principles of non-violence were giving way to forced confrontations. The teachings of Ghandi, so eloquently expressed and passionately lived by Martin Luther King, were quickly becoming dissipated. They were being replaced by the choleric protestations of Elijah Muhammad, a wisp of a man who claimed he was divinely inspired to put forth the Doctrine of Black Supremacy and who foretold of an apocalyptic conflict with the white race; Stokely Carmichael who advanced the cause of Black Nationalism; and Eldridge Cleaver, an angry black intellect and writer who espoused revolution.

Violence was in the air, lurking behind every encounter between a cop and a ghetto resident. The issuance of a ticket, the shutting down of an outside crap game, intervention in a street fight, the incarceration of a drunk, a simple arrest, just about anything could spark a confrontation or a riot. Boston had been spared so far, but the gig was up!

From what I heard, it started right after the first demonstrators were arrested. The police used bolt cutters to free them and were descending the stairs with their prisoners when the first rock was thrown - first one and then another and another. After about the fifth rock the police moved into the crowd and began to push the participants down Blue Hill Avenue. That's when all hell broke loose. As the crowd dispersed down the Avenue some of them began to smash the windows of small businesses on both sides of the street.

That was the beginning of a week and a half of riots. They began in Roxbury, a predominantly black neighborhood, and moved out to the South End. They were a nightly occurrence. There was violence, widespread looting and fire-bombing. The Tactical Patrol Force handled the brunt of it and the National Guard was called in to assist. The city had never experienced anything like it before and they were unprepared.

The department purchased a large supply of ax handles from a local hardware store and issued them to the cops. I was temporarily reassigned to District 3 for the duration of the disorder as part of the police suppression force. I made one arrest of a rock thrower, the result of a foot chase that propelled my partner and me into a third floor apartment on Columbia Road. I was caught on television coming out of the building with our prisoner.

There were injuries on both sides, but no one was killed. I will never shake loose the memory of these riots. I can still remember, as though it was yesterday, standing in the middle of Grove Hall, hitherto a hallowed market place in Roxbury, as it burned to the ground. All the while the firefighters, who were attempting to control the blaze, were being pelted by rocks. Large parts of Roxbury would remain a cultural wasteland for years to come.

Other than the destruction that I had witnessed in Beirut, Lebanon in 1958, this was the closest thing I had ever seen to war, and it was happening in the United States. A violent contagion was spreading across America - Cambridge in Massachusetts, New York's Spanish Harlem, Detroit, Maryland and Milwaukee would soon be ravaged.

Smaller scale, similar type racial eruptions would rack the city right into the Seventies. Black neighborhoods became feared places for white people. A young white woman, whose car ran out of fuel in the Grove Hall area, was doused with gasoline and lit on fire by a group of neighborhood kids. She lived long enough to tell the story. They didn't want her in the neighborhood, she said. Before the violence was over a white motorist would be pulled from his car at the intersection of Eustis and Zigler Streets in Roxbury and crushed with a large cinder block. His assailants could only be prosecuted for assault and battery by means of a dangerous weapon because the victim lived longer than the 'one year and a day requirement' necessary to seek a murder complaint.

Kids were responsible for most of the disorders. It was almost always kids, but that didn't make any difference. Whole groups of people were stereotyped - fear set in, neighborhoods crystallized, white flight was accelerated and the entire section of Dorchester that comprised District 3 was finally abandoned by the Jews. Before they left they turned over the Hecht House, on the American Legion Highway, and their Temple Mishkan Teflia on Seaver Street to black associations and neighborhood residents for small change. Some charged that the cheap sale of real estate, I believe it was one dollar for the temple, was equivalent to extortion. The press began to refer to this area of the city as North Dorchester to distinguish it from the white side.

The black prostitution action gradually shifted from Columbus Avenue to the Combat Zone. Bad money is like water - it finds the path of least resistance. La Grange Street, a small section of connecting way between Washington and Tremont Streets, received the brunt of it. The street traffic was so bogged down with prostitutes soliciting motorists that eventually the city had to reverse the direction of vehicular traffic, making it one-way out of the Zone from Washington Street to Tremont. Enrico's became the next hot spot and the Combat Zone became an equal-opportunity employer.

The summer of '67 witnessed thousands of young hippies invade San Francisco. Calling themselves 'flower children,' they set up in a six block area of the city known as the Haight-Ashbury section and declared that season to be the Summer of Love. Most of them were in their late teens and early twenties. They wore long hair and raggedy denim pants, Indian beads, multicolored shirts and fluorescent body paint. They engaged in a seasonal long 'love in' during which they slowly chipped away at the sexual conventions of the times. They smoked dope, ingested mescaline and tripped out on LSD. Doctor Timothy Leary, the high priest of the League of Spiritual Discovery, who advocated the mystical use of hallucinogenic drugs, was to become their Guru. At one time he had taught at Harvard University. One of his professional associates, whom I met in a chance encounter, commented to me that Leary had written a book on statistics. He offered this tidbit of information as evidence that the Doctor had acted differently before he started abusing drugs.

Boston was one of the other cities targeted for a downsized hippie celebration of communal love. The city has always regarded itself as the eastern twin of San Francisco. It is similar in many respects. Not drastically different in size and population, it is a cosmopolitan town built on hills and seeded with democratic values. A generally liberal oriented, educationally elite class combined with radical traditions has historically operated to open it up to eccentric behavior.

The cops figured that we were in for a hippie invasion, but their timetable was off. Only a couple of hundred of them made it to Boston and most of them assembled on the Boston Common, a large tract of land in the middle of the city consisting of forty-eight acres set aside in 1634 by the early colonists for the grazing of cattle. They frolicked around and washed their clothes in Frogg Pond. A few of them even jumped in.

I peeked in on them, but I failed to see them at the time as 'love people.' At best, I regarded them as silly and at worst, a social aberration. They were the spawns of affluence - the brats of the middle class. I disagreed with those who believed that they were the next phase of the beatnik movement. Beats were unconventional and it's true they used drugs, but they were an artistic underground literary movement that affirmed sensation and life. They challenged the shibboleths of conventional society, but in their own odd way they made a contribution. This was not true of the hippies who struck me as weird, unattractive and shaggy.

I would come to understand them differently in my maturity. Counter-culturalists to be sure, they turned out to be an antidote to the gut-wrenching effects of the impending clash of issues that would be played out in the streets of urban America during the late Sixties and early Seventies. They put on a face of love in a world that had turned to violence. By the end of the year, 500,000 U.S. troops would be involved in Vietnam.

On October 10, 1967, Deputy Superintendent Ed Blake retired from the Boston Police Department. He was pushing the limits age wise, but it nevertheless came as a total shock to me because Deputies never discussed retirement plans with patrolmen. This man had shaped my professional life for the past twenty-eight months and tomorrow he would be gone! He was a tough guy, kind of a hard-ass, but he was honest and decent and he had taught me the ropes. He had said that I was a "digger" and I was deeply proud of that. He went out on a Tuesday - the slowest day of the week.

The Red Sox won the American League Pennant. The fans flipped out, and Blake slipped into the upper regions of the Boston Police Department's memory bank.

FOUR

Man can climb to the highest summit
but he can not dwell there long.
----------G.B. Shaw

Twenty-Three

My boss, for the next several years was a cigar chewing, balding, middle-aged genteel Sergeant Detective named Jimmy Lynch who, in the beginning, amounted to little more than a disembodied voice who answered the phone and received my reports for the next few days after Blake retired.

Lynch had been assigned to the Intelligence Unit for some time and it was he that I had reported to when the Deputy was on vacation or on a day off. I would not meet up with him until sometime during the beginning of the next week. I thought it was strange that suddenly the guy I was now reporting to was three full ranks below Blake on the chain of command.

In reality, Jimmy Lynch was a first-level supervisor and that's the way it was generally done on the department. The Deputy had been an anomaly in that respect, preferring a strong hands-on approach and failing to delegate. It went along with his secretive nature. Information was power to Blake, and keeping it close to the vest put him in a priory position with others in the department who never knew what kinds of guilty knowledge he possessed. It gave him a lot of leverage.

And of course I was not the only one feeding him. He was also tuned into guys like Tommy Mitchell and Peter Ryan, whom I have already mentioned, and Larry Murphy and Eddie Walsh, two others of whom I was only vaguely aware of at the time, but who would come to impress me. All of these guys were excellent investigators.

Larry had an innocuous look about him - almost a double for Norton played by Art Carney in the *Honeymooners*. He was so disarming that on more than one occasion he got bets into the same bookie, re-arresting him on the same offense.

Eddie Walsh was something else. A medium framed, gravelly voiced, eagle eyed police detective, he cut to the caricature of the mythological Hollywood Detective and was destined to become a legend in his own time. The first time I met him was at Blake's retirement party on the first Friday in November.

He sort of shuffled around the place talking to one person and then another. I could see that he was absorbing the whole scene. He introduced himself and assured me of his help if I needed any. His slightly baggy, brightly colored sport jacket and pants gave him a flamboyant quality. Eddie was a born cop. He emanated like one, not hard, but street wise. I didn't know it then, but I would learn a lot from him. Eventually he would be assigned to the newly formed Organized Crime Division where he would share many of his insights with me.

Looking back over the years, it was Walsh who would fan the embers of Blake's street level criminal genius and carry on in his tradition. That's how it happens on police departments. There is always someone who sparks the neural connection and keeps the movement going. I'm getting ahead of my story again.

Bill Hogan was another investigator assigned to the unit, an intense guy who would eventually become a Captain Detective on the Massachusetts State Police. And there was Jackie Long, a thinly-built, well dressed, good looking man who had the inside on major organized crime activity: affiliations, business fronts, loan-sharking, bookmaking, extortion and murder - a phenomenal amount of information close to the core of the operation, information whose source would be doubted. Information the department came to suspect the officer could only have traded by having gotten too close to the other side.

That sort of pitfall has always been a malady of intelligence work. Distinctions and roles can become blurred in the quest for information.

Intelligence Officers are evaluated on the basis of the information they develop and sometimes they over-step their bounds. The requirement to maintain one's ethical and professional identity becomes even more critical during undercover investigations. Long was not working undercover, but he was close to the wise guys. He called them informants but in some respects they were friends. They used each other, embraced in an endless dance that I would see stepped out a thousand times in the years to come among the feds, the cops, the wise guys and the hoodlums, usually with benign results.

There was a murder investigation, a cover-up, in which Long was suspected of having been peripherally involved, an investigation that produced few results followed by the eventual transfer of the officer to the Traffic Division. And that was it. I didn't know much more about it than that. Blake had a lot of wires in his head but there was a new quarterback and the game was about to change.

I was slightly apprehensive with Sergeant Lynch in the beginning. I went through the standard rap every morning at the same time, producing bits and scads of criminal information concerning my activities of the night before. He listened quietly and thanked me each time before he hung up. Otherwise, he didn't say much. I was still careful to allow him, like Blake, to put the receiver down first. My anxiety lifted the first time I met him face to face in the office - especially after he told me that he was a friend and former partner of Lieutenant Billy Burke of the Police Academy. Lieutenant Burke was the reason I was assigned to the Intelligence Unit to begin with.

Lynch said, "We were looking for a certain type and you fit the bill." (I still didn't know why Burke selected me. Perhaps he was amused by my audacity with the oral sex detective.)

Lynch was a pretty ordinary-looking guy in most respects. About five feet nine inches tall, his large frame carried only a few more pounds than it was intended to. Weight and proper diet was always something that he struggled with. He had a curious little way of peering over his reading glasses and looking at whomever he was speaking to whenever he was engaged in a confidential conversation. He lived with his delicate wife Midge and slender co-ed daughter Eileen in a modest white house in Hyde Park's Bel Nel Village, a small protectorate totaling about a half a dozen streets nestled between Boston and the town of Milton. He was scrupulously honest, soft spoken and shared Blake's penchant for secrecy. He was a college guy, financially sharp and also a former Marine, a fact that delighted us both. I liked him.

Nothing changed right away as far as my work was concerned. I continued to work nights - by this time I was all over the city. I had any number of projects going. My assignments were few. Tuesdays were still slow and I continued to deliver Friday night's report at 11:00 AM on Mondays.

Sergeant Lynch lacked Blake's obsessive interest in pimps, prostitutes, B-girls and strippers. I think part of it was due to the fact that he lacked the clout with the Vice Squad that Blake had been able to enjoy. At one time in his career the Deputy had been assigned to the Vice Squad. Consequently he knew all their tricks, and being a member of the Command Staff had afforded him a lot of positional power. I think he enjoyed being able to intimidate them into doing their work with no games being played. Simply put, a report generated by Blake was received differently from one sent by Lynch. Consequently, I had the sense that Lynch was just politely hearing me out during our late morning sessions. I sometimes felt that I was speaking into a hollow drum and listening to the reverberations of my voice bouncing around; then I got involved with a porno investigation with organized crime implications which seemed to pique his interest.

It started with some of the Porn shops in the Combat Zone getting busted up. One of them was even fire bombed. I wasn't sure who actually owned it, but I suspected it was Joe Zamba, one of the original smut dealers in town. I ran into Popeye a few days later and he told me that the word in the street was that the firebomb was a present from the mob because the owner had been resisting the heavy payments that he was being forced to make.

That didn't surprise me - protection money was an organized crime staple in the Zone. The way Popeye put it, the wise guys were coming in real heavy on the Porn shops because they were a sleaze bucket operation to begin with and the cops didn't give a fuck what happened to them. "Who were they going to complain to?" he asked.

There was probably a little truth to that, but the firebombing was another thing. The cops would have liked to get a good hook into the investigation.

Somebody, even a passerby could have gotten hurt, but nobody was talking. Not too long before that a women had been murdered and her body was found on the roof of the nearby Casa Mia restaurant. A couple of local hoods tied up with the 'Office' would eventually be indicted for that one, but a clear motive was never established and one of the witness/hoods was murdered and the case went south. The streets were heating up and these incidents made me uneasy. Dirty money invites dirty tricks.

There were better than a half a dozen porn shops scattered around the Zone back then. The main ones were the Booknest at 54 Kneeland Street; The Bookmark Annex at 623 Washington Street; the Leisure Time Book Shop across the way; the Book World at 8 Beech Street; and the Boylston Book Shop at number 10 Boylston.

I maintained a casual interest in these places as it was part of my job to check the type of material they were dealing in. Most of the magazines on the shelves could be described as Soft Porn by today's standards. Occasionally some of the harder stuff slipped in and it was my job to alert the boss when it did. The police department considered any kind of cover that featured a naked female exposing her vagina as having crossed the line. (They were called 'spreads' in the business.)

If I came across something flagrant I was authorized to buy a copy and deliver it to Headquarters for their inspection. (They never complained when I did.) The Vice Squad would take it from there. Most of the magazines were wrapped in plastic, making it difficult to check. Some of the so-called nudist magazines weren't, and they often displayed pictures of naked pre and post-pubescent children at play, which the department considered legal. Neither did they move on depictions of women being tortured nor on the dead body scenes.

They were principally concerned with 'spreads' or nude adults portrayed in intimate scenes involving sexual penetration. Sex toys were also making their debut at the time and their display in store windows was forbidden.

The type of material set on the racks was generally sectioned off according to sexual propensity. There were heterosexual and homosexual display materials along with the sadistic and masochistic variety, right down to the women and animals stuff and on through to the necrophile depiction of women posed in caskets (which I thought were the sickest of them all). Most of these stores maintained a quantity of hard-core stuff, usually under the counter, for their special customers. If I spotted that kind of a transaction I reported it the following day including a description of the magazine, if possible, and most importantly, the location of the stash.

Popeye was right about porn being a sleaze-bucket operation. He was right about a lot of things. He also remarked that the Homicide Unit was looking at a suspect in the Paramount Hotel explosion - that it might not have been an accident. As it turned out, he was right. Lieutenant Detective Bob Hudson, one of the sharpest investigators the department has ever produced, verified Popeye's take years later. Apparently one of the prostitutes who lost her life had a brother named Ken Harrelson, a serial killer. He was also known as 'The Giggler' for the hideous, contorted and shrieking laugh he emitted one evening after he called the police emergency line and informed the operator of the location of his last body. Eventually convicted of four murders, one of which had occurred near the Combat Zone, he was a principal suspect in the hotel explosion - but nothing ever came of the investigation and the cause of the incident remained officially an accident. Popeye knew his stuff all right and he regarded porn shops as further proof of the Zone's deterioration.

I was never comfortable checking the stores out. A porn shop was not the kind of place that I would have wanted to have a friend or acquaintance to see me in. The only times I dropped in was when asked by the department or on a slow night when I knew I wouldn't have much to report the next morning.

For that reason, in addition to the rough stuff that had been going on, I ended up nosing around one night in the Kozy Book Shop located at 74 Stuart Street on the southern perimeter of the Combat Zone. I got into a conversation with two young brothers in their early twenties who worked there. Both of them were extremely bright, especially the older one, who was hung up big time on the theory of evolution. On the first night we began to discuss Darwin, admittedly one of my own preoccupations, and that began a long-term association with John.

I actually looked forward to our conversations and on one occasion almost forgot why I was there to begin with. Neither he nor his brother seemed at all interested in the business of pornography. It was just a job to them. John knew his customers well, and he commented to me that most of them were married professionals from outside the city. He surprised me when he confided that many of his customers were doctors.

"You would think that they would see enough real-life 'bollicky' broads to last a lifetime, but they're over here looking at pictures," he remarked. I thought to myself that the concentration of doctors might be due to the nearby proximity of the New England Medical Center located just a couple of blocks away and nothing more than that, but I didn't respond.

John kept the hard stuff under the counter and his private customers knew it was there. I witnessed him make a number of sales. He told me that they also sold movies that were secretly stored in lockers in the nearby Motor Mart to selected customers. Their basic supply of literature occupied a large part of a building on Beech Street. He didn't have access to snuff movies, but he mentioned that they were floating around. (A so-called snuff movie was a photographic representation of women being killed. No one to my knowledge has ever verified their authenticity.)

According to John, the Kozy was owned by Chicky Kandaras, who also owned the Booknest and was associated with the Hub Book-Shop at 675 Washington Street. I never met Chicky and no one ever really knew who owned what in the Combat Zone. The real owners were buried under layers of subterfuge. The phonies on record with the Secretary of State's office were referred to as 'straws.' The Kozy was loosely managed by a guy named Barry Reisner, a piggish looking character, who I learned through extended surveillances drove a white Ford with Rhode Island registration MJ-306 and periodically delivered literature to the store.

I also learned that the Hub Book Shop did business with a Rhode Island company named Books In Storage. The FBI suspected this was an organized crime front, tied in with the Patriarca branch of the New England La Cosa Nostra. If this were true it would serve as the first piece of hard evidence that the pornography industry was controlled by organized crime.

Lynch congratulated me for what he said was a nice piece of work. I could see clearly that the key to getting along with this supervisor was higher level criminal investigations, especially ones that plugged in the Feds. He encouraged me to keep on digging.

I was in the store another night when I met a porno-photographer who introduced himself as Herbie. He was a thin, pockmark faced sleaze ball whom I took an instant dislike to. Actually, I don't think he had anything to do with the Kozy Bookshop - he was just checking to see if his work was being displayed. It was evident to me, almost as soon as I engaged him in conversation, that he was obsessed with money. He was on his way back to Framingham where, I would later learn, he kept an underground studio in his residence set up for pornographic photographic sessions.

We continued our conversation as we left the store and I persuaded him to have a cup of coffee on me at the Saxony restaurant near the intersection of Boylston and Stuart Streets. He was pretty open with me from the start for two reasons. Firstly, he mistakenly believed that I was in tight with the Kozy Bookshop because he had seen me talking to John (this was another trick that I would use more than once - act friendly with one person to gain the confidence of another) and secondly, because I laid the fabrication on him that I had just inherited a load of dough and was looking for some way to invest it. (That was the bait). I would like to open up a porn shop, I told him; it was the up and coming thing and if he would help me with his skills and connections (the ego pump) I'd be willing to take him in as a partner.

He actually started to drool at this point and I was getting sicker by the minute talking to him. He assured me that he was interested and we set up another meet about a week later. He showed up on time; I bought him another coffee and he told me that he had met with a guy and was setting the deal up. He was looking at a store close by and I could get into it for ten grand. He instructed me that I would have to give a piece of the action to the locals (mob connected guys) but that was the price of doing business, and I would have to purchase the books from certain people, but he could arrange for that. If I were still interested he would set up a meeting with Louie, a guy in the Intermission Lounge - but I had to act fast because someone else was looking at the deal.

At this point I begged off, angrily denouncing any deal with the mob. A look of disappointment swept across his face.

"Look, that's the way it is," he argued, hoping to change my mind. "That's the only way you can operate in this business - it's like that all over the country. I know, I've been doing this a long time. They're behind every fucking thing anyway. You don't believe in that school-boy First Amendment crap, do you?"

That was the last time I met with him - I had heard enough. My job as an Intelligence Officer was done. I had pretty much substantiated what had only been suspected - that organized crime controlled every facet of the smut trade in Boston and more than likely across the country, from the location of the business, the purchasing of the magazines - to the extortion payments off the top.

It would be up to the detectives or the feds to carry the investigation any further. For me to go any deeper would have forced me to play my final hand - and that would have ended my usefulness and my job. It wasn't worth the trade-off. I had an idea who Louie was anyway.

I walked Herbie to his car, parked near the Kozy. It was a cold night and he kept rubbing his hands together. He was driving an old Pontiac with the metallic stripe down the front and a dealer plate on the rear. I shook his hand - it felt dry and wrinkly. He gave me the willies.

"Take it easy, Herbie," I said, "and by the way, I do believe in the First Amendment." He looked at me like I had two heads and drove away. I remember thinking that it's too bad that scum like him and the rest are able to hide behind it.

I found my way back into the Kozy and spent the rest of the evening talking to John about the evolutionary development of the ordinary tapeworm. John said that at one time they had had legs.

On January 28, 1968, a political bomb exploded over America. Its explosive force reigned down principally upon the major cities but nothing escaped its fury. Almost every town, village and hamlet experienced some effect. It was the Tet Offensive, the single-most devastating enemy initiative ever launched throughout the Vietnam War, one calculated to both undermine the confidence of the American people that the war could be won and to erode the morale of the troops in the battlefield.

The Viet Cong moved across South Vietnam, first capturing the city of Hue, and worse, they penetrated the protected grounds of the U.S. Embassy in Saigon. It would take almost another month to drive them out. Although there were other great battles in addition to the Tet Offensive, such as

Hamburger Hill and Hanoi Hilton to name a couple, none compared with the depressing consequences of this action.

Before Tet the American people had been led to believe by the Government that the war was being won - that it was just a matter of time and the Viet Cong would be crushed. That's the way the Secretary of Defense, Robert McNamara, made it sound when he rolled out his charts and plugged in the numbers indicating that a U.S. victory was inevitable. And how could this trim, bespectacled intellect with the slicked back hair be wrong? He had given up a job as the President of Ford Motor Company the day after President Kennedy was elected for a position in public service. This was a man of intelligence, veracity and purpose. How could he have been so terribly mistaken? Or was he lying?

Tet accelerated the expanding anti-war sentiment to heightened levels. Demonstrations proliferated across the country. The Students for a Democratic Society, an increasingly revolutionary 'New Left' anti-war protest group on the nation's campuses reached 100,000 members and General Westmoreland's request for an increase of 206,000 men was denied, signaling the end to the escalation of the war. The Beats crossed over to Haight-Ashbury and Allen Ginsberg would be pushed to new levels of artistic and political dissidence.

The radio talk shows were buzzing for weeks with controversy. The 'Doves' asked how could this have happened. Wasn't the enemy almost beaten? How could such a massive operation have been pulled off without a single intelligence leak? Were the South Vietnamese in the countryside, who we were protecting, in league with the Communists in the North? Didn't this demonstrate that the Communists could strike at will? What business did we have intervening in a civil war ten thousand miles away against a small country that had successfully pushed back foreign invaders for two-thousand years? Would the U.S. be defeated in the end, just as the Chinese, Cambodians, French and Japanese had been?

The "Hawks" countered that the U.S. had to stay the fight. Tet was only one battle and the enemy had eventually been dislodged. Our failure to prosecute the war would result in a Communist take-over of Southeast Asia beginning with Cambodia and Laos and following through with a 'Domino Effect'. This would strengthen the hand of Communist China and give them access to the Mekong Delta region, potentially one of the world's great breadbaskets. And what about the men who had already died? A victory would give meaning to their sacrifice - a defeat would render their deaths meaningless.

I was taking all this in one evening, sitting stone cold bored on a routine surveillance, listening to the Steve Fredricks talk show on WMEX radio when he introduced a controversial guest named Tim Whitman, the founder of the newly formed Boston Draft Resistance, an anti-Vietnam protest group set up to counsel young men on methods of beating the draft.

I was appalled by Whitman's open appeal to gain support and recruit anti-draft counselors in the city of Boston. I wasn't sure if his group was violating any state or local laws, but I clearly considered this guy's efforts to be an attack against the national security.

Draft resistance was nothing new - the practice had been going on for some time and had been well publicized in the media. It ranged from opposition to military induction based on matters of conscience, such as in the case of Muhammad Ali (the former Cassius Clay), a convert to the Black Muslim Faith, who had refused on moral grounds to be inducted, to outright and defiant public draft card burnings for which some individuals had been arrested, tried, convicted and imprisoned. As it turned out Doctor Benjamin Spock, the famous baby doctor, would be sentenced to two years in July for counseling draft evaders though the sentence would be eventually overturned on appeal. That was in the script.

I had no trouble with a guy who was willing to accept punishment for his beliefs. Ali ended up losing his title over it and others went to jail. However, this talk show guest sounded like he was into teaching people deceptive tactics to avoid their military obligation. This violated everything I stood for. I knew guys over in Nam, including a few of my friends, who had shipped over in the Corps and ended up there. Jesser was no warrior but he did his time. Nobody enjoyed it, but duty called. This guy had me fuming!

Admittedly he had some balls, getting on the radio and risking exposure, but the ragbags and cowards that he would attract were something else. They were like the ten thousand Americans who had immigrated to Canada, self-centered and gutless. I wanted to get a peek at this guy. Perhaps I could get his registration number and give it to the Feds - "Yeah, Lynch would like that" I muttered to myself.

I broke off the surveillance and headed over to Broadway in the South End where the broadcasting studio of WMEX was located. I parked in a position that afforded me a full view of the front door. I was about a half a block away from Kerry's Village when who should appear but Sal Frachata himself, crossing the street. He spotted me right away, and more than likely believed that I was watching his place. He was wearing a scowl, probably still smarting over the police closure of the upstairs gay bar (probably the shortest-lived nightclub in the city's history) which I had learned he had named the Orchid Room. He couldn't have come up with that name on his own, I thought. He was too fucking dumb.

I put the car in first gear and quickly drove away in an effort to elude Sal. Just before I turned the corner I looked in my rear view mirror and caught him following me in his own vehicle. Trying to act nonchalant I parked on Tremont Street and walked over to the LaSalle Hotel hoping to shake him on foot. I sat at the bar and ordered a beer. Tanya Rienza was performing - she was bumping and grinding and pulling at her tassels getting them ready for the big spin. She was giving the boys a real good show.

About five minutes passed and Sal came in. He stood at the door a few moments, probably waiting for his eyesight to adjust to the darkened conditions. He spotted me; he walked over to where I was positioned at the bar and sat next to me. He never ordered a drink. He just waited - five minutes passed and then ten. I felt menacingly engulfed by his presence. I shot over a sideward glance and I could see that he was staring at me.

I ordered another beer - by this time my expense money had increased to fourteen dollars a week. Tanya was followed by Emerald, an emaciated looking female who was no wider than the pole she was attempting to wrap herself around - that's when I felt a light tap on my shoulder. It was Sal. I turned to my right and our eyes locked.

"Hey kid, how long have you been on the police department?" he asked.

I feigned indignation and shot back "Don't bother me, pal. I don't know who you are and I ain't gonna talk to you unless you're some kind of a cop or something."

He sarcastically retorted, "I'm not a cop, kid - you are." And he left the bar.

He had me good - my cover was blown. I reproached myself for having parked so close to his joint. Normally I wouldn't have done that. It was the guy on the radio whom I was interested in and not Kerrys Village, but Sal couldn't have been expected to know that. I was had, but it wouldn't be the first time. I'd had a couple of other near misses also. One evening I walked into the Dip and ran straight into a high-class, good-looking whore sitting at the bar. We recognized each other at the same instant. Ironically, Beverly had baby-sat for her children right about the time we were going out. Pam was a friend of Beverly's last boyfriend. I recall suspecting right away that she was a hustler from the weird hours she kept. I had met her once in her Emerson Place apartment just before I got on the police job. She let Beverly go the next day.

Another time I was hanging around the Big M when I overheard 'the Dog' involved in a conversation with the bartender about guns.

He commented, "The State Police are always checking my car so I stick it up my sleeve. One of these days he's going to come up to me, and I'll have it in a bag instead and I'll put two of them right behind his head."

That was just a lot of bluster meant for my benefit. He must have come to suspect that I was a cop and decided to test my reaction. They were catching up to me all right - I was heading toward being 'made.'

I left the LaSalle and headed back to my car. I was relieved to see that it was still in one piece. I flipped the radio back on and the talk show guest was getting ready to leave. He repeated his phone number a couple of times for anyone who wished to call him for further information: 547-9197.

I jotted the number down and that would become my ticket to the kaleidoscopic world of the radical Sixties. I felt dumb about having blown my cover - it was only a matter of time that the word would get around and I would be neutralized in the Zone. However, it wasn't going to make any difference because I was about to leave the 'pasties,' the 'G-strings and the 'behinds' - behind!

Twenty-Four

Jimmy Lynch gave me the green light on this Whitman guy the next morning.

"Give him a buzz, Phil, and see what he's up to."

I called the number a couple of times, finally connecting with Whitman in the early evening around dinnertime. He sounded friendly and we agreed to meet about eight o'clock.

He lived in a rundown apartment building at 138 River Street, about a mile from Mattapan Square. I rang the bell once and less than a minute later a guy who looked to be about twenty-six years old answered the door.

"You must be Mike Russo," he said.

"Yes," I responded, "and you must be the guy on the radio."

"I sure am. Come on upstairs Mike, and be careful where you step. The light is broken, like a lot of other things are around this place."

Whitman lived on the second floor with his pretty wife Freida, a conservatively dressed woman wearing dark slacks and a white nylon blouse. She had a feline quality about her, moving noiselessly around the apartment performing small chores, while hanging in close enough to hear our conversation.

I ended up wondering where she stood on the issue of draft resistance. I had a sneaking suspicion that she might not have been in sync with her

286

husband who, by the way, turned out to be a soft spoken and likable guy and whose opposition to the Vietnam War and commitment to what he was doing was unmistakable. He was good looking and, save for a passionate grasp of contemporary issues surrounding the war bordering on obsessive, he seemed pretty regular. He was the opposite of what I had expected - there was nothing of the disheveled hippie look that I had anticipated.

After a brief introduction, in which I explained that I worked at the Boston State Hospital as a psychiatric aide, we got down to business and I laid it right on him.

"I'm a former Marine having second thoughts about the war and getting involved with your group might be the answer, but I'm a little unsure at this point and would like to know more about what you are doing." He took the bait. An honorably discharged Marine would be a prize catch for his draft-dodging operation. I went on.

"On the other hand, it's hard to see myself doing this - it's so contrary to my conditioning." I paused, and he answered.

"We are a draft-resistance group that counsels people on the options open to them to avoid the draft. Those options include conscientious-objection status (which he explained needed to be religiously-based and well-documented), medical and psychiatric exceptions and lastly, emigration."

He commented that draft-card burning was a highly personal option that carried with it a five-year penalty. I had the impression that he was emphasizing the educational, rather than the inspirational orientation of the group. He underscored the enormous value of a military veteran being in a position to help people sort through their reservations, but he reiterated that the ultimate choice belonged to the prospective draftee. I suspected that he was deliberately downplaying the radical nature of the group to avoid turning me off.

We chatted a bit more, touching on the philosophical underpinnings of civil disobedience, starting with Thoreau, on through to Gandhi and more recently Martin Luther King. (He would never think I was a cop with the load I was laying on him - thanks to college, Jesser, Murphy and Memos.) When I was sufficiently convinced that he didn't suspect my intentions I asked him if he had any literature that I could look at which might help me to decide.

I was set back when he handed me a thick packet of information describing the mission and operation of the Boston Draft Resistance, including the names, addresses and phone numbers of its members. I was even more astonished when he explained that it was the only packet he had and asked would I mind returning it to him after I had looked it over?

"No problem - I'll return it tomorrow night." Meanwhile, I would make up a copy for the Department. Lynch would like that! I flashed him the victory sign and was getting ready to make my flight when I looked over and noticed Freida staring at me. She wore a troubled look on her face. I wondered if she were more put off by her husband's zealotry or my intrusion. Perhaps it was both, or something else altogether. When she realized I was looking back at her she smiled, a delicate tight little smile that left a lot to interpretation.

"I'll see you tomorrow." And with that I made it down the stairs and out the front door - I was anxious to be out of there. I had done my thing and I didn't want to push my luck.

"Not a bad guy," I remember thinking. "It's too bad he's so fucking misguided."

I clearly crossed a line that night. From the underbelly of the Combat Zone I ascended into the world of 'domestic intelligence gathering,' but I didn't give it much thought. I had no reservations about laying the con on Whitman. The country was being attacked from within and he was part of the assault forces. I felt like a Marine basking in the glow of a successful reconnaissance mission and I couldn't wait to deliver my paper trophy to Berkeley Street (Police Headquarters) the next morning.

When I handed him the packet, Lynch smiled, acknowledging his tacit approval. The following day he told me that he had slipped copies of the material to the Feds and they were highly interested. I was amazed at the impact that it had on them. After that, whenever I surfaced at Berkeley Street with information, a couple of FBI agents would be hanging around the office to see what I had. Peter advised me that anything I said or gave to the Bureau would end up in a report to Washington.

"That's FBI standard operating procedure," he commented. He had no problem with that - he just wanted me to be aware.

This marked the beginning of a seriously intensified inter-agency effort which included federal, state and local agencies in a cooperative network of sharing information while attempting to stay one step ahead of the cascading events that would rock the country over the next few years! The clearest manifestation of this union became evident to me one evening at an arranged dinner party at Liberty Mutual, a private insurance carrier neighboring Police Headquarters. There, police officers from Boston, the State Police and various campus police and security outfits dined with agents and their supervisors from the Federal Bureau of Investigation, Secret Service, the Bureau of Alcohol, Tobacco, and Firearms and Naval Intelligence. This impressive gathering had been put together by Jimmy Lynch, himself a graduate of the FBI Academy, and clearly the original catalyst for the modern day task force in Boston.

Back to my story. On the following night I returned the original packet to Whitman, thanked him for the information and explained that I needed more time to think about it. The Boston Draft Resistance was eventually absorbed by the New England Draft Resistance Movement and draft evaders ceased to be viewed as an aberration. I never attempted to contact Whitman again.

Unless additional information was needed, repeated contacts would have resulted in overexposure, which would have increased the risk of detection. I had learned early in the game to reveal only that amount of Mike's personality as necessity required to obtain the needed info. Staying believable also meant retaining as much of my real self as the situation permitted. (I wondered if they taught that in actor's school.)

Included among the literature given to me was a leaflet put out by the Student Mobilization Committee (SMC) with an address of 7 Brookline Street in Cambridge promoting a May 6 anti-war demonstration at the Boston Common. Although still a ways off, this bore looking into. That was the first time I crossed a municipal line to conduct an undercover police investigation of a proposed event intended to take place in Boston.

In a figurative sense, the Student Mobilization Committee would become a pinwheel from which I would be ejected into a topsy-turvy, stroboscopic world that I hardly could have imagined, and one foredoomed to forever alter the way I would perceive of Government in the future.

Cambridge is one of the larger cities in the Commonwealth of

Massachusetts. At that time its population exceeded one hundred thousand residents, not including the thirty thousand or so Harvard and MIT students who made up their campus populations. Cambridge is separated from Boston by the Charles River, whose headwaters are located twenty-eight miles upstream in the rural town of Hopkinton, which also serves as the starting point for the famous Boston Marathon. The city has undergone a number of changes through the years but to this day it has retained some of its old mansions and baroque characteristics.

The two main bridges connecting Boston and Cambridge are the Longfellow Bridge, an ornate structure named after the poet who wrote a poem about the Charles River in 1841, and the more heavily traveled Harvard-Mass. Avenue Bridge which is 364.4 'Smoots' and one ear long. (Smoot was the name of the MIT student whose frat brothers laid him out across the length of the bridge that many times to measure it.) The campuses were lighter in those days - more innocent and mischievous. Panty raids and booze parties were about as wild as it got. Harvard boys chased Radcliffe girls (and occasionally scored). MIT students gained notoriety for their electronic pranks and engineering gimmickry. They were memories now.

In 1968 the party was getting wild and Tet was the most unruly guest. This event would fully ignite the campuses and weld together the colleges on both sides of the river. At the time there were more than forty colleges in the Boston Metropolitan Area, a relatively confined and densely populated region. Boston University, Boston College and Northeastern combined would add another fifty thousand students to the mix. There was a growing awareness among the authorities that the city, because of its unique demographics, could potentially suffer serious damage from the ongoing civil unrest although this perception was more of an implicit understanding than a concrete and well thought out professional projection.

The Protest Movement was heading in the direction of a collision with organized society, especially its symbols 'the Deans, the Cops and the Feds.' The campuses were bursting at the seams with dissent. The abolishment of the ROTC (Reserve Officers Training Corp) and the barring of military recruiters on campus became the activists' rallying cries and the Student Mobilization Committee became the center of their off-campus network. I happened to walk into the place just about the same time that things were really rolling.

I felt strange at first, but the feeling soon passed after my initial encounter with a staff person, an impish guy with an oversized pair of glasses. He asked if I needed help. I told him that Whitman had given me the information on the demonstration and that I was interested in learning more about the group. He explained that the Student Mobilization Committee was a non-ideological umbrella group for anyone and everyone opposed to the war in Vietnam. "Or at least that's the way it should be," he added. I wasn't sure how he meant that.

Like Whitman, he was casually dressed and came off as a sober-minded dissident who clearly stood against U.S. military intervention in Southeast Asia. Once again this student's hard rock commitment waylaid me. It wouldn't always be this way - but my first two contacts with political radicals were disarming.

The office itself was fairly large and was conveniently situated near the corner of Brookline Street and Massachusetts Avenue, a large commercial thoroughfare piercing the center of Cambridge like an elongated shaft. Hand-made, multi-colored signs and an array of anti-war literature calling for the immediate withdrawal of U.S. forces from Southeast Asia were casually displayed all over the place. Their messages were clear: 'Stop the bombing; Stop the national genocide; End the draft; Direct action; Say No to war; Solidarity with Indochina; and Bring the troops home!'

I walked around the office emitting a steady stream of political patter, punctuated by subtle questions about the upcoming May 6 event, while simultaneously scanning the literature for anything else that I might pick up. Something similar to that would become my Modus Operandi (MO) in the days ahead.

I asked the staff kid what he meant by his "or at least that's the way it should be" remark. His answer was enlightening. He commented that the Student Mobilization Committee was becoming increasingly dominated by members of the Socialist Workers Party (SWP), which he described as an American Communist Group formed in the late twenties as a result of the Trotskyite split. I knew Trotsky was a big time Commie who had been assassinated by Stalin loyalists because of differences that separated them, but I had no idea of what those differences were, nor did I care. The significance of the staffer's comment, if it were true, was simply that a Communist group was usurping the influence of a so-called umbrella organization and using its widespread non-ideological appeal to generate influence far beyond its numbers. That would mean that Secretary of State Dean Rusk was not totally off when he accused the protest movement (or at least in this case, the Student Mobilization Committee, the main organizing body of anti-war sentiment in the U.S.) of being run by Communists.

"Except one thing," the staff kid said in response to that very question by me, "they are American Communists, not Russian or Chinese."

Nevertheless, he confided in me in an unexpected gush of truth, that he was sufficiently distressed about the ideological impact of this development to consider severing his ties with the group. He commented he didn't mind openly acknowledged Socialist Workers Party members,

"They have a right like everyone else to be involved with the SMC". It was the surreptitious ones who bothered him. "Some of them are even being paid by the Party," he said," and that's not above board." He lamented that he had reservations about "copping out" as it would only further the SWP takeover.

At that time I wasn't in a position to confirm what this guy was saying; that in effect the Student Mobilization Committee was being taken over by the Socialist Workers Party. Later I would be convinced that this was true - that was how the Socialist Workers Party operated!

I would come to learn that the Socialist Workers Party enjoyed an estimated eight hundred members nationally, with a local membership of less than one hundred party faithful. The Student Mobilization Committee was only one of the Socialist Workers Party's front groups - others included the Young Socialist Alliance, the National Peace Action Coalition, Female Liberation/Gay Liberation, the Fair Play for Cuba Committee and the Militant Labor Forum.

The Student Mobilization Committee was their greatest success. It would serve as a vehicle for the wild expansion of their influence by multiples of tens of thousands. It would evolve and change over time, eventually relocating and becoming known as the Greater Boston Peace Action Coalition, affiliated with the larger National Coalition for Peace and

Justice, but their tactics remained consistent - overt and covert penetration and control. They were the undercover ideologues of the protest movement. I came to learn a lot from them!

As far as the May 6 Peace Demonstration was concerned, he revealed that the only thing that had been set so far was the date. I thanked him and returned to the street, knowing implicitly that my fate was sealed. From that night on, and into the foreseeable future, I would be the Department's basic protest movement spy. That's how it worked out - the City was soon to be ravaged and the Department needed to plan. A little more than a week after Tet the order came down assigning me permanently to the Intelligence Division - it blew my mind!

In the beginning of my new assignment I moved between criminal work and the 'subversive-activity' side of the operation, but by the time spring rolled around events were spinning out of control. The campuses were jumping; the streets were electrified; Government was stymied; and the Boston Police Patrolmen's Association signed their first contract with the City.

I felt good about the union - it spelled the end to slave labor. The city would soon have to pay us for overtime and court - no more freebie crap (not that I would earn much as an undercover cop). Kevin White, the former Massachusetts State Secretary, had been elected Mayor and he handed the cops a good raise and a hell of a contract - ninety percent of it has remained in effect to this day.

The cops and the dissidents were on the march. It was inevitable that they would meet in the battlefield where they would be mutually ground down in a clash between tradition and change!

Senator Eugene McCarthy, a declared anti-war candidate, challenged Lyndon Johnson for the Presidential Nomination. Five thousand supporters, mostly students, inundated New Hampshire to prepare for the nation's first primary. On March 12, McCarthy, a lackluster politician from Minnesota, captured twenty of the normally conservative state's twenty-four electoral delegates and almost twenty-nine thousand primary votes. Public sentiment against the war was soaring.

A beleaguered Johnson, worn down by the struggle of having to choose between 'guns and butter,' beat McCarthy to the punch and soon after the

New Hampshire upset announced his retirement. In a speech that would stun the nation he said,

"I have ordered our aircraft to make no attack on Vietnam except in the area north of the demilitarized zone. Accordingly, I shall not seek, and I will not accept, the nomination of my party for any term as your President."

The President's announcement worked to pump up the level of anti-war activism to new heights. The dissenters had beaten down this jowly dude - they had him on the ropes and their victory served as inspiration to intensify their efforts and broaden the movement. Their hatred of Robert McNamara, Dean Rusk and National Security Advisor McGeorge Bundy intensified. Branding them as the contemporary equivalents of the 1950's EC Comic's monsters, the Crypt Keeper, the Vault Keeper and the Old Witch, they painted their distorted features in a satirical portrait of shocking torture, sadistic gore, debauchery and death.

A coalition of people rose up against the government. They moved across the political spectrum from classical liberals, who politely protested that 'War was not healthy for children or other living things,' to radicals who defiantly engaged in sit-ins, teach-ins, building takeovers and civil disobedience, on through to the more dangerous and revolutionary elements of the movement who saw 'imperialistic war' as a product of an economic system that placed profits before people, a corrupt system managed by the few against the many, a system that inevitably produced a plethora of social ills - poverty, racism, sexism, homophobia and pollution. Their solution called for a fundamental restructuring of the entire system - through the use of force and violence. These were the really desperate (and dangerous ones). One such group referred to itself as 'Ben Moria and the Up Against the Wall Motherfuckers.' They spelled **Amerika** with a **k**.

Any one of these groups could have been planning anything, from a simple demonstration to a bombing. Government, more specifically the police department, had no way of knowing. Good intelligence was essential to planning. Otherwise the police would fail in their protective role. How many cops would it take to control an unruly demonstration? Would traffic be effected? Would there be civil disobedience - blocking doorways, seizing public offices or damage to property? Who were the leaders? What were their track records? What was the issue and how much pulling power did it have? The police needed numbers, tactics, duration and other pertinent information in order to develop a logistical response.

It was essentially the job of the Intelligence Unit to develop this information and forecast possible outcomes of protest actions and other contingencies. These units were fairly new and anemic innovations in most big city police departments and the smaller ones lacked them entirely. Blake, without ever anticipating this social upheaval, had started the Boston operation back in 1961 and the time had arrived for the big test. In turn, the Boston Police Department Intelligence Unit would expand its ranks in a kind of knee-jerk reaction to the challenge.

New officers were added to the complement of personnel - about a half a dozen guys over time who would guide the city through the turbulence of the late Sixties and early Seventies. They were young and personable, college guys mostly, hip enough to be able to connect with the campuses. None of them would be working undercover, but it took a lot of different people to do the job. I amusingly pointed out to Mike Flammia that all but one of them was Irish.

"Are you surprised?," He asked.

"No, Mike," I answered, "but our jobs will be safe. As an absolute minimum, an intelligence operation requires an undercover cop and a clerk - one guy to report what's happening and the other guy to write it down." He got a chuckle out of that. He knew what I meant.

Actually they were pretty good guys and I formed a bond with them that would transcend the department. Pat Brady really cracked me up. A hefty five foot ten, he possessed an inquisitive mind, classical good looks and a sense of humor spiced with Irish wit and searing insight. He saw irony and humor in everything, from the bumbling bureaucracy in which we worked, to the self-serving nature and hypocrisy of the command staff.

Bobby Dapkas was another guy who understood the system. He came with Brady. Tall, slender and savvy, he possessed clean-cut good looks accentuated by a slightly flushed, bashful expression that subtracted years from his age. He had given up his Harley Davidson police motorcycle to become an intelligence cop but eventually the lure of the road (and a better shot at details and overtime) would get to him and he would return to his machine, but not until we had done our thing.

Jimmy Cox, a former Boston College High School starting Fullback, was a later addition. A tough, remarkably strong and resilient guy, he was slightly older than the others. He was also quieter and harder to know. I recall his good-natured prodding of me on my being naive.

"You really think the job is legitimate," he would joke.

I would routinely reply "The job is legitimate, Jimmy. It's some of the people on the job that aren't." Jimmy would just grin.

Detective John Schroeder, the brother of Barney Schroeder, my academy instructor, was our investigative/tech man. He was older and more subdued than the others. We enjoyed a family connection - my mother and aunt were girlhood friends of his wife Wanda and helped put on her wedding shower. (Years later I would learn that my mother made the shower bell from crepe paper that she had purchased at Dennison's.) The two families, the Schroeder's and the Volante's, came from the same Brighton/Allston neighborhood although I didn't know a lot of the particulars at the time. What I do remember about this slightly balding, moderately built man is that he had no shortage of guts. He would invariably position himself in the violent middle of chaotic street disruptions in order to perform his job and photograph the principals.

In addition, there was Arnold James, a big strapping black guy with large brown saucer eyes, the first student to graduate with his Bachelor's Degree in Law Enforcement from Northeastern and one of two in our unit who would be gunned down in the Seventies in armed robberies. He would live, but John Schroeder would die. Those events were blowing in the wind.

The most memorable character had yet to arrive - Gerry O'Rourke, a Mickey Spillane/Mike Hammer-type tough guy. I remember Gerry for a whole lot of things, not the least of which was his having assisted the statuesque Raquel Welch strap on a shoulder holster in preparation for a movie she was making - with measurements reaching 37-22-35, who could forget? - More of him later.

The unit was eventually headed by Deputy Superintendent John Donovan, a tall, slightly bug eyed, distinguished-looking man, formerly the lead investigator on the Boston Strangler case, a two year investigation of a serial killer named Albert DiSalvo who had confessed to murdering thirteen women but was found not guilty by reason of insanity. He was jailed for non-related offenses and the killings stopped.

I recall asking Donovan just how many of these homicides did he believe were attributable to DiSalvo? "Most of them" he answered, "because DiSalvo was able to recall incriminating details that only the killer would know but others were copy cats." (Translation - who knows?)

Donovan lacked the interest that Blake had in the Intelligence Unit. Once, when referring to Abbie Hoffman who, together with Jerry Rubin, had founded the 'Yippies' - an acronym for the 'Youth International Party' - in 1967 (a bizarre and sometimes violent group of freaks, one step devolved from hippies), Donovan asked, "Who is *she*, anyway?" Pat Brady and I shared a lot of laughs over that.

Donovan was a Civil Service Lieutenant, unlike Blake who was a Captain. Appointment to the Command Staff was, and still is, a managerial prerogative that fell outside Civil Service regulations. Politics almost always prevailed. He enjoyed the trappings of power, and that came equipped with a chauffeur. Straight from the sod, his driver, Matty Kilroe, was a kind and sensitive guy who took advantage of this opportunity to land an investigative position. Matty always wore a big smile and stayed on top of whatever was happening. Eventually he made detective.

Peter Ryan, who had been Blake's driver, moved over to the 'subversive activity' side of the unit where he functioned as an unofficial mini-boss because of his longevity, brazenness and good counsel.

There were a couple others who would eventually be assigned to the unit but these were the originals. I didn't meet them all at once, nor did they arrive on the same day. It wasn't like the Intelligence Unit had undergone a planned reorganization in preparation for the massive upheaval that the city was already beginning to experience, rather they were grudgingly assigned to the unit over a relatively brief period of time, after the need for them was clearly established.

For the next several weeks I became totally immersed in my job. I grew a beard and gradually took on the look of the streets. This was the 'now generation.' Initially I saw them as an undisciplined generation of whiney brats who demanded instantaneous gratification; otherwise they would pout and stamp their feet and possibly fuck up the city in the process. I viewed the 'peace-niks' as a non-violent group of self-absorbed individuals whose motivation grew more out of a survival instinct than an intellectual process. However, I was still young enough to make the moves and talk the talk. I was able to connect to what was happening. Movement paranoia was becoming pronounced. The word went out to distrust anyone over thirty. I had more time on that note - I had just turned twenty-nine.

It didn't take long to get the routine down. There were literally hundreds of places where I could drop in and pick up literature. The whole thrust of the protest movement was to attract as many people as possible to the cause. The main informational distribution points in Cambridge were: Lobby 7 in MIT's William Barton Rogers Building on Massachusetts Avenue - a massive cement structure fronting eight massive Corinthian Columns (I have always viewed this place as a concrete symbol of the power of education - I was so impressed with the building as a kid that I hooked school to wander through its many lobbies); the Julius Adams Stratton Building across the street (this was the MIT Student Center and the location of many protest actions); the numerous buildings of Harvard University; the National Headquarters of the Students for a Democratic Society - 639 Mass. Avenue (the Tab Building); University Action Group at 60 Fairmount Street; Female Liberation at 552 Mass. Avenue.; Center for United Labor Action at 639 Mass. Avenue. and of course, the Student Mobilization Committee and several other smaller offices on the same block and across the intersection on Prospect Street. The basic energy source from which the protest movement gained its momentous vitality flowed from the Central Square area - especially Brookline Street.

The main distribution points on the Boston side included Boston University's George Sherman Union, a student center located on Commonwealth Avenue; Northeastern University's Ell Student Center; The Young Socialist Alliance at 655 Atlantic Avenue.; Free University at 68 St. Steven Street; and a slew of smaller offices around Huntington Avenue and the Washington/Green Street area in Jamaica Plain.

Offices were always springing up, closing down and relocating. I read numerous underground publications to aid me in keeping track of the action. There was Boston's own *Avatar*; the Student Mobilization Committee's *Student Mobilizer*; the *Old Mole*, a Cambridge by-weekly and the *New Left*

Notes, the official publication of the Students for a Democratic Society. There was even a *Peoples Yellow Pages* containing hundreds of informational listings including addresses and phone numbers of activist, informational, political and radical groups such as draft counseling organizations, birth control operations, Female Lib and Gay/Lesbian associations, Black, Indian and Puerto Rican Nationalist groups and various sanctuaries and cooperatives.

The streams of informational pools were endless. They provided me with a spot to drop my hook, a place to begin, so to speak. However, how I fished the waters or the way in which I developed my catch was another matter. Picking up a handout promoting a demonstration was just the beginning. I usually followed that up by a phone call or a personal visit - eye-to-eye contact was important. Eventually I was able to pick up the telephone and get a run down on the proposed action, though predicting the level of support and actual behavior would take more time.

In the beginning I skittered the periphery of the movement. I passed myself off as a quasi-academic attending University College, Northeastern University's part-time program for adult education. I, or Mike Russo at this point, retained the cover story that I was also a Psychiatric Aide at the Boston State Hospital and a union organizer, a passionate one at that, in the State Hospital Employee's Association. The union part was the delicious little tidbit of bait that I offered in exchange for information.

One of the great thrusts of the peace movement was to enlist the support of as many unions as possible. I came across as a fence-sitter, willing to lend the support of fellow union members to various actions but as a prerequisite to any decision I would goad them that I needed to know as much as possible about the action and the reasons for it. I didn't mind getting busted, of course, I'd been there before. But if they were planning on civil disobedience or if there were a good chance of disruption, for example, trashing a building, I wanted to have an idea so I could advise other union members of this possibility, better enabling them to reach a more informed decision.

This student/teacher con was another highly effective technique for obtaining information. Movement organizers tended to be bright. They functioned in a world of ideas and many of them were proselytizers by nature - they were unable to resist the opportunity of making another convert.

I was astonished at how well it worked. They'd really spill their guts out to get a crack at real union support, especially the Progressive Labor Party members who sported hand-made signs portraying a red fist superimposed over one of their common slogans declaring, 'When students strike there is no school, when workers strike there is no war!' It wasn't hard to figure out whose support they valued more, nor was it hard to figure out that they were bad news!

The Progressive Labor Party was the most radical and dangerous component of the Students for a Democratic Society. Originally similar to the Socialist Workers Party, they enjoyed a national membership of about eight hundred people and a local following of about one hundred hard-core soldiers. Also, like the Socialist Workers Party, they infiltrated and operated behind front groups such as the Worker Student Alliance, the University Action Group and the Student Committee for Travel to Cuba. In terms of violent propensity, however, the Progressive Labor Party beat the Socialist Worker's Party hands down.

Originally the Stalinist faction of the American Communist Party, the Progressive Labor Party had evolved into an independent Maoist, pro-Castro operation, which had become increasingly frustrated with the slow pace of the revolution. Though they both were Marxist-Leninists, upholding the eventual triumph of the Proletariat (the working class) over the Bourgeoisie (the ruling class), their timetable for action was disparate. The Socialist Workers Party believed that the ultimate revolution was still a way off. The Progressive Labor Party believed that it was imminent!

The Socialist Workers Party believed it was their role to gradually and persuasively educate the working class to bring about the revolution, while the Progressive Labor Party believed that the time was ripe. The Socialist Workers believed they should work with others, such as gay and lesbian groups, in a common front against the establishment, while Progressive Labor held these groups in disdain. The Progressive Labor Party was the more doctrinaire, militant and volatile of the two. I regarded the Socialist Workers as the tea-totaling propagandists of the movement and the Progressive Labor Party as its out-distanced guerrillas. I learned early on to distinguish between the two.

A story coming out of the New York City Police Department reported that the Progressive Labor Party had staged a 'chicks-up-front demonstration.' They had intentionally pushed women to the front of the crowd, allowing them to be hurt by stampeding police horses. The demonstrators had deliberately spiked the backs of protest signs with protruding nails to jump-start the horses in order to film the chaotic results for propaganda purposes in a trumped up demonstration of police brutality.

The Progressive Labor Party was trouble and my antennae went up whenever I suspected they were involved with any kind of action, like the night I learned that they intended to trash a Back Bay computer store. I didn't have much time, nor did I know the reason why this store was targeted. Nevertheless I was able to slip away from the marching group long enough to drop a dime in a public telephone and notify night operations of their intentions. Officers of the Tactical Patrol Force arrived on the scene seconds after the first rock had been thrown and the group scattered. The chase was on and a couple of the participants were arrested for disorderly conduct.

It would have been a lot worse if the police had failed to arrive at all. I made a lot of those crisis-type, public telephone calls before it was over. Jimmy Lynch was right when he advised that, "a good investigator should always carry a pocket full of dimes." These small coins spared the city a lot of damage back in those days. Eventually I was humorously referred to as the 'Night Deputy' because of my unofficial power to have the night operations Duty Supervisor call out the troops, on short notice if necessary. However, it would be a long while before I had earned that distinction, and it only came after the reliability of my information had been repeatedly verified.

Many aspects of my situation were still no different from when I had worked in the vice end of the operation. My longevity in the unit was still directly correlated with the timeliness and accuracy of my reports. The bosses were still looking for more than mere rumors, scuttlebutt and horse shit - nothing had changed in that regard.

Over time I became painfully aware of the myriad dissimilarities among peace activists. I came to view the simple act of protest as a harmless exercise of basic Constitutional rights and nothing more. It was a painful awareness because it carried with it an accompanying obligation that somehow I must educate the brass that distinctions among movement elements had to be made, rather than allowing everyone to be thrown into the same mix.

The police, for the most part, reflected a particularly hard view of conservative America which held that protest against the war was largely the consequences of self-indulgence, cowardice and ignorance. These perceptions shared a common consensus throughout the ranks. To a large degree, this attitude was steeped with class bias - most cops, like me, were products of the working class which didn't permit us much time for either social reflection or military avoidance. We had no choice - get drafted or join up. There were no deferments for guys in my neighborhood. The 'Boys from Somerville' were the first ones they grabbed. Following discharge it was 'get-a-job time, keep your mouth shut and take advantage of whatever incremental opportunities the work place made available'.

The behavior of these youthful college protesters flew in the face of those notions. Many of them were the products of wealth (at least from many cop's point of view) and had no idea what deprivation or work was all about. They didn't have to defer gratification to obtain social standing because they were already there! (I wondered what Doctor Coggan would have said about that.)

I felt the same way in the beginning, but like I said, I had to make some uneasy adjustments over time. At some point I arrived at the conviction that my role as an undercover operative in the peace/protest movement required an educational as well as an informational component. I was just a Patrolman, but I was the only guy on the department who was living the action out on the street where it was happening.

Over the next few years I would experience the radical Sixties from a unique perspective. One that permitted me to view unfolding events from all parts of the movement, from its planning levels on through to enactment, for several hours a day, in all of its manifestations, irreconcilabilities and ironies - before the television media or print journalists had time to feed bites of it to the general public, government officials, political pundits and future historians. In short, I saw it the way it came down, before anyone else could screw up the story. I was at ground zero and the shock waves from Tet were reverberating, except this wasn't the Combat Zone - it was America!

Twenty-Five

On Thursday, April 5, 1968, the Reverend Doctor Martin Luther King was felled by a sniper's bullet in Memphis as he stood on a second floor balcony talking to supporters. Riots, looting and fires ripped through many of the major cities across the country. The war cry, "Burn Baby, Burn!" was resurrected and echoed far into the night. Washington, D.C. was placed under martial law!

Boston was not spared. The tumult started in Roxbury and spread up and down Blue Hill Avenue and Washington Street, between Mass. Avenue and Dudley. About thirty small businesses were set ablaze. Firefighters were pelted with rocks as they struggled to extinguish the fires. Absent police protection - they simply gave up - allowing the stores to burn, opting instead for a strategy of containment. Fully armed black business owners set up shop outside their establishments to protect their property! Homemade signs sprung up in store windows advertising that the businesses were black-owned.

The city was no more prepared for this riot than for the one before. I was called off my normal assignment and given sentry duty under the El (elevated railway trains) directly across from Big Jim's Shanty on Washington Street (the South End bookie joint, where the big black guy had toyed with the idea of dropping me on my head). There I stood, casually dressed and unarmed, clutching an ax handle for protection and in full view of the customers exiting the front door. I felt completely misplaced, exposed and stupid.

The disruptions continued on a smaller scale for several more days. By the time the violence was over Roxbury would have lost the remaining few white merchants who had salted the neighborhood.

The firebrands wouldn't miss them. "They're blood sucking Jews," they charged, adding "it's better that they're gone." That wasn't how a lot of the older residents felt, especially those who didn't have access to a car to go shopping.

Anti-Semitism was on the rise in black neighborhoods! Jewish merchants and landlords were vilified as being 'price gougers' and 'slum lords.' It was fueled by the rising tide of Black Nationalism that was storming the nation. Stokely Carmichael was a leading proponent of this philosophy of black self-determination and pride. He coined the words 'Black Power' in a raging denunciation of the shotgun wounding of James Meredith in 1966 on a Mississippi highway. Meredith, a fiercely individualistic and eccentric ideologue into his old age, was the first black who cracked the color code of Ole Mississippi U.

Sometime after Lynch took over the Intelligence Unit I had an opportunity to hear Carmichael speak. Actually, I didn't have much choice; an assignment landed me in Franklin Park on a Sunday afternoon in front of the main loudspeaker, adjoined to the podium from which the speaker elaborated on the principles of 'Black Power.'

I was really nervous, being one of the few white guys in the crowd, and the only one who was wearing a wire. The brass panicked when they learned that Carmichael would be visiting the city. They hung a tail on him and when they learned that he was scheduled to make a public speech on the Roxbury side of Franklin Park they ordered Lynch to outfit me with a recording device to tape what he said.

I wasn't thrilled with the assignment, but I didn't have much choice. I suspected it might have been the Commissioner himself who had been behind the order. He was an ex-FBI Agent and that was right up his alley. I rejected the first two devices the tech guy strapped on me because of their bulk. I accepted the third, a small microphone attached to a ballpoint pen.

Not wanting to blow the assignment, I maneuvered my way through the sea of black faces surrounding the outside staging and positioned myself directly in front of the main speaker. Stokely was tall, slender and light-skinned. He was kind of a jaunty looking guy and could have been easily mistaken for a jock. Save for the depiction of a black panther on his sweatshirt, he didn't appear in the least bit menacing (as he was sometimes portrayed in the media). He engaged in some light-hearted chatter with a couple of people in the crowd just before he stepped up to the microphone. Once he began to speak the levity around him melted away exposing the submerged pain of an angry black intellect. Like many of the dissident leaders of his time, Carmichael was an articulate, brilliant and charismatic speaker.

In a speech spliced with eloquent rhetoric and piercing wit, he called for blacks to unite and oppose the forces of racist oppression - to develop pride in who they were and foster the ties that bound them. He cried out for black control of black money, businesses and neighborhoods. Most of all, he demanded that blacks should take control of their own lives and not rely on whites to define them.

The thought occurred to me that he wasn't saying anything a whole lot different than more moderate blacks were saying. That was the 1967 Christmas message of 'Kwanza,' a uniquely Black-American creation stressing seven principles reinforcing black pride. That had never created a stir. Perhaps, I reasoned, it wasn't so much the message as the messenger. Stokely Carmichael bathed his message in revolutionary oratory - and that made the powers nervous!

If I hadn't been so shaky about the prospect of getting made and ending up being buried somewhere in Franklin Park I would have enjoyed his speech even more than I did, but as it was, I couldn't wait to get out of there while I was still in one piece. This pervasive fear of exposure is something that an undercover cop has to learn to live with.

I was relieved once the speech was over and I was on my way back to the office. I had successfully completed my mission and was anxious to deliver the recording to my superiors. I parked about a block away from headquarters and headed down Columbus Avenue, being careful to ensure that I wasn't being tailed by one of Carmichael's security people (they looked like goons to me), or some wise-guy who had spotted me in the street. When

I finally arrived at the office several cops were standing around waiting. Most of them were detectives, but there were others whom I didn't know. Lynch beckoned me into the huge walk-in safe located behind the left wall. That's where the cops assigned to the unit went to discuss private business when they didn't want to be overheard, or to view pornographic movies or literature for their criminal content or whatever.

The tech guy removed the tape recorder from under my shirt and jacket and carefully placed the cassette into a separate device and pushed the play button. Jimmy Lynch and a couple of the others bent over the machine to listen. After more than thirty seconds had passed and nothing came out they tried once again with the same depressing results. Apparently the jack connecting the microphone to the tape recorder failed to make a good connection; hence the machine had never recorded a single word.

The cops remained silent in their disappointment. I was embarrassed, but after I thought about it I realized that it wasn't my fault. They should have checked me out before I left to determine if the tape recorder was in good working order. Had they done that they would have learned that the jack had failed to make a tight connection with the receptacle. The funny thing about it was that the radio guy had checked out the first two devices but didn't follow through on the third in the interest of time. I ended up making out a written report and learning a good lesson - that nothing should be left to chance!

The country was being torn by the question of race as well as war. It was hard sometimes to distinguish between the two because the adherents shared the same beliefs, mainly that it was the so-called 'establishment' that was at fault! The establishment was a sort of amorphous conglomeration of government, businesses, economics, laws, values, mores and traditions.

Cops were regarded as the brutal protectors of the corrupt mix and were often referred to as 'pigs' in an adaptation of George Orwell's novel *Animal Farm*, in which a successful revolution spear-headed by pigs was waged by farm animals against their human masters. Once victory had been achieved the animals settled down to enjoy the benefits of an egalitarian society - in which the pigs regarded themselves as a little more equal than the other animals. Get the point?

The Black Panther Party was the most poignant example of cop loathing in the country. A black power revolutionary group based on the principles of Marxist-Leninism, they featured themselves as protectors of the black community in its efforts to achieve freedom and eliminate police brutality. In Boston they were located at 123 Winthrop Street in Roxbury, an old wooden residence that doubled as an armed barricade. They consisted of about a dozen hard-core members. Their leader was a guy named Bobby Pruit, a six foot two inch, 210 pound thug who, like many of the others, possessed a criminal record. Their national headquarters was in Oakland, California and they were formed along the lines of a government in exile.

A much later published Black Panther newspaper article began with these words: "The only way to get peace is to withdraw oppressive forces right here in Babylon," and continued "Marxist-Leninism is a philosophy for any people moving against the oppressive power structure." David Hilliard, the Chief of Staff of the Black Panther Party, summed it up like this "Fuck the motherfucking man. We will kill Richard Nixon. We will kill any motherfucker that stands in the way of freedom." Bobby Seale was Party Chairman and Huey P. Newton was its Minister of Defense.

They wore green berets and worked to endear themselves to the black community by participating in breakfast programs for kids and voter-registration drives. Like any well-entrenched gangster group they believed that good works were the key to enlisting community support. The La Cosa Nostra had perfected the method.

The cops were onto the Black Panthers ever since a police officer was killed in Oakland in 1967 in a shoot-out which left Huey Newton wounded. Newton was arrested, giving rise to the 'Free Huey' movement. Newton eventually beat the rap, but that only made things worse. The cops regarded the Panthers as treacherous. Before a year would pass almost two dozen party members would face charges of conspiracy to blow up property, murder and kill cops.

The Panthers were not unwilling to work with whites on specific issues, unlike Carmichael and other black nationalists, like H. Rap Brown, who argued that Blacks should go it alone. The Panthers supported the 1967 California-based white-leftist Peace and Freedom Party nomination of black comedian,-turned-activist, Dick Gregory for President. Their first choice, Eldridge Cleaver, was too young. Cleaver ended up in a shoot-out with the cops and skipped town. He left the country and was banned from the party after falling out of favor.

The Boston faction of the Black Panther Party would house, on one overnight occasion, Bernadette Devlin, a revolutionary member of the Irish Republican Army who was in the U.S. on a speaking tour. She was photographed going into the front door of Panther headquarters by Jackie Spencer, a young civilian investigator for Gordon Hall, a part-time journalist and lecturer on the subject of political extremism.

Spencer and I, along with Peter Flynn who also worked for Gordon, would work closely together in the future. I can't recall how I met them, nor under what conditions, but they were two really sharp guys whom I came to trust implicitly. Cops don't generally confide in civilians, but these guys added to the efficiency of the intelligence operation. Eventually they both became cops anyway, Spencer in Boston and Flynn in nearby Quincy.

The enmity between the cops and the Panthers ran deep. It was reinforced at all levels by the nation's Police Chiefs, right up to J. Edgar Hoover - Director of the Federal Bureau of Investigation, who referred to the Panthers as "the greatest threat in the history of America". In Boston, as in other cities, the Panthers reported hostile police gunfire and suspicious fires at several of their properties, and while I never doubted that a renegade cop might have let go a few rounds under the cover of nightfall, nothing was ever proven.

The cops and the Panthers shot it out all over the country. Before the final curtain came down twenty-eight Panthers and fourteen police officers would have died in exchanges of gunfire! The Panthers were the cannon fodder of the Black Nationalist movement: Stokely Carmichael, H. Rap Brown, J. Edgar Hoover and the rest of the chorus hummed the tune - the battle went on, and the bodies fell.

We escaped the worst of it in Boston, due in part to the ultimate good sense of a lone Sergeant who made a decision that was later proven to be wise, but at the time was highly unpopular with the troops. Time has dulled my memory as to exactly when it happened but the story itself has remained embedded in my mind.

The local headquarters of the Black Panther Party was located at 123 Winthrop Street in Roxbury, the city's largest black neighborhood. The

Department was well aware of the site and the Intelligence Unit possessed floor plans of the interior of the house. Information supplied by informants also revealed that the two-story wooden structure contained a formidable supply of guns and ammunition. At that time it was legal to possess rifles and handguns on the premises without the benefit of a Firearm Identification Card or any kind of screening process. Every window in the house was barricaded half way up with sandbags that were clearly discernible from the outside. The message was clear 'Fuck with us at your own peril!'

Every cop on District 9 was well aware of the address. Most of the cops in the surrounding districts also knew, that is, all except for two rookies assigned to the adjacent District 10 who were sent over to District 9 to cover a one-night shortage. (That's always the way.)

The house had been rented to the Panthers by a white Doctor who also owned a nearby pharmacy. The Doctor had lived in the house at one time but long since had moved to a plush suburb. However, he had never notified the police of his change of address, so when his pharmacy was broken into it was simply routine for the cops to notify him of the intrusion at his last known address.

The two cops, having never worked this district before, and being rookies to boot, dutifully checked out the 'owner of record' on the old yellowed address cards that were kept behind the front desk and came up with the Winthrop Street location. The hour was late so when a phone call failed to raise the owner they decided to pay him a visit - and that's when the shit hit the fan!

The bell rang and an occupant of the house looked out of the second floor window and saw the cops at the door. He must have thought it was all over, that the cops had come to make a bust. He alerted the others and panic spread through the house like wildfire!

This was the day they knew would come and for which they were well prepared. The revolution had begun! Several armed Panthers descended the stairs - others manned their positions behind the windows.

In a few moments the front door opened and the two rookies felt the terror of veteran cops staring down the barrels of two fully loaded, double-barreled shotguns.

"What do you want, motherfuckers?" one of the gunmen shouted.

The cops never bothered to answer. They leaped away from the line of fire and retreated for the cover of their cruisers where they called over the radio for help!

The way I heard it, within moments every available cop from Districts 9 and 10 had responded to the scene. Two fellow officers had been assaulted by mean of firearms (an on-sight arrestable offense) by Black Panthers with whom they knew a confrontation was inevitable. They, the Panthers, must not be allowed to get away with this! The cops were chomping at the bit to avenge the incident.

By the time the Patrol Supervisor, a short white Sergeant, arrived on the scene mass mayhem was about to take place. He was apprised of the incident and quickly surveyed the situation. Painfully aware of the movement of armed profiles silhouetted behind the moon-struck windows, he was pitifully conscious that any sort of aggressive action by the police would be met with a barrage of Panther gunfire and death.

I don't know all that he was thinking but the next thing he did was to have the radio dispatcher order the officers, who by this time were all over Winthrop Street, to get back in their cruisers and leave the scene. It was a highly unpopular decision at the time and for a long while it was hailed as an act of cowardice by the officers.

I never met the Sergeant face-to-face, but several years later, when I was being interviewed by an assessment board for promotion to the rank of Sergeant, I was asked,

"What was the most courageous command decision made by a Patrol Supervisor of which you are aware?"

I told them this story. That was the closest it came to a bloody battle between the Boston Police and the Black Panther Party in the city of Boston.

Though I have never been an uncritical fan of command-level decision making within the department, it should be pointed out that the enlightened Boston Police policy of not singling out the Panthers for disparate enforcement action yielded positive results. The policy of selective enforcement, practiced in other cities, which directed enforcement action against the Panthers for trivial offensives such as spitting on the sidewalk or minor motor vehicle equipment failure, etc. would have worked to make martyrs out of them in the black community, which naturally may have resulted in a show of visceral support. Given the revolutionary mind-set of the group, this could well have been misconstrued for ideological support of their revolutionary aims. In short, even treatment by the police had denied the Black Panther Party victimization status in Boston, thereby lessening the possibility of open rebellion. Those were Spencer's later on comments on the subject - and I agreed.

The race thing was really cooking. Blacks and whites were clearly more divided than ever and King's untimely death accentuated the differences between them even more. Most of the cops, at least the white cops and especially the FBI, disliked King anyway. In a classic example of a logical fallacy (putting the cart before the horse) they blamed King for the racial unrest that seemed to follow him wherever he went. They never took into consideration that the cities he visited were already at the verge of exploding. It's no different than blaming traffic cops for vehicular congestion because they are often present when the condition occurs, and failing to realize that is why they are there to begin with, to remedy the problem.

And there were the persistent rumors coming straight out of Washington that J. Edgar Hoover had King on tape hustling prostitutes and working with members of the American Communist Party. Although nothing was ever really proven about any of this at the time, it was enough to tarnish King's image among lawmen and refute his program of non-violent direct action. Don't forget these were men of the Fifties, myself included, and that stuff didn't go.

Four years on the job had made its mark. I had learned to accept very little at face value. I wasn't sure about anything anymore, much less where King might have been coming from. The air was filled with dissension - the streets were becoming more dangerous and the country seemed to be coming apart at the seams. Martin Luther King had been moving around the land in the midst of all this chaos, denouncing the war and calling for white America to change its course - and now he was dead!

Perhaps I wasn't always sure where he was dealing from - for a long time I had trouble separating the man from the myth, but I innately knew that he was a decent man who stood towers beyond the other guys at the table. It wouldn't get any easier without him. I didn't need the Kerner Commission to tell me that 'Our nation is moving toward two societies, one black, one white - separate and unequal.' That was obvious.

The day following the King assassination members of the Black Panthers joined with white leftists and staged a demonstration outside of Police Headquarters. They were protesting police brutality and some of the arrests that were made on the previous night. In spite of it being an impromptu action, about a couple of hundred protesters showed up. The cops took a lot of pictures and the rally broke up without any incidents.

The May 6 demonstration at the Boston Common attracted a few thousand anti-war demonstrators. It was the biggest action to date on the site. I mixed in with the protesters and listened to the speeches - the war was denounced in a stream of continual damnation. The participants sang, chanted and waved their fists in defiance of an American Flag that some kid was unceremoniously running around the field.

It pissed me off and I would have liked to kick the kid's ass, but there was nothing I could do about it. I busied myself picking up anti-war literature, especially the sort that promoted future actions. Most of the larger protests were geared for spring and fall to take advantage of the weather and the increased campus activity.

There was one scheduled for the next day at the John F Kennedy Building in Government Center. I notified Jimmy Lynch over the phone and he in turn alerted the FBI and Secret Service. This presented another opportunity for the guys in my unit to work together with other agencies and to coordinate the police action with the district cops. The other Intelligence Officers did their thing with the cameras and radios while I moved around the crowd sponging up bits and pieces of information associated with future activities, meetings, discussions and actions. This was also an opportunity to learn the makeup of the various groups and individuals who were participating. Sometimes the other agencies had their own guys infiltrating the crowd. In the beginning I wasn't sure who they were. Eventually I got pretty good at making them - it wasn't hard, especially the ones who wore 'clip-on' earrings.

Things were happening on the home front also. Before the month was out I took advantage of newly enacted State legislation that allowed police officers to reside within a ten-mile limit of the city and purchased a duplex house in a Boston suburb named Woburn. We had been saving for the down payment right along and I was interested in purchasing rental property. I had grown up in a couple of multi-family houses and I believed that that was the way to go. The house, which was only eight years old, was being listed for $29,990.00 by a Woburn broker who advertised that, after collecting the rent it would cost the owner only eighty dollars a month to pay the mortgage. It was a good deal, especially since it was costing me thirty bucks more a month to rent.

The town of Woburn was ideally located halfway between Beverly's hometown of Andover, where her family still lived, and my aunt's house in Somerville. Like most people of my generation, I was attracted by the lure of the suburbs. Although the construction of Route 93 would eventually cause Woburn to lose its small town atmosphere and become a city it was a good compromise at the time. I slid in just under the wire with a V.A. backed, ten-percent down payment and the house was ours.

I recall once, just before we moved in, sitting alone on the second floor and rubbing my hand across its newly polished hardwood surface and feeling wonderfully ecstatic about this new possession. Not bad for a Somerville kid! I felt confident that I was coming up in the world. Beverly seemed to take it in stride. In spite of what she said to the contrary, I wasn't sure if she really liked the house. I wondered if perhaps it wasn't rural enough for her.

I didn't really expect her to jump for joy, especially since she had just learned that her only brother was expected to die from an untreatable malignant tumor in his stomach. It was "as big as a grapefruit," the Doctor said, and he was unable to remove it. We were still living in Roslindale when he was diagnosed.

Beverly was devastated. A couple of weeks after we learned the distressing news I returned from work one night to learn that Beverly, in a bout with depression, had painted the living room a solid blue - the walls, the ceiling, the radiator - even the border. In a radical departure from her normally meticulous nature she had even painted over the wallpaper. I became more sensitive to her behavior after that, fearing that she could be lapsing into a mental breakdown, but apparently this painting incident was an isolated stress reaction that didn't impair her ability to function or to take care of Kimberly. I also worried about what the landlord's reaction would be.

I felt pretty broken up myself. Kenny was a great guy and he had hardly turned thirty. He was tall and thin and shared Beverly's blonde hair and good looks. As sick as he was he managed to drop a lawn mower off at our new house for our front lawn and removed a broken overhead branch from of an old oak tree in the yard.

"It's dangerous," he said. "It's got to go." He performed these chores early in the morning, making a special trip to my new house before I rolled out of bed and could stop him. He eventually died and Beverly was never quite the same.

On June 5, exactly two months after the King assassination, Robert Kennedy was murdered - shot in the head by a fanatical Jordanian shortly after emerging victorious in the California Democratic Presidential Primary!

None of this went well for the nation. Kennedy's assassination was regarded by many as another senseless act of violence against a man of peace. His violent death marked the end of the Great Society, and more specifically, classical liberalism in America.

It also had a pretty chilling effect on Eddie Jesser, who after his short flirtation with 'enlightened conservatism,' had fully reverted back to his Boston-Irish democratic roots. And who, by the way, had graduated college, married Dell and was getting ready to attend Graduate School at Michigan State on a full scholarship, including a twelve-thousand-dollar fellowship. That was more than double my annual salary and typical of what I would come to understand as the leitmotif of Ed Jesser, his central tendency so to speak - minimum input, maximum yield. He had also been accepted into Yale Law School, but had chosen not to attend because he disliked lawyers.

Jesser's concentration of courses would be in public relations and journalism. He was so embittered by Kennedy's death that he lapsed into political exile for the next three years, refusing to work on anything that touched of politics - an astounding reaction for a political junkie like Ed. It was as though the assassination of this man from Massachusetts, the brother of a slain President, had invoked nightmarish images of some ghoulish memory. During the next few years we exchanged letters and post cards and I saw him occasionally on return visits, but for the most part he was off the radar screen.

Kevin Murphy was still around. By this time he had been honorably discharged from the Army where he had served a two-year stint as a Lieutenant in the Signal Corps. He had graduated law school and had married a delicately crafted, pretty art teacher from Connecticut and was living and practicing law in Bedford, Massachusetts. I hadn't seen him for a while.

Before the summer was over there would be another inflammatory event played out in the national arena. It happened in Chicago on August 28 at the scene of the Democratic National Convention. The cops were sucked into a major street battle with anti-war protesters which ultimately provided months of ugly media footage of violent street scenes portraying 'cops gone wild,' chasing and beating demonstrators in one cluster-fuck of an operation.

It was admittedly an undisciplined overreaction on the part of the police who were ill-prepared to handle the several thousand unruly demonstrators who had flocked to Chicago from all over the country to protest the nomination of Vice President Hubert Humphrey, who had been selected to head the ticket, and whom the protesters considered to be an extension of Johnson's abominable war policies.

Their overreaction, however, did not stem from a lack of information. For weeks before the event the Intelligence Unit of the Chicago Police Department, referred to by anti-war dissidents as the 'Red Squad,' received police reports from across the country reiterating the likelihood that their city would be inundated with thousands of protesters between August 25 and August 30 bent on disrupting the National Democratic Convention.

I had learned that a significant element of this massive protest clearly intended to provoke the cops, as evidenced in an August article on the upcoming Democratic Convention published in Boston's underground newspaper, the *Avatar*, which concluded with this warning,

"Don't come to Chicago if you expect a five day festival of life, music and love. Chicago may be a festival of blood!"

A couple busloads of political activists left Boston to participate in this action. I knew from their backgrounds, even before they were photographed on the bus, that a few of them intended to create disruption at the Convention. This projection was replicated by other departments across the country and reported to the Chicago PD. It is likely that the cops and Mayor Daley were pretty revved up by the time the thing went down.

The rest is history. Tired of the chanting, worn down by the taunts, angry at the disobedience and infuriated by the rocks, bottles and bags of shit that had been hurled at them, the outnumbered police broke ranks and the streets surrounding the Chicago convention hall became a battlefield covered with blood. Scores of people were injured, including cops, and many others were taken into custody.

Eight participants were eventually indicted and charged with crossing state lines to incite a riot. Included among them were Bobby Seale, Chairman of the Black Panther Party; Abbie Hoffman and Jerry Rubin, the outrageous duo who had co-founded the Yippies; and Tom Hayden, the inspiration for the Students for a Democratic Society. Seale would later be rendited to Connecticut where he would be tried for murder with several other members of his party, giving rise to the 'Free Bobby Seale' movement.

Others spawned the 'November Action Coalition-the Day After,' a Progressive Labor Party front group who promised violence in the streets as soon as the expected guilty verdicts were handed down.

The images of police violence and wild student protesters sickened ordinary Americans and worked to hand a victory to Republican candidate Richard M. Nixon on November 6, 1968. He had billed himself as a man with a plan to end the war, although he had never made the details public. The dissidents weren't buying it.

A great many American citizens were tired of the war, but they were even more turned off by the 'New Left Movement' which the FBI charged was "made up of beatniks, hippies, disenchanted intellectuals and some over-awed students still on campus," which they concluded "has mushroomed into a major security problem."

A lot of things happened that summer. I was exhilarated to learn that Beverly had become pregnant again! I was ready this time - I had a three-bedroom house and a good job. I hoped that another kid would strengthen our marriage, which was showing some early signs of strain. Stupid arguments for the most part, which we got over pretty quickly, but nevertheless left me with a residue of doubt concerning Beverly's feelings toward me. I sensed that she might have been experiencing some second thoughts about our marriage.

I graduated Northeastern in September with a Bachelor of Science in Law Enforcement. It had been a long grind. I had attended winters and summers, right up until the end. I felt more tired than triumphant. I skipped the official graduation ceremony, opting to have my diploma sent in the mail.

Two weeks later I was accepted as a graduate student in the Department of Sociology. To my surprise I was recruited by Professor Stephen Schaefer, the head of the Criminology Division, a renowned scholar and past Chairman of the International Criminological Association.

Schaefer was a transplanted Hungarian Jew who had fled his country because of Communist persecution. He was, at one time, the head of the Budapest prison system and had authored several books. He was well known for his early contributions to the study of Victimology, an emerging discipline that focused on the criminal/victim relationship.

I wasn't sure why he had selected me. Although I had managed to graduate with honors, it was more the result of perspiration than inspiration. Perhaps, I mused, it was because I laughed at his jokes. Actually, he was pretty funny. I also liked him for his down to earth style. I recall him addressing the subject of the death penalty during class one day. He argued that no amount of research would ever be able to prove whether or not it was a deterrent. He explained that the only method that might be reliably employed to determine the truth would require successive periods of execution, to be alternately carried out between periods of relaxation on the same population over time, thereby establishing the incidents of greatest murder frequency. That, of course, was highly unlikely. In the end he concluded that "It's just a matter of personal taste" or "aesthetics" as he sometimes referred to it.

Schaefer was personally opposed to Capital Punishment because of its macabre nature. He had witnessed many executions in his official capacity as a prison administrator and it had turned him off, but unlike many social scientists who pandered their values to the public clothed in pseudo-science, he was unwilling to compromise his principles.

As an interesting side-note - he commented that the most humane form of execution was "death by hanging." He said that it was quick and relatively painless, providing that it was done properly. He was a colorful teacher and I enjoyed his tutelage.

I didn't sweat the cost of the program because by that time I was enjoying the benefits of the G.I. Bill. By a single swipe of the legislative hand anyone who had been honorably discharged from the military service since 1955 would obtain veteran status. In addition, any veteran who was discharged since 1961, the year that one hundred combat ready U.S. Special Forces were sent to Vietnam to join the advisors that were already there, was considered a Vietnam Era Veteran. Veteran's status didn't help me get on the job, nor did it pay for most of my undergraduate work, but it was sure coming in handy now.

The first thing I did was inform Dean Tim Moran, who had since been promoted to Director of the Law Enforcement Program, of my good fortune to have been selected for graduate study. I had grown close to him over the years and I admired him profusely. I was anxious to share the good news with him.

He was sitting behind his desk, going through a deluge of paperwork, when his secretary quietly escorted me to the door leading to his office. A large print of Norman Rockwell's 1958 Saturday Evening Post cover featuring *The Runaway* was prominently displayed on the wall behind his desk. Tim knew both Rockwell and the State Cop who was featured in the painting and had something to do with arranging the meeting that had made it all happen.

He waved me in and invited me to sit down. He always had time for his students, many of whom, including me, stopped by frequently to chat with him. He had already laid the cornerstone of many professional careers. He was a full Dean now and enjoyed primacy of the most rapidly growing program at Northeastern University. His warm countenance didn't detract from his serious demeanor. Tim enjoyed that rare quality of causing each person he encountered to feel special.

He didn't act at all surprised when I told him the good news. He was pretty nonchalant about it, leaving me with the impression that he had expected that something like that would happen. In fact, he offered me a part-time teaching position. I was awed by the offer and could hardly believe that he made it. I thanked him but politely demurred, explaining that I preferred to wait until I had completed the requirements for the Master's Degree in two years. Tim promised me that the job would be waiting for me. We shook hands on it.

I visited Paul Memos at the Male Home and expressed my anxiety about my not having majored in Sociology or Criminology (which I would be specializing in) and we discussed what I might do to remedy that deficiency with little time remaining. He gave me some solid advice, counseling me to become facile in learning to speak the language of the science, pointing out that a lot of it simply amounted to fancy phraseology.

I purchased a *Dictionary of Sociology* and steeped myself in its jargon. Paul was right - it helped me immensely. His final comment on the subject served to reinforce his cynical view of sociologists. He asserted that when they weren't pushing their personal views on the world, and even when they were doing pure research, their findings did little more than to document the obvious. Paul believed that social scientists were an extravagance of an affluent society - peel away the layers of cultural subterfuge, he inferred, and their importance would become increasingly blurred.

Cops, on the other hand, held a special fascination for him because they functioned on a survival level. They were part of the tenuous divide between barbarism and civilization and were keyed into the dark pools of instinctual behavior and primitive reality that man, throughout the ages, has constantly sought to suppress, but which have nevertheless bubbled up everywhere. Cops were spectators to the archival footage of man's follies and Paul, his immense intellect eternally curious, enjoyed the recount.

My own faith in humankind was also beginning to wear at the edges - four years on the job was enough time for that to happen. It wasn't only social scientists whose truth I doubted, it was some of my own fondest beliefs.

On November 23, 1968, Patrolman Charles McNabb was killed in the line of duty. He was shot in the chest by one of two men during an attempted armed robbery. The poor guy had just finished a paid detail and was on his way to work when he came on the incident.

Twenty-Six

Kenny died. Kristin was born. I was sidetracked for a short time with a bookmaking operation. And the anti-war movement took an ominous turn.

Beverly and I rushed to the Massachusetts General Hospital as soon as we got the call. Kenny's impending death had been a certainty to us right along, but now the time had come. The rush hour traffic, expectedly, slowed us down and by the time we got there it was too late. He had slipped away less than two minutes before we arrived. Beverly's sister Thelma, an RN by training, gave us the grim news. She was standing by his bedside when we entered his room. She lifted her head away from Kenny and tearfully informed us that Kenny had died.

"He's gone," she said.

I thought, *"His pain is gone too."* Kenny had fought the demon until the end. There was nothing left to him. His body was ravaged and his face was gaunt. His once strong athletic physique had been worn down to a rack of bones. I don't think he weighed a hundred pounds. I wondered what he might have been thinking about when he drew his last breath.

I was concerned about Beverly's father Jimmy. He had suffered a couple of heart attacks in the past and I feared that the news might kill him. He had never made any attempt to conceal the paternal obsession that he held for his son from either of his two daughters. Kenny was the light of his life - it was obvious for anyone to see. Perhaps, as sons often do, he had embodied his father's unfulfilled expectations, a one time superb athlete, a good family man and a hard worker who in his late twenties had already begun the climb up the white collar ranks at General Electric.

Jimmy arrived right after us. I hit him with the bad news, but he didn't have to be told. His initial reaction was disarming. He placed his hands in his front pockets and ambled around the corner in search of a public telephone. He found one and dropped a coin into the slot. I dutifully trailed him to his destination, fully expecting him to move into cardiac arrest at any moment. I was in the ready.

Apparently Jimmy was notifying his employer that he wouldn't be reporting to work that evening. I overheard him say in a flat, unemotional, monotone voice,

"I won't be coming in tonight - my kid just died."

He hung up the phone and closed his eyes. Cupping his bald head with his right hand, he leaned against the wall and ratcheted out a long, sorrowful wail that came from deep down inside his gut. No! I mean his soul, a baneful cry of irreplaceable loss and inconsolable despair.

It was chilling and out of character for this normally constrained, white Anglo-Saxon Protestant. What's more, I felt powerless to help him. I put my arm around his shoulder and muttered the standard heartfelt condolences that people make during these times but I knew that nothing would help. Only time itself could soften his agony. It's not easy to bury your child. I have seen it happen too many times. I don't think anyone ever fully recovers from the experience.

By the time Jimmy returned to his family he was fully composed. They never knew what had happened around the corner. I felt terribly saddened by the whole scenario, especially the calloused way that the hospital had chosen to handle a dying patient. They had put Kenny in a room by himself in an isolated section of an unoccupied ward on a lower floor (I think it was the basement), perhaps so that he wouldn't disturb other patients. They left him there to die.

Kenny's wife Audrey, a strikingly beautiful woman with seductive good looks, sat next to his mother outside the death room. They looked vacant.

I reflected on what it must have been like for my mother right after my father died. It was even tougher in those days, especially without doting grandparents, (they were also dead) a house or insurance money. I hoped that Kenny's three kids, a boy and two girls, would have a better shot. I was certain the boy would anyway - he looked like his father when Kenny was a child. That's what Jimmy said. He was soon to become the apple of his grandfather's eye.

My daughter Kristin was born in the early afternoon on January 23, 1969. I was pretty jittery and went through some of the same vigilant, repetitive behaviors that I had with Kimberley: practice runs to the hospital, neighbor updates, phone numbers for emergency assistance etc., but this time there was less pressure.

The circumstances were different now. We owned our own home and had a room waiting for the new baby. It was easier getting around the suburbs - there was less congestion and the streets to the hospital were fairly direct. The Winchester Hospital, which specialized in maternity, was located in the next town. It sat on the rustic crescent of a huge hill that bordered the Middlesex Fells Reservation, two thousand and sixty acres of woodland that I had been hiking and camping in since childhood, so I was familiar with the area. This patch of woods has always provided me with solace from the tensions of life and it was applying its chrism back then.

Beverly's labor was less intense this time and Kristin's birth was normal. She came on time - right on the button. She had escaped the malady of her sister and was born without colic. The world was an easier place for her and she responded as pleasantly as any comfortable baby would. She rarely cried and loved to sleep.

My sister Jeanette and her husband Eddie were among the first to visit Beverly and view the baby while they were still in the hospital. I looked at Jeanette as she peered through the nursery window. She was an aunt again and she beamed with pride as she stood there gazing down at Baby Girl Vitti.

I drifted back to our lives together as children and for a brief moment I was overcome by a strange sensation. It felt as though I had fallen into a time crevasse and had been catapulted back into the past. The years had melted away and there we were standing on the front porch of a house, about three blocks from where we lived on Broadway, waiting for someone to open the door so that I could pitch the sale of school Christmas cards to the unsuspecting occupant.

We both attended the Little Flower School around the corner. The neighborhood boys referred to it as Saint Theresa's to avoid the 'sissy' connotation. It was one of the oldest parochial schools in the Boston area, and together with Saint Benedict's Church, maintained a pervasive influence in the lives of the parish youth, many of whom were the products of low income, violently charged, broken and alcohol soaked homes. Confession on Saturday afternoons, Mass on Sundays, novenas and school dances, which we referred to as 'record hops' on Friday evenings; for the males, it was also the Altar Boys, CYO Baseball, Boy Scouts - the whole nine yards; for the females there was nothing, it was all about their brothers.

I was in the eighth grade and Jeanette was in the fourth and on that day she was helping her big brother sell Christmas cards, helping me to win the first prize for the most sales. I could see her standing there as though I had arrived back at that moment. It was late autumn and the fallen leaves were swirling around the street in one last dance with the wind before the advent of the season's first snow.

Jeanette was getting cold and she wrapped her coat securely around herself. She was a pretty kid, tiny and fragile. She wore bangs and her large brown expressive eyes lent her the appearance of a kewpie doll.

We were in trouble. The streetlights had blinked on more than fifteen minutes ago signaling that we were late for supper. I couldn't recall if I had made the sale, but what had lingered in my mind was her willingness to risk being sanctioned for my delinquency and to share the consequences. It was a crystalline moment - though in a few short months my world would fall apart upon learning of my mother's death. I have always savored the memory.

That's the kind of kid she was and now she was married with a daughter of her own. Still delicate and pretty, she had married a neighborhood kid named Eddie Harrington, a good guy whom I liked and respected. He had recently graduated Northeastern University's Graduate School of Business where he had attended on a full Fellowship.

Eddie was a hard driver, a former football player at Somerville High School, a no nonsense kind of guy who strove toward success. He had already landed a good job at General Electric where he was employed as a traveling auditor. He was so good at his job that he was allowed to skip the three-year apprentice program that generally preceded that position. This employment would take him abroad. His conservative politics didn't stop him from coming down pretty hard on the police - overweight, gruff and uncivil cops angered him beyond comprehension. Some of his antipathy was his own doing - like a lot of young people in the Sixties, regardless of their position on the political spectrum, he wrestled with authority. (So did Jesser for that matter).

Eddie was no more mechanically inclined than I was so when the time came to put the crib together it would take us more than eight hours to follow the 'simplified' instructions. I had dared not construct the monstrosity before the baby was born for fear of bad luck.

If Kimberly, who was by now three and a half years old, was the slightest bit jealous of her new sister she masked it well. She took to her instantly. She absorbed her and communicated her every need - to the extent that Kristin hardly talked until she reached four years old. She didn't need to; her sister did it for her. When she finally spoke it was only because I had insisted that Kimberly not be allowed to interpret for her. Amazingly enough, Kristin began to verbalize in full sentences.

Things were starting to move along again. Graduate school wasn't that difficult, except for a course in advanced statistics that almost did me in. Kristin's birth, in a classic demonstration of the balance of nature, diverted Beverly's attention from her brother's death. It also helped when I was reassigned to the day shift for the next five weeks (as long as it took me to complete my new assignment). This way I would be home in the evening, at least for a while.

I was a little surprised when I learned that I would be going back to a gaming investigation. I was the only guy working undercover on this subversive stuff and things were becoming more dire. In January the Progressive Labor Party had begun to do some serious saber rattling, deriding other elements of the Students for a Democratic Society for their lack of discipline. They accused the more moderate factions of being 'dope smoking, do your own thing-anarchists'. They urged their comrades to become more actively and visibly involved with strikes, especially those involving third world workers such as campus cafeteria employees, and openly campaigned for support of 'ghetto rebellions.' More ominously, they called for black and white workers to engage in an armed struggle against imperialism. In short, they were campaigning for an 'open revolution against the establishment' and that meant the cops. As a Marine I knew the powerful difference that focus and discipline could make and I took the threat seriously.

It seemed to me that bookies should have taken a back seat to this new danger, but that's never the way it goes on police departments. The mix of personalities, bosses, events, personnel requirements, staffing levels, politics and plain stupidity results in a constant shifting and realignment of priorities. I would become more deeply and bitterly affected by this in the latter part of my career, but back then I was merely perplexed.

Jimmy Lynch sensed my bewilderment and remarked,

"It'll only be for a short time, Phil, and you won't lose your contacts. I'm doing the guy a favor. He's looking for somebody with a little imagination who can be trusted and you fit the bill."

The guy turned out to be Captain Joe Jordan, the Commanding Officer of the Vice Control Unit. I was instructed to meet with him secretly in the pharmacy section of the Statler Hilton Hotel, next to the Arlington Street entrance. I was intrigued by the cloak and dagger stuff and began to look forward to learning more about what I would be doing. Of a practical concern, I was hoping this new mission wouldn't affect my classes in the late afternoon. It didn't.

I first met Joe Jordan back in the early Sixties at Northeastern where we occasionally attended classes together. He was a handsome guy, kind of dapper, who struck the image of a cool cop, right down to the dark sunglasses. He always sat with the same guy - another Lieutenant on the Boston Police Department and rarely spoke to anyone else. I wasn't in his league and I kept my distance. He projected a professional image that reflected a contradictory blend of insularity and flamboyance. He liked Tim Moran, which made him all right in my book.

The next morning we enjoyed a cup of coffee and he laid it right out. As best as I can recall he said,

"Look, I'm getting some serious tabs (complaints) from the State Police on some local bookmakers, mostly horses and number guys and I'm having a problem answering them. One guy has been operating for more than twenty years and has never been pinched. What's worse, he owns a small meat market next to District 11. It's a real eyesore. The cops like him and are in and out of the place so watch out."

"The other guy has some serious action going in the back room of the Riverway Cafe at Huntington and South Huntington. Gerry Angiulo has an apartment upstairs."(Angiulo was the local La Cosa Nostra boss in the city.) He continued, "It's going to be hard to get a bet into the guy because the bartender only allows people he knows in the back room."

None of this sounded very easy to me.

He went on "I've got a couple of other places too. These guys are tough but they have to take some chances - that's how they make their money. Maybe you can trip them up. Jimmy Lynch tells me your pretty good - do you mind doing this?"

I agreed, of course (I had no real choice). But I informed him that,

"I've never played a horse with a bookie and I'm not sure how to go about it."

"No problem," he said. "Show up here tomorrow at 10:00 AM and meet with a cop named Ralph Ryan. He's a thin guy and he'll be wearing a red coat. Tell him who you are and he'll take you through it." He handed me an envelope containing expense money and target locations.

His final admonition was not to discuss this investigation with anyone at all. "You'd be amazed at how this stuff gets around, so be careful who you talk to. As far as anyone is concerned, you're still working on the hippie stuff. Jimmy Lynch will cover you on that angle."

Lynch covered me all right - he never even briefed the big boss. He fed him a line of crap about what I was doing. He told him that I was still hanging around the campuses. It amazed me that a Captain and a Sergeant would have the balls to keep a Deputy Superintendent in the dark. That wouldn't have happened with Blake. He called all the shots. Actually, I didn't really care. I figured they had their reasons and my loyalty was to Lynch anyway. He was my immediate supervisor and that's the way it worked. I just hoped that I wouldn't end up in the middle.

Ralph Ryan was an honest, street wise and ballsy cop. I liked him right away. He had a soft nasal sound to his voice, a combination of a pronounced Boston accent punctuated with a neighborhood twist, similar to his friend

Joe Jordan. He was evenly tempered, cynical and one hundred percent willing to work with a young inexperienced investigator. Fiercely loyal to Jordan and good at his work, he had knocked off his share of bookmakers, but the constant court exposure was doing him in. They saw him coming.

So did I. He was standing at the cash register the next morning, about ten minutes early, buying a pack of butts. His fire-engine red coat made him easy to spot. I waited until he was finished with the transaction before I approached him and introduced myself. He followed suit and we shook hands. Ralph struck me as an easygoing guy and I felt at ease with him right away. By the time we finished our coffees and doused our cigarettes I was pretty revved up and raring to go. My gaming education was about to begin.

This investigation presented a new challenge. In the past I was simply expected to root out and document gaming behavior. It was purely an intelligence undertaking and while it called for a lot of discipline, some flexibility and a modicum of creative thought, it never was intended to culminate in an arrest or criminal prosecution. Now I was expected to get bets into the bookies, arrest them and prepare the subsequent court cases for prosecution. Some bookies were more careful than others were and my targets were among the most difficult. I was either going to make it or not.

Over the next several weeks Ralph taught me the basics of the betting game. For a good part of the time he hung around street corners and store fronts to confer with me. Nothing sophisticated, that came later, but enough to give me sufficient confidence to make a wager and understand just what was going down. In the beginning I didn't know much more about horse racing than the differences among the positions of win, place and show. I knew a little about the numbers game (demeaningly referred to as 'the nigger pool' in my old neighborhood) but only enough to make a straight bet. I came to learn the distinctions among a 'lead number bet' (a bet on a single number) and a 'bleeder' (a bet on any two numbers) a 'parlay' (a bet on two selections of horses with the winnings of one wager bet on the other) a 'quinella' (the selection of two horses in one race to finish in order) and a 'trifecta' (the selection of the first three finishers based on their win, place, and show positions).

I learned that bookies who, for the most part, were regular guys and well liked were tied in with organized crime. They were the patsies who took the fall, front guys for the syndicate. They served as conduits for the movement of raw money to big time mobsters, money that would be used for loans-sharking, extortion, union racketeering, invasion of legitimate business and murder. They weren't big into drugs in the Boston area at the time. In years to come, however, drugs would supersede gambling as the principal activity of organized crime.

I learned that so-called 'bookies' were simply 'writers,' one of any number of individuals employed by a true bookmaker who functioned as a manager. I learned about 'odds makers' and 'runners' (who picked up the cash and betting slips), 'lay-off men' (bookmakers who accepted bets from other bookmakers to avoid getting hit with a big win) and 'offices' where the bets were called in and tallied. Syndicated gambling was big business and required the normal compliment of technical people and accountants to run it. It was a well-oiled enterprise supported by ruthless men, ready and willing to use violence, up to and including killing, to keep it profitable. And I learned more about cops - crooked cops - who would sell out their brother officer for a payoff. Blake wasn't wrong about that.

The list that Jordan handed me included four places. Three of them, including the Peerless Market, were in the Fields Corner area of Dorchester and one of them, the Riverway, was located on a major intersection in Roxbury, a few blocks from Jamaica Plain. In reality, most of the major sections of Boston are designated postal zones and the boundary lines are subject to interpretation.

The Riverway was by far the most difficult to crack and I almost gave up before I got lucky. Ralph Ryan coached me every step of the way, especially for the first couple of weeks, but the bookie was running a tight operation. He sat in an enclosed booth section in a room to the rear of the bar. Only known bettors were permitted to enter and there were plenty of them. There was a constant line, especially during lunch hour. The bartender, a big Jewish grandfatherly-type guy named Arnie, also functioned as the 'gatekeeper' and wouldn't so much as allow me to sit at the rear of the bar which would have provided me with some limited visual access to the bookie.

I dropped in the place every day at different times for the first couple of weeks so that the bartender would get to know me. I assumed the cover of a Northeastern University student living with roommates in an apartment across the street in one of the old and deteriorating brownish brick buildings which, to this day, casts a depressing effect on that section of the avenue.

I brought in textbooks and did my homework at the bar. I deliberately forgot one of the books and returned the next day to pick it up. It was the second edition of the Harbrace College Reader and not something cops generally carried around. I did everything I could to dispel the image of a cop. Although Arnie seemed to buy my cover, he still relegated me to the same blind side of the bar.

My lucky break came one early afternoon after a coat rack in the joint fell apart. It turned out that Arnie was a pretty compulsive guy. (I was familiar with that syndrome!) He liked things to be in working order and was having a tough time putting the rack back together without the benefit of any tools. Screw drivers work better than dimes so I leaped at the opportunity to fill the gap.

I abruptly left the bar, leaving my beer and promised that I would return soon with some tools from my apartment across the street. When I was sure no one was tailing me I moved as quickly as I could in the direction of my car which was parked a few blocks away near Northeastern University.

A February storm had blanketed the area with about six inches of snow and the going was tough. Time was essential and I cursed myself for having parked so far away from the joint, a precaution that I generally took to avoid being followed. This time it was working against me. I was wet and breathing hard by the time I returned to the bar with my dented brown metal tool case. I waited outside for less than a minute to regain my composure, then nonchalantly walked back in the front door carrying the implements that in time would pry open the bookie.

Arnie was pleased that I had returned with the tools and the both of us got busy right away on the coat rack. It was a skit reminiscent of the Eddie and my crib fiasco except this time I kept bumping into Arnie. We weren't making much progress and finally the bookie emerged from the back room and took over the job. It took him about ten minutes to get the thing back together and that was the first time that I got a good look at him. He was a guy in his late thirties, a six foot four inch, two hundred and sixty pound meat-house.

It was 3:00 PM by the time he finished - just in time for Lefty, the second shift bartender, to begin his shift. Arnie thanked me for my help and, in Lefty's presence, handed me a free high ball for my efforts, then began to chat with his relief. I gulped it down on top of the Bud and got out of there before I felt the effects of the alcohol. I had a strategy, and also a class that was soon to begin.

The next day I dropped in after three in the afternoon, when I knew that Lefty would be working and Arnie would be gone. I ordered a beer and took up my usual place behind the bar. A short time later two working guys came in from the street. They sat next to me and put in two numbers with Lefty. He took the action in front of me with no attempt to conceal what he was doing. I took advantage of the moment and played two bucks on number 364. He took my dough, wrote the number down on a small pad of paper - and that was the beginning of the end.

I couldn't wait to tell Ralph that I had scored. I called him at his house that evening and he congratulated me. In a thinly disguised veneer at self-depreciating humor I remarked,

"I just got lucky, Ralph - without luck I wouldn't even have been able to find the place."

His response stuck with me for the rest of my career.

"Every undercover guy needs a little luck, Phil. It's the way you manipulate your luck that counts. You could have just sat on your ass at the bar when the coat rack broke and you'd still be sitting there. Instead, you saw it as an opportunity to get into the action and it worked. I'll tell Jordan the good news in the morning."

Following Ralph's instructions I continued to put in number plays with Lefty. I also wrote everything down just the way it happened, including notations of other guys making bets, incriminating language, phone calls, behavior and personal observations such as the all-important location of the hide. I jotted everything down in a notebook that I updated daily in preparation for the case down the road. I kept the notebook in my car. On the third day Lefty blew my mind when he told me to by-pass him at the bar and go straight in to see Big John if I wanted to play a horse, or if ever I came in and saw any 'cop types' hanging around. He said the place was getting hot and you could never be too careful. That was my second break.

The time was ripe. The next day was Friday and I knew the action would be hot and heavy. It always was on payday. I slipped in the joint and walked past Lefty right into the back room. John was sitting in a rear booth writing furiously on a sheet of paper. Before him stood a long line of gamblers. He was clutching a roll of bills that would have choked a racehorse and it kept getting bigger as he accepted bets from his customers. Two television sets were on and after each race he would busy himself paying off the winners.

I picked up one of several *Armstrongs* that were scattered around the place and pretended that I was reading it. Actually I had my selection all picked out. Ralph was secreted in a doorway outside and had prepped me on who to pick before I went in. This was the big test.

It took a few minutes before I reached John. When I finally got there I looked down at him and in a voice as subdued as my quivering heart would allow I played five bucks on a horse to win in an upcoming race.

He gazed up at me and asked, "You're a friend of Arnie's?" He had also witnessed Arnie serve me the free drink.

It was a rhetorical question, but I answered it anyway. "Yeah, I know him," I said.

He accepted the fin and wrote down the information. I sat down at a booth and breathed a silent sigh of relief. I had him by the balls!

The race went off a few minutes later and my horse came in. He was a heavy favorite so he didn't pay much. I was astounded that I had won. This would give me a more solid case. The same thing happened a few days later, but this time I had played a pony in the 'show' position. All total, I won thirty-two bucks and that was more than enough to move in on Big John.

Joe Jordan and the crew, armed with a search warrant, arrested Big John and Lefty about noontime on Friday, March 7. I made my final play with him just before the squad came in. John wrote the 'number' down and when I saw Richie Cox coming around the corner I latched onto John and placed him under arrest. He was startled and jumped up. I was completely off the floor and still holding on to his massive bulk, when, in a pre-arranged maneuver, he tossed the paper containing evidence of my play into an adjacent booth where he anticipated that a confidant would torch it with his lighted cigar. Come to find out it was 'flash paper,' chemically treated writing paper intended to fully ignite at the touch of a burning object.

He was too late. Richie Cox, his nimble body in the ready, had scrambled over the partition and retrieved the 'master sheet.' Richie saved the day - this evidence of play was needed for a successful court prosecution.

I got the Peerless too. It took me about the same amount of time although I encountered a slightly different set of problems. I don't want to bore you with the details. Suffice to say this meat market dealt strictly with neighborhood people. They sold a good quality product and handed out free chickens to some of the cops in the district on the holidays.

For at least three weeks I did the family shopping there - talking to people and getting known. On a couple of occasions I brought Kimberly with me. She was a really cute kid and Soucey, the owner, in full view of the meat man behind the counter, gave her a couple of avuncular taps on the head. I deliberately maneuvered her in that direction so that the guy behind the meat counter would think we were friendly. All's fair in love and war.

You know the rest of the story. The meat man took the bait and figured I was in with the owner and when Soucey was absent I started to play numbers with the meat man. I kept on playing number 269 and number 990 for a half a buck each. On two occasions Soucey was present and observed the meat man take the action. That showed complicity in the same offense.

Joe Jordan constructed an affidavit based on the information I had given him and applied for a search warrant. He put together a raiding party and we headed out to Dorchester. He didn't tell them where we were going - that sort of secrecy was standard operating procedure. The members of the raiding party never knew where they were headed until they got there. This was a precaution intended to prevent anyone from tipping the place in advance that cops were on the way. Jordan wasn't able to trust some of the guys who worked for him nor was he able to get rid of them. They had connections. I supposed that was the biggest reason I was there to begin with.

We hit the place at 3:30 in the afternoon. It was pretty clean, which lead me to believe that somehow they had been tipped anyway, despite our precautions, but by whom? There were still a few slips lying around which the bookie had overlooked and Eddy McHale, a gaming expert and Joe Jordan's side kick, located most of them. The way Jordan put it, "They never completely clean the place up." Eddy was a court-sanctioned "expert witness" and a real character in his own right. In the years to come he would take my gaming education to new heights.

I have always suspected it was the bookie who operated in the bowling alley around the corner, another one of my targets, who had dimed the meat store. He was a tall lanky guy who always dressed in sneakers, dungarees and a sweatshirt topped with a baseball cap which he never took off; a sort of eternal teenager type, who in the beginning came to trust me enough to take steady action right in front of me, especially on Saturday mornings, a sure sign that he didn't think I was a cop.

That's probably what Jordan was thinking when he insisted that I had seen enough and that I should attempt to make a play. I think he was buoyed by my other two scores and believed that I could do it again.

He commented, "You have to move at some point Phil - he's either ready or not."

It was premature and I didn't feel comfortable with any attempt to make a play just yet. I felt that I needed more time, but I had no choice. I gave it a shot anyway and, as I expected, the bookie turned me down. I asked him if I could play a half a buck on number 269 and he looked at me like I had three heads. "I don't know what you're talking about," he said.

The action shut down in the Peerless right after that. I attempted to make a play and the meat man told me that they didn't book anymore because it was too much trouble. That was prophetic to say but it didn't make any difference, I had them good.

The bowling alley bookie must have been putting my description around Fields Corner. A couple of days later I was sitting in Mallows on Dorchester Avenue putting the peek on the little tough-guy bookie in the corner. He also had been operating pretty openly in front of me until then. That day everything dried up - the money, the slips on the table, the whole bit. Mallows was my fourth and last target.

I was sitting at the bar getting ready to wrap it up when two tall, grossly overweight red-faced cops walked through the door. The broken blood vessels that lined their scowling faces told an all too familiar story. The bulbous nose on the beefier one looked as though it had been run over by a truck. They were still wearing their uniform trousers underneath their civilian coats. They didn't have the decency to fully change into plain clothes. They didn't care who knew them, least of all me. They walked straight up to where I was sitting at the bar and looked me over, making no attempt to conceal their purpose. They made me sick. They were two big drunken slobs and I knew that they were there at the bookie's request to identify me. However, I don't think they succeeded.

I sat there in silence peeling away at the Budweiser label on the bottle that I was fingering in front of me. The whole joint went quiet. The patrons at the bar knew what was going down and I was burning inside. I couldn't believe how brazen these cops were. They didn't give a fuck. They must have felt insulated. Just how corrupt could a system be that would tolerate this kind of outrageous behavior? Who did the bookie call to ID (identify) me? Who put them up to it? And how far up the ranks was he positioned?

It wouldn't have mattered if I had known the answers. No one would have done anything about it anyway. Gambling was as much an industry on the police department as it was in the underworld. Gaming money was a staple - it was indigenous to the police world, and it moved around the city like a low-grade virus, steadily debilitating the system but never completely destroying it.

Ordinary cops rarely benefited from it - but all of them were affected. Some bookies wielded as much power as their commanding officers. The bookies took care of the decision makers, a great many of them headquarters brass, district captains and sergeant detectives. I'd heard of cases where cops approached bookies to get transfers. Years later I learned of an instance where a District Captain ordered a recalcitrant bar owner to reinstate a bookie whom the owner had expelled from the premises. It was incongruous that the department placed more of an emphasis on saluting the front desk of a police station, or taking off one's hat in the presence of a District Commander, than it did on honesty. This was the kind of stuff that stripped away at a young cop's faith.

There were straight captains, of course, but as I would come to learn, they rarely got a district. Most of the time they ended up with some sort of a staff position, like Captain Cadegan at the Police Academy, or buried somewhere in headquarters. There were straight lieutenants, sergeants and detectives who knew what was going on but never took a piece of the envelope. There was even a sergeant who quit the department out of disgust for corruption. However, men like him were few and far between, and even he ended up coming back on the job.

There were also men like Blake, Slattery, Jordan and a score of underlings beneath them in the chain of command who didn't play the game, but ironically they were needed to maintain the profitability of the system. They were the boogie men who kept enough tension on the gaming operations to keep the payoffs coming. In retrospect I suppose that I was one of them.

The stoolie cops eventually left the bar and my assignment was finished. The four defendants were found guilty of various lottery violations. They included the manager of the Peerless for 'allowing the premises to be used for gaming.' Jordan said that was the only time in twenty-four years that the guy had taken a hit.

In the Roxbury Court, Judge Wilder, after I had provided the court with about fifteen minutes of uninterrupted chronological testimony, forced me to repeat my entire Riverway Cafe testimony including the thirty-two dollars of winnings, the master sheet and marked betting money - he inferred that I was lying

These were his exact words. "Do you expect me to believe that a cop walks down the street, goes into a bar, makes a bet with a bookie and has a couple of pieces of change to prove it?"

"No, your honor, I don't," and without his requesting it, I reiterated my testimony. That obviously irritated him but he had no way out. He found the defendant guilty and fined him fifty dollars. That's about what the others got. None of it seemed worth it to me.

However, Joe Jordan was pleased. "It cost them a bundle with their lawyers," he said, "plus we inconvenienced them. We hit Gerry Angiulo where it hurts and knocked off the meat-market next to the police station. We look for small successes in this game, Phil - that's all we can hope for." Personally, I was relieved it was over.

I bumped into 'thirty' over the weekend and I wasn't too happy about it. That was the only time I ever experienced such utter depression on a birthday. Maybe I was buying all that stuff the movement people were dishing out about this irrevocable divide. I felt as though I had crossed over a chasm and there was no going back - my youth was gone.

Police Officer Francis Johnson was killed in a Combat Zone bar the next day. He was killed by a drifter who was attempting to rob the bartender when the police officer interrupted him. Johnson was called from his traffic post at Tremont and Boylston Streets when the patron began threatening other patrons in the bar.

He was shot to death in the Tam, a rundown, derelict-type joint on the western side of the Zone. It was a Monday evening and I was back on nights. After the police officer was removed from the bar and the investigation was finished the bar continued to do business as though nothing had ever happened. That's what a cop's life was worth to the owner of this gin mill.

I threw the vice squad one last bone after I went back on nights. Richie Cox and I tipped over the Coliseum, a heavy action after-hour joint in the North End believed by Jordan to be owned by Sammy Granito, a mustache Pete, Revere based Mafia Don. We slipped right by Pinocchio, the doorman who was stationed outside with a walkie-talkie ready to alert the club upstairs whenever he spotted a cop lurking around. He never figured that a black and a white guy doing the town together might be cops. There were less than seventy-five black cops on the job back in those days and Richie was the only one working vice. Richie was a cool guy, good looking, straight and willing to work.

We partnered on a lot of capers over the years, but this one was the most fun. We sat in the joint every night for almost a week, drinking, laughing and talking to the waitresses. For short periods of time we almost forgot why we were there - to familiarize ourselves with the operation and note the identities of the individuals who were running the establishment.

Captain Jordan and other members of the Vice Control Unit hit the place early in the AM on Saturday morning. Richie and I fingered the main offenders and a number of them were arrested. We saved a couple samples of the booze for analysis and obtained an easy conviction in court for the unlawful sale of alcohol. The Coliseum was shut down and never reopened. And by the way, Pinocchio was the door-man's true name.

Twenty-Seven

The anti-war movement was still humming when I got back. A proliferation of activity had begun. Increasingly, colleges were becoming targets of radical action and the Ivy League schools were no exceptions.

On April 9, 1969, hundreds of Harvard students clashed with police and occupied University Hall in a siege that would result in many injuries to both sides, several arrests and the expulsion of sixteen students. Mike Ansara, the founder of Harvard University Students for a Democratic Society (SDS), had returned to his alma mater for this action and, by the accounts of many who were present, cast an eerie influence on the unruly students.

The newspapers played up the incident and the sixteen students became a 'cause celebre' on the campus. This was the culmination of a series of violent protests at Harvard. One of the first entailed an SDS attack against Secretary of Defense Robert McNamara who had been invited to speak at the college. Despite security, he was forced from his car by protesters and beaten on the head with sign handles until he was rescued by Cambridge Police and escorted off the campus.

Things got so out of hand during this volatile period that the revered Fogg Museum and Widener Library required twenty four-hour police protection. The President of Harvard came under intense criticism from many members of his own faculty for calling the cops during the University Hall action. In response, San Francisco State President Hayakawa, an outspoken foe of the SDS, repudiated the critical faculty members for their betrayal.

The Progressive Labor Party (PLP) continued their vehemence with a couple of staged demonstrations on the Boston Common followed by successive marches to the State House on Monday and Tuesday, April 14 and 15, but they failed to engender a sizable crowd. They carried signs portraying big red fists, but no one seemed to be paying much attention. I attended the first day's action and managed to pick up a good sampling of literature. I listened to the rhetoric and it was frighteningly obvious that the PLP were heading down a dangerous path. They were quickly becoming the political isolates of the anti-war ensemble.

Conversely, the Student Mobilization Committee (SMC), which had continued to fall under the insipid influence of the Socialist Workers Party (SWP), was experiencing great success at galvanizing a good portion of the anti-war sentiment. The major political parties of the time, namely the Democrats and the Republicans, would have been well served to see how the Student Mobilization Committee operated. They had an agenda to mobilize support for a planned anti-war demonstration heralded as 'Moratorium Day,' scheduled for October 15 on the Boston Common. The planning for this event had begun in the early spring. I had missed the first meeting, but I was there for the second. About two dozen people, mostly students, were in attendance.

The leaders of the organization, all of them sober minded dissidents, laid out the strategy explaining that the Boston Moratorium was intended to be a part of a huge national rally, a one day massive protest directed against the war in Vietnam - an unmatched public outcry against the United States Government complete with all the accouterments - public speakers, entertainment, informational tables, literature, signs, posters and placards.

"That's the objective," one speaker concluded. "The challenge is getting there." In capsule form he instructed his audience that the success of the rally would depend on their energy and organizational abilities.

"There's a lot of anti-war feeling out there," he said, "but it's up to you to mobilize it."

He emphasized that the ultimate success of this big action would be dependent on the outcomes of a series of smaller actions planned to take place along the way. He was referring to other forms of protest demonstrations, lesser actions such as teach-ins, sit-ins, and building takeovers. The mission, for this core of activists, would be to return to their colleges and high schools and shape the anti-war sentiment that was drenching the campuses.

The second speaker, whom I knew to be a dedicated member of the Socialist Workers Party, handed out literature and a compact organizational booklet illustrating techniques of organizational development and methods of mobilizing student opinion against the war. The rest of the evening was spent dividing the participants into groups based on their political and geographical spheres of influence.

Mike Russo, as I had expected, was assigned to work with the Boston State Hospital Employee's Union and he was urged to return for the next scheduled meeting to report his progress. I provided my contact person with the main phone number of the institution, GE-6-6000, and instructed him on how to connect with the Male Home. This necessitated that I tighten up on my cover in the event that he actually attempted to contact me (Mike Russo) as I fully expected he would.

I, in the role of Mike Russo, had laid an almost airtight rap on him. I explained that I resided at the male residence of the Boston State Hospital where I was employed as a Psychiatric Aide. I further elaborated that I had been evicted from the building because another attendant had used my room for the showing of a pornographic movie.

I never disclaimed that it happened, but I vehemently denied that I ever approved of it. "It was something the guy did without my permission," I said, assuring him of my disgust of pornography. "As far as I knew," I added, "the attendant who used my room intended to show a short eight millimeter clip of Second World War news footage entitled *Bombs Over Tokyo*.

Continuing this stream of gibberish, I explained that once the Administration had gotten wind of the pornographic movie they had used the incident as an excuse to punish me for my union activities by expelling me from my room at the Male Home.

Predictably, my contact person was becoming bored, which was exactly the effect that I had wished to elicit. He just stood there looking down at the floor and shuffling his feet around. I continued, confiding in him that I had moved surreptitiously into a vacant room in the basement of the Male Home where I intended to remain until the matter, which was under appeal, had been successfully resolved.

This was the kicker - only one guy knew that I was still living in the building. If my contact person needed to get in touch with me he would have to dial the main number and after being connected to the Male Home, ask for Paul Memos who would deliver the message.

It was a wildly believable, eccentric tale and it worked every time that I used it. It had even gotten me past the 'movement detectives,' individual members of radical groups dedicated to uncovering infiltrators.

I dropped in on Paul Memos the next evening and he agreed to take any messages for Mike Russo with no questions asked. I doubted at that point he would get any - it just wasn't worth their effort.

Things hadn't changed a lot in the Male Home - just some of the faces. There were three or four conversations going on in the front lobby. I ran into a couple of the old timers and one of them told me that a woman whom we both knew from the Reception Building back in '62 had plunged to her death from the top of a building in New York City. She had been a beautiful and extraordinarily talented woman. She had performed in the Metropolitan Opera -- her name was Andrianna Tranquillo.

And the beat went on.

Twenty-Eight

S ome other things happened around that time. Dan Sweeney officially took over the reins of the Boston Police Patrolman's Association (BPPA). He had finished filling the un-expired term of his predecessor, Dick MacEacern, and had been elected President. MacEacern had retired due to a leg injury, reportedly the result of a gunshot wound received in an incident on the Boston Common.

The headquarters brass were happy to see him go. MacEacern had turned their police department upside down and they didn't appreciate it. In a typical illustration of comical Command Staff hypocrisy they had showered him with official deference after he was elected President, going so far as to attend a family funeral; but in truth they despised him, denouncing him as a wild card.

They regarded Sweeney as a more rational, moderate choice and while they still hated the idea of a union, they preferred Dan to Dick. I don't think they ever realized how tough the little red-head could be.

Dan was my man and I figured I had a big connection in the union. I enjoyed calling him occasionally at home on Saturday mornings to discuss union business. I had been doing this for a while and whenever I did he was always willing to kibitz. During one of those calls I talked to his son Al who was a psyche major at the University of Massachusetts. It was obvious that he was a pretty bright kid so I encouraged him to come on the department "because a college degree could make a big difference in the near future".

I urged him to "Get on the elevator on the first floor before degrees become common, or perhaps even a necessary entry requirement." (Of all the naive professional assumptions of my young career, that one turned out to be the most disappointing).

In spite of some misgivings concerning the quasi-military nature of the police department (Al was never in the service) he eventually came on the job. He was different from his old man from the start, decidedly more of a management type, but no less controversial. His issues were still in the wind.

Of a more immediate impact, I was assigned a partner. Lynch called me in early one afternoon. There he was, standing and looking out the window, Gerry O'Rourke, also known as 'Rockball.' He was an agile-minded, swashbuckling, two fisted, scotch drinking South Boston Irishman, a personality every bit the envy of the most colorful Mickey Spillane character, and one of the least likely to perform well in an undercover capacity.

Gerry was a cop fashioned by birth, pure and simple. The guys sometimes referred to him as 'Gerry the Cop.' He loved the job - he was tough, quick, smart and fast on his feet but the Department would have had a better shot at stuffing a genie back in the bottle as having Gerry work undercover, especially in the anti-war movement. It just wasn't his bag.

For the past four years I had worked alone and I had come to prefer it. I had no wish to get saddled with a partner, and if I had to bite the bullet it wouldn't have been with Gerry. He would not have been my choice. He was simply too obvious. I would have selected a laid-back type, like Richie Cox, a guy made for undercover work.

Gerry was a traditional cop and good at what he did, but the stuff that I was doing was anything but familiar. It was uncharted territory and I was making up the rules as I went along. I had no wish to trip along that labyrinth with a five foot ten inch, wavy-haired, rock-hard, ever ready super-cop, particularly not one as profuse as Gerry O'Rourke.

In a transparent attempt to assuage me, Lynch explained that the brass didn't want me working alone. However, I suspected that the true reason was that Gerry had requested first-halfs because a night job would afford him the opportunity to attend law school.

"Things are changing for the worse out in the street," Lynch said. "It's getting more dangerous and the department doesn't want you out there by yourself."

He didn't have to tell me things were 'getting more dangerous!' I could see what was happening and that was an understatement! *Society was disintegrating* would be a more accurate statement. The ghettos were burning; crime was spiraling out of control; cops were getting blown away; the intelligentsia were ripping up the streets. Traditions were being overturned: men of peace - killed; government officials - assassinated; flags - burned; and veterans - humiliated. Gays were seething, and women - women - only God knew.

As I was out there every night I was deeply affected by these changes. The emotions evoked by these conflicts poured through me through me like a torrent. I knew just how dangerous it was getting and I felt pretty uneasy with it all, paranoid perhaps.

I can still vividly recall an incident that occurred one evening while walking up the south side of Beacon Hill. I was following a man whom the Secret Service suspected of having authored several threatening letters to the President. He was a gargantuan guy, real crazy and known to be dangerous. I was getting ready to turn right onto Park Street in the direction of the Paulist Center, a politically radical Catholic chapel where this 'cuckoo' was heading, when I became astutely aware of a small pick-up truck coming up on my left hand side.

As the truck moved slowly past me I could see that it was carrying several ragbag-type rowdy young men. They were laughing and carrying on badly. The truck slowly came to a stop on the narrow street, no more than a couple of feet from my left shoulder. One of the passengers suddenly pulled a hand gun from his waistband and pointed it at me.

"See you later!" he said.

The ensuing fear of an imminent death instantly transformed my body into an adrenaline-soaked power pack. I quickly moved toward the bay of the truck and reached for his extended arm. I grasped his wrist and yanked him over the side panel. The gun and his head hit the ground at about the same time. His head sounded with a clunk and the gun landed with a clink, unlike the sound of metal. I pinned his head to the street by pressing down on his throat with my left knee and reached for the gun that had landed close by.

Once I had grasped it I knew from the feel that it was a plastic water gun! To my chagrin and to his horror I had mistakenly believed that I was being threatened with a real 'piece.' My assailant turned out to be an adolescent prankster, a foolish one at that, but I was so pissed that I didn't care. His friends leaped off the carrier and surrounded me.

I stood up, remaining steadfast in my opposition. An explanation or an apology would have invited attack. I defiantly challenged them. "Who's next?" I shouted.

Nobody moved! An anxious minute passed. Then his friends eased the terrified kid back onto the rear of the truck. Once he was safely on board the others followed - two of them got in the front. The water gun kid was crying.

"Fuck you!" he blurted, his voice painfully rising over the roar of the engine as it turned over. The truck began to move and the 'cowboys' drove away in a chorus of obscenities. I mentally burned the registration number into my brain and checked out the listing the next day. The truck belonged to a twenty-two year old kid from the state's richest town, Weston, Massachusetts. His first name was Lesley. Evidently he and pals were out for a night in the city, playing guns.

Once I had cooled down I felt a twinge of guilt about what had happened, but the way I resolved it, the prankster had gotten what was coming to him. I wondered about how many other people he and his silly band had terrorized that night before encountering an up-tight undercover cop.

Here's the point! I was well aware of what was happening on the street and sometimes it got to me, but I had grown to cherish the freedom that I had become accustomed to while working alone. I also enjoyed the demands of the job: the immersion in current events, the intellectual nuances of movement leaders, the ideological differences among political philosophies, the acquisition of activist information, the sorting and grading of radical groups and most of all, the obsessive challenge of having to accurately project their future actions. I was quietly doing my own thing, unsupervised and unencumbered by department clocks, cruisers, radios and reports. And I wanted to keep it that way.

I didn't want to get saddled with a partner, not any partner, much less the irrepressible Gerry O'Rourke! Unfortunately patrolmen must follow orders and since it didn't look like I would have much choice in the matter I caved in and accepted the inevitable. There was no point in alienating the guy before we even started. Gerry wasn't a bad guy and besides he was an ex-jarhead.

Eventually there would be some other changes that I would have to adjust to. It would be necessary to meet Gerry in the Intelligence Division office in Police Headquarters at the beginning of the shift. Lynch explained that working odd hours was out. With the ratification of the new union contract it had become necessary to work established shifts. Our new shift would start at 6:30 PM and end at 2:00 AM (although occasionally we would volunteer to work days). The administration was taking the hard line by forcing the union to play by the new rules even if it meant thwarting investigations that overlapped the time constraints.

The new rules didn't make much difference to me. I pretty much worked those hours anyway. There was an added benefit to my meeting Gerry at Headquarters - it removed the requirement of my having to call Lynch every morning to receive my assignment. I had started to tire of that. Now the boss could just leave us a note. Ed Blake wouldn't have gone for these changes. He would have thought that they reduced his flexibility, but as it turned out, I came to prefer the new routine.

I gradually came to feel much more integrated into the life and fabric of the Department. I had never realized how much I had missed, especially the never-ending rumor mill which continuously spurted out information throughout the three shifts, for seven days a week and fifty-two weeks a year. Police departments never close their doors and cops never stop talking to each other. Roach had been an exception to that rule, or maybe he just didn't talk to me. I still wasn't sure.

I was careful to avoid being seen entering the building by bad guys or radicals. At that time in the evening things were pretty quiet around Berkeley Street. Headquarters stopped doing business with the public at five o'clock in the afternoon and there was no lock-up in the building.

Prisoners were handled by the eleven District Stations. I soon got used to reporting there although it felt somewhat strange in the beginning.

My partner and I were assigned an unmarked police car, a Chevrolet Malibu, which was also a first for me and promised to save a great deal of wear and tear on my personal vehicle. I had purchased a new Chevrolet Biscayne in 1967 but the constant wear and tear, resulting from its continual use, caused it to break down frequently. This was the second car that I had burned out on the job and Gerry was forever helping me to get it started. There was one drawback to the department vehicle, nonetheless. Basically, it was an unpainted cruiser, which made it easy to spot. That difficulty would have to be worked out. Eventually Gerry and I would work out many problems - partners usually do.

Gerry was a punctual guy and never tried to beat the department for time. We both worked a full shift, so we never experienced a problem on that score. We would meet in the office at the beginning of the shift, bang out a few phone calls and then head out onto the street. In the beginning Gerry would dutifully drop me off at a selected location where I would do my thing: pick up literature, attend meetings, talk to informational sources, etc.

However, we soon tired of that wearisome arrangement. Neither one of us liked the idea of having Gerry wait for me so we made our first big adjustment, namely that for at least a good portion of the time we would work separately. I would do my thing and he would do his. For me, that meant the continuation of what I was already doing (collecting domestic intelligence). For Gerry, it meant the gathering of criminal intelligence.

At the end of each shift I would dictate my portion of the report to Gerry. He was a proficient typist and I did not learn to type until years later. We'd place the finished product and any pertinent literature underneath the Sergeant's desk blotter for him to read in the morning. Occasionally I would call the boss at his house if I had unearthed information that couldn't wait. A few times, if I had come on something really heavy, I would travel to Hyde Park to see him. Jimmy Lynch would become my confidant over the next several years.

The radical scene was pretty much over by late evening, usually around ten o'clock. By that time I had collected most of my information. Sometimes

Gerry would pick me up at an agreed upon spot and we would cruise around noting registration numbers, tailing the wise guys or performing brief surveillances. Occasionally we worked on assignments that were given to us by our bosses, and sometimes we worked the Combat Zone.

Gerry often worked with the Vice Unit guys or the District Detectives as they moved in and around the Zone putting the peep on the joints or talking with the hoods. A favorite tactic of ours was to have 'Mike Russo' follow Gerry around and eavesdrop on the conversations the wise guys would have after Gerry left. We uncovered a great deal of valuable information that way, including the whereabouts of a fugitive who was wanted on a murder warrant. Between the two of us, we stayed on top of the action in and around the city.

In some respects Gerry and I complemented one another. His strengths were my weaknesses and conversely, his weaknesses were my strengths. Irascible by nature and generally regarded as impatient and brash, he had an amazing facility for absorbing his surroundings and the instinctive knowledge to act quickly and decisively in out of control and perilous situations. One of his favorite sayings was, 'Strike when the iron is hot.' I supposed that is another way of saying 'He who hesitates is lost.'

He also had an excellent sense of direction and possessed an intricate knowledge of his surroundings. Both of these qualities continued to be monumental obstacles for me. One evening, several months after we had begun working together, we were cruising the city when the most dreaded of radio calls interrupted our conversation.

"Shots fired! Two officers down outside the Big M on Mass. Avenue!"

Apparently two District 4 cops, Officer Dennis Ross and his partner Peter Muse were working the wagon that night and had stopped outside the Big M to tag a vehicle that was double-parked near the front door. They were simply doing their job. They went inside to get the driver and ended up in a dispute with one of the patrons. The argument had spilled onto the street. Suddenly the disputant reached for a concealed firearm and shot both of the officers.

Ross, who was severely wounded, managed to empty his gun at the fleeing assailant, but it was not known if he had hit him. The other officer lay wounded underneath the wagon, his swivel holster pinned under his body and a bullet in his spine.

Gerry pressed on the accelerator and the car jerked to life. He took advantage of every short cut through the surrounding neighborhoods and in a few minutes we were approaching the scene. Police cars were everywhere and the whine of sirens overwhelmed the night.

Gerry stopped about five hundred feet from the crime scene and I jumped out of the car as quickly as possible. This was a pre-planned tactic and one that would work again and again for us.

An 'Officer down' or 'Officer in trouble' call never fails to result in a massive police response in the direction of the officer, but it's also important to work the crowd from the outside in. That way, an alert investigator may be in a position to write down registration numbers of vehicles leaving the scene, and/or pin suspects trying to flee the area. I maneuvered my way through the widening crowd, scratching down license plate numbers and searching for any face that might hold a clue as to what had happened.

The wounded officers were en route to the hospital by the time I reached the front door of the Big M. I spotted a flamboyantly dressed guy wearing a gaudy jacket outlined in red sequins. He seemed excited and was talking incessantly to anyone in the crowd who would listen. People are more likely to ramble on after viewing a violent incident, particularly the shooting of two cops and even more so when they are exhilarated by the result as this guy obviously was.

"What happened man?" I inquired.

Momentarily thrown off by my beard and white sneakers, he blurted, "Two pigs got offed! That's what happened! They got into an argument with the dude over a parking ticket and he came out the joint. First he shot one motherfucker, and then he ran around the wagon and shot the other one. Bang! Bang! Bang - right in the stomach! They didn't know what hit them and those pigs were gone!"

Before I could entirely assimilate the full horror of his remarks he abruptly stopped, apparently realizing that he already had said too much. He reproached himself and spitefully commented, "Why am I telling what happened to a white man in a black man's neighborhood?"

But it was too late - I knew that I had an eyewitness. I had to locate

Gerry immediately, before the guy disappeared. I frantically searched for Gerry in the crowd, finally spotting him just as my eyewitness was slipping away.

"Gerry, quick!" I warned him. "Get another cop and grab that guy over there. He's a witness and he's leaving! Don't say anything about me - just take him to the station and I'll meet you there."

Gerry never wasted any time asking me for an explanation, nor did he look for an assist. He locked onto the guy, grasping him underneath his left arm and marched him to an available cruiser. He jumped in the cruiser with the witness and instructed the driver to take the suspect to the station while I picked up the unmarked car.

A half an hour later I walked into District 4, deliberately delaying my arrival to achieve the best psychological affect. The witness, who still did not know that I was a cop, was perched on a table in the detectives' room looking real belligerent. This was a hard, street-savvy guy. He held all the cards and he knew it. The cops would have to release him or charge him with a crime, and he had been blameless in this incident. Gerry and a couple of detectives were questioning him.

According to Gerry, the witness insisted that he hadn't seen anything and had demanded to know why he had been picked up. He claimed that he was a late-arriving bystander and that he "didn't see nothing." As evidenced by his smug look, he believed that the cops had already overstepped their bounds. It was also pretty evident that he hated cops, and no wonder. A record check revealed that he had just been paroled from Walpole State Prison where he had served a couple of years on an armed robbery conviction. And that's how we jammed him up!

The minute he saw me he knew that he was screwed. His mouth fell open in astonishment. He realized that, in the excitement of the moment, he had spilled his guts to a cop. How could he continue to argue that he didn't "know nothing" when he had already told a cop the whole story? I reveled in his anguish, as he had reveled when the cops were shot. His joy became mine.

It didn't take him long to assess his position. His failure to cooperate would have placed him in violation of the conditions surrounding his parole. Just being out that late at night in an area habituated by known felons would have been enough to send him back to the can, but to have witnessed the shooting of two police officers, then refuse to cooperate with the investigation, would have buried him.

In his own words he lamented, "I ain't gonna be no mother-fucking accessory." And with that, he identified the shooter.

The suspect turned out to be a local boy named Eugene Knox, a big fearsome-looking bruiser who loathed cops. A warrant was issued for his arrest, but was never served. Knox fled the state and headed for Atlanta, Georgia. The way I heard the story is that shortly after he got off the bus in that southern city he got into a beef with a couple of police officers and attempted to shoot them down, just as he had done in Boston. But this time he would lose. The cops got the drop on him. He was cut down in a hail of bullets and when the dust settled Knox lay dead on the pavement. The cops had won this battle, releasing our reluctant witness from ever having to testify.

Dennis Ross returned to the job after his injuries healed. He was lucky. Eventually he was promoted to the rank of Sergeant. He became an excellent and street-wise Patrol Supervisor. Peter Muse wasn't so lucky - he never returned to duty. The surgeons were unable to remove the bullet from his spine.

Twenty-Nine

Police work entails long hours of boredom punctuated by periods of extreme excitement. Gerry was an action cop - they don't come any better. He fed off danger and chaos like an enlivened wire. During the boredom phase, however, he could become oppressive. Extended surveillances were not his thing, especially if I were inside some enclosed place where he feared that I might be in danger.

Gerry and I had partnered up while I was half way into a subversive/drug investigation that had begun in a head shop on Charles Street and ended in a yippie commune at 690 Mass. Avenue in the South End. It was this investigation that caused us to realize, early in our partnership, that it would be impossible for two people, especially Gerry and me, to work undercover together.

Head shops were small businesses that existed within the gray shadow of the law. An intricate part of the Sixties counter-culture, they purported to heighten human sensation, but in reality they profited by catering to hippies and drug users.

'Roger's' was a typical head shop consisting of an outer room set up for the sale of drug paraphernalia such as pot pipes, incense burners, cigarette rolling papers and small accessories such as Indian beads, head bands and amulets. The inner room was painted in psychedelic colors and bathed in black light. The surrounding walls were adorned with fluorescent posters that glowed in the dark and served as a backdrop against the measured pulsations of a strategically positioned strobe light. This room was designed to elevate the drug highs of the various customers and was not generally accessible to the public.

Drugs were a staple of the times. They were imbued in the culture and inextricably interwoven into the lives of a cross-section of young America. For some they were a sacrament that promised sublime personal pleasure and expanded awareness as espoused by Timothy Leary. He wasn't the only one pushing this crap. The Beatles and other musicians repeatedly glorified drugs in their music. It was widely believed that the use of the term *Yellow Submarine* was a metaphor for an amphetamine, although the drugs of choice back then were mainly pot, hash, mescaline, peyote and LSD. Most were classified as hallucinogenic and were regarded by their adherents as possessing mind-expanding capabilities.

I scouted out the head shops as part of my street scam and that's how I happened to meet Christopher, my connection to the commune at 690 Mass. Avenue. It was before I was teamed up with a partner and I was just shuffling around the city doing my thing.

I was sitting on the floor of the inner room of Roger's Head Shop when Christopher came in with a really messed up looking chick who, as it turned out, had been tripping out for the past four hours. As her hallucinations escalated she went from seeing music and hearing colors to experiencing the utter horror of being ravaged by snakes and spiders. She was convinced that they were invading her body orifices. She writhed painfully around the floor, frantically passing her hands over her mouth, ears, naval, crotch and behind.

The intermittent flashes from the strobe flicked off her frail body, seemingly locking it into a thousand positions of brilliantly displayed animated movements. The florescent posters beat synchronously with each illuminated seizure contributing to the demonic effect that permeated this small room. She struck the image of a wounded chickadee flipping over and over on one wing. Suddenly she held her hand between her legs and discharged a wretched scream.

Christopher lost it. He slowly rose to his feet, his progress measured in rapidly escalating lighted intervals, and stood there looking helplessly down at his friend. He was frozen. Perhaps it was a combination of my state hospital and police training, call it what you wish, but I instinctively swung into action. This time I would need to be a blend of cop, psychiatric aide and exorcist! I shouted to the kid in the front of the store to turn everything off, switch on the regular lights and to call an ambulance.

The clerk took more than five minutes to locate the light switches and turn off the strobe and he never called for medical assistance. That would have been bad for business. Meanwhile, I continued my feeble efforts to reassure the terrified girl that these horrors were only imagined.

The interval that passed before normalcy returned to the room constituted the single most eerie episode of my entire undercover years. The electrified images of the four of us: me, the writhing girl, the fear struck boyfriend and the bumbling manager coruscated off the walls in a tumultuous dance tantamount to a macabre discotheque.

I began to make progress once the room was restored. The girl looked up at me from her fetal position and tightly grasped onto my wrist. Her hand was wet from a combination of sweat and urine. Soothingly, I continued to talk her down until her nightmare had passed. I cannot recall everything I said or how long I had pleaded with her but eventually it worked - she came out of it. She was wiped out, exhausted but lucid. She thanked me and introduced herself as Katrina. I offered to give her and Christopher a ride home - they accepted and gave me directions to 690 Mass. Avenue.

The building itself was a four story bow-front Victorian set on a busy street in a neighborhood that was still in the middle of its decline. I dropped them off at the front door. They both thanked me and invited me to stop by the next day. I took advantage of the opening and dropped over the next evening. When I mentioned Christopher and Katrina's names the creep who answered the door ushered me in. He was wearing a tattered Army dress jacket with an upside down American Flag sewn on the back. Neither of my friends were home, nevertheless, it didn't take me long to make a connection.

The apartments housed a band of drug using yippies whom I suspected might have been involved in a national 'Trick or Trash' event on the past Halloween night. (On that evening marauding groups of longhaired freaks had engaged in an escapade of vandalism against private property.)

During the next several weeks I would make significant in-roads into this revolutionary collective which was destined to become one of the most infamous hippie joints in the country.

I tied in with a guy named Rich Burch, an honorably discharged Naval Officer whose name I suspected was a pseudonym. There was something not real about this guy and I thought perhaps he was a 'mole'; he was too clean in comparison to the other denizens in the house. His lightly speckled soft white hair flowing down his shoulders in long cascading waves just didn't make it with me. Rich was a friend of Christopher's and lived on the top floor with the messiest, most unkempt, freakiest people I had ever witnessed under one roof. I doubted that the bathtub got much use.

Rich wrote madcap revolutionary articles for various underground newspapers, but paradoxically enough, he came across as a peaceful sort. He was also meticulously clean - that condition compounded by his military background made him a real anomaly when compared to the rest of the communal group. Apart from the nightly intelligence information that I was getting out of him, I came to really enjoy our conversations.

I returned to this fishing hole repeatedly and got to know many of the people in the commune. Lynch told me that the Bureau (FBI) had been tracking some of them for their radical affiliations. He provided me with a list of named subjects. They were: John James Fraser, Mary Jane Grayson, Sharon Marie Steele, Sonia Robinson, Lawrence Legore, Jeff Courtney, Mark Phillips and Russell Burroughs. Several of them would become suspects in the emerging weather underground. Apparently the Feds had penetrated the commune and had an undercover guy in the mix, or at least they had a source in the group. Amusingly enough, the source reported Mike Russo's commune visitations to the Feds. Mike Russo was described as a 'guest' of the commune and thought to be 'dangerous'.

Among its most notorious guests were Jerry Rubin and Abbie Hoffman, the outrageous founders of the Youth International Party. I never saw them in the place but I learned through Rich Burch that they were planning to move there in about one month. They were considering the possibility of buying the building. This was big news and I was excited to learn of it. The consequences for the city could be immense. These screwballs were nothing but trouble.

I was picking up information on this duo the night I got exasperated with Gerry. I sneaked a peak at my watch and realized that I had over-stayed the time that Gerry and I had agreed upon. He was waiting outside for me, probably getting increasingly more jittery by the minute. I envisioned him bursting through the front door like gangbusters in an effort to rescue me. I understood his concern but I couldn't be pressured like that.

As it turned out, I was right about Gerry's anxiety. When I finally met up with him, he told me that he hadn't intended to wait any longer. He thought that I might be in trouble and he was getting ready to go in. This event precipitated our first big compromise: that, at least for the biggest part of the night, we would each go our own separate ways. I was pretty tactful in maneuvering the deal while taking great care not to antagonize Gerry in the process. I assured him that I would keep him advised of what I was doing, especially with regard to dangerous missions. In such instances we would continue to work together.

I got my space and Jerry got the cruiser. A police car was of no use to me anyhow - a bicycle was a better idea. I had a three speed Raleigh gathering dust in the basement which could be better used for transportation at work. I decided to try it out. The bike turned out to be a superb undercover device. Police officers never rode bicycles in those days and it worked to dispel the image of a cop.

I mapped out an approximate six-mile route that covered most of my intelligence sources: down Commonwealth Avenue to Boston University and over the BU Bridge to Brookline Street in Cambridge (Gerry had showed me that shortcut). I'd pass through Central Square to Prospect Street, then to Washington Street in Somerville, on through to the McGrath Highway, over to Broadway and then to Rutherford Avenue in Charlestown. From there I'd cycle through downtown Boston, stopping occasionally in the Combat Zone, and then on back to headquarters. I blended into the shadows of each night and rode its rhythms until pleasantly fatigued. At the end of each tour I would secure my bicycle in the lower basement of Police Headquarters.

I stopped at the appropriate points to pick up literature and gab with movement people. Occasionally I would ride up and down Mass. Avenue from MIT to Harvard. I would sometimes sit and talk with the hippies stretched out on the public benches or camped in the Cambridge Common. Occasionally I checked out the literature posted on the bulletin boards in the campus dormitories of Harvard University for notification of protest actions.

I picked up a lot of information that way and the job soon became second nature. Before it was over I was monitoring over forty locations including apartments, schools, storefronts, churches, groups, tribes and collectives. I was really cracking!

Most of the major organizations operated through fronts similar to the Progressive Labor Party and the Socialist Workers Party. The Protest Movement was made up of a mosaic of groups, a virtual paradox of mostly New Left political diversity. It took me a long time to learn just whom it was that I was dealing with. The leaders typically exaggerated their groups' numbers and many of them played a smoke and mirrors game to amplify their influence.

I kept a loose check on the Communist Party USA and The Young Worker's Liberation League and their two principal committees: to Free Angela Davis and to Fight Political Repression.

The Workers Party Guild was the mother organization of the Youth Against War and Fascism who, similar to the Progressive Labor Party, were considered fanatical and dangerous. On the shaded end of the continuum was The Black Panther Party and its two principal organs: The Committee to Combat Fascism and The Committee to Defend the Panthers. Their Caucasian ideological counterparts were known as the White Panther Party, although it seemed to me that their relationship was more superficial than real. There was also the Spartacist League - a component of the SDS, and a militant women's group known as Bread and Roses, many of whom were hard left lesbians.

Woodstock Nation, a huge open air love fest involving over 400,000 young people, occupying rented land in New York State would spawn a multiplicity of smaller tribes and collectives. Sorting them out wasn't easy.

Woodstock was a festival of raw love, music, dope and naked kids. It was one of two momentous events of the summer of '69. The other was the disintegration of the Students for a Democratic Society.

Rubin and Hoffman never did move into 690 Mass. Avenue. I had entrusted the information to a part time *Boston Globe* columnist with whom I sometimes swapped information and he broke the story, which probably scared them off. It also jeopardized my safety and clipped my ability to gather any further intelligence at that location.

Before summer arrived I had received my first Police Department Commendation. Captain Joseph Jordan wrote the request for commendation to the Police Commissioner in recognition of my having successfully concluded investigations at the Riverway Cafe, the Peerless Market and the Coliseum. The Commissioner's Commendation became a permanent part of my personnel folder.

On May 22, 1969, Black Panther member Alex Rackley was murdered in Connecticut. The main suspect was Bobby Seale. The Chicago 8 was reduced by one.

In June 1969, the New York City Cops raided the Stonewall, a Greenwich Village gay bar, for various licensing violations including same sex dancing and a three day street battle ensued as a result. This was the official start of the Gay Power Movement and its reverberations were clearly felt in every major city in the U.S. Its echoes may still be heard.

Several hundred gay men and women marched in Boston. Their parade route took them past Police Headquarters. The brass peered out the windows and stood on the steps outside the front door gaping at the spectacle of people of the same sex openly embracing one another as they walked down Berkeley Street, flaunting their homosexuality and holding signs advertising their 'perversion.' The command staff didn't know what to expect and as a precaution they ordered a heavy police presence along the parade route.

I was required to infiltrate the parade for intelligence purposes so I rode alongside the marchers on my bicycle to see what I could pick up in the way of loose conversation or planned actions. I attached a helium balloon to the rear carrier for effect.

The demonstration was peaceful and there were no incidents. I couldn't help but note the physical cues of gut wrenching fear that racked some of the participants. They were fearful - the cops were astounded - and I was embarrassed!

357

Thirty

The Students for a Democratic Society (SDS) was by far the major student group on the nation's campuses. What had started off as an anti-nuclear testing group founded by Tom Hayden in the early Sixties had grown into the most formidable student organization the world had ever produced. By 1965 they had openly broken with what they believed were the simplistic and naive assumptions of the New Frontier and had begun to move down an increasingly explosive revolutionary path. They were the first to have organized an anti-war demonstration in Washington during that year attracting thousands of protesters.

The SDS grew more radicalized with the intensification and continuation of the war. For each moment of each day that the conflict continued, for each scaled escalation, for each deliberate expansion, there was a direct and proportional effect on the size, rationality and temper of this student organization.

Senior Washington officials threw gasoline on the fire by deriding and insulting the student leaders in an effort to isolate them from the so-called 'Silent Majority,' a term coined by Dean Rusk in '67 to describe the vast amount of people who stayed home from demonstrations. Vice President Spiro T Agnew, whom the dissidents despised and charged was the 'bag man' for President Nixon, would come to define their members as 'effete impudent snobs'.

The U.S. war leaders might just as well have injected the dissidents' bodies with a powerful serum that stimulated their growth and twisted their minds. The War Policy of the United States Government had created the monster and by the end of the 1969 Spring Semester I could plainly see that this organization was beginning to fragment and some of its members were going off the deep end.

The seemingly never-ending war groaned on in spite of the students' best efforts to call attention to its futility. The draft continued, Vietnam was being destroyed, its people slaughtered, and the body bags kept coming. It was pushing many of them into a state of frenzy and despair. The Progressive Labor Party gradually emerged as the most volatile component of the SDS. And it was they who most clearly annunciated the credo of the New Left - simply stated that nothing less than a total revolution would cure society's ills!

Their primary organizational antagonists were the Socialist Workers Party, who shared their Marxist underpinnings, but disagreed vehemently with their methods and timing. As their differences became more accentuated, the organizations edged toward the brink of open war. Lesser political components of the SDS entered the affray and the clash among philosophies, tactics and strategies would become unbearable and non-resolvable. These differences metastasized during the national SDS Convention held in Chicago between June 18 and June 22. I attended simultaneously informational SDS meetings at Boston University during this tumultuous period and spent time in the Ziskind Lounge reviewing position papers and witnessing confrontations and arguments. At some point into the convention the members of the Progressive Labor Party and the Socialist Workers Party entered into a rancorous dispute. Their hatred for one another reached a white-hot intensity and boiled over into pitched battles on Commonwealth Avenue and Brookline Streets. These 'gang' fights continued well into the Seventies.

One of the local conferences was held in the Morse auditorium. Each person who attended, including me, was searched and once the meeting began the rear doors were closed and secured from the inside. SDS sentries guarded the doors and no one was permitted to enter or leave until the meeting was over. I can tell you - I sweated it out. I feared that I was about to be uncovered and resoundingly beaten. I was immensely relieved once it was over and the members of the audience were permitted to leave.

I can't remember the specific issues under discussion although I do recall the Progressive Labor Party as having a lot to say. They struck me as modern day fascists and I questioned the wisdom of the University's Open Door Policy. (What did the school gain from opening their doors to people with divergent political views, but closing them to others with opposing political views?)

The main body of the national SDS eventually spit out a complicated agenda and a plan for action. They reached a general consensus that Capitalism was the root cause of all social problems and that imperialism, which they described as "the monopoly phase of Capitalism," had to be destroyed. They assumed a multi-pronged approach and agreed to support:

(1) The liberation of Black and Latin Colonies within the U.S.,
(2) The right of national self-determination and the right of political succession,
(3) The struggle for National Liberation of the people of South Vietnam led by the South Vietnamese Provisional Revolutionary Government,
(4) The Democratic Government of Vietnam led by President Ho Chi Minh,
(5) The Democratic Government of China,
(6) The Peoples' Republic of Albania and Korea and
(7) The Republic of Cuba.

They called for the people to 'Come to Chicago in September for the trial of the Chicago 7, to force the power structure to bring the war home, and to build major actions in the fall against the war in Vietnam.' They rallied for actions against racism and for support of the working class, open admissions to universities and a one hundred-dollar minimum wage.

They supported Women's Lib and denounced 'the sexual myths and stereotyped ideas of masculine and feminine' that obfuscated the truth and led to gender differences. They denounced 'the use of women to bring down wages by the performance of free services,' particularly housework. They argued that 'for justice to come to black people there must be black economic and political self-determination.' They demanded 'an end to militarism and business control of society,' especially the military industrial complex, a nebulous set of relationships between the government and private sector that these radical adherents abhorred and firmly believed was the root cause of the Vietnam War!

Jared Israel and Mike Schartz, two local guys representing Harvard and Radcliffe, set out a tactical program for the SDS which emphasized among other things, 'the smashing of racist courses and institutes, especially pig institutes, counter insurgency institutes and riot control programs such as the ROTC and the police.' (This proposal would eventually lead to student demands to eliminate the College of Criminal Justice at Northeastern University.) Also included were the remarks of the youth components of the Du Bois Club, the Communist Party and the Independent Marxists which generally emphasized similar positions.

The presence of what many believed were a disproportionate amount of Jews in the anti-war movement fueled the right wing prejudice that Jews were disloyal. Jews couldn't win - they were sought after by radical elements on both sides of the political spectrum. This hatred was later encapsulated in various pro-war and anti-semitic literature distributed in the student lounges of the local colleges. One such handout, containing a statement denouncing Jews, ended with these words, 'Kill for peace, kill for freedom, kill Vietnamese, kill, kill, kill.' I suspected that the source of the information was a Nazi storefront on Brookline Street, the only one of its kind in the Boston/Cambridge area, and that the pamphlet was a direct reaction to the SDS convention.

This was the credo of the New Left as it was articulated during the SDS Convention. Simply stated, Capitalism polluted everything and was at fault for every social malady from poverty to war. Only a complete top to bottom restructuring of the economic system and a reversal of the power relationship between the Bourgeois and the Proletariat could cure the problem. The dissidents called for a cleansing of the system and a total reordering of the political and economic values that supported it. It was straight Marxism served with a New Left twist - none of it was new.

The participants had a lot going for them. They had a lot of goals and a few good ideas, but how to accomplish all of it was where the Convention broke down. The extremists called for joint revolutionary violence among workers and students.

The Black Panthers, the Communist Party, the Independent Socialist Club and the Cambridge Movement for a Democratic Society supported the general SDS positions but added demands for the abolition of taxes and rents, the end of imperialist schools and the end of cops. They struck at the very essence of America and called for 'the end to art, literature, design, music, social and individual values, the entire culture,' and the implementation of a pure communist society. They signed off on their position paper with 'All power to the People!'

At some point during the convention disharmony struck. The SDS accused the PLP of being Trotskyite, challenging their belief that the Proletariat, as opposed to the national or ethnic forces, should be the primary force in the revolutionary struggle. I interpreted this to mean that the PLP was losing faith that students could make a difference in effecting change and wanted to carry the fight to working people.

The Socialist Workers Party further intensified the criticism of the Progressive Labor Party, accusing them of being both racist and reactionary and in opposition to open admissions, black studies, community control of police, the Black Panther Party and Ho Chi Minh.

The Sparticist League denounced the PLP as being against the Black Panther Party and joined with the Revolutionary Youth Movement who emphasized the fight against 'white supremacy' and called for mass militant actions against imperialist aggression in Vietnam. They also opposed gun control arguing that 'the people had to be prepared for self-defense and eventual armed struggle!' They argued that they were on the side of Socialist Revolution while other members of the SDS were not.

Their differences with the main body reached a point where they walked out of the Convention behind their leaders, Bernadine Dohrn and Mark Rudd. (Seven months later an accidental explosion would drive Bernadine and a comrade named Cathlyn Platt Wilkerson out into the street naked from a Greenwich Village townhouse that was being used as a bomb factory. Two men and a woman were found dead inside.) The Progressive Labor Party and the Workers Student Alliance added to the furor and were expelled! The SDS also kicked the Labor Committee out for supporting what they considered to be a racist teacher strike in New York. According to the *New Left Notes*, this amounted to about a one-third walk out. Street fights were said to have broken out among warring factions.

The Revolutionary Youth Movement split into two factions: the RYM-1, clearly an underground insurgent organization, and RYM-2, their propaganda arm that was deemed better able to deal with people.

The most dangerous group to be spit out of the convention was the 'Weathermen,' an offshoot of the Progressive Labor Party who aligned themselves with the RYM-1 movement. They were reported to be Jim Reaves, Henry Olsen, Carry Kazio, Ivan Handler, James Kilpatrick, William Geoghran and Boston's own Eric Lavin, a national SDS coordinator and among the most persuasive and magnetic speakers of the movement.

I once heard Eric speak to a group of curious students at Northeastern University. Though it was outside in the Quadrangle, not even the sounds of passing streetcars and automobiles on Huntington Avenue could muffle his message. He was powerful! When he finished I understood how his oratory could move young people. I remember thinking that perhaps a few of Boston's own Revolutionary War colonists had possessed the same sort of mesmerizing charisma. I have no knowledge that Eric or any of his cohorts were ever involved in specific acts of violence. I have little doubt that it was the Weathermen (or the Weather Underground as they were later called) who fueled the beginning of the violent underground phase of the anti-war movement.

They were firebrands and their principal enemies were The ROTC, cops on the campus, Firestone, Delmonte Corporation, United Fruit and Chase Manhattan! They charged that the police had beaten the people in Grant Park at the Democratic National Convention. They argued that, as protectors of the corrupt system, the cops served to ensure continued exploitation, protection of bosses and brutalization of blacks. They demanded that police cadet training programs be abolished. The Weathermen envisioned themselves as elitist revolutionaries primed to lead the masses in the final assault against Imperialism and the worldwide victory of Socialism. Their bible was a palm-sized red book containing the quotations of Chairman Mao and their operating guide was the *Mini*

Manual of the Urban Guerilla, a blueprint for revolutionary violence, which contained the following two statements:

1. Any citizen who wants to become a guerilla can go into action on his own and thus become a part of our organization. This decentralization makes it more difficult to locate the source of the action.
2. The urban guerilla is an armed person who struggles against the military dictatorship by non-conventional means. Political revolutionary and valiant patriot, he struggles for the liberation of his country. Large cities are his battlefield.

These mothers had definitely flipped!

The controversies that fragmented the SDS Convention that summer mirrored the differences in the larger movement across the country. The anti-war movement was permeated with tensions - squabbles were breaking out all over the place. Blacks and whites enjoyed little more than paper relationships, and 'movement women' remonstrated against their devaluated status in the anti-war effort. This was borne out by my own observation, that women in general performed a disproportionate share of the more servile jobs, such as answering phones and making posters. They made few speeches, did little writing and were rarely involved in ideological development and strategic planning.

They didn't appear to have made much progress since the day they threw their bras in trash-cans on the Atlantic City boardwalk protesting the 1968 Miss America Pageant. (A lot of non-movement, macho guys ridiculed them on that day, sneeringly referring to the condition of bra-less, bouncing breasts as a turn-on.)

One radical feminist group, which was affronted by more than just the restraining influence of bras, editorialized in their newspapers for pants with an elongated, zippered fly allowing women to piss like men. Their issue was that male-designed female clothing fostered sexist oppression.

Black women were unashamedly defiled by male black nationalists who openly proclaimed that black men had to develop individual self-respect before women could be regarded as equal. Stokely Carmichael took it one step further and stated graphically that "The only position for women in the movement is prone." Stokely didn't like a lot of things, especially working with whites. His position softened in the late Sixties, but like many other Black radicals, he was never able to overcome his distrust of Caucasians.

The stresses in the movement that generated the greatest controversies sprang from the area of tactical development and the fault line that provided the greatest concern for government was the one that split the 'time for action'. The 'Violence Now' people worried me most. Though only a small fragment of the peace movement, the results of their actions were devastating.

The summer of '69 marked the beginning of the most violent phase of the anti-war movement in Boston and the nation. Demonstrations turned violent, private properties were destroyed and police officers were assaulted. The Cambridge Police tripped off an early warning signal when they raided a Franklin Street apartment decorated with pictures of Che Guevara, an icon of the Cuban Revolution. They arrested seven persons, most in their early twenties, for various gun and drug violations and they confiscated four shotguns, one rifle, a pistol, six machetes and 844 rounds of ammunition along with a store of amphetamines, marijuana and hashish.

The name of the collective was the 'Peoples Information Center' and the apartment was fully adorned with radical symbols including paper Viet Cong flags pasted on the ceilings.

Of more concern to the members of the raiding party were two lists that were prominently displayed on the wall. One, a 'Watch List,' included the times of police patrols in the neighborhood and the other, a 'Pig List,' displayed the registration numbers of both unmarked and personal cars operated by police detectives who were thought to be undercover operatives by members of the collective. Actually, I don't think they were undercover cops. More than likely they were ordinary plain-clothes men, but it didn't make any difference, they were still targeted and that meant their lives were in danger.

I had been to this pad a couple of times before the place turned sour but fortunately I had escaped detection. The raid was led by Detective Dominic Scalese, a handsome five foot ten inch two hundred and twenty pound powerhouse who smashed the door down with a battering ram. Dominic, whose favorite weapon was an axe handle, had earned his reputation as the 'Scourge of the New Left'. His name alone was enough to spark fear - his presence was deadening. I didn't know him personally but by all accounts he was a tough and fearless cop who stayed on top of the militant scene.

For every Dominic Scalese there was a Richard Picariello, a New Left underground operative, just as committed, who would eventually be arrested and convicted of blowing up a Prop Jet Electra at Logan Airport in Boston, two National Guard trucks at the Dorchester Armory and a courthouse in Rhode Island.

Boston's own Suffolk County Court House would be bombed and one of its employees would lose his leg. That happened toward the end of a reign of terror and violence that ripped the city apart over the next few years - a crushing siege that challenged the department to its very core and would continue unabated until the war ended for the United States in 1973. The Boston-Cambridge area was hit hard during this period and would eventually total up millions of dollars in property damage, thousands of people arrested, scores of protestors hospitalized and dozens of injured officers. Armories were broken into, banks were robbed, buildings were vandalized and one ordinary police officer would pay the ultimate price - his life, the result of a planned revolutionary bank robbery.

The entire movement was affected for the worse. I sensed the change - I felt it in the air. I could see it in their faces and hear it in their voices. Their expressions were more serious, their smiles less frequent, their conversations more muted. They were less trusting and more somber. I read it in their literature; it was more critical, more poignant and more inflamed. I discerned it in their attitude - they were less friendly, less embracive and more suspicious. The distrust among groups bordered on paranoia. I learned that the hard way soon after the convention was over.

It was still the middle of the summer. It had been a hot day and the pavement was still warm. It was early evening and I was sitting with about thirty young people in an austere room located in the Transit Building, an old concrete structure located at 108 Mass. Avenue near the fringe of the Back Bay

I was there in response to a Progressive Labor Party flyer inviting people to a meeting to discuss convention related issues. Gerry O'Rourke was hanging around outside in a back-up position. True to our agreement, we worked together whenever it came to the PLP. They were dangerous and I appreciated having him around. The one thing we didn't figure on was that their security people would close, bolt and guard the door once everyone was inside.

I had a bad feeling from the start. I realized that the meeting participants all knew each other and I was the only stranger. The PLP was regarded as bad news to most committed dissidents and the ordinary anti-war activists avoided them like the plague.

The meeting had barely started when I found myself surrounded by several members of the organization. One of them challenged me and demanded my name and identification, charging that I had come to infiltrate the meeting. At first I believed that someone must have recognized me and blown my cover. Now I was in really in trouble! Unless Gerry could receive telepathic messages and push through a locked steel door I was about ready to get my head knocked off. That is if I didn't get killed.

I had a phony Northeastern University Student I.D. card identifying me as Mike Russo; a campus cop had made it for me as a personal favor, but I refused to show it. Perhaps this way I could buy more time until the situation got hotter, suddenly displaying it at the right moment, thereby diffusing the tension.

Suddenly the guy who zeroed in on me shouted, "I know who you are - I've seen you before! You're a revisionist rat from the SWP spying on us!"

I couldn't believe what I was hearing. I thought that I'd been made as a cop, when in fact this guy thought that I was a card carrying member of their principal adversary, the Socialist Workers Party! I felt slightly heartened by this even though the two security goons had left their station at the door to join the others who were circling me.

These were guys designed to do the job. Both exceeded six feet and one of them was pushing two hundred and forty pounds. They began to puff their chests up in a male ritualistic manner, signaling their intention to do me in. I decided to play my final card - my crazy card. The one that I would use to act as a hopeless and mentally disturbed eccentric fixated on attending anti-war meetings.

I hit them with a mix of protestation and salad talk, insisting on my right of free speech while simultaneously denying any involvement with the Socialist Workers Party. I sounded like Mumbles McJumbles. At some point, in the midst of this loosely connected stream of unintelligible verbiage, my tactic worked. The big guy grabbed me under my left arm and escorted me to the door. The other guy opened it and they broomed me out. I had convinced them that I was crazy and not worth the effort of a physical beating. Cops do the same thing whenever they want to avoid arresting a disorderly person. My State Hospital training had paid off again.

I was deliriously buoyant to be back out on the street! Gerry spotted me right away and followed me in the unmarked car to Mass. Avenue and Boylston Street where I hopped in the back seat.

He remarked, "You're out early. Did you pick up any information?"

"Yeah Gerry, I did," I responded. "The Progressive Labor Party are real motherfuckers."

That happened toward the end of the third week in July. A couple of days later, on Sunday, July 20, 1969, a manned spaceship landed on the Moon. I was awe struck by this single event. I snapped a picture of Beverly sitting on the floor of our living room in front of the television at the precise time the spacecraft touched down in the late afternoon. I wanted to capture the image on the screen at the precise moment of impact - however, it didn't come out.

Forty-five days later Ho Chi Minh died. He was one of the great revolutionary heroes of the radical left. Jane Fonda would go on to earn the eternal damnation of American veterans for her one woman, unauthorized North Vietnam propaganda tour in 1972 for, among other things, the purpose of raising blood supplies for wounded *enemy* soldiers. She embodied the New Left's allegiance to this communist leader when she lovingly referred to him as Uncle Ho.

He was so deeply imbedded in the culture of political change in the U.S. that it had been rumored since the middle Sixties that his profile was hidden in the giant splash of blue paint that beautified the Boston Gas Company's huge rainbow colored tank on Commercial Point at Freeport Street in Dorchester. The basis of the rumor originated with Sister Corita, the artist responsible for the design. She was a former Catholic Nun with a scant history of social activism. This tank has remained a permanent part of the Boston skyline and can be clearly seen by motorists traveling on the Southeast Expressway. It has been repainted since those days but the design has never changed and the rumor has always persisted.

Celebrities, like Jane Fonda and other outspoken anti-war critics who carried their extremism to the zenith, were the prime wellspring of the anti-hero status that awaited the ordinary Vietnam veteran upon his return from Southeast Asia. American fighting men were demonized and vilified at home as much as they were by the enemy. This pronounced hostility affected their morale in the battlefield. Reports were coming back from the war describing incidents of racial tensions and drug use among American troops. The use of marijuana was wide spread. 'Mommasan' sold foot long joints to Soldiers and Marines in the jungle. Others dropped acid and shot heroin. There were even reports of fragging incidents detailing the deliberate murder of unpopular military officers.

Military personnel openly complained of low morale and poor leadership. They protested that they were being forced to fight a war with their hands tied behind their backs. They moved around in an endless circle of casualties and death, taking and re-taking the same objectives. They charged that the anti-war protests back home served only to restrain the military and invigorate the enemy. I couldn't have agreed with them more.

Some of the guys who I had been in the service with were over there. And it turned out that Charlie Cosgrove was one of them. When I served with him in '62 he was a young hopeful Marine from Malden, a blue-collar town not far from my neighborhood. I don't think he weighed much more than 140 pounds. He was a smiley kid with animated features. His large brown freckles and lively movements blended together with his youthful naivety so uniquely as to remind me of Howdy Doody, a celebrated icon of the times.

A black kid named York was another. He had been a gunner in my 106 Squad, a quiet Marine with dark boyish good looks. He was thoughtful and brooding and passionate. Like Charlie and me, he had been orphaned at an early age and like Charlie, he didn't have much going for him - he shipped over, too.

The Marine Corps was full of guys like these, desperate at birth and desperate in life. I swore that I would never desert them. I was in a war also, a slower more diffuse domestic war which was sapping the spirit of the nation and the life of my department, but I would stay the action.

The trial opened for the Chicago anti-war demonstrators on September 8. It would last a long time and serve as continual anti-war forum for dissident propagandists.

Thirty-One

The police department's first encounter with the Weathermen occurred during the beginning of the Fall Semester 1969. San Francisco State President Hayakawa, an unbending and outspoken foe of the New Left, visited Boston and was scheduled to give a speech to select members of faculty and students in the Ell Center Student Lounge at Northeastern University.

Hayakawa was a flash point! His name alone sparked controversy and a huge demonstration had been planned for outside the building. On the day in question I went to work early and began to scout around the campuses of both Northeastern and Boston Universities. I began to hear muffled rumors of a violent Weathermen-led protest planned for Northeastern University. As I learned more I found that the Weathermen and their supporters intended to trash the building where Hayakawa was speaking. It was a whispered event, but well advertised just the same. It would be their first demonstration of violent protest following the tumultuous SDS Convention and they intended on making it good.

The plan called for participants to move into the crowd carrying knapsacks full of rocks and bottles. A partner, whose role it would be to remove the projectiles at a given moment and fling them at the building that contained the feisty speaker, would accompany each person carrying a knapsack.

I passed the information to Sergeant Lynch who made appropriate notifications to the various departmental units that would be affected. These specifically included the Commanding Officer of District 2 and the Tactical Patrol Force (TPF), an increasingly higher profile unit which continued to function as the department's main line of defense against violent disorder. The information was also conveyed to the President of Northeastern University and plans were jointly made with the police department to contain the anticipated disorder. The initial part of my job was done, but the acquisition of intelligence doesn't end at any one point - there was more waiting in the wings.

The Tactical Patrol Force moved onto the campus well before the arrival of Hayakawa. They marched to the ROTC Center and waited for their next move, and during that interlude of time a serious misjudgment was made.

Apparently, while the cops were standing by, Northeastern President Asa Knowles was meeting with selected Deans and members of the faculty - at least that's the way I finally pieced the story together. The regularly assigned Commanding Officer of the TPF was not working that day; hence, the officers assigned to the unit were placed under the command of the District Captain who was untrained in their tactical procedures.

The select core of University Advisors recommended to the president that the police should provide the necessary protection for Hayakawa and the building, but should do so without their riot gear. (The academicians clearly wished to avoid the Gestapo image which they feared that riot gear would convey.) Contrary to police procedure and the dictums of common sense and logic, someone in the chain of command conceded to this naïve face-saving request and the cops were subsequently ordered to leave their helmets, face masks and long 24-inch batons in the ROTC building.

The officers marched to the Ell Student Center and took their positions around the perimeter of the building. They looked like plucked chickens and I was astonished and disheartened to see them standing there without their equipment, especially since I had come in on my own time to develop the information. The police higher echelon and the University Deans had been apprized of the information and knew that the Weathermen had intended to incite violence. The Command decision to disarm the officers and leave them unprotected was indefensible. I was seriously pissed and headed to a telephone to give Lynch an earful.

"Hey Sarge," I complained as soon as he picked up the phone, "None of these cops have helmets on and there are knapsacks all over the fucking place - I'm sure some of them are loaded with rocks." Lynch was authentically caught by surprise. His voice was tinged with disbelief. He responded,

"I told them Phil. I told them every last word. I don't know who's making the damned decisions over there, but they know about it. I'll give them another call."

I hung up and headed back to the Quad. I was red hot mad and with each advancing step back to the school I coined a new vulgarity for the brass. By the time I got back the Quad was spilling over with protestors. They must have come from all over the city. There were so many of them occupying the street that traffic was stopped on Huntington Avenue.

I slowly and methodically slipped into the crowd and joined other plainclothes cops who had infiltrated the rowdy group for the purpose of bumping up against the many knapsacks that were scattered around to determine which ones contained rocks. Gerry was behind me ready to lock on to the first offender I detected, but it was like trying to find a needle in a haystack. The crowd got even bigger. Several hundred participants pushed their way to the front stairs where the TPF were positioned.

The herd, trampling over some of their own members, began to forcefully push their way up the cement stairs in an attempt to muscle their way into the front door. They were successfully repelled by the police on the first attempt. They regrouped and made a second try. On the second attempt, as if by cue, the rocks and bottles started to fly. One of the first cops hit was Brad Jones. Brad was a quiet, kind-hearted guy. He was one of the three Blacks in my academy class and one of the least likely candidates I would have thought to join the TPF.

The TPF were the elitist shock troops of the police department. They moved in where lesser cops feared to go. They got off on danger and violence and were trained to intervene in the most chaotic situations. They were feared and hated by the revolutionary left and this would be the incident that forged this unit in fire. Some boss had fucked them good this time and placed them in peril, but it would never happen again.

The way Brad would later tell the story; he saw the rock coming out of the corner of his eye and was able to defensively jerk his head from right to left avoiding a direct strike. It nevertheless hit him with great force on the jaw and shattered six teeth. He said the physical damage would have been a lot worse had he not seen it coming. Brad fell to the ground and was removed by an ambulance to the emergency room of the Boston City Hospital. Several other officers were also injured and transported to the hospital. Scores of rioters were arrested and many of them would also require medical treatment. The addition of police reinforcements eventually quelled the riot but at a great physical and mental cost to many who were involved.

In one well-publicized case, a defendant would claim that his career was destroyed as a result of a false arrest that caused him to lose his grant. More than twenty-five years later a higher court would eventually affirm this.

Many people were hurt that day, on both sides of the fence. I was hurt also, hurt because of the careless way that the brass had acted on my information, information that I had gathered on my own initiative. Brad had been my academy classmate and his teeth were knocked out because a lightweight Commanding Officer had permitted elements of the University Faculty to bully him into a defenseless position. This was a clear example of aesthetics substituting for sound police judgment.

The TPF cops would never forget the ferocity of the day and the careless way in which they were managed. Pay back was a couple of weeks away.

Thirty-Two

omentum was gaining at a furious pace for the planned October 15 National Anti-War Moratorium. I had been attending meetings for several months and I was increasingly impressed by the expanding levels of commitment, energy, organizational ability and overall efficiency of the SWP dominated Student Mobilization Committee which would eventually blend into the nationwide People's Coalition for Peace and Justice.

Each college in the Boston/Cambridge area, plus a number of high schools, was assigned a minimum of one campus organizer. In addition to their organizational efforts to mobilize support for the Moratorium at their respective institutions, it was also their responsibility to report back periodically to the mother body, the SMC, and provide projections of their current estimates of support. These estimates grew larger at each meeting which were held principally at Boston University.

The BU location was selected because it was a mid-way point between the two cities. Every major university and most of the smaller colleges were represented. I sat in on these meetings and added up the estimates. Harvard University, Radcliffe, MIT, Boston University and Northeastern were the predominant institutions - with each of them projecting thousands of participants. And there were the smaller ones - Emerson, Boston State, Wentworth, Emmanuel, Simmons, Wheelock, Suffolk, Wellesley, Babson and Lesley Colleges, to name a few. The Mass. College of Pharmacy, several high schools and countless professional associations - lawyers, doctors, nurses and ministers 'against the war' added to the mix.

Support was gushing in from everywhere and it was not limited to the Boston area colleges, high schools and professional associations - the circuitry was sparked by the efforts of forty or more political groups. The underground newspapers were really pumping up the action and even the fringe radical collectives were getting involved. The Yippie Rainbow River Tribe put out information on the upcoming action, as well as *Sundance,* a yellow, white and blue publication of the White Panther Party, and the *Juche,* the principal organ of the outlaw Peoples' Information Center. These were the people I feared would be trouble.

Cesar Chavez, the union boss of the victorious grape workers and leader of the United Farm Workers, would also lend his support to the anti-war movement. Chavez was visiting Boston for a brief time when I initiated a meeting with him. He was staying at 173 Harvard Street in Dorchester and working with Andrea O'Malley and Phil Rodriquez leading marchers down the city's historic Freedom Trail to the A&P Headquarters at 530 Atlantic Avenue in support of non-union farm workers.

His was just one of hundreds of individuals and groups that I, as Mike Russo, would check out to determine their degree of danger potential. I have singled out Chavez because I must tell you that I became fond of him almost immediately. I found him to be a gentle and dedicated soul who acted selflessly and out of genuine concern for the disadvantaged. I chatted with him for a couple of hours. We talked about the war, the plight of farm workers and third world people in general. I was amazed that he would give me so much time. He made me feel that talking to me was the most important thing he had to do that day.

There was nothing phony about this guy. He was short and slightly stubby and possessed an oval face that hinted of rounder and fleshier times. He spoke with a soft voice. His deep brown eyes mirrored the pain of a thousand generations of Mexican farm workers. He struck me as a simple and decent man who acted out of a higher order conviction. I felt a twinge of guilt for laying the con on the guy. But what else could I do - what other way could I separate the good guys from the bad guys?

I can't recall his specific words but their import jolted me. He saw the whole wrap up - the war, poverty and union busting, along with the conditions of the lettuce and grape workers, as the inevitable result of one prolonged assault of the *haves* against the *have-nots*.

It was not the people like Chavez who worried me. It was the November Action Coalition TDA who would become my principal concern. I kind of stumbled onto their office on Brookline Street one evening. A couple of them were talking to a young radical, a good looking eighteen year kid named Bob Stoddard, whom I had met in the street one night while working undercover.

Stoddard was a member of the Revolutionary Youth Movement which, following the SDS Convention, had set up a storefront office next door. Stoddard had served time at the Billerica House of Correction for breaking and entering into an MIT Professor's house. He was basically an affable kid who got his rocks off playing revolutionary. I suspected that his hard core opposition to the war and membership in the Revolutionary Youth Movement was spurned more out of romantic defiance than ideological positioning.

I had enjoyed a casual relationship with Stoddard and it was about to pay off in huge dividends. As a result of his introduction, the 'Day After People' gradually took me into their confidence, initially referring to their plans to create havoc in the streets the day after the verdicts were handed down on the Chicago 7.

Of a more immediate concern were their specific plans to wreak havoc in Cambridge on the late afternoon and early evening of October 15! It had taken me two weeks to develop the information but I had hit it lucky and before the infamous day arrived I had their blueprint of destruction down almost to the last detail.

For some strange reason their leader, Frank Lobar, entrusted me with the intimate details of their plan. He claimed he was on the faculty of MIT. I doubted that he was but I didn't know for sure. Some of the MIT faculty were really weird, just like some of the students.

I remembered a student that Mike Weinburg had introduced me to, back in my bachelor days when I was living in the South End and just before I got on the job. He was a sinister looking character with greasy slicked-back black hair and dressed in a black metal-studded motorcycle jacket, dungarees and black leather boots. He boasted that he carried a gun and reveled in his hatred of cops. To make a long story short, I ended up ordering him out of our apartment after he expressed satisfaction following a televised news item that detailed the shooting of a police officer. I felt like punching his lights out!

As it turned out, this tough-talking eccentric left over from the Fifties, was a brilliant graduate student at MIT. He was part of the research team that produced the 'Boston Arm,' an artificial limb that could be physically manipulated by electrical energy generated by thought processes. Apparently he had contributed to the engineering aspects of the device.

I don't mean to knock MIT. I have a profound respect for the institution, but it has been known to house some loonies, and Frank may well have been one of them. I never did find out. Time constraints and the crushing business of identifying, projecting and policing future actions prevented the Intelligence Division from conducting in-depth investigations. We left that for the Feds.

I never met more than eight people who made up Frank's group, but he was clearly the boss. I knew that the November Action Coalition was tied in with the Progressive Labor Party, the Revolutionary Youth Movement and the Weathermen. In fact I had tailed a couple of their members to the 'Red Book Store,' just outside of Central Square, whose cellar served as a meeting place for the bad-assed Weathermen and to another at 173-A Mass. Avenue, a Progressive Labor Party Office.

Frank was a serious ball breaker. I knew that as soon as I met him - especially after I asked him if the November Action Coalition intended to support the Moratorium. He turned his shaggy head toward me and with an expression that seeped with canned sarcasm replied that 'demonstrations were a fucking tool of the power structure to mask the real issues'.

"Our organization has plans," he said, "but they're different. We will deliver a real message! One that the pigs will understand - one that will hit them where it hurts."

This guy had a program but he was being real cute about the details. It would take me the biggest part of two weeks to tie them down.

At some point he took me into his confidence and revealed that his comrades were planning an afternoon of violence following the October 15 Moratorium. I sat in the middle of a meeting that he conducted with seven members of his organization, most of whom I knew to be members of the Progressive Labor Party as well as their appendage, the November Action Coalition.

He pinned an enlarged map of the Greater Boston Area, including Cambridge, on the wall and pointed to several locations along Massachusetts Avenue between the Mass. Avenue Bridge and Central Square which, he ranted, were part of the military-industrial complex and had to be neutralized. He placed a large X over each of these buildings, most of which belonged to MIT and were in some way involved with government research, and looked self approvingly back at his audience. He waited a full minute before he went on - a malicious expression crept across his face and seizing the opportune moment when the room fell completely silent, he continued.

"There will be thousands of people at this Moratorium. Before it is over we will attempt to attract as many of them as possible to a further action down Beacon Street to Mass. Avenue and across the bridge and past these piss holes. After they are liberated we will march to the pig station in Central Square and destroy it."

My chest tightened up when I heard the last part of Frank's instruction. There had been any number of demonstrations at police stations before, but this was the first instance in which I become aware of a planned effort to destroy a police facility. Lobar never elaborated further on the plan but I took it to mean that his supporters had intended to at least trash the station (throw rocks?) and perhaps something even worse - I didn't rule out explosives.

As soon as the meeting was over I beat it to Lynch's house in Hyde Park and delivered the news. There was no doubt in my mind that the Progressive Labor Party and their cousins, the Weathermen, were behind this and I expected big trouble. For the next few days I spent all of my working time developing information on the planned Anti-War Demonstration on the Boston Common and the smaller but more violent action in Cambridge that was sure to follow.

The air was brittle with excitement. I had never witnessed the level of enthusiasm or flurry of anti-war activity that was taking place. Just about every college and anti-war organization intended to play some sort of role. Sometimes I rode my bicycle and other times I walked - but wherever I traveled - no matter where I trolled - and whomever I rapped with, I kept on coming up with related information - the sum total of which reinforced my conviction that the city of Boston was about to get hit with the biggest anti-war demonstration in its history!

By this time my analytical skills were so honed by my prolonged immersion in the movement that I consistently and accurately predicted ninety percent of the social protest actions around the city. I spent my entire working - plus hours, tracking events. I experienced the peace movement in all of its richness. I was obsessed by it. I marked its parameters. I identified its leaders. I analyzed its make-up. I noted its differences. I discovered its tactics. I learned its strategies and I absorbed its vibrancy. I was affected by its disappointments and maddened by its rage. I danced to its music and was inspired by its dreams.

I believed that it was theoretically possible to develop a mathematical construct which would accurately predict the size, temper and tactics of a protest action - by simply plugging the proper values into the equation - such as the pulling power of the issue, the amount of people working on it, the length of time involved in its planning, the degree of social acceptance and adaptability of the sponsoring group's, and the personal appeal of its leaders. The one thing that could screw up the result was the weather and in New England that was always an unknown.

My mathematical limitations prevented me from reaching the point where I was able to develop such a formula, but it didn't really make any difference. I went through that sort of a mental process whenever I projected the size and temper of a demonstration for the department. The other guys assigned to the unit underwent a parallel process. They worked with the other agencies, especially the FBI and outside police departments, and particularly the Campus Police, Deans, informants and other sources and in a few cases even students, who for their own reasons, ratted out their classmates.

The Boston Police Intelligence Unit was a small part of a huge network spread throughout the country, an interrelationship among federal, state and local agencies connected by phone. (Computers were still in the future.) Phone calls were usually limited to an inquiry or a heads up on an impending action. This was particularly true with the Washington D.C. Police who were the most ravaged department in the nation.

I kidded around a lot with the day guys assigned to the unit, asserting that I was their principal source of information and that they probably knocked each other over every morning to read our nightly report, in hopes that I would have projected a serious action in the evening, or on the weekend, justifying overtime compensation for them.

Back in those days overtime was not distributed on an equal basis. I'm not too sure how the districts operated, but that was certainly the case with the Intelligence Unit. Because Gerry and I worked nights and received a night differential of about sixteen bucks a week, Deputy Donavan reasoned that the day guys should get the lion's share of the available overtime. I never was a big money guy, but the thought of the day guys cashing in on my work on a Saturday afternoon while I sat home making zip irritated me.

Things had been done fairly in the Marine Corps. Conversely, police departments had always been riddled with inequities - any cop knows that.

Thirty-Three

The closer it came to Moratorium day, the more convinced I became that Boston would be hit hard. Moratorium days in the past had never generated more than a few thousand supporters and they had tended to be well behaved. I was sure that wouldn't be the case on Wednesday. On the evening of October 13, two days before the proposed event, Gerry and I put the finishing touches on a comprehensive report detailing the proposed involvement of more than forty groups who intended to play a role in the national anti-war action.

I put my reputation on the line and predicted that upwards to one hundred and ten thousand demonstrators would participate. Cooler heads prevailed and Peter persuaded me to scale it down to about ninety thousand to avoid embarrassment in the event that we had overestimated.

Peter was the senior man and an original in the unit so I bent a little. Ten or twenty thousand individuals wouldn't make a big difference at this level anyway. The city would be seriously impacted one way or the other and the department needed to plan. Traffic would be disrupted and both lives and property, including the safety of police officers would have to be considered. It would be necessary for the department to move into a large-scale mobilization effort, utilizing officers assigned to other districts to support the plan. The Tactical Patrol Force would have to be called in and overtime personnel would be needed to cover the shortages.

I had a lot riding on this and I was fully aware of the consequences of a miscalculated projection, especially where money was concerned, but I stood by my guns. I preferred to err on the side of safety - there was too much at stake. I was not about to assume the guilt of an under prepared police department - one Brad Jones was enough. The job of the Intelligence Unit was to forecast events and we were about to be tested. The entire unit was together on this.

In summary, the overall plan of the Student Mobilization Committee called for the establishment of several assembly areas for demonstrators to gather. There would be at least a dozen of them. The main ones were located outside the major universities and colleges. These included Harvard and MIT students who would gather on different sections of Mass. Avenue in Cambridge. Boston College and Boston University participants' assembly areas would be separated by several blocks on Commonwealth Avenue, and Northeastern University marchers, along with Wentworth and a number of smaller college supporters, spread out at alternate locations on Huntington Avenue.

The protesters were estimated to begin marching at different times in the morning, based on their respective distances from the Common. Harvard had the longest way to go, approximately three and a half miles - that meant they would begin first. They planned to march down Mass. Avenue, meeting up with MIT a mile and a half down the road. Boston College would kick off early and join with Boston University somewhere on Commonwealth Avenue. Northeastern and her neighboring smaller colleges would move out last as they were the closest to their destination. They were located about a mile and a half from the Common. They all intended to converge on Mass. Avenue with half of the complement turning right onto Commonwealth Avenue and the other half turning left.

Commonwealth Avenue is a large tree lined boulevard in the city of Boston. It is approximately 220 feet wide and includes a pedestrian walkway in its center. Its most beautiful segment majestically divides the historic Back Bay right down the middle where, in one straight shot it links Mass. Avenue to Charles Street which forms the southern boundary of the Boston Common. Traffic moves in opposite directions. It is one of Boston's few planned streets, and as fortune would have it, the only one capable of providing a sufficiently wide thoroughfare for the mass of humanity that would use it on October 15. The rest of the outline included a list of speakers and planned events that were scheduled to take place around the staging area in the vicinity of the war monument.

The final portion of my report contained the most ominous implications. The guts of it read that 'Members of the November Action Coalition TDA, the Weather Underground, the Progressive Labor Party, the Revolutionary Youth Movement and possibly other unknown collectives and members of the radical fringe intended to provoke a further violent demonstration at the conclusion of the Moratorium.'

It continued, 'The organizers of this effort intend to attract other individuals to their cause by signs, placards and word of mouth. It is suspected that bullhorns will be used. The organizers will wave red flags at various assembly points to call attention to their march. These flags are intended to identify assembly areas for individuals who wish to continue their protest. The marchers will proceed down Beacon Street, turn right onto Massachusetts Avenue and cross over the Mass. Avenue Bridge into Cambridge where certain individuals plan to trash a number of locations along Massachusetts Avenue, which they assert are associated with the military industrial complex. Most of these buildings are associated with MIT and a partial list is included at the conclusion of this report. The ultimate objective of the organizers is to use the crowd for cover and to incite the participants to ultimately trash the Cambridge Police Station in Central Square. It is likely that several thousand demonstrators will participate in this march.'

Sergeant Lynch and Peter Ryan met with the Commanding Officer of the Bureau of Field Services, Superintendent Herbert Malowney and his assistant Deputy Superintendent Charles Barry and advised them of the Intelligence Division's projections. To their credit they accepted the unit's recommendations. (Years later Peter would acknowledge these command staff officers for generally approving the unit's estimates. I was not aware of these higher level machinations at the time as I was still groveling around the streets.)

The TPF were put on alert - Officers from other districts were notified to report to District 1. Overtime expenditures were authorized and a command post near Boylston Street on the periphery of the Common would be established. Channel 1 would be cleared for all communications concerning the event. Plans were laid out and the North Side Commander, Deputy Superintendent Warren Blair, was placed in charge.

Blair was a highly regarded member of the Department Command Staff. He was an Army veteran of the Second World War and in spite of not having graduated high school had achieved the rank of Captain. I didn't know much about him at the time, but I shared the respect that most cops had for him. He was renowned for his work on the Felony Squad back in the Fifties where he had been assigned as a Sergeant Detective. It was said that in one month he had amassed over two hundred and fifty arrests of the most dangerous criminals in the city.

His six foot two inch, two hundred and forty pound body lent force to his command presence. There was an aura about this man. He enjoyed high communication skills and his tactile manner and personal spontaneity, combined with an ability to quickly analyze a mass of information and make the right decisions, made him the perfect man for the times. In a vintage Blair statement he had remarked to Mel King, a well-known social activist and a group of supporters who had taken over a small tract of land in the South End to protest displacement of poor people by rich land interests, "I believe in your cause and I am with you but I have a job to do. Clear the area!"

Mel King eventually won the war. 'Tent City', the name given to the action, emerged victorious over time, but Blair won the battle. He was an open minded and brilliant tactician, and the city lucked out for having him. The curtain was about to rise on his first big act.

I sweated Wednesday big time. I was forecasting a heretofore never experienced massive action combined with predictions of later violence in Cambridge. I would have looked really bad if I were wrong, not to mention the embarrassment that I would have caused the unit, including Jimmy Lynch who had supported me. There were certain intangibles that I could not calculate for, such as the weather, which could have messed up my forecast.

Cops believe that bad weather is oftentimes their best friend because it has a depressing effect on street crime. I have reiterated that belief many times throughout my career and have wished for rain or poor weather conditions to put the damper on some event - but not on October 15.

I wanted the police departments in Boston and Cambridge to be ready. I wanted them to be able to suppress any violence that might occur and I certainly did not wish anyone, especially a cop, to get hurt, but I desperately wanted to be right. Different variations of this conflict remains a classic dilemma of undercover work - the worst case scenario, the very thing the agency is attempting to avoid is precisely what its prognosticating operative wishes to happen. The ideal balance would be achieved with the problem being put down because of the information supplied by the undercover operative and the proactive strategies undertaken as a result by the affected agencies, but that wouldn't be the way this story was going to unravel.

As it turned out I had nothing to worry about. Wednesday proved to be a comfortably warm day. These balmy fall periods in New England are often referred to as 'Indian Summer.' I rose about 7:00 that morning and went to the office early. I don't recall the point at which they put me on overtime, but it wouldn't have made any difference; I would have gone in no matter what. I wasn't about to miss the show. I had too much hanging on the outcome.

Soon after I arrived at the office the guys fanned out to the various assembly areas and were reporting back that the buildup was already underway. People had begun moving onto the Common as early as 9:00 AM. Many of them were carrying picnic baskets in preparation for a long day. Pat Brady was at BU and he transmitted over his portable radio that several thousand students were milling around outside the University. (Hand held radios were still a new thing in the department, and believe it or not, some of the old time cops resented them because they believed that it was just another method the department used to keep tabs on the walking officers).

The march was under way before noon. I selected a position at Commonwealth Avenue and Dartmouth Street where I stood hypnotically transfixed by the seemingly never ending chain of protesters pushing their way down the avenue in the direction of the Common - a relentless surge of humanity, possessed of a singular spirit, intent on arriving at their destination where they would stand together on a common piece of ground and howl their protest.

By two o'clock a virtual sea of people had surrounded the War Monument and there were no signs of a let up. I had never seen that many people in one place in my life. Their numbers already exceeded the entire population of the city of Cambridge and more was yet to come. I remember thinking just how helpless the police would find themselves if the crowd turned on them. I fully appreciated, at that point, the natural law abiding instincts of the general population.

The protestors sang and chanted and listened to speaker after speaker denounce the war. They carried signs and posters and wore buttons that conveyed messages flashing the whole panoply of issues underlying the anti-war/social justice movement. The messages were varied. Some of them read: *The subways belong to the people; Fight racism; Abolish the ROTC; Legalize marijuana; Support strikes; Smash racist unemployment; End the draft; Black power; Yellow power; Women's power; Workers' power; People power; Citizen power; Gay power; Flower power; Ecology action; Give earth a chance; Amnesty is justice; The people will free the panthers; U.S. out of South Africa;* and *For a Nuclear Moratorium.*

The most repetitive message, however, sprang from some variation of the anti-war theme. It was plastered all over their signs, posters, placards and buttons - it was reiterated in their speeches and put to song in their music. It dominated their literature and was illustrated in their handouts. It was reflected on their faces and portrayed in their expressions.

It was the force that brought them to this historic place to begin with - to this hill - in this park - to wage this protest - to shout out this collective demand to end this war - now, now, now, now - not tomorrow, or next week and not according to some secret Nixon time table, not gradually, not piecemeal and not with honor but now, now, now - right fucking **now**!

I was captivated by the prevailing bond that united this quivering and burgeoning mass of flesh. It grew larger and larger. Throughout the afternoon marchers continued to pour across Charles Street and onto the Common. Demonstrators came from everywhere, from Boylston Street, from Tremont Street, across Park Street, up the maze of winding roads that comprise Boston's elegant Beacon Hill and down Beacon Street onto the

Common. The war monument disappeared in the center of the widening crowd. Picnickers gave up their ground and stood up to make room for others and still they kept on coming.

I was mesmerized by the immensity of the expanding action and blissfully relieved to know that I was already vindicated. By two o'clock my projection of ninety thousand participants had been surpassed and the crowd continued to increase. At its high point it exceeded one hundred and ten thousand demonstrators. That was a lot of people and it stood as testimony to the work of a small group of political dissidents, namely the Student Mobilization Committee and its dominant core, the Socialist Workers Party, who had orchestrated the entire show.

The behind the scenes power of this small group of American Communists has always mystified me and has remained one of the hidden truths of the 1960's Anti-War Movement, at least in the Boston area and, I suspect, the entire country. I am referring to the covert power of a small group of unconventional political dissidents to influence the actions of a hundred people, multiplied by a thousand, in a wild geometric progression whose end, in the case of this demonstration, was still not in sight.

I sat under a tree on the sun-scorched side of a grassy knoll and took it all in. I smoked a couple of butts and recovered my energy for the next event which I knew was waiting in the wings.

The red flags literally started popping up about 3:00 PM. That's how Lobar had planned it. I didn't know how many there were going to be but I had spotted about a half a dozen of them. A couple of the flag holders were wearing white sweatshirts fronted with red fists, confirming the influence of the Progressive Labor Party. There were two individuals in each team of flag wavers. One member held the flag high while the other exhorted the demonstrators to continue their protest by following them to Cambridge.

This action, as planned, coincided with the approximate time that the larger demonstration commenced to wane. The last significant speaker had left the monument area and the demonstration started to break up. Thousands of people began to leave the Common and return to their dorms and their homes. These were the legitimate ones who were by far the majority. They had done their thing - they had made their point. Their story would now be carried across the country and it was time to call it a day.

These were not the ones that Frank Lobar and the November Action Coalition knew they could attract. They were after the extremists, the sickos, the drunks, the potheads and the cuckoos. It was mainly these troublemakers, along with the curiosity seekers and the revelers who wished to keep the party going, who would make up the bulk of the secondary action.

I was amazed at how easily a handful of people holding red flags and speaking through bullhorns could organize a seemingly spontaneous action and lead thousands of people, at least ten thousand, down the primrose path. But that was exactly what they were able to accomplish in the space of about a half an hour. As the leaders began to move down Beacon Street, the rest of the herd took up the rear. This experience reinforced my notion that most people were simply followers.

Peter Ryan advised the Bureau of Field Service to hold the Tactical Patrol Force over to provide a motorcycle escort for the demonstrators along the march route ending on the Boston side of the Mass. Avenue Bridge. He had correctly calculated that this tactic would contain any acts of violence along the way. Peter saved the city a lot of dough that day, however Cambridge was not destined to share in Boston's good fortune.

I fell into the march at the very beginning and walked down Beacon Street with Frank Lobar (the Pied Piper) and a dozen or so of his supporters. I recognized some of them as Weathermen. They led the march carrying their red flags high in the air. I intermittently fell slightly back into the crowd, deliberately minimizing my presence to avoid detection. The scary consequence of the PLP meeting that I had attended in the Mass. Transit building was still fresh in my mind. You could only get so close to these people before they became paranoid. In addition, I was afraid that one of them might recognize me from that evening.

The march participants moved steadily along the several blocks to Mass. Avenue passing Berkeley, Clarendon, Dartmouth, Exeter, Fairfield, Gloucester and Hereford Streets, a distance of about a mile, where they turned right and continued onto the Bridge. I caught up with Lobar and his scurvy crew on the small section of Mass. Avenue that served as a connecting road to the bridge. I had regained my position next to Lobar when a small advance party of three male supporters came running from the opposite direction, hastily approached him and breathlessly stated,

"The pigs are everywhere. They're on both sides of the street right up to Central Square and the pig station is surrounded!"

Lobar closed his eyes for a moment and laughed. "Then we will liberate Harvard Square," he responded, signaling a change of plans that would substitute this new location for their previous objective in Central Square.

The two squares were situated about a mile apart. They still had two and a half miles to go and that would give me plenty of time to sound the warning (at least I thought it would).

I gradually broke away from the march and high-tailed it to a nearby liquor store. I flashed my tin on the manager and urgently requested to use the phone. He led me to a back room covered with pin-ups and I dialed the private number of the Intelligence Division as I had done hundreds of times in the past. This time the fate of Cambridge would hang in the balance.

As always, the boss picked up the telephone. Lynch dryly asked as he had so many times in the past, "What have you got Phil?"

"Sarge, listen carefully. I don't have a lot of time to talk. Call Cambridge and inform them that the demonstrators are approaching the Bridge. There are at least ten thousand of them, maybe more. It's hard to tell because I can't see the end. But get this! Because of the heavy police presence on Mass. Avenue and around the station in Central Square they're changing their plans - instead of MIT and the police station, they now intend to trash Harvard Square. They're moving pretty slowly and it will probably take them an hour or so to get there. Cambridge better be ready - there are a lot of crazy fuckers in this group. They're smoking pot and drinking and getting higher by the minute!"

A moment passed, giving Lynch enough time to digest the message and mentally calculate its import. He hoarsely responded, "I'll call them right away Phil, and watch yourself out there."

That ended our conversation for the time being. I continued to contact the office by pay phone to report the progress of the march whenever I had an opportunity.

The liquor establishments started to fill up with scraggly-assed marchers making purchases of cheap wine. This pattern of abusive drinking and

frenzied booze purchases (and thefts) would be carried out whenever the marchers passed a liquor store. The owners were either intimidated or possessed by the profit motive; in any event, they didn't close down. I broke into a small run and regained my position up front. I felt really good about picking up that latest piece of crucial information. Cambridge was probably already getting ready.

In the very beginning of the march things stayed relatively under control and the participants remained strangely quiet. Most of them didn't know each other and didn't have a clue as to where they were going or what might be lying in store for them once they got there. The powerful presence of so many motorcycle officers skirting both sides of the marchers deterred any serious acting out and was reassuring to me. Police officers riding Harleys have always been obdurate reminders of police authority and they were used extensively in the Sixties and early Seventies.

The marchers were noisier once they began to congeal, but the real problems wouldn't occur until the police escort was discontinued at the Boston line. This turned out to be a mistake. The shit hit the fan soon after the marchers began to cross over the bridge into Cambridge. It was an understandable oversight, but poor planning nevertheless, and it almost cost an old man his life.

Oncoming traffic began to move slowly against the body of marchers, who by this time were completely spread across both sides of the street. I cursed myself for not having anticipated this contingency. The Intelligence Division should have notified the State Police, who had jurisdiction on the bridge, of possible problems and traffic should have been diverted from the Cambridge side.

Once the marchers realized they were free from the cops many of them became wildly celebratory. They began to chant, "Ho, Ho, Ho Chi Minh," and openly smoked pot and swigged down crappy wine. They cursed at motorists, challenged drivers and vandalized 'pig cars' (luxury vehicles) with hands, feet, bottles, rocks and pocket knives. The action at this point ceased to be an anti-war demonstration and instead became a celebration of violence and debauchery.

A small gang of unruly freaks stopped an older black Caddy being operated by a neatly dressed man wearing a sports jacket and tie who appeared to be in his late sixties. One of them, a tall skinny guy with a matted beard who struck me as an elongated version of a maniacal Mick Jagger, forcefully opened the driver door and jerked the terrified man out from behind the wheel. Another guy assisted him in roughly jamming the old-timer against the door. They angrily referred to him as a 'pig motherfucker' while two others hopped on the car and started jumping up and down on the hood in a frenzied effort to damage the vehicle. As far as these punks were concerned, any kind of luxury car regardless of age, symbolized capitalistic extravagance and hence was a justified target for 'revolutionary force!'

The poor bastard had probably just retired from the workforce like a million other guys and purchased his dream car, a used Cadillac. In a couple of years he wouldn't be able to afford the gas anymore but for now he was flying. And this cowardly gang of four pieces of shit would cut short his dream. I looked over at the guy - his arms were pinned against the car, his tie was blowing in the wind and his eyes were full of fear. He was scared and so was I - really scared!

I wasn't as concerned about his car being busted up as I was for his physical safety. At any moment I expected that these guys would start laying into him. I worried that they would kill him, if he didn't have a heart attack first. I also feared that if I interfered I would not only invoke their suspicion but would be setting myself up for a big fall. It was a long way off the side of the bridge into the cold and polluted waters of the Charles River - that's if I made it that far!

My hands began to sweat and my feet felt cold. I could feel my heart beating against my chest. I thought to myself that I was either a cop or I wasn't. My moment of reckoning had arrived. Even the radical Mike Russo wouldn't forgive me if I failed to help this guy. I had to do something. I frantically searched my mind for a remedy or tactic that I could use to save the old timer and get out of this jam, but I kept on coming up with blanks. None of the marchers seemed to care. Some of them were busy busting up other pig cars and the old man meant nothing.

No one but one guy - a medium framed, curly haired and athletically built dude with steel blue eyes and a serious demeanor who stepped out of nowhere and moved in the direction of the struggle. It happened in a matter of seconds and I am haunted to this day with the question - did I move on my own or was it this act of isolated courage that jogged me out of my paralysis and prompted me to act? In any event, the stranger and I imposed our bodies between the old-timer and his attackers. I implored the batterers to lay off the guy. I hollered "Leave him alone - He didn't do anything. Let's not forget why we're here. There's a lot of shit we can do and this ain't the way to make our point. We wanna shut the war down - not this old motherfucker."

My newly found partner was hardly as pleading or as conciliatory. We pried off the old man's assailants and pushed them away. He just stood there with his arms crossed over his body, forming a human shield between us and any other would be attackers. He remained remarkably strong, silent and resolute throughout the whole ordeal.

God knows we didn't plan it that way, but it was a perfect Mutt and Jeff routine - hard guy and soft guy - and it worked. The rats backed off and slipped into the crowd muttering obscenities as they disappeared.

It turned out that my ally was a devout Quaker and a practicing member of the American Friend's Service Committee. His name was John and he worked out of an office on Brattle Street in Cambridge where he served as a draft counselor. He commented to me that he was a pacifist and that's why he opposed the war. He was a peaceful guy, I could see that, but I was convinced that he would have resorted to violence if necessary to save the old man.

John was misplaced in this group. He didn't realize that he was marching along with the detritus of the crowd that had dominated the Common earlier in the day. These were the remnants, eternal celebrants who didn't know when to call it quits, the malcontents, the phonies, the true subversives - the dangerous ones. He shouldn't have been there, but I was grateful that he was.

We did our best to console the old-timer, who in his own right was a pretty tough guy. I believed him when he remarked that he was a former boxer and assured us that he would have made short work of those guys in his earlier days. (Age takes a special toll on tough guys.) The old man was forced to abandon his car and walk against the crowd to the Boston side of the bridge. John and I chatted for a while and eventually split. I had a lot of work to do.

I steadily moved to the front of the marching crowd, carefully working my way through the maze of people, who by this time had begun to raucously advance down Mass. Avenue. We passed alongside the scattered structures of MIT. I was relieved to see hundreds of out of town police officers lined up and down both sides of the artery and heavily positioned in front of the targeted buildings.

The Cambridge Police Department numbered about two hundred and sixty sworn officers at that time and would have been hard pressed without their help. I was satisfied that they had accepted our projections and had hired hundreds of police officers from surrounding towns to supplement their ranks and help fortify their city against the planned violence of the radical fringe that was presently invading their territory.

This was the first big test for the State of Massachusetts' recently enacted Mutual Aid Compact and its irony was not lost on me - namely, that the revolutionary left's attempt to fracture government would instead work to unify it. Not only would it expand municipal government's power base exponentially by solidifying these local bodies with other municipal, state and federal agencies, but it would also provide further evidence of the need for domestic intelligence. I wasn't about to complain - it was keeping me in a job and out of a car with Roach.

The head of the serpent slowly made its way past Albany Street and into Central Square. The marchers were crazier now - they were deliriously wilder and drunker and higher. Western Avenue was cordoned off with police preventing access to the station. Nobody cared - the party was getting better all the time.

It would take another half-hour before the first marchers would begin to enter into Harvard Square. I will never forget it. I was right up front standing alongside Lobar and his demented circle shortly after the first demonstrators began to pour in. And to the march organizers' utter amazement, and to my complete astonishment, not a single police officer could be seen anywhere. The place was ripe for the picking!

I asked myself 'how could it be possible that Cambridge would fail to respond to the information that I was sure Jimmy Lynch had transmitted to them.' Information that advised the police department that several thousand violent scab-bags of the first order intended to trash Harvard Square, one of the most business-packed, cosmopolitan, intellectually elite localities in the entire country. It was either a colossal failure of communication or poor planning. Somebody in the chain of command had fucked up real bad and this small city was about to pay the consequences.

Lobar's eyes widened and his mouth sagged! He looked hideously dumbfounded. There we stood on the threshold of the most hallowed square in the world, the famous 'People's Republic of Cambridge', and not a single cop could be seen. He must have felt like Pinocchio entering the forbidden land of bad boys - an unchecked territory of unbridled behavior where any kind of delinquency was tolerated. Or perhaps he might have delighted, as a wolf certainly would, in finding the chicken coop unguarded. I lost sight of Lobar after that - he and his friends became lost in the crowd. They had work to do.

The disorder started as I knew it would. The first rock was thrown right after a couple of guys lit a fire in a barrel they had hoisted up onto the top of a small underground transit station's flat roof that jutted over the surface of the street. At first the rioters selectively smashed the windows of banks and finance companies with rocks and bottles but as time passed, and the cops still hadn't arrived, all hell broke loose. Windows were shattered everywhere, cars were overturned and small fires began to break out all over the place.

I slipped away from the crowd, located a public telephone and contacted the office. I asked Lynch if he had passed on the information that I had given him. He assured me that he had. He was at a loss to explain why Cambridge had failed to develop a plan to simply transport half the available troops from MIT and Central Square to Harvard Square. They had the buses to do it and they didn't lack the personnel.

I also called the Cambridge Police and informed the officer who answered the phone that Harvard Square was literally being destroyed. "I'm a Boston cop," I blurted. "I'm working undercover and there's a riot going on in Harvard Square and there aren't any cops here. You better get as much help as you can down here before they level the place."

His response boggled my brains. He answered, "Yeah we're getting complaints on that."

By the time the troops arrived it was too late. The situation was completely out of control. The cops chased the rioters down the connecting streets to the square but the rioters continued to return to the battleground in a ceaseless motion of confrontation and retreat. The destruction continued on unabated and both cops and rioters were injured. Scattered arrests were made but they were insufficient to control the disorder. In fact, the arrests only worked to depress the levels of police coverage because the prisoners required transportation and booking.

The State Police moved in and marched down the avenue firing tear gas at the rioters, but a downwind shifted it back on the police and disabled their efforts. At some point, later in the evening, a decision was made to call in the Boston Tactical Patrol Force. (They didn't take prisoners.)

Two busloads of about seventy uniformed officers and supervisors, clad in full battle gear including jump suits, helmets and long sticks, arrived in a quiet area located about a block from the transit station which had continued to mark the center of the upheaval. About two thousand hard-core individuals continued to defy the police, taking advantage of every opportunity to break windows, throw stones and light fires.

The officers fell out into the assembly area and stood in formation. Their Commanding Officer, Lieutenant Bill McDonald, a five foot eleven inch bull of a man called them to attention and barked out their instructions. I wasn't able to hear what he said but the grim look on the officers' faces underscored their interest. I didn't know McDonald at the time but I would come to respect him as a well organized and compassionate man who was, nevertheless, willing and able to use force whenever the situation warranted it. And this was one of those situations!

Lieutenant McDonald marched the officers up Mass. Avenue to the subway station, counting cadence all the way. The steady beat of the officers' boots as they hit the pavement sounded their serious intent. A large contingent of officers in the rear of the formation carried their service batons in the port-arm position and sang God Bless America. The officers took up positions near the station. McDonald got on the bullhorn and ordered the demonstrators to leave the area, clearly warning them three different times of the consequences of an unlawful assembly.

Hardly anyone complied - instead they persisted to chant and jeer the police, directing obscenities at them and pelting them with rocks and bottles. At the conclusion of the third warning a deadpan look came over the commander's face. He looked directly at the crowd and in a steady and resonant voice he ordered his troops to **Get 'em!**

And get 'em they did! Still smarting from the beating they had taken at Northeastern at the hands of many of the same people, the cops broke ranks and penetrated the crowd, flailing their sticks as they moved. No arrests were made. There were countless injuries - bodies went down like ten pins all over the place. Members of the Tactical Patrol Force exerted their might and kicked ass. The crowd panicked, fleeing the square from every direction.

I got packing myself. Most of the TPF guys didn't know me and they lacked the time to make distinctions. I wasn't about to become a casualty of my own stupidity. It's time to start moving when the cops get rolling; that's a truism of the street and most undercover operatives don't have to be told. I had experienced some pretty hairy near misses in those days, but fortunately, I had usually managed to stay one step ahead of the cops. However, my luck was about to run out!

I quickly walked into a Paperback Booksmith store located at 25 Brattle Street. I figured I'd get a breather and at the same time fish around for the location of a molotov cocktail workshop that was rumored to be located somewhere in the area. This place had possibilities - I knew the night manager had connections to the revolutionary left. Perhaps I might overhear something or get lucky and learn that they were making these firebombs down in the cellar. It was a long shot but it was a place to start.

There were about ten people in the store, not counting the manager. He sat high on his perch to the left of the entrance surveying the customers. He wore a long dark beard and couldn't have been more than twenty-two years old. His name was Randy and I had the impression, from previous conversations with him, that he was a dropout from Harvard. That in itself qualified him as a curio-piece as far as I was concerned. Contrary to popular perception, it's not easy to flunk out of Harvard once you get in.

I speculated as to the reasons why. I guessed that he was so consumed with the tenets of the revolutionary left that he let everything else go. Perhaps his involvement with the politics of the New Left was so compelling that it had blotted out any other interest, including formal education. There were a lot of kids like that floating around back in those days.

The first time I met Randy he was standing behind a table in Harvard Square giving things away, mostly books, beads and radical literature. He referred to his small place on the sidewalk as a 'free store,' a sort of anti-business that rejected the profit motive.

Apparently, at some point, he ran out of his parents' money and landed a real job in the Paperback Booksmith. He was kind of a closed mouth sinister sort and that led me to suspect that he might have been tied up with the Weathermen. Whenever he was working a large assortment of free radical literature, along with various handouts, sat on the desk in front of him. This was his own personal display and I dipped into it on frequent occasions. It was a lucrative well.

The first person to catch my interest was a well-dressed delicately framed woman wearing a long brown suede coat. She was standing at one of the racks browsing through a display of books. She wore dark nylon stockings set off by two-inch high heels which contributed stature to her long flowing figure. She was a pretty woman in her early twenties with dainty features and long slender hands which she used selectively to finger through the titles. She possessed a self-contained look and seemed beautifully traditional and out of place in an environment like Harvard Square in the Sixties.

I wondered what might lie behind her ladylike exterior - was she as inwardly alluring as she appeared to be? First impressions could be terribly deceiving - I knew that first hand.

My thoughts were brutishly interrupted by the multiple sounds of hundreds of feet running down Brattle Street. The cops were pushing what remained of the crowd out of the square. Most of the crowd had been decimated by the TPF who had literally broken the back of the resistance but apparently hangers-on continued to create sporadic incidents. I looked out the door and the cops were right behind the running mass.

It is a mathematical certainty that someone must always be last. This is especially true in disorderly situations. Frank Lobar and his freaks had long since made their flight and the bulk of those who remained had been clobbered. The cops were more or less conducting a mop-up exercise.

I didn't know who the last dude was or why they were chasing him, but he was running just ahead of the cops when I stuck my head out the door to see what was happening. Instead of remaining with the stampede he made an abrupt left and turned into an alley across the street from the bookstore. This was a mistake.

He must have believed this tactic would have allowed him to elude the cops. He didn't realize that a solidly built wall at the end of the alley would block his access and force him to turn back into the direction of the oncoming cops. I don't know what happened when he did, but about two minutes later he bolted back out of the alley and scrambled onto Brattle Street with the cops still on his tail.

The manager of the bookstore opened the front door and gestured for the kid to come in, in essence offering him the store as refuge. It was an act of compassion - that's the way Randy saw it. The cops saw it differently - to them Randy was acting as an accessory after the fact or in the very least, defiantly.

The fleeing subject bypassed the offer and continued to run down Brattle Street. He flashed a terror-stricken look at the bookstore manager as he ran passed the front door. By this time one of the riot cops had caught up with him and landed a couple of glancing swipes across his back with his twenty-four inch service baton, but nothing was going to stop this kid, he just kept on going. He rounded the corner with the cops still in pursuit. He may have even gotten away, but the rest of us didn't. The bookstore would become our prison for the next several hours.

The manager might just as well have thrown a bottle at the cops as to offer the store as refuge to a fleeing rioter. What's more, Randy slammed the front door in the officer's faces as a couple of them attempted to enter. Before the cops could react he locked and bolted the door from the inside and repeatedly refused their demands to open it.

His defiance triggered their rage and for the next several hours the Paperback Booksmith would become a place of hell for all of its occupants, including me, while Randy and the cops played a dangerous game of cat and mouse. The police sealed the front entrance by posting a sentry outside the door.

Randy further infuriated the cops when he shut off some of the lights and suggested to his customers that they crouch down. They complied

- they didn't have much choice. These, the intellectually elite of Harvard Square, didn't have to have it spelled out to them that the guys in blue on the other side of the glass door were itching to get at them. It didn't make any difference that they were innocent, that they were shopping at the time and that they didn't have anything to do with the riot. They were being made to suffer for the bookstore manager's intransigence and they knew it. The consequences could be dire.

Randy refused to open the door. I got the impression that he was getting off on the whole thing. An overweight police sergeant, whom I had never laid eyes on before, approached the door and repeatedly ordered in an increasingly loud and booming voice for someone to open it, but his demands were left unanswered.

The belligerence and bellicosity of these two antagonists, the bookstore manager and the police sergeant, provided a volatile mix whose dangerous product saturated the room like an incendiary gas threatening to explode at any moment. The customers were terrified that, without warning, the leather-booted and helmeted police might crash through the door and bash them into eternity.

Randy turned off a few more lights and the innocent occupants hid under book tables like children playing 'hide and go seek'. "Perhaps," one of the customers suggested, "if we wait long enough, the police will leave."

I looked over at the classy chick who was huddled in a corner of the store not far from where she had started out. Even the subdued lighting was unable to conceal the clear lines of horror that connected the fine features on her face. She struck me as a person who lived in an inner world of rationality and polite social discourse. I'm sure she read good books, attended the theater and listened to classical music. Her small psychological enclave of intellectual civility with its moral and ethical underpinnings was being threatened now in a way that she could not understand. These were the police - she trusted them. They were her protectors - why were they so angry and what did they intend to do?

I was in a real jam - the cops didn't know that I was trapped inside. I wanted to get out of there and at the same time I felt compelled to rescue the others. I shared a bond with them, a bond of innocence laced with fear, and I would not let them be arrested or harmed if I could help it.

I peeked out the glass window encased in the wooden frame surrounding the front door and oddly enough, I was unable to recognize a familiar face among the squad of police officers who were stationed outside. I thought this strange considering that my academy class made up the core of the Tactical Patrol Force. Eventually the guard stationed outside the door was relieved by a cop whom I believed to be Dennis McKenna, a popular member of my recruit class. Dennis was a tough ballsy cop, an attractive quality in the police world, especially considering his slight stature. He was one of the first guys to volunteer as a decoy to snag robbers in the Combat Zone. Certainly, if somehow I could speak with him away from the others, I could work something out without having to blow my cover; but how?

I gave it about ten minutes thought and came up with an idea. I would inform the manager that I knew the short cop outside the door, explaining that I met him in the Combat Zone and had interviewed him for a graduate school paper on street level prostitution. I hoped that I could convince Randy to persuade his customers to hide out in the basement so that I could speak to the cop privately, increasing our chances for an agreement.

Surprisingly enough he agreed to the plan. We spent the next ten minutes convincing the fearful customers to wait it out in the basement. Once I was sure that everyone was downstairs, especially Randy, I approached the door and looked directly at the cop whom I believed to be my classmate.

"Dennis," I pleaded, "it's me, Phil Vitti. I'm working undercover. Nobody did anything in here - they're innocent - take my word for it. Just leave and I'll tell you more about it when I see you."

He looked at me like I had two heads and acted as though he didn't know me. Perhaps it's my beard I thought. He doesn't recognize me. Feeling disappointed, I turned around to ascertain that I was still alone. Once I was certain that Randy or any of the customers had not come upstairs, I reached through the waistband of my dungarees and freed up the police badge that I had taped to my right inner thigh. I removed it from my clothing and pushed it against the window. The front of the badge could be easily read, **Boston Police Patrolman - 2079.**

The officer looked at it and did a double take. He immediately walked across the street and returned with the heavy Sergeant. At about this point I became sickeningly aware that the cop look-a-like in the window was not Dennis McKenna, and in fact was a Cambridge Police Officer dressed in a riot uniform identical to that of the Boston Police TPF. This realization came over me like a nauseous avalanche, diminishing me for my own stupidity.

If the cop had been wearing a badge I would not have made this mistake. It was not unusual for the TPF guys to remove their tins when they were engaged in street combat. Though it was a violation of the rules and regulations, this dereliction prevented rioters from ripping it off their uniforms or identifying them, rightly or wrongly, in a future disciplinary hearing for excessive force. I would've liked to have kicked myself in the ass but it was too late for recriminations. I had to do something now and get back out into the street. I again displayed my badge for the Patrol Supervisor, but it didn't faze him.

"Open the fucking door!" he ordered.

I responded, "Look I don't have the key - the manager has it and he won't give it to me. No one did anything wrong in here - leave them alone. I'm a Boston cop and I'm working. This is my badge," and I pointed to it with my right hand as I continued to press it against the window, all the while fearing that Randy was going to come up on my back and discover who I was. I literally had a small window of opportunity to make my point.

Any half-intelligent cop, at that point, would have written down the number and checked with Boston regarding its authenticity. Had he done so he would have learned that the badge belonged to an undercover police officer named Phil Vitti who, the last anyone knew, was working in Cambridge that very evening. But this guy was anything but bright. He was an obese, thick featured, contentious oaf of a man with a hammer like brain and a bullhorn voice. He shouted, "I don't give a fuck if you have a badge - anybody can have a badge nowadays." He once again ordered, "Let me in or I'll break the fucking door down!"

There was no talking to this guy. He was so pissed he couldn't think straight. His most pressing desire was to be allowed to enter the store where I feared he would take out his frustrations on the luckless customers inside. Perhaps he would have arrested them or whacked them around - there was no way of telling. I looked over at the other cop whom I could tell was embarrassed by the actions of his boss and receded back into the shadows.

I sat alone in the dark for the next ten minutes in a vain attempt to corral my torrid anger. I abhorred that dumb fuck! He was the living depiction of a cop pig and fulfilled the most disgusting qualities of the metaphor. For one fleeting moment I felt embarrassed to be a police officer. Perhaps the militants were right - maybe I was on the wrong side. This was one ugly night that I wouldn't readily forget. Here I was, a Boston Police Officer, working for the City of Cambridge free of charge - imprisoned in a bookstore with a dozen innocents by Sergeant Bluto and his crew who lurked outside threatening to smash the door down at any moment.

Eventually I descended the stairs and entered the basement where the others were hiding out. They were sparsely separated and were not talking to each other as they feared the cops might detect their voices and break through the rear door. The elegant woman was there too. She was sitting on a small stepping stool with her arms tightly locked around her knees. In a clumsy attempt at reassurance I asked her what her name was. "Debbie -- my name is Debbie," she answered and we both fell silent.

"I couldn't talk to the cop" I whispered to the prisoners, "we're going to have to do something else."

The distinct body odor of fear wafted through the basement. I was able to detect it. I had smelled it once before, on the second night of boot camp at Paris Island when I was assigned to fire watch duty which required me to walk around the barracks in stocking feet while other members of Platoon 218 shared a tortured night's sleep.

More time passed - it seemed like an eternity. Randy remained insistent. He wasn't about to let the cops in and the cops weren't about to leave. This game could go on all night and I was getting tired of playing it.

Sometime around nine-thirty I decided to make a move. I quietly opened the rear door and peaked out into the alley. I fully expected that a cop would jam his stick between the door and its frame preventing me from closing it and giving them the wedge that they needed to enter the basement. I didn't see any cops, but that didn't mean they weren't out there. It could have been a trap. On the other hand, the Patrol Supervisor wasn't exactly bubbling over with smarts and perhaps he had never thought to post a guard at the rear door. If that were the case it was worth the risk to attempt an escape. I stepped out into the rear alley and when nothing happened I quickly returned to the protection of the bookstore.

I figured it was worth the gamble. I decided to make a break for it, but by this time I had developed an affinity with the entrapped customers. I felt as though I were one of them. It was clearly us against them (the cops). I intended to do anything I could, short of violence, to help the customers escape. I surveyed the rear alley and made a quick mental map of a possible escape route.

Randy explained that anyone wishing to escape would have to scale a garage roof before gaining access to the street. I thought of the classy chick with the high heels and in an oblique offer to her, I advised that the men could help the women make the climb. I detailed the risks but assured the group that at least this way we had a chance. I had no comers - they just sat there in stone cold silence, numbed by fear!

I couldn't wait any longer. I bolted out the door and was ecstatic to learn that there were no cops in the rear alley. I made it to the street in a few minutes and was on my way down Mass. Avenue to Boston and Police Headquarters. It was about ten o'clock and the streets were silent.

A couple of fire engines remained in the square to deal with the aftermath of the earlier fires which continued to smolder. The streets were littered with rocks and broken bottles and a small contingent of police officers guarded the hundreds of broken windows that lined the sidewalks. Public telephones were ripped out and it was obvious that some looting had taken place. I was affected by the pungent odor of stale tear gas which the State Police had directed against the crowd earlier in the evening. I was so unglued that I hardly noticed the hour and a half it took me to walk back to the office.

The rest of the crew was anxiously waiting for me when I arrived late in the evening. My anger subsided slightly when I saw them. I could see that they were genuinely concerned, especially Gerry. They could have gone home earlier but they hung in there, plainly worried when I had failed to check in or return from Cambridge. Mike Flammia made a hasty phone call and when he hung up he told me that the Police Commissioner was personally relieved that I made it back safely.

"He was worried about you," Mike said. "In fact, he sent me out in the middle of the riot to look for you. He was worried once you stopped calling in. At one point when he was being advised of the riot's progress, he (the Commissioner) said, 'I don't give a damn about the riot, that's Cambridge's problem. Where is Phil Vitti?'"

I was impressed with the Commissioner's concern. I had never met the guy and was not aware that he knew I existed. He was appointed Police Commissioner in 1962, a couple of years before I got on the job and he had a pretty solid reputation of having been a great athlete. He had played football for both the New York Giants and Baltimore Colts. He had also served as a PT Boat Commander in World War II and was rumored to have known John F Kennedy. He was a retired FBI agent, which added to his luster, and with all this, he was personally concerned about me. That took the edge off things, but still in all I entertained a real mad against the Cambridge Police Sergeant for his failure to acknowledge a legitimate police badge, in spite of my having risked my safety by displaying it twice.

The Deputy was also in the office when I arrived - he was the next person I talked to after Mike. I let loose and told him the whole story. I came on really strong at the end and just short of a demand, I urged him to contact the Cambridge Police and complain about the way I had been treated and also to inform them to call off the dogs outside the Paperback Booksmith.

He squinted his eyes and looked at me with a quizzical expression as though he was searching for something to say. A soft compassionate smile broke out across his face and he entered his office. About a minute later he emerged carrying a small bottle of whiskey and a glass of ginger ale. He poured two shots of whiskey into the drink and mixed them with an old bent spoon. He handed the glass to me and encouraged me to drink it. This was the first time that I had ever seen any booze in the office.

Obviously he wasn't taking me very seriously, so I did what he failed to do. I called the Cambridge Police myself and pissed all over the poor bastard who answered the phone. "Leave the people in the bookstore alone," I demanded after besieging him with a rambling account of my role in the evening's carnage and the events that led up to the bookstore incident. "The customers are all innocent. They were just in the wrong place at the wrong time," I reiterated. I wasn't sure if he believed me, but he assured me that he would get the word out on the street. I thanked him and breathed a sigh of relief as I hung up. Pat Brady put the final touches on the evening by adding a little humor in with my high ball.

I was finally able to put the whole thing in perspective. I attributed the poor judgment of the police to the actions of the Patrol Supervisor, a single sergeant driven mad by the destruction of his small city by long-haired shaggy looking freaks playing hard at revolution. He desperately needed to get even - it didn't make any difference who I was or what I had to say. I was wearing a beard and I was dressed in dungarees and sneakers and that made me fair game.

I met the Dennis McKenna look-a-like Cambridge cop a year later in the cafeteria of Northeastern University, introduced myself, and reminded him of that night. He apologized for the incident, explaining that he had disagreed with his supervisor but was simply following orders. The sergeant was also there that morning. The patrolman pointed him out, standing by the bulletin board. He was enrolled in the Law Enforcement Program. In all likelihood, I thought, sucking up the government grants that were being awarded to police officers for furthering their education under the Omnibus Crime Control Act.

This historic legislation had resulted in a deluge of police officers attending college. Some of them were less committed than the students who paid their own way. I figured that this guy was one of them. However, by that time I had become a new member of the Northeastern Faculty and the attendant role expectation of a lecturer inhibited me from telling him what a genuine asshole I thought he was.

The day after the Moratorium, the *Boston Globe* ran a front-page story with these headlines, "*100,000 on Common Cry 'Peace Now' As Boston M-Day Rally Tops Nation*". Other actions included 30,000 in New Haven, 15,000 at Rutger's University, 10,000 in Minneapolis, and 30,000 at the Washington Monument. Even rain-soaked San Francisco had attracted 1,500 demonstrators. A photograph taken from Beacon and Charles Street captured a sea of people spread across the front page.

The underground newspapers recounted slanted and inflammatory incidents of violence occurring across the nation. The city of Cambridge was racked with damage estimates exceeding one and a half million dollars. The Weathermen had made good their threat - these were indeed the promised 'Days of Rage.' The legitimacy of the Boston Police Intelligence Division was established and I would breathe a long sigh of relief. I had earned my title as the Night Deputy.

A month later it happened again. November 15 was declared as National Moratorium Day - 750,000 demonstrators from across the country assembled in Washington DC to denounce the Vietnam War. It was the most immense protest action that had ever taken place in the U.S.

About this same time the Silent Majority waged a nation-wide counter offensive. These were a tiny fraction of the two hundred million people that Rusk had referred to as normally staying home and not participating in demonstrations. Several hundred pro government demonstrators congregated on the Boston Common. American flags could be seen from everywhere. They dotted the landscape and small replicas were worn on the clothing of the participating patriots. It was a notable national turnout and there was no violence. The crowds were large but orderly and they even picked up after themselves. It all pointed to the huge divide that was splitting America.

Before the year was out 300 American insurgents visited Cuba to cut sugar cane and demonstrate their solidarity with the Cuban people. The total eventually reached five hundred and fifty. They were heavily penetrated by government agents and CIA informants.

I knew one of them - his nickname was Zimmy, a conservative Jew with a strong patriotic flair. He would have made a great re-con man. I liked Zimmy and he eventually assisted me in an undercover investigation of an organized prostitution ring, but that was almost five years down the line. Suffice to say there were plenty of Zimmys in the movement. They participated for their own personal reasons. In any event, they were indispensable to the Government, even on the local level.

One of the responsibilities of the Intelligence Division was to cultivate and maintain a relationship with as many informants as possible. Some were amusing eccentrics such as Mrs. M who called the unit constantly to report on a wide variety of suspicious relationships and questionable activity (none of which could ever be pinned down).

Others were highly positioned professionals such as a well-known physician who plagued the unit with calls documenting Communist activity everywhere. He saw the enemy behind every tree and pole. He wasn't altogether wrong; he had been the object of a few demonstrations by a combination of protest groups including the PLP dominated 'Mental Patients Liberation Front' for his use of a medical procedure which could be described as a modified pre-frontal lobotomy for the purpose of controlling rage. He hot-wired the brain rather than relying on straight surgery to deaden villainous tissue. Most of the informants, however, were run-of-the-mill type sources that enjoyed passing on information for whatever it was worth.

Nineteen hundred and sixty-nine was a watershed year for a lot of reasons. Many things were happening simultaneously. Aside from the marked escalation of domestic violence, official peace negotiations began in Paris and Nixon signed the first draft lottery bill. Student deferments would no longer provide a way out of the draft. Now anyone could go, including the college elite. That spelled even more trouble on the campuses.

Somewhere in the middle of all this tension the well- known Smiley Face button was born. It was comprised of two eyes and an upturned mouth against a round yellow background surrounded with a black border, an indication that someone still had a sense of humor.

Thirty-Four

The cool hand of winter gradually stilled the region and quieted the level of street unrest. Believe it or not, I spent the next several weeks assigned to the Traffic Division directing traffic in Keaney Square in the North Station area, the second most difficult post in the city. The first, at that time, was Andrew Square in South Boston. The traffic assignment resulted from a union conflict with the city over a stalled contract. The Keaney Square post was pure punishment duty.

Dan Sweeney, in what eventually proved to be an effective tactic, recommended to the members of the Patrolmen's Association that they refuse to accept paid details, especially in the busy downtown area in an effort to put pressure on Mayor Kevin White by the local businesses to resolve the contract dispute and end the police embargo. These businesses, especially the big stores like Jordan Marsh and Filenes, desperately needed the services of individual traffic officers to assist their delivery trucks. Except for a few scabs, most of the union members complied with the detail boycott, resulting in temporary traffic tie-ups throughout the day.

The department countered by assigning all non-rated plain-clothes officers to the Traffic Division to cover the vacant details. The entire personnel of the Intelligence Division with the exception of Gerry O'Rourke and Peter Ryan, who by this time had received his detective's rating, were transferred to the day shift of the traffic division. Gerry was excused because he was attending law school (though I was under the impression that he had dropped out by that time). Even Tommy Mitchell, who was number one on the Sergeant's list and destined to be promoted in the spring, had to go.

In the middle of all the political chaos of the late Sixties, the Boston Police Department chose to transfer most of their Intelligence Officers to the Traffic Division, a unit that would be considered extraneous and abolished in just a few short years. I saw this as the completely stupid act of a largely comatose command staff which spent too much time playing politics and indulging themselves and not enough time in the street. Dapkas, Cox and Pat Brady saw it for what it was, an act of revenge against union members - busting balls!

Whatever the motivation, it didn't make much difference. While Boston was burning, the emperor was amusing himself. Variations of this theme would be played out repetitively throughout my career. It would have been funny, I suppose, if so many people hadn't been hurt or killed. Many corpses have been buried throughout the years between the murky layers of time and faulty government decision making. This was small time stuff.

When I complained about losing my contacts with the underground movement the word came down from one of the brass that I could keep my beard. This guy equated successful intelligence gathering with the presence of a beard. That astonished me but I resigned myself to make the best of the situation. (The movies were still free.)

In the beginning I was assigned a walking route on Chauncey Street, near the center of the city. I walked up and down the sidewalk between the intersections of Essex and Summer Streets and was required to remedy any traffic problems that resulted from truck deliveries to the assorted businesses in the area, especially in the rear of Jordan Marsh. For the most part they got along without any help and I only assisted when the safety of the public required it, such as an old lady walking across the street. I was careful to adhere to the unofficial agreement among the supplementary officers assigned to traffic to avoid the performance of free details. We refused to be used as scabs. This route was a choice assignment and I enjoyed walking in and out of the stores gabbing with retailers and customers.

The Keaney Square assignment was simple retaliation for a dispute

I had with a bigoted Irish police lieutenant. He misconstrued my sincere effort to correct the way he had pronounced my name as impertinence. In truth, I was not offended with his pronunciation. I was accustomed to my name being mispronounced by all kinds of people, including Italians. That was routine. But what pushed me off the edge was his retort after I clumsily attempted to explain to him why I had failed to respond at roll call. I contended that I was not aware that he was calling me because he had mispronounced my name - and after giving him the correct version - he sarcastically remarked,

"Is that the Roman pronunciation?"

I bristled at the comment. I took it as a wise ass ethnic slur. To add insult to injury, he had shouted it out while standing behind an elevated podium in full sight and hearing of more than thirty police officers. I was embarrassed and my ears began to heat up. I was sure that they had turned cherry red, a sure physical cue that I was losing it. I was besieged by conflicting thoughts as I stood there waiting for roll call to end.

I considered how well I had been treated since I had been on the department. It truly was an Irish dominated department. And the Irish held most of the good jobs, which was inevitable. On the other hand, I had one of those good jobs and I had gotten it without politics. I had been treated well all the way down the line beginning with Blake and on through to Donovan. Jimmy Lynch treated me like a son and I had a great relationship with everyone in the unit, most of whom were Irish. And of course there was Tim Moran, my academic mentor and friend - just being around him was an uplifting experience.

Conversely, a lot of the old time Italian cops harbored grievances against the Irish, believing that the Italians all too often ended up on the short end of the stick. More than one had recounted stories of Irish bosses deliberately mispronouncing their names in an effort to denigrate them. I had no reason to believe that this was Lieutenant Shawn O'Brien's intent, but I had little doubt that the 'Roman' inference remark was a put-down and I intended to call him on it.

I lingered in the guardroom a few minutes after roll call. I was getting more irritated by the second, especially when I considered the reputation of this particular superior officer. I suspected that O'Brien was one of a diminishing breed of individuals who believed that the badge gave them a right to shake people down. In this case, that meant putting the arm on businesses in his assigned area for everything from bananas to small appliances. The downtown area provided a rich and fertile environment for the movement of this boss sponge. The retailers were only too happy to accommodate him. One hand washed the other, especially when it came to parking tickets.

My patience was wearing thinner by the minute. It seemed like he was never going to break away from a conversation he was having with a couple of sycophant traffic men, so I intruded into the circle. I waited until he acknowledged me and in the presence of the two officers I reproached him for the ethnic slur.

"Lieutenant, I don't mind you screwing up my name but I didn't like the 'Roman pronunciation' remark."

He was a big guy with reddish-orange hair and a pleasant smile - a sort of 'Andy' type in *Mayberry RFD*, but it was evident that he didn't like what I had said to him. He scratched his head and flashed me a curious look that evolved through all the stages of humiliation from perplexity to anger. He was not accustomed to patrolmen talking to him like that. Actually, I had surprised myself by this breach of discipline. I had the most peculiar feeling that 'Mike Russo' was inside of me, peering out through the corner of my left eye to view the Lieutenant's reaction. What made it worse is that I had challenged him in full view of his admirers. That was tantamount to insubordination back in the Sixties!

The Lieutenant just stood there, coyly scrutinizing my features and mulling over my remarks. Finally, he asked, "Is that right?" (I think it was meant to be a rhetorical question.)

"Yes Lieutenant," I responded. "That's right."

Not wishing to inflame the situation any further, I backed off. I respectfully thanked him for hearing me out and went on to my assignment, hooking a ride in a cruiser to the intersection of Summer and Washington Streets.

Predictably, my assignment the next morning was changed from a walking route on Chauncey Street to a traffic post at Keaney Square, and that's where I remained until I was reassigned to headquarters a few weeks later. With five separate movements of traffic to handle, this was a tough enough intersection under normal circumstances, but the cold weather, along with the noise and dirt raised from construction in the area, compounded the problems.

The proper management of traffic requires a good deal more training and experience than most people realize. I was an undercover cop and not a traffic man and I had a hard time of it. The most difficult part was allowing drivers to make rights and lefts before releasing stopped traffic. I botched some of my signals which resulted in opposing lines of traffic entering the intersection at the same time causing a couple of minor accidents that took place right in front of me. I was almost struck in one of them. Although they were just fender-benders, safety considerations prompted me to reduce the movement of traffic to its most basic components, allowing only one stream of traffic to move at any one time.

There I stood in the middle of a five-spoke hub exercising simple-minded control over four lanes of stopped vehicles. This irritated a lot of motorists and a few of them swore at me as they drove by. An irate cabby shouted out his window that I was a "fucking rookie" and didn't know what I was doing; but in spite of their protests, this method prevented any future mishaps. Traffic backed up of course, but that wasn't my problem. As for the Lieutenant, he just kept on smiling.

Dan Sweeney got his contract under which the officers of the Intelligence Unit would be rated as 'Agents.' This was a new and goofball designation designed to emulate the FBI and no one was too happy with it. We saw it as a curve ball to get around the provision in the new collective bargaining agreement which mandated that plain-clothes officers be rated as detectives following the completion of one year of investigative work. We asked ourselves why this provision didn't apply to us. If we weren't doing investigative work, what were we doing?

Sweeney explained that the city wanted to keep the total percentage of detectives to below ten percent of the department and that Intelligence Officers were excluded from the provision because they didn't go to court. This was bull, especially in my case, but there wasn't much we could do about it.

We blamed the union for this failure. We had been screwed from the start. The union hard-heads regarded the personnel of the Intelligence Division as college boys whose connections had won them 'tit' jobs. They weren't totally wrong about this, but it didn't apply to everyone. In any event, the coveted detective's rating would remain as elusive as ever.

The spring offensive was underway by the time I returned to the domestic intelligence scene. A day after the Chicago conspiracy convictions were announced fifteen thousand young people took to the streets for a demonstration in Boston which ultimately turned violent. The rioters started at Government Center and moved down Tremont Street smashing the windows of numerous banks and insurance companies along the way. The First National Bank of Boston took a good hit and a police cruiser was overturned.

Judge Julius Hoffman was burned in effigy for handing out the sentences and several rioters were arrested before the TPF squelched the outbreak. This disorder was mild compared to what happened in other parts of the country where police stations were blown up and courthouses and financial institutions assaulted. Although it had taken a year and a half, the November Action Coalition TDA had fulfilled their promise. Riots were only a part of it.

I came into possession of a list of companies being surreptitiously distributed around college campuses containing several businesses in the Greater Boston vicinity accused of being part of the military-industrial complex, and therefore fair game for various actions beginning with simple protest demonstrations and escalating into acts of civil disobedience, up to and including sabotage. I suspected that the Weathermen were the true authors of the unsigned list because I had initially discovered the handout in the Red Book, a bookstore just outside Central Square, where many of the insurgent members continued to meet.

A sampling of the businesses included Block Engineering Inc. at 19 Blackstone Street in Cambridge, a firm who allegedly had contracts with the Army Research and Development Agency at the Edgewood Arsenal in Maryland, a central headquarters for the development of chemical warfare techniques and materials; Aerospace Research, Inc. at 130 Lincoln Street in Brighton - involved with the development of foliage penetration radar systems to detect people roving through jungle cover; and Cryogenic

Technology in Waltham, which made parts for infra-red detectors. A total of sixteen businesses were named.

A partial list of fifteen corporations included IBM, 520 Boylston Street - computers; Gillette, 3900 Prudential Center - sales; Sony, 393 Totten Pond Road, Waltham - an assembly plant; and Retina Foundation, 20 Staniford Street, Boston - involved with research on the enhancement of night vision.

The most ominous section of this hit list identified ten individuals charged with being war criminals by the authors. Some of them were: Samuel P. Huntington, 52 Brimmer Street, Boston - formulator of the "Forced Urbanization Policy"; Arthur Smithies, 85 Dunster Street, Cambridge - designer of the "Post War Stabilization Policy"; C.W. Spangler, Executive Vice President of the Honeywell Corporation - the major producer of anti-personnel weapons; and the most well-known of them all, Henry Kissinger, whom they listed as 'on assignment in Washington' and who they charged was an architect of Vietnamization policy and an advocate of the continued air war. Kissinger was a central political figure of the Vietnam Era. He had begun as a foreign advisor to the National Security Council and had ended up as Nixon's Secretary of State. While many people perceived him as brilliant, eccentric and enigmatic, the New Left regarded him as a dangerous double-dealing fuck.

It was among the duties of the Intelligence Unit to notify each company and individual named on the list of the impending danger. The sheer magnitude of the problem stymied the police department from setting up any kind of real security, beyond routine police patrols, to protect the endangered targets or from conducting an intensive investigation to determine the provocateurs behind the publication. This stuff was becoming commonplace.

The suspects could have been any one of multiple individuals or groups hell bent on destruction. The very subject of the military-industrial complex was a flash point of anger and unfathomable hatred on the campuses and among the radical community. Their number was legion, although I continued to suspect the Weathermen. Any business perceived to be contaminated with government influence was deemed fair game for sabotage.

The Black Panthers were still awaiting trial for a bizarre conspiracy to blow up department stores, the Bronx Botanical Gardens and various railroad lines. A couple of Catholic Priests broke into a company that produced napalm, busting up the furniture and spreading blood all over the offices. The war was coming home - it had become personal. The faces behind the conflict were being unmasked. The players were in danger - their personal safety jeopardized - their homes and offices imperiled.

Many businesses in the Boston area hired their own security. The Sixties sparked a long trend that turned out to be a bonanza for the security industry. Bob Johnson, a decent guy and a college buddy of mine, picked up on this and in partnership with a former state cop created First Security, a top-notch security outfit that would grow into a wildly successful multi-million dollar corporation. I lost my shot at getting in on it from the start. Bob gave me the opportunity. I needed some modest cash up front but I had some personal problems at the time and I couldn't afford it. (I'll get to them later, the personal problems that is, but I don't want to get ahead of my story.)

The warmer weather served as a catalyst for a series of actions across the city. The Boston Black Panther Party and the Beacon Hill Revolutionary Action group sponsored a march in support of Bobby Seale, beginning at 3:00 PM on Tuesday, April 14, which started outside the Federal Court House in Post Office Square. Their purpose, as stated in their own words, was 'to confront the pigs who beat and brutalized Bobby and had killed 28 Panthers.' I infiltrated the march which ended up at Police Headquarters on Berkeley Street. Deputy Superintendent Warren Blair handled the Headquarters' action. Years later he confided to me of his strong intention to arrest Mike Russo (me) once the demonstrators began to block the front stairs.

"I wanted you real bad," he said. "I had no idea you were a cop. I was convinced that you were trouble."

I had a dim memory of two cops moving toward me once the demonstration had gotten underway but I didn't hang around long enough to get knuckled. I had become an expert at evasive action.

The following day there was a 'God Bless Amerika Anti-war March' beginning at Massachusetts and Commonwealth Avenues and ending up on the Boston Common. A small ultra left contingent consisting of Black

Panthers and their allies planned to carry the action to Tech Square in Cambridge to confront the CIA whom they accused of killing Che Guevara and running a secret war in Laos. They also intended to continue the march to the draft board, culminating in Harvard Square where they planned to spend the night in the streets. "Our streets," they snidely remarked to their members, signaling their secret intention to incite violence.

Cambridge continued to be a favorite target of the violent left but it didn't take long for this small police department to learn from its mistakes. This action was intended to be a scaled down version of the Harvard Square riot but the cops acted decisively and nipped it in the bud. The police moved on the insurgents quickly, made a few arrests, and it was all over before it had started. I wasn't there, but I heard about it.

Boston University was hit hard with a number of demonstrations designed to cripple its administration. Many of the incidents had emanated from a larger action, executed the previous winter, which had resulted in the arrest of 62 students for trespassing in the George Sherman Union. This was followed by a student strike on February 23 and 24 in which students demanded the release and reinstatement of the jailed students and an end to proceedings against two popular professors, Zinn and Fleischman, darlings of the New Left.

The students were tough, but John Silber, the President of Boston University, was tougher. A straight-laced intellectual and classical scholar, he stood his ground and plainly refused to accept lawlessness. He called the cops as many times as he had to and the TPF was called out several times to quell disturbances. The Boston Police tired of it and eventually demanded that the Boston University Campus Police get their act in order - and so they did. (To paraphrase Ricco Cappuci, a former TPF cop and subsequent Deputy Superintendent of the BU Campus Police, the spring of 1970 was the crucible from which the early notion of Boston based professional campus police had taken form.)

But getting back to Silber, he had a lot of guts. The day guys enjoyed working with him. Peter, himself a very straight-laced guy, said Silber was fearless, straight forward and willing to back up the cops when necessary.

Perhaps that doesn't sound like such a startling statement, but consider the times. Cops were not welcome on college campuses - many students and faculty considered them the equivalent of foreign invaders.

President Asa Knowles was another notable exception to this mind set. He clearly supported the Law Enforcement Program at Northeastern University and continued do so, despite it being lumped together, by campus radicals, with the ROTC, and made to be a continual object of vandalism, threats and scorn. It was so hot for Knowles that he had to employ a bodyguard.

Other than Silber and Knowles, it seemed that most of the academics in the surrounding colleges, from Dean down to Lecturer either held the cops in disdain or feared to publicly support them. The police had become the scapegoats for an unpopular war. To make matters worse, a slim majority of U.S. citizenry, by 1970, had come to support the anti-war demonstrations. The cops were getting screwed all the way around, pumping up the notion of 'the thin blue line,' a collective feeling of social isolation which, by then, had become heightened to an almost insufferable police belief that they alone stood precariously perched on an eroding ledge between civility and anarchy.

I experienced the alienation big time, especially as a graduate student in the Department of Sociology, an area of study historically dominated by liberals and social engineering types. A couple of the faculty and more than a few of the students were to the left of Castro, and I had the distinct feeling that they would have shoved me off a building if given the opportunity.

There was one big glommy blonde haired guy who constantly glared at me. He reminded me of an inflated 'Lil Abner' with just a little more brains. He was about six foot five inches tall and easily tipped the scale at two hundred and sixty pounds - he wasn't anybody I wanted to tangle with. He was a teaching fellow in the undergraduate school and refused to acknowledge me even when I said hello to him.

One day I snatched a brief look into his messy looking small office. The door was partially ajar as I walked by. Apparently he had just finished advising a young undergraduate student. There, hanging on the wall over his desk, was a life sized portrait of Chairman Mao. It became clear to me that this guy was a 'run in the red radical'. Doubtless, he saw me as a 'dyed in the blue cop'; in his mind a defender of the corrupt economy, an oppressor, a pig. It was curious how this academic's thin veneer of sociological objectivity crumbled so badly in the mere presence of an off duty cop. I didn't think Memos would have been surprised. In fact, this big goof fulfilled the most negative characteristics of Paul's impression of social scientists. Need I say more?

Unfortunately, he wasn't the only one. There were a couple of others who shared his animosity toward me, though they were subtler. As a result, I enjoyed few friendships at the graduate school.

There were some notable exceptions. Vinny Basile was one of them. Vinny was a formidable guy. He was built like a fire hydrant, hard, short and compact. He dressed well, smoked cigars and spoke in a hoarse staccato voice laced with Italian undertones. He was a Probation Officer assigned to the East Boston District Court. This was a predominantly Italian neighborhood at the opposite end of the Callahan Tunnel. Vinny was fiercely patriotic and proud of his commission in the National Guard. His rough exterior disguised an analytical and innovative mind. I liked Vinny - he was an establishment type like me and we hung together.

Glen Pierce was another good buddy. He was well on the way to his Doctorate Degree when I first met him in class. Glen was an intellectual purist. True to the tenets of the scientific method, he produced good research and went on to become a co-director of Northeastern University's Policy Research Bureau. Glen was a pure drink of water in a muddy stream. I admired him for his simple life style and intellectual integrity. He later publicized research findings that undercut the popular notion that capital punishment was a deterrent to murder. The research caused a national ripple and pissed off more than a few cops but that did not make Glen a bad person.

Then there was Judy, the ineffable Judy. Pert, pretty and chaste, she embodied the fading values of the vanishing fifty's women. She was a curious mixture of Dorothy in the Wizard of Oz and the all-American girl, delicately blended into a unique personality and animated by a lively mind.

"I'm a Catholic from Kansas," she proudly pointed out within the first two minutes of our introduction. She was engaged to a man who lived and worked in another state and for the two years that I knew her I do not believe she ever dated.

I was the beneficiary of that relationship because she knew I was married and she felt safe. We talked a lot and shared a lot. We came to know each other over the two years of classes. We were in simpatico - she was my pal, my soul mate. She was the first woman I was ever able to communicate with on a rational level, absent the nuances of gender. Our relationship was friendly, intellectual and perfectly circumscribed. Anything more would have exceeded the bounds of propriety and that would have disappointed us both. But there was no denying the way she made me feel, nor the second thoughts that had come to plague me concerning my marriage.

It just wasn't the same way with Beverly - neither one of us had ever shared that elevated sense of trusting intimacy. Ours was a marriage of convenience. (At least that was the way I believed Beverly felt about it.) There was little empathy and even less communication. We had never really connected from day one.

I was an Italian Catholic street kid with a lot of rough edges whose biggest professional hope was to acquire a detective's rating. I was everything that Beverly loathed. I just didn't make it in her eyes. Perhaps if I had possessed an MD, or even a doctorate, and had worked in a professional setting things would have been different, but a Combat Zone undercover cop didn't quite cut it with her. About the only feeling Beverly and I were sharing by this time was the gnawing awareness that things weren't getting any better.

On Monday, May 4, 1970, four students were shot and killed by National Guardsmen who panicked and shot into the crowd during a campus demonstration provoked by the United States invasion of Cambodia. The heavily outnumbered guardsmen fired into the demonstrators after being pelted with rocks and bottles by an ever widening crowd that threatened to engulf them. Many of the soldiers were no older than the students they felled and most of them were inexperienced at crowd control.

The news of the students' deaths and the wounding of nine others was instantaneously transmitted around the country and students on college campuses from coast to coast staged a nationwide strike! The campuses exploded and were simultaneously melted into a solid front against the war, the machinery of the United States Government, the state of Ohio and the suffering Governor Rhodes.

The events at this mid-western university further vilified government and inspired campus activists to wage protests everywhere, not simply in the big cities and places like Chicago, Watts, Boston or Columbia. Kent State would serve as a mainspring for thousands of anti-war demonstrations throughout the country which would continue unabated until the war's end.

People were saddened by this event all across the political spectrum. Even the cops, many of whom defended the soldiers, knew in their hearts that the National Guard had fucked up. The incident served as positive proof that cops, and not soldiers, should handle internal strife.

By way of comparison, Warren Blair was confronted with a similar incident outside Boston University. The cops were attempting to arrest an unruly demonstrator for disorderly conduct when an angry crowd of students surrounded the officers and demanded that they hand over the prisoner. It would have been easier for the cops to simply shove the prisoner into the back of the wagon and take their chances than to release him, but that was not the option Blair chose. Instead, he released the prisoner, inviting serious criticism from the police on the scene who condemned him for caving into the protesters' demands.

In my mind, and I suspected secretly in theirs, Blair had exercised good judgment. Had he chosen to force the issue and maintain custody of the prisoner, in spite of the overwhelming odds, someone surely would have been killed. These kids would never have backed off. They intended to take advantage of their superior numbers to rescue their friend. Deadly force would have been the only way to stop them - a dead student, and for what, a disorderly conduct pinch? (This was one of the least important and overused misdemeanor pinches in the book.) Police commanders are trained to exercise discretion, soldiers are not. Sorry for the lecture - it's all hindsight anyway.

Getting back to the events of that time, the campuses were further inflamed when the state chose to indict twenty-five students for their role in the disorder. The 'Kent 25' became a national rallying cry for students everywhere who were against the government. The campuses shifted into overdrive and the flames of open revolution threatened to spread into the streets.

The campuses became the main planning bodies against the war. At Boston University, the George Sherman Union was the locust of student activity. In Chicago, the Art Institute functioned as the hub for the planning of a citywide strike. Wayne State was radicalized and substituted as a tool for the expansion of anti-war activity. At Antioch, the school radio became the broadcasting center for social protest. College phones across the country facilitated a vast network of inter-connected informational sources and the Boston campuses erupted all over the place. The Student Mobilization Committee got a shot in the arm and I spent a lot of time moving between their office and the local campuses, mostly on bicycle.

Newspaper pictures of Kent State were flashed across the country. One depicted a young female coed, her face etched in grief, bending over a dead student. This photograph would join another, the execution by gunfire of a Viet Cong prisoner in a public street in Saigon in 1968, to become icons of the war. The most poignant picture of all was yet to come; a devastating photograph of an hysterical nine year old girl running naked through the streets of Trang Bang with napalm burning her flesh. The girl made it. She lived, but the memory still haunts me.

It seemed to me that at the point when the protest began to level off, some other event would be unleashed to escalate the tension. Kent State was a profound example of this. Not only did it solidify student opposition to the war, but it galvanized middle class domestic opposition as well. The country never settled down after that - events started to really spin out of control.

The city was racked by minor disorders throughout the summer. The largest one took place around the streets of Northeastern University. It started off as a simple protest action and wound up as a full-scale battle followed by smaller eruptions which kept the TPF busy for several days. At its high point individuals were throwing lighted mattresses off the tops of buildings onto the police who patrolled the streets below.

Northeastern dormitory students were blamed, but as it turned out the real culprits were transients who occupied apartments in the multiple family brick buildings in the area. I suspected that many were professional agitators drawn to the neighborhood as a result of the initial disorder. However, I was never able to confirm my suspicions, mainly because I was busy working ten hour shifts for several evenings. I was on the roof of the Hemenway Hotel on Westland Avenue surveying the tops of surrounding buildings through binoculars to protect the officers below.

Gerry and I relieved the day guys who spent the hottest part of the day on this boiling hot tar roof. There were two hours of overtime built into the shift for every member of the unit which made the assignment more palatable. Nothing much got beyond Gerry's acute vision, and while the assignment was boring, the night vision binoculars occasionally provided us a real show - it was like being back in the Downtown Lounge absent Delilah.

Demonstrations, open air pot parties, unruly concerts and scattered disorders continued to punctuate the summer months. Domestic violence was becoming a part of urban life. I feared the disruptions would never be over. The smallest incident could provoke a major crisis. Cambridge continued getting whacked pretty good too. By this time I had left my grudge in the Paperback Booksmith and was fully involved with developing intelligence for both cities.

In August, Janis Joplin, acclaimed as the 'Queen of Rock and Roll,' appeared before an overflow audience of more than thirty-five thousand young people at the 'Summer Thing Concert' in Harvard Stadium. Cambridge held its breath - they had suffered a number of disruptive actions over the summer months and they feared for the worst. Gerry and I penetrated Joplin's inner circle and posed as security agents. This provided a good vantage point from which to view the crowd and report any incidents or problems by radio to the police department command post outside.

Joplin was a big raw-boned chick with a slightly pock marked face. She had been riding high in the recording world since 1967 when she shot to the top of the charts following her appearance at the Monterey Music Festival. She referred to her style as 'comic blues,' a sort of white rural blend of country music and black blues. She dazzled the audience with her booming voice and electrifying style, but despite their thunderous applause from the very beginning when Joplin and her 'Full Tilt Boogie Band' walked on stage, she was clearly nervous. I couldn't help but notice her, between numbers, gulping down shots of whiskey being dutifully poured from a bottle by a friend waiting in the wings.

I was standing right next to her when I first noticed her doing this. I must have been wearing a puzzled expression because she turned toward me and smiled.

"Do you know why I do this?" she asked. And without waiting for an answer she explained, "Because I am afraid they will hate me. Can you read the headlines of the *Boston Globe* tomorrow? Janis Joplin ridden out of Boston on a rail!"

On the contrary, the fans ate her up. She drove them to ever higher levels of ecstasy, especially with her deliverance of *Piece of My Mind* and *Ball and Chain*. The crowd was verging on hysteria before the concert was over and I feared that Cambridge was in for another pounding. There was no way that the Cambridge Police Department and the TPF combined could have handled the avalanche of trouble that I anticipated was soon to fall into the streets. It seemed imminent!

Suddenly she stopped singing, the instruments ceased and the crowd fell silent. After a long empty pause, Joplin began to speak and then sing a measured farewell to her audience. Her message was dramatically interspersed between interludes of music with pleas of peace that soothed her audience and guided them down from their dangerously heightened emotional levels.

To make a long story short, the concert ended and everyone went home. There were no incidents, thanks to the bewitching influence of an awesome entertainer who had no idea of the power of her presence. She died a year later from an overdose of drugs. I was not surprised, just saddened.

I was awarded my Master's Degree on Thursday, September 10, 1970, at a select ceremony at Northeastern University. The Fall Graduation was always smaller and more intimate than the formal and expansive June exercise traditionally held at the Boston Garden. I enjoyed the ceremony for that reason and felt especially buoyant knowing that I had reached the end of the long academic road on which I had set out in 1962. Beverly and her mother Milly, and my Aunt Mary and my sister Jeanette were present to see me receive my diploma. The guys in the unit gave me a monogrammed oversized leather briefcase accompanied by a card congratulating me for receiving my Masters Degree. They signed it: James Lynch, Peter Ryan, Bob Dapkas, Pat Brady, Matt Kilroe, Bob Howland, Larry Murphy, Tom Mitchell and Gerry the Cop.

True to his word, Tim Moran had already given me a teaching assignment. I was scheduled to teach 'Police Community and Public Relations' beginning the following week at Northeastern's University College. I thought it was amusing that an undercover cop would be selected to teach this course - it was the opposite of what I was doing. (Eventually I would teach courses more related to my field of study, Sociology/Criminology, but this was my first assignment.)

The book said that good community relations involved the open application of professional police techniques on the overall police operation, and the public relations aspect had to do with the specific focus of public attention through public programs and the media on these same operational techniques. Conversely police undercover operations were, by their very definition, deliberately based in subterfuge and shrouded in mystery.

I was shaky about the whole prospect of teaching, especially in an area in which I had so little experience. Tim assured me that my sociology background made me a natural for the course. Most cops thought that sociologists were out of it, and they still do to this day. I couldn't say that I blamed them but I wasn't about to argue that point with Tim. In truth, I was dazzled by the offer which I viewed as a solid achievement and a great opportunity. I wasn't about to blow it.

I was so uptight before I delivered my first lecture that I gulped down a shot of whiskey and swallowed an aspirin just before class. That was out of character for me. I wasn't a big drinker and I had no particular fondness for whiskey, but someone - I can't remember who, told me it would help me to overcome any initial anxiety I might experience from encountering my peers in a structured classroom situation.

I can still recall a few of the students that made up my first class. One of them was Richard Pugsley, one of 7 brothers and a father, all of them sworn members of a distinguished Boston Police family who would serve to the end of their careers without the slightest hint of scandal. Their offspring would keep the tradition going. I often think of their quiet dedication in the midst of police media abuse.

Another was Moe Flaherty, a Hollywood-handsome and no-nonsense TPF cop and prescient student who would eventually go on to fashion an innovative form of policing beginning in the late 1970s. It was called Team Policing back then and would eventually, in the Nineties, be renamed Neighborhood Policing. The changeover was a tough fight and to begin the transition Moe would have to bend many of the encrusted bureaucratic rules that stultified the police department. Moe would go about his work like a driven artist, shaping, coloring and twisting the scant and calcified resources he had to work with. He would pay a personal price for this - to be robbed of his bounty by a transient Police Commissioner who would unashamedly take full credit for Moe's creation. That's a whole other story.

Getting back to September 1970, my first class went pretty well. I enjoyed the classroom and stuck with teaching on a part time basis until the end of my career.

The night after I graduated, and for the next few weeks, I became immersed in a deep undercover operation involving narcotics and the theft of guns by a revolutionary leftist group who, as I would learn, supplied weapons to the Black Panthers for the expressed purpose of murdering police officers. It started early one Saturday morning as Gerry and I were getting ready to wrap it up. We had just put the finishing touches on our Friday night report when the harsh ring of the phone interrupted our conversation. Gerry picked it up and after listening intently for about a minute, he handed the receiver over to me saying, "Yeah, Phil's here."

Late night phone calls were unusual. I was hoping it wasn't anything heavy because I was looking forward to the weekend and a graduation party my aunt was planning for me on the following night. Brian and I were getting ready to tie one on.

"Who's this," I asked?

Joe Smith, a hard-working, street-wise detective assigned to the Narcotics Unit was on the other end. He didn't have to introduce himself. I easily recognized his voice. His rapid-fire manner of speech left little doubt as to his identity. Joe requested that Gerry and I meet him at District 4 to possibly identify several individuals whom the Drug Unit had just arrested for narcotics violations.

While searching the suspects' car the arresting officers had discovered six 30-30 rifles and a store of ammunition in the trunk. The occupants of the vehicle, including the registered owner, denied any knowledge of the firearms and the detectives weren't sure of just what they had or the purpose of the guns.

"Ya mind dropping over?" Joe asked, his words tumbling out all over the place. "They're dirt bag hippies and maybe you might know them."

Too bad that they didn't grab these guys earlier in the evening I thought, but I didn't have much choice. "On the way Joe," I answered.

I didn't have to say anything to Gerry - he was already going out the door. It didn't take much to recharge him. He possessed a deep reservoir of restless energy that could be tapped into in an instant. I hung up the phone and we shot over to the district to assist in the investigation.

A total of six people had been arrested; four of them, including one female, looked (and smelled) like they had crawled out from underneath a dung heap. They were attired in the uniform of the Sixties underground, complete with oily hair, matted beards, soiled clothes, ripped dungarees and worn out sneakers with holes.

One guy, a short dude with dark brown curly hair, was clean looking and neatly dressed. He was wearing dress pants and a madras jacket. He was markedly different from the rest. It didn't take an Einstein to figure out that he might be the guy to press for information.

After secretly viewing the motley crew from a distance, Gerry and I put together a half-assed plan that called for a detective from the Criminal Investigation Division to march me (as Mike Russo), into the booking room in handcuffs like any other Friday night prisoner, and sit me alongside the four dirt balls to eavesdrop on their conversation while the clean cut guy was being booked. (The female arrestee was already in the process of being transferred to the Women's House of Detention.) Ralph Ryan was working that night and agreed to place me in the cell with the clean guy in hopes that he might inadvertently drop some tidbit of information providing me with an opportunity to pry him open.

It was a long shot but we had nothing to lose except sleep. For the next six hours I remained locked up in a dark, dirty, urine saturated, eight by six-foot cell pumping this sharpie for all he was worth.

My cell mate introduced himself as John Bell. I told him that I had been busted for pot and spiced my story with a slew of obscenities directed at 'the pigs' that had arrested me. I casually commented that while I was waiting to be booked I'd overheard one of the guys he was arrested with plotting with the others to hang some kind of rap on him.

I said, "Look man, I don't know what your game is but I overheard one of the dudes you got busted with say to the guy he was sitting next to, Hey man it's his car - we don't know shit about any guns." The other guy laughed and said "Yeah, fuck him!" This was a complete fabrication of course.

I was amazed at how easily I had sucked him in. Despite the lateness of the hour and the exhausting pressure of the arrest process, his reaction was acute. In one simultaneous physical response his eyes widened, his mouth opened and his chin dropped. He was rip-roaring mad! Standing to my right, he turned his head in my direction and tightly grasped the bars in front of him. He began to speak, first slowly and then more quickly, his words sodden in anger.

"I knew those motherfuckers would try to jack me up! I knew it as soon as the cops grabbed my license. All I was, was a fucking chauffeur - they asked me to use my car because it has a big trunk. They stole the motherfucking guns and now they're tryin' ta hang it on me."

This guy was bleeding real bad. Throughout the night and early morning he regurgitated the plot of how he had gotten tied up with the others. He spilled his guts, but there were still some holes in his story. It would take a little while longer and a few more meetings to fill in the gaps.

The cop in charge of the prisoners removed me from my cell three times during the night, ostensibly to make a phone call, to speak to my lawyer and to make bail. During these interludes I joined Gerry in the detectives' office and poured out the details of what Bell was telling me.

Gerry quickly jotted the details down in his own inimitable clear style on a blank piece of paper, after which a uniformed police officer would return me to the cell where I would continue to siphon the unsuspecting Bell. It was a tense and draining night and although we were never authorized overtime for our work, it paid off in dividends.

The following Monday I contacted Bell at a prearranged meeting in the Stuart Diner in Worcester, a city about forty-five miles outside of Boston, supposedly to make arrangements to buy a large quantity of grass. Bell told me that he sold heroin in Worcester and Montreal, Canada and that he had connections in the marijuana market and could get his hands on sizable quantities of the stuff if I could come up with the cash.

Over the next few days I met with him at various locations for short periods of time, in cellars and garages where I was introduced to a number of low-lives, all of whom sold drugs and none of whom held a professional interest for me. I was concerned about guns, not dope.

I got into a shoving match with a motorcycle creep from the Iron Cross Motorcycle Gang who harangued me with questions regarding the discrepancy between my name 'Mike' and the tattoo 'Phil' on my upper left arm. I was in the middle of an old coal bin in a dirt cellar when the dispute started. After repeatedly refusing to accept my explanation that Mike was my middle name and the name that most of my friends called me, I feigned frustration and told the guy to go fuck himself! He shoved me in anger and I pushed him back. The jam was broken up really fast but it worked to lessen the others' suspicions of me.

Bell told me that he had met three of the guys he was arrested with about a month before when he had stopped on an isolated Vermont road to provide them with mechanical assistance when their car had broken down. Apparently Bell was a skilled mechanic.

During this brief encounter with the stranded motorist and his passengers, one of them offered him money as an inducement for the use of his car in staging several breaks in and around the vicinity of Burlington, Vermont.

Bell agreed to the proposal, and as a result the three men broke and entered into fifteen gun shops in the area. These breaks had taken place the week of August 30 to September 5. Bell had acted as a back-up guy and had used his Caddie with the large trunk to transport the stolen firearms.

I also learned that they had intended to break into a large gun shop located in Lancaster, New Hampshire in the early morning hours of September 11, but their plan was foiled by their arrest in Boston on Thursday, September 10 by the officers of the Drug Unit.

Bell said that the guns and ammunition seized by the police at the time of the arrest had been designated for transport to Cambridge, Mass., to an unknown location near Harvard Square where they would be sold to a group of black militants whom he believed were members of the Black Panthers. They had also planned to meet an unidentified black male who promised to take them to another location where they could purchase heroin.

He said that three of the guys were professional B and E men who specialized in the theft of guns, ammunition and dynamite exclusively for the Black Panthers. They had conspired to break into gun shops all over New England and as far west as Phoenix, Arizona. Bell said they were responsible for similar break-ins in that state and, in addition, had cases pending for similar crimes in Massachusetts and California. He even supplied me with the names of several New England gun shops where the thefts had taken place. It all checked out.

One of the people who had been arrested, a guy named Bubba, was only there for the ride according to Bell. They had picked him up earlier that evening in Cambridge. Bell said the broad was a prostitute and heroin user. She was basically a 'blow job,' he added. Neither Bubba nor the prostitute, was criminally involved with the other three.

As it turned out, not one of the gangrenous crew he was busted with had ever attempted to contact him since the multiple arrests, which convinced Bell more than ever that they were setting him up. That, of course, was exactly what I wanted Bell to believe.

Eventually I included all the information in a comprehensive report and submitted a copy to Sergeant Detective John Doris of the Drug Unit who was handling the case. I also kept him briefed on each new detail.

Doris arranged for an interview with Bell and laid it on him. He reviewed all the information I had given him, which was enough to convict Bell of narcotics violations and gun trafficking charges, and then offered him a possible alternative to prison. Cooperate with the police, testify against the others, and Doris would put in a good word for Bell with the District Attorney.

Bell knew that he was had. He flipped and even supplied additional information beyond what the police had already known. He told Doris of a specific plot by the band to blow up a radio station and kill a police officer. That underscored the dangerous nature of the group. Bell said that, "They wanted to get in the headlines."

And that's the way Doris quoted him in court. The main culprits did receive some notoriety, but they also got slammed with some serious time. Bell, Bubba and the broad ended up with suspended sentences.

The Globe played it up big once the case was tried. The caption over the story read, *Plots to Kill Hub Policeman Told in Court.* It was a speedy trial. Neither the Intelligence Division nor Gerry or I received any credit for the role we had played in the investigation, but that was par for the course. A cop's life possibly had been saved - that's all that was important. It had been a team effort and things had worked out all right but it wouldn't always be that way. Our luck was about to run out.

Thirty-Five

O n Wednesday, September 23, Patrolmen Walter A. Schroeder, 42 years old and a father of nine, was gunned down in a Brighton Bank Robbery. It was late morning when Jimmy Lynch called and notified me at the house. His information was pretty sketchy at the time - just that Schroeder was hit while responding to a hold-up alarm at the State Street Bank located at the corner of Western Avenue and Everett Street. Lynch said Schroeder was seriously injured and that he might not make it.

The information hit me in the pit of my stomach with a sickening thud. All cops hurt when any one of their own is seriously injured or killed. Cops suffer a familial attachment to one another and the bond is never more intense as when one of them is murdered.

I knew the family and that made it tougher on me. His brother Barney, my former recruit instructor, was still at the Police Academy when it happened. His other brother John, a former member of the Intelligence Division, had been transferred recently to District 4. It was a voluntary move. John preferred the action in the district to the more specialized work of the Intelligence Division.

As I said earlier there was the relationship between the Volantes (my mother and aunt's family) and the Schroeders that spanned the years when they were living and growing up in Brighton. My aunt had worked for their father Frank in the Hood Rubber in the late twenties and early thirties. She referred to him as Mister Schroeder and said he was a good boss. Finally, what really threw me was Lynch's remark that the incident had all the earmarks of a movement bank robbery. Apparently there was a female among the robbers. That was one of a number of clues that hinted of a radical leftist action and that made it even more personal!

I didn't waste any time getting into the office. Peter had just dropped his wife off at Saint Elizabeth's Hospital when he got the bad news. They were expecting their first child and Mary Ann had gone into labor. (Ironically, the wounded officer was rushed to the same hospital.) Peter was already in the office when I arrived. He looked pretty grim. His eyes had lost their bright luster and his eyelids drooped a little. I could tell by the deadly serious expression on his face that he had given up hope that Walter would survive.

We had a lot of work to do. Cops pull together during these highly stressful times. They put in as many hours as the task requires and money is never a consideration. They work tirelessly day and night, especially during the initial stages of the investigation when the evidence is the freshest and the likelihood of arrest the greatest.

The Homicide Unit had come up with the names of two suspects who might have been involved - Susan Saxe and Katherine Ann Power, graduate students at Brandeis University, a small but distinguished, Jewish founded, nonsectarian college in Waltham, Massachusetts. Among its alumnae Brandeis includes Abbie Hoffman, who had graduated in 1959 and the infamous Angela Davis, a black communist revolutionary who became a New Left cause célèbre after her imprisonment in connection with a gun smuggling scheme that had resulted in the death of a Corrections Officer at Soledad Prison.

The bank robbery investigation would reveal that Saxe and Power had gotten tied in with a couple of hard core ex-cons named William 'Lefty' Gilday and Robert Valeri at a school based, government sponsored educational reform program. They had been sucked in by the pumped up and machismo rhetoric of the swaggering con-men who offered them the opportunity to engage in something more than endlessly frustrating and futile protest actions that never lead to anything and failed to stop the war.

The men talked them into the idea of participating in something that was genuine - a real action calculated to demonstrate their zeal for the revolution. So as the story goes, the two broads, who featured themselves as vanguards of the revolution, and the two scumbags who regarded the broads as simple props to pull off a criminal action, along with Power's boyfriend Stanley Bond, planned and executed the armed robbery of the State Street Bank in Brighton.

Lynch supplied me with the names of the two Brandeis females and asked me to see what I could find out. The other guys in the unit went to the scene of the bank and canvassed the neighborhood for witness information. The way the investigators eventually put it together, Saxe was inside the bank with Stanley Bond and Robert Valeri when Walter Schroeder and his partner Frank Callahan responded to the bank to investigate a hold up alarm. Gilday, decidedly the most evil of the five criminals, was secreted in a nearby get-away car and Katherine Power was holding down the 'switch car' a further distance away.

Adhering to police procedure at the time, the two officers emerged from their cruiser and Walter took the front of the bank while Callahan went around to the rear. At that point they were still investigating the complaint. Most of the time these incidents turned out to be false alarms but that wouldn't be the case this time.

According to witnesses, Gilday had always harbored a wish to kill a cop and he got his chance that morning. Walter never saw it coming. In a matter of seconds Gilday opened fire with an automatic weapon and cut Walter down. Shot him in the back. Walter fell to the ground clutching his mid-section. Gilday kept on firing to cover the escape of his fellow bandits. Some of the rounds smashed through nearby windows and imbedded themselves in neighboring houses - almost three dozen rounds were recklessly fired into the air. The robbers escaped with twenty-six thousand dollars.

Walter died soon after he entered the hospital. An interval of time passed before the officer's death was broadcast to the public providing me with a small opportunity to track the women. I made about a dozen phone calls to established connections and came up with the name of a

Brandeis student who was the director of the 'Brandeis Regional Strike Force.' Her name was Melinda. I spoke with her on the phone and with a put-on quivering voice I pleaded with her to put me in touch with either Kathy Power or Susan Saxe. I confided to her that I possessed sensitive information that was of vital importance to them and necessary for their safety.

She swallowed the bait but apologized that she had no idea of their whereabouts. However, she did say that both women were scheduled to address a secret meeting later in the evening for the purpose of sharing with the participants the details of a dramatic action taken earlier in the day. I believed her when she added that she had no idea what the action entailed. It was obvious that she hadn't connected up the two events.

Melinda summarized that the two women were part of an anti-war student group whose motto was 'keep the pressure on' that was associated with a college professor named Paul who resided at 236 Bay State Road in the Fenway. She gave me his address and phone number. I didn't waste any time dialing his number. It was a solid piece of information and I desperately wished to expand on it.

The professor answered the phone but I failed to confirm much more than his name. I gave him the same line as I had given Melinda but he wasn't biting. He sounded pretty shaky to me, causing me to suspect that he didn't trust me or that he knew more than he was admitting. He insisted that he had no idea of where the women were and refused to say anything beyond that. For a brief moment I considered having Mike Russo visit his apartment and choke the truth out of him. I even discussed the tactic with police investigators but wiser heads prevailed. That had been raw emotion bubbling up and nothing more. When it came right down to it, I didn't know if the professor did know anything. It was a far better idea to let Homicide handle it - that way there would be no complications down the road.

I gave the information on the professor to the detectives. I don't know to this day what he might have told them, if anything, but not long after that they put the case together. They even pinned the Back Bay apartment where Bond, Valeri and the two women were living. However, by the time they hit it the culprits had blown the scene - the apartment had been abandoned.

The robbers purchased a new car with their loot. Not a penny of the dough was ever given to the movement as was promised. That justification was bullshit from the start. It didn't take long for the cops to arrest the three guys. Valeri flipped and testified against the others. Bond and Gilday got some serious time but the women remained at large for many years. Bond blew himself up in his jail cell in 1972 in an accidental explosion caused by a homemade bomb. Saxe was captured five years later in Philadelphia. She was spotted by a sharp, uniformed police officer who had committed her features to memory from a wanted poster he had viewed.

In 1993 Power turned herself in. She was married by then and had cultivated the image of the perfect, but dowdy looking housewife. She had been leading a double life for twenty-three years. After several years of running she tired and ended up in Eugene, Oregon where she sold homemade pies out of a small restaurant. She admitted her guilt and apologized to the members of the Schroeder family. Both women got short time and Walter Schroeder stayed dead.

Thirty-Six

Roxbury was rumbling again. The trouble started after a group of white kids from the Curley School in Jamaica Plain chased a black kid down Center Street to the Bromley Heath Projects. Several neighborhood black youths intervened and the resulting jam spilled out onto the street.

The police responded and locked up a thirteen year old black kid named Larry Palmer for a violent offense. Palmer was transported to old District 10 in Roxbury Crossing, and according to handouts widely distributed by the Black Panthers, was threatened by the police.

The Panthers alleged that the youngster was brutally beaten by the cops while in transport to 'Pig Ten' (District 10). Allegedly the cops said to the kid, "Mr. Nigger, we're going to throw you in Jamaica Pond and no one will know the difference." The Panthers embarked on an extensive propaganda campaign against the police. They displayed pictures of fully outfitted cops lined up along the school route charging that the police were occupying their community.

Soon after, about fifty black kids retaliated by throwing rocks at passing white motorists on Center Street, smashing the windshields of innocent people. Cars were forcibly stopped and the terror stricken occupants were pulled into the streets and beaten. The district cops and the TPF responded but several people were injured before order could be restored. That evening's carnage set the stage for weeks and months to come. A multiplicity of seemingly spontaneous hit and miss attacks against predominantly white motorists erupted throughout Roxbury on an almost nightly basis. The cops played an endless game of tag with the marauders. They made a few pinches here and there but it was usually too late before the police arrived. Somebody was invariably injured.

Eventually fearful whites refused to enter the area. The dwindling pool of white inhabitants dissipated. Blacks became leery of the night; attitudes hardened; neighborhoods rigidified; the final nails were driven through white solicited vice; the militants were jubilant; the bigots-titillated and the ordinary folks got fucked.

Developing intelligence on the Black Panthers was a pretty difficult task for a white cop. About the best I could do was call their office on the phone and pump them for information on scheduled demonstrations. Even that was not so easy. The Panthers were a closed society in spite of their supposed alliance with the militant left. They didn't trust anyone, especially strange voices over the telephone. Over time, I cultivated a black southern accent together with two or three cover stories that at least got me to first base.

Once Jimmy Lynch sent me to the old Campbell School in Roxbury to cover a community meeting called to discuss a singular instance of professed police brutality which centered on a juvenile arrest. The Panthers were present and they invited interested members of the audience to a further meeting at the Orchard Park Project. I put my balls in my head and my brains in my back pocket and decided to attend.

The Orchard Park Project was a dilapidated, crime infested, turbulent public housing development located in the heart of Roxbury. Economic prosperity had robbed it of its previous working class tenants and it had deteriorated over the years to a cluster of stained red brick buildings that housed the most desperate of the city's black poor.

It was late in the evening when I arrived at the publicly announced address. I had walked most of the distance, having left my car parked several blocks away. I experienced a deep sense of foreboding as I entered the building and sidestepped my way through the rubbish strewn hallways to an apartment on one of the upper floors. I felt completely cut off from even a semblance of security. Any sensible cop would have blasted me had he known what I was doing. Unfortunately, the challenge of learning the Panther's game plan had exceeded the bounds of my common sense.

The apartment door was open and the meeting was in progress when I arrived. Several young black males were congregated in the living room. I must have shocked them when I walked in and seated myself on a nearby metal folding chair. I was the only white guy in the place. I was gripped by the fear of exposure. I could well imagine the consequences of the Black Panthers having discovered the presence of a white cop spying on a meeting centering on police brutality. I prayed that they would buy my cover - simply put that I was a naïve white liberal concerned with injustice in the black community.

Suddenly one of the conversants broke off from the group and walked across the room to where I was sitting. He was tall, athletically built, good-looking, neatly dressed and unmistakably serious. He looked down at me as I sat stupidly in the chair. He allowed a moment to pass causing me to feel increasingly awkward and out of place. In a metallic voice that stripped the room of its hushed silence he politely asked, "Would you please leave." Actually, it was an order and not a request.

He didn't have to say it again! I thanked him and I was out of there like a bat. I watched my ass all the way back to the car and when I was sure that I was not being followed I let go with a long sigh of relief and beat it back to my neighborhood. That was the most asinine caper I had ever pulled off. I learned something that night which surprised me and its lesson has persisted through the years - there is civility everywhere, at least with a little bit of luck.

In another scam I penetrated the outer skin of the Jewish Defense League. The JDL was a nationalistic militant group of pseudo religious thugs led by a recalcitrant Rabbi known as Meir Kahane. They numbered about a thousand members nationwide and enjoyed a local office at 3 Linden Street in Brookline. This group based their principles on 'Love of Jewry, Dignity and Pride, Iron Discipline and Unity and Faith in the Indestructibility of the Jewish People.'

I saw them as a kind of Semitic right wing reaction to the abuses suffered by Jews over the years. No matter, they acted more like the Nazis they despised than the Jews they professed to be. They hated the Soviet

Union, Moslems and Blacks, and were known for their security patrols in Jewish neighborhoods which frequently erupted into street clashes with anyone who disagreed with them.

They were the prime suspects in the recent bombing of a New York City Russian musical performance; (I didn't know any details). They became a target of police interest when the city was graced by a visit of the Siberian Dancers of Omsk, a Russian Ballet directed by Yuri Yurovsky, as part of the Boston University Celebrity Series. The performance was scheduled for the late afternoon of Sunday, January 24 at Boston Symphony Hall. (This meant overtime for the Intelligence Division.)

My involvement with the JDL on that day was quick and fleeting. It started at noontime outside Symphony Hall, at the intersection of Hemenway Street and Mass. Avenue, where the members stood on the sidewalk and conducted a brief meeting discussing their tactics for the demonstration and ended with my being assigned the role of passing out protest literature to passers-by.

I stood on the street corner wearing a dark overcoat wrapped around a white shirt and brightly striped tie. My hair was combed straight back and my beard was purposely scraggly. I wore sunglasses and occasionally puffed on a cigarette. From time to time I slipped away from the group to report bits of information to Gerry, who remained at a secondary location. He passed it on to the boss.

Gerry and I ended up on the stage during the actual performance, the same as we had for Janis Joplin. We wanted to ensure that none of the street characters got that far. I enjoyed the production but was surprised to note that a few of the dancers were seriously overweight. Beverly would have been aghast. In any event, it turned out to be a pretty decent day, light and financially lucrative and the only instance that Mike Russo would be forced to change his name to Mike Weinburg.

The U.S. military incursion into Laos in January 1971 fueled the anti-war movement's assertion that the United States secretly intended to take over all of Southeast Asia. Nixon was further vilified and plans were made for additional domestic disruption and increased violence. (The American troops reportedly entered Laos to stop enemy activity around the Demilitarized Zone, the DMZ.) When the government announced that the troops were withdrawn in February, the anti-war activists refused to believe it. The militants were no more satisfied with this government declaration than they had been on June 29, 1970, when the government announced that the last U.S. troops had been withdrawn from Cambodia.

The New Left believed that the government was embroiled in a tissue of lies and corruption and could not be believed under any circumstances. They pointed to the death of Military Officer Captain Bush in Laos as proof that the government had lied about its presence in this tiny country. The militants charged that the U.S. had 'undeclared a war' on Laos. They were seriously pissed and seriously right. It would later be proven that the United States Government lied to the American people concerning the times of military intervention in both Laos and Cambodia.

Earlier in the year returning Vietnam veterans had met in a motel in Detroit and formed the 'Vietnam Veterans Against the War.' They established a national office at 156 Fifth Street in New York City and a New England office in Cambridge at 65A Winthrop Street. Members recounted stories of American atrocities in Southeast Asia and illegal military intervention in Cambodia and Laos.

They called for congressional hearings and laid down plans for a 'National Action Bivouac' scheduled between April 19 and April 24 of 1971, in Washington D.C. They entitled it 'Operation Dewey Canyon III' and issued an internal document labeled 'Top Secret' describing their proposed action as 'an invasion of Washington D.C. by Vietnam Veterans, Veterans, GIs and Reservists, aimed at the American Government Policy of Genocide in Indochina' and calling for an 'Immediate withdrawal from Indochina.' The final day of the action would coincide with a massive national peace Moratorium being planned by the People's Coalition for Peace and Justice.

The way I would hear about it later, from a federal agent, was that more than two thousand battle weary, rag tag Vietnam veterans camped on the green between the Capitol and the Washington Monument. Most of them were in full combat attire, stripped only of weaponry. Some were in wheel-chairs. All were deadly earnest. They ranted and raved, demanding that the government listen. They were deemed to be trespassers and about a hundred of them were arrested. But still they persisted.

An honorably discharged Naval Lieutenant named John Kerry led them. He was tall, slender and well spoken. As I watched him on national television, he struck me as a cross between an aristocrat and a Beatle. I was impressed to learn that he had earned a Silver Star. I knew that didn't come easily. I really didn't know what to make of so many veterans defying their government. Perhaps they were the 'ten percent' I reasoned, relying on an old military explanation of the expected percentage of screw-ups in any given unit. I hoped that none of them were Marines.

Before it was over Kerry would win the right to address William Fullbright's Senate Foreign Relations Committee. He asked them, "How do you ask to be the last soldier to die for a mistake?" (As it turned out, that would be a guy from Woburn, Mass.) On the final day he tossed his war medals on the cold steps of the capitol - the others followed. Eventually it was revealed that Kerry had thrown someone else's medals, but it probably wouldn't have made a difference had the truth been known. The symbolism was there and it was powerful.

By March 20, 1971, both the Gallup and Harris Polls indicated that 75% of the people wanted out of the Vietnam War. This finding drove the war movement to new heights. The Peoples Coalition for Peace and Justice began to immediately lay out plans to connect the publics disfavor with the war to other social issues. They developed a multi-pronged propaganda program geared to convince the American public that the Vietnam War was simply a poignant manifestation of a decadent system based upon economic exploitation and political repression.

The more moderate members of the group generally argued that ordinary Americans would have a hard time dealing with the complex of issues that purportedly lay at the root of American Capitalism. I couldn't have agreed with them more. The extravagant claims and myriad protests of the far left turned regular people off. They came across as anti-everything.

After a lot of internal haggling, movement leaders produced a written agenda that narrowed the foci down to three issues: immediate withdrawal from Southeast Asia; a sixty-five hundred dollar minimum income for a family of four; and the freeing of all political prisoners. The last issue demonstrated how disconnected the people from this segment of the movement really were from ordinary Americans. Not too many people gave a rat's ass about political prisoners, a definition few of them would have agreed with anyway. Nevertheless, increasing popular sentiment against the war stimulated the movement and continued to push it toward unprecedented levels of political activism.

Anti-war activists believed this happening was the stress point in the system that they were searching for, the light at the end of the tunnel. The people were finally coming around, awakening so to speak. They had turned against the war. And that presented an opportunity for movement organizers to make lasting political and economic changes in America. All power to the people!

Millions of protesters poured into Washington for a plethora of spring actions beginning on April 15, continuing through to April 24 and climaxing three days later. The Mayday Tribe, an out-of-control group of Yippies, attempted to shut down the Capitol and almost succeeded. They ran through the streets laying siege to West Potomac Park, blocking bridges and occupying buildings. Thousands were arrested. Simultaneous demonstrations broke out across the country. Cops were stretched thin everywhere, especially the D.C. Officers - they were overrun but somehow or other they managed.

There was great turbulence in the country and the thin blue line was getting thinner. It felt like the war would never end and the shit would never cease. The air was saturated with the threat of violence and the streets became more dangerous. The conventional crime rate also rose to an unprecedented level. Reason was all but lost and my self-imposed professional attempts to clarify the differences among groups to the police brass became more academic than real.

I was especially distressed by this development because I knew it would result in more police and demonstrator casualties. A personal benefit from the fractionalization that went on was the cover it provided me, thus enabling me to move more freely among the dissident groups with greater immunity. No one talked to each other, including elements of the peace movement, and that worked to my advantage. I was astonished that I could still pull this off even after I had assumed a part time faculty position with Northeastern University. But then most of my students were law enforcement types and they didn't talk to political dissidents.

443

I was doing well to fulfill my many roles, although I almost blew it once when an MIT cop stupidly revealed my true identity to a campus radical during a building takeover. I was there on an intelligence mission and the highly positioned Superior Officer commented to the student that he had attended school at Northeastern University's Department of Law Enforcement with me. I don't know if his head was stuck up his ass or if he was out to gain points with the guy, but I was forced to melt away after the student began to ask me questions. Otherwise my cover would have been totally blown.

Other than this one instance, I bounced around the radical network pretty well. I even found time to perform conventional criminal work late at night after the dissidents had wrapped it up for the day. I prided myself at being able to adapt quickly to a wide variety of people and situations. The longer I worked at it, the better I got. My biggest challenge was soon to come.

Just after I turned thirty-two my home life took a nose-dive. I'll never forget it if I live to be a hundred. It was late Sunday evening and I had just dropped my aunt off in Somerville after arriving back in Boston from Schenectady, New York where we had spent the weekend visiting my sister's family. Beverly had wished to stay home that weekend, explaining that she had housework to do. She had thrown me a nice party for my thirty-second birthday just before I left, and I felt like I was falling in love with her all over again.

I opened the front door and walked into the kitchen. Everything was immaculate. Nothing was out of place. The floor was freshly waxed and the counter tops gleamed. Even the wallpaper had a fresh look to it. I was happy to be home after the long ride. I had not even taken time to share a cup of coffee with my aunt, as was our usual practice, because I was anxious to get home to Beverly and the kids.

Beverly greeted me. "How's the kids?" I asked.

"They're sleeping," she answered.

"It's nice to see you, Bev. Her blonde hair shone and she was wearing her best Andover Shop slacks and blouse. She didn't respond. I hugged her and rubbed the side of my face against hers. She felt stiff and cold. I was puzzled by her unreceptiveness and moved my head away to get a better look at her.

She took advantage of the newly created space and pushed up a white envelope between our bodies, over the top of her head and just under my nose. She might as well have hit me between the eyes. I knew something was terribly wrong. I opened the rear flap and removed the contents. I could hardly believe what I was reading. I read it three more times to be sure. My throat thickened and my heart began to pound like a jackhammer. I felt like I had just been kicked in the stomach. It was a letter from a lawyer, whom I had never met, ordering me to leave my home. It happened as suddenly as that! I guessed the reason why.

Thirty-Seven

Things hadn't been going well for Beverly and me for a long time. Our marriage had long since grown cold and we were living more like siblings than man and wife. Even her mother Milly joked that we acted more like brother and sister than married people. Beverly's sexual furnace had shut down (on me) soon after the birth of our second child. I rationalized that part of the reason had to do with her fear of another pregnancy. Perhaps the death of her brother had also contributed. I tried to be understanding but it was pretty tough sometimes. I made light of my anguish by recalling my academy classmate Billy Quinlan's remarks about having to make an appointment for sex after marriage. It was precisely Beverly's failure to have kept her appointment on the past New Year's Eve which brought our problems to a boil. I burned that night. I burned real bad!

The next morning I had calmly explained to Beverly that I was unable to continue living as we were. I drove the point home, that had I wished to live in a celibate state I would have become a priest and would not have chosen to marry. I professed that I had no knowledge of what was causing our problem, and if there were no solution soon, I would be forced to look for sex outside of our marriage. I asked for her understanding and permission to do so. I promised that it would not be something that I would go about doing right away, and assured her that I would be careful and selective once I did.

It was more of a threat than a promise, so you can imagine my surprise when she consented to my request. She just as well might have knocked me out. I never would have believed that she would have agreed to such an outrageous proposal, but she did. She asked only that I not grace her with the details. Of course I agreed.

That understanding was worked out on the first day of the year. Forgive me if I sound too much like a cop with this explanation but it was not made under coercion, threats or false promises. It was not made in the heat of anger or agreed to in a humorous or sarcastic vein. I fully believed that I was free to seek my own adjustment. I stuck to my word and eight months passed before anything happened.

The affair started innocently enough. I had been assigned a course scheduled to begin sometime in September. Tim Moran asked me to submit a syllabus outlining my course of instruction before the first lecture. My inability to type increased my anxiety about getting it in on time.

My sister, who had typed most of my papers throughout college, lived in another state so Beverly suggested that I ask her cousin, an undergraduate at Northeastern University, to perform the task. Cynthia was sort of a plain Jane athletic type, kind of pensive, who had enjoyed a comfortable adolescence in an affluent home in the suburbs with loving doting parents. Now in college, she was living away from home for the first time in her life.

Coincidentally, I bumped into Cynthia in the cafeteria. She was accompanied by her roommate - a busty little brunette with quick eyes who introduced herself as Cassandra. When I requested her help in preparing the syllabus, Cynthia apologized and explained that she had never learned to type. Without any prompting by me, Cassandra interjected and agreed to type my work. She appeared more than willing.

A few nights later I dropped by their apartment on Wait Street, a few blocks down from the university, to pick up the finished product. I had called first and talked with Cassandra and fully expected that both roommates would be home. The only thing I had on my mind at that point was obtaining the completed syllabus.

I entered the front door of the sooty yellow brick apartment building and walked up the stairs to the second floor. Cassandra opened the door.

She was wearing a white lacy see-through negligee. She told me that Cynthia had left for the evening and that my syllabus was ready.

She invited me to sit down and offered me a glass of wine. The whole room seemed wonderfully seductive. Cassandra turned some soft music on the radio and after some polite chatter, she asked "What is your greatest fantasy?"

I answered, "Hiking the Appalachian Trail from one end to the other." I went on to expound on the delights of nature and briefed her on the length, time and difficulty of the trek. "What is yours?" I asked, half suspecting that she was going to throw me a bomb.

She paused, as though to reflect. Her soft white features seemed all the prettier in the dimly lit room. I don't recall her exact words but they floored me. She said something about indulging in unmitigated sex, enhanced by the use of body oils and powders.

Man, this was a-real come on! I was being seduced for the first time in my life and I loved every minute of it. Most ordinary guys, married or not, would have taken the bait and I had more compelling reasons than the ordinary guy, not to mention the support of an oral agreement with Beverly giving me permission to compensate for the lack of sex in our marriage. I wasn't about to lose this fish, especially after the long drought I had experienced. She sounded a little bizarre but so what? I decided to press my option.

"Where's the oil?" I asked.

Our relationship was a hamburger and coke affair consisting of about eight sexual encounters spread over the next six months. I was clear about my intentions, stressing only the physical basis of our attraction and downplaying any romantic motives. I never gave Cassandra any false hopes.

Our rendezvous were hastily arranged, usually brief snatches of time calculated to take advantage of small interludes of privacy either at her place or my friend John's apartment in Winthrop, a small coastal town on the North Shore (sort of romantic, actually). Free love was the battle hymn of the Sixties and had come to replace the free speech movement as the sensual lubricant of social protest.

Cassandra was a novice creature of the liberated Sixties and she exulted in the excesses of her newfound freedom. She was young, nimble, playful and uninhibited in her lovemaking and joyous in her good looks. She was new at it, having reached her early twenties still intact, and neither she nor I could foresee the consequences of our trysts.

For her, I suspect it was the blooming of romantic feelings followed by the pain of rejection. For me it was the misuse of a human being as I crossed the line over to legal adultery. I came to sense that Cassandra had developed feelings for me, feelings for which I could never reciprocate. The weight of the relationship became more pressing and I began to feel like I was living a lie (much like the lie Mike Russo was living).

At this point my whole life was a lie! My combat zone/political/radical professional life, my empty married life and my cheating personal life were all a lie. Something had to give, so I started with Cassandra. Her removal was the easiest and perhaps the most immediate solution to my dilemma. I arranged to meet her on Huntington Avenue. I pondered her possible reactions and I fervently hoped that she would understand.

I took her down as gently as the circumstances permitted. I ended my explanation of why we had to part with the standard line about it being "best for the both of us." She seemed to understand although she never responded. I dropped her off at her apartment, said "good-bye" and walked back to my car. I was enormously relieved that it was over.

The way Beverly told it, Cynthia came to her and related her suspicions regarding her roommate Cassandra and me. These suspicions were supposedly based on the way Cassandra acted whenever I visited their apartment and Cynthia was present. She had no proof of anything mind you, just suspicions, but Cynthia thought it was important to share her concerns with Beverly.

Perhaps that was how it happened - Cynthia, acting out of an exaggerated sense of girlish loyalty to her older cousin, blew the whistle on a relationship that she had no factual knowledge existed. Or maybe Cassandra had confided the relationship to Cynthia, expecting some comfort, but instead was betrayed. Or it just might have been that Cassandra deliberately informed her roommate of our affair because she knew that Cynthia would tell Beverly and she wanted to get even. I doubted this version. More than likely Cynthia, acting out of naiveté, put the screws to both of us.

A few weeks before my New York trip Beverly conceded that she had reason to suspect that I had been involved with another women and begged me to tell her the truth. She had a feeling about it - she could sense it, she explained. Beverly repeatedly assured me that there would be no consequences if I just confided in her.

I mulled it over for a couple of minutes and decided to come clean. I trusted her assurances. Reminding her of our earlier agreement, I confessed that her suspicions were right on. I told her that I had been involved with a woman but that I had ended the relationship because of the immense guilt I had felt. I apologized, explaining that I felt "really bad" about the whole thing and guaranteed her that it would never happen again. I secretly hoped that this revelation would jar her into understanding that my promiscuous behavior was linked to her neglect. I refused to identify my partner though Beverly repeatedly demanded that I should. That would have constituted a breach of loyalty and I wasn't about to burn Cassandra. Beverly finally seemed to accept that explanation.

Imagine my sick chagrin a few days later when I returned home from a day tour and was startled to see Cassandra coming up the basement stairs into the kitchen, sobbing hysterically, with Beverly trailing behind her. I can't recall how Cassandra got there or how she returned to her apartment. Eventually I was able to piece together that Beverly lured Cassandra to the basement and in a manner approximating the most evocative techniques of a masterful interrogator, pulled the truth out of her.

Apparently Beverly had made Cassandra the same kind of promise that she had made me - simply that she would not take any action against her or me providing that Cassandra would just tell the truth. (Unfortunately, the truth was a vagary that Beverly was never able to fully comprehend. That indeed had placed a far greater burden on our marriage than lack of nookie.)

The rest can be surmised. While I was away for the weekend applauding Beverly's understanding to my aunt, with whom I had confided the whole story, Beverly was engaging a lawyer and with assistance from certain members of her family, whose help she had sought, had indeed plotted to do me in. I was particularly disappointed with her father with whom I enjoyed a good relationship. I had even escorted him on a couple of guided tours of the Combat Zone. The problem with that, however, was that he looked more like a cop than I did and I feared he might blow my cover. I asked myself how could he have forgotten the good conversations and fun times we'd had together. As it turned out, he never did. Years later we resurrected our relationship, but of course it was never quite the same.

The State of Massachusetts, at that time, required 'cause' to effect a divorce. Beverly had her cause - adultery, should she decide to push it. Next, she needed to get me to voluntarily leave the house to fulfill the other requirement. The law also required that an individual applying for a divorce must live apart from his/her spouse. Somebody had to go and it wasn't about to be Beverly.

When I finally regained my composure, I refused to leave. I knew that the lawyer's letter was not worth the paper it was written on. As a cop I was aware that it lacked any real legal authority. It amounted to a legal bluff.

So Beverly left - kids and all. The only other time that I could recall having felt so desolate was the day I got the news that my mother had died, which had left me with the same feeling of sudden abandonment. Now, twenty years later, it was happening all over again.

I toughed it out for a couple of days by 'banging in sick', something I had never done before. I refused to leave the house even for a moment, fearing that Beverly would slip in behind me and lock me out. There wasn't much food around and I was forced to eat whatever scraps I could find.

On the third day Beverly returned. She rang the doorbell and I allowed her in. She wore a cheerless expression and didn't bother to waste any time. In an exasperated rush of words she pleaded with me to voluntarily meet with her lawyer and sign a temporary agreement to move out. She needed time to think she explained. It wouldn't be forever, perhaps just a week or two at the most.

I didn't believe her, but I didn't have a lot of choices left. The kids needed to live somewhere and I had to go back to work. I needed a paycheck and things were happening back in the city. I thought about it for a short time and dejectedly agreed to cooperate. I reluctantly packed my clothes and moved in with two former Marines - John MacNeil, one of my former roommates on Balsam Street in Dorchester, and his kid brother Allen. I knew the apartment well - I had been there with Cassandra.

It was the likely thing to do. John and I had become close friends over the years. We featured ourselves as a kind of a 'Mack and Myer' comedy team and he had helped me out a lot around the house. We had shared a lot of laughs while fixing things. John was an electrician and a skilled technician and, unlike me, he was handy with tools.

At my urging, he had installed an array of multi-colored flashing bulbs illuminated further by two overhead six foot long black-lights in the basement of my duplex. The inclusion of fluorescent posters and globs of phosphorous paint smattered all over the place further enhanced the desired effect. It looked like a real hippie pad, minus the dope.

We had some great parties there, good rock and some heavy dancing. We moved to the beat of the Supremes and the sounds of James Brown, Tom Jones, Elvis and a variety of artists from the Sixties. Notably absent were Arlo Guthrie, Paul Simon, Bob Dylan and the MC-5s - they were more geared for Mike Russo and the rebellious 'under thirty' generation.

The parties, though raucous, had never gotten out of hand. The only casualty was Jutta, the beautifully statuesque and exquisitely dressed wife of the broker who had sold me the house. Even her German accent was unable to mask her mortification when she looked down and realized that her pale white chiffon blouse failed to block the black light from fully illuminating her silver toned bra. Normally staid and stoic, she fled the basement for the first floor and the redeeming light of the kitchen. That was about as wild as it ever got.

John got wiped out a few times, we all did, and he slept over on a cot in the basement. Now it was my turn. I needed somewhere to go and John pulled through for me. The brothers MacNeil lived in an old sprawling apartment house on Shore Drive right next to the ocean.

I met Beverly's lawyer at the dilapidated Cambridge Courthouse at the pre-arranged time. Beverly and I obediently sat together across from her like two children about to be counseled. The lawyer was a middle-aged and weary looking woman with auburn hair, brown eyes and a shapely overly proportioned butt. I didn't like her from the start. She struck me as being coldly aloof, calculating and completely indifferent to my feelings. I suspected that she hated men and I wasn't about to do anything to change her mind. Her continued insensitivity pushed me over the edge and I asked her, "Do your male partners allow you to do any other kind of legal work besides divorce?"

It was a cutting remark intended to provoke her. However, she stayed cool and never responded. Instead, she laid a phony rap on me about the need for a short cooling down period. She was full of crap and we all knew it. This lawyer was working for Beverly and her only intention was to persuade me to willingly move out of my house in order to clear the way for a divorce action.

They had me hung up and I knew that, too. I felt like one of Ben Moria's 'Up Against the Wall Motherfuckers.' I caved in and signed the papers which marked the beginning of the official end.

Two weeks passed and I began to press Beverly to allow me back in the house. She consistently refused, arguing that she needed more time to think. Although I had learned over the course of our relationship that many of Beverly's promises were written in sand, that didn't prevent me from being enraged at this particular breach of faith. I became painfully more frustrated and futilely threatened that if I wasn't back by the beginning of May, I would begin to live as a single person, meaning that I would pay John rent and begin to date other women. The situation started to get nasty.

Beverly countered by hitting me with a formal divorce notice. A local constable delivered the papers in hand after he called and verified my address. I would be the first person in my entire family, right down to my second cousins, to get divorced. I was deeply ashamed of this failure and felt diminished as a human being but I wasn't alone. My lifelong friend Brian Gill had already started the same process. He and his wife had also separated. The curtain had finally descended on our pantomime.

After that I fell into a deep melancholy which lasted for several weeks. Strangely enough, I never missed Beverly. In fact, I had grown increasingly bitter toward her. In my mind she was quickly taking on the dimensions of Cruella de Vil. I was appalled by her treachery and revulsed by her deceptive tactics.

I yearned for my children, and I deplored the loss of my home and all of its belongings which I had worked so hard to obtain. Kimberly was just six, brilliant beyond her years and already my good little buddy. Kristin was only two and as cute as a button. Her secrets were still locked inside of her. I feared that she would never come to know me as her dad.

I suffered a deep-rooted need to be a good father. Much of it stemmed from my own orphaned status and the deep feelings of despair and loneliness I had experienced as a child. I remembered the stories my mother told me about my father before she died, about how much he loved me and how proud he was to push me down Broadway in a baby carriage. Imagine a big husky guy, an athlete, a former professional wrestler, gaining satisfaction from pushing an infant in a baby carriage on the sidewalk of a main boulevard in a congested working class city back in 1939!

I never knew my father - at least not after I turned six months old. But, for all my waking consciousness he had existed as an ideal - as did the love my parents had shared. Perhaps they also had shared a prophetic realization that my father's days were numbered. From all the accounts of everyone who knew them, they truly loved one another and lived each day like there would never be another.

I had never experienced that kind of relationship with Beverly. I believed that she had married me out of necessity, a marriage of convenience that would ultimately come to oppress her. Any allusions I had to the contrary disappeared soon after the wedding ceremony. We hardly related to one another. We were from two different neighborhoods and had been brought up in entirely different ways. I had never experienced the candy colored world she fantasized about and she was never comfortable in the hard scrabble world of a street kid. Six years later it was over. Beverly pulled the plug. She didn't need me anymore and now she was tossing me out into the street. I felt emotionally drained, empty, hurt, busted and broke. Mostly I pained. I pained for my children whose dreams I feared would never be fulfilled.

Kevin Murphy, by then a practicing attorney who had since moved to the neighboring town of Melrose, referred me to another lawyer. He apologized that morally he couldn't take the case because he knew us both. Kevin, unlike most lawyers that I would meet over the years, operated from a full set of standards.

His colleague also turned out to be a pretty good guy. He charged me just three hundred bucks for the divorce, perhaps because I had done my own negotiating with Beverly to keep the price down. Arriving on a settlement had been excruciating psychological agony. As soon as we came to a general agreement her mother would throw a wrench into the deal. At one point Milly caused Beverly to refuse my full offer of the house, including the rent, along with alimony and child support.

Finally Beverly and I settled on a contract. We agreed that we would continue to jointly own the property. I would be responsible for the expenses and the general maintenance of the tenant's side. The principal, interest and taxes amounted to eighty bucks a month after deducting the one hundred and sixty dollars for the rent that I collected from the other side. In addition, I agreed to pay Beverly sixty dollars a week out of the one hundred and forty that I cleared from my paycheck.

That left me with about sixty bucks a week to live on, in addition to the hundred dollars a month I earned at Northeastern, which could not be guaranteed. Things were pretty tight for a while, but I managed. All I could afford on some evenings were coffee and donuts for dinner. It couldn't have been too easy for Beverly either, but somehow she managed to avoid having to get a job for the next year and a half. Perhaps her family helped her - in any event it relieved me to know that the girls were getting her undivided attention.

Things weren't about to get any better. Soon after I had moved into my furnished room in Winthrop my car was broken into and my freshly laundered clothes were stolen. I had just picked them up at my aunt's house. She had resumed doing my laundry again, like she had when I was single.

About a month later I was involved in an automobile accident. A strung out junkie chick driving on the wrong side of the road hit me head on. My head went through the windshield and I ended up in the hospital for a week with a serious concussion. My late model Chevrolet Impala was totaled. All I ended up with was the bill. And worst of all, my black three-speed Raleigh bike was stolen after I stupidly chained it to a parking meter in Harvard Square. I was so intent on continuing my surveillance of a guy, who I knew was wanted on an interstate flight warrant, that I unconsciously fastened it to a five-foot parking meter. I never stopped to think that a thief would simply have to lift the entire bike and the chain up over the meter. It was such an easy maneuver that the thief probably feared it was a police sting. The FBI got their man, but I lost my bicycle.

In the end it was Gerry who busted me out of my depression. I was riding around with him a lot during this time, especially after my bicycle was stolen. (Eventually I would buy another one, of course, but I was financially strapped at the time.) Gerry picked me up and dropped me off while I did my thing, halfheartedly scooping up bits and pieces of intelligence at different locations.

We continued to do our Combat Zone routine, hunted down registration numbers and performed short surveillances. We picked up some new Black Panther addresses: 33 Montrose Street and 81 Centre Street in Roxbury, 201 West Springfield Street in the South End and 264A Western Avenue in Brighton. Some of them were given to us and others were tail jobs.

Gerry particularly enjoyed the criminal side of the operation. However, I'm not sure how much he enjoyed me. I was slipping down a mental mineshaft into a deeper abyss.

I was pretty depressing to be with. I didn't say much while I was in the car. I just looked out the passenger window and remained silent. (Roach had trained me well at that.) I was sad, morose and unlike my usual self. I had no wish to speak. I was absorbed into my own thoughts and those thoughts usually centered around Beverly and the synthetic sugar-coated world of deceit, subterfuge and manipulation that I believed she lived in. As far as I was concerned, she possessed more personalities than an undercover cop.

That's what I was doing one night - being silent, sullen, gloomy and preoccupied - when Gerry's patience, short lived to begin with, finally gave out.

"Get yourself together!" he barked. "You're no fucking good to anyone like this!"

He jerked his head around speedily, as if it was on a swivel, and like an eagle swooping down on his prey his eyes narrowed and focused in on me. I was sitting in the passenger seat with my hands folded together on my lap. The look on his large Irish face was unmistakably serious and tinged with genuine concern. Something inside of me snapped. It was as though Gerry had tripped a buried psychological spring release that had ejected me back into the real world. The inner feelings of guilt and anxiety that were imprisoning me began to peel away and my depression slowly lifted. I thought about what he said for a few minutes and remarked "You're right Gerry - I'm Sorry. Do you mind dropping me off near Central Square?"

"No problem," he responded, his voice plainly unburdened. "When do you want to get picked up?" he asked.

"Don't worry," I answered. "I'm walking - it's a nice night. I'll see you back at the office."

Thirty-Eight

Plans for the fall anti-war offensive were already underway as summer ended. Time seemed to move more quickly now as I grew older. My seven years on the police department had passed at twice the speed of the four years that I had spent in the Marine Corps. I picked up some more information on Weather Underground meeting places and got involved with a non-affiliated group of gun harboring radicals in Jamaica Plain who had bragged about wounding a Boston cop.

Jimmy Lynch handed me the assignment. He told me he had information that guns were being stored in a Myrtle Street apartment in Jamaica Plain. He believed that the apartment was occupied by the remnants of a West Coast commune that for some undetermined reason(s) had broken away from the other members and had headed east. My assignment was to somehow get into the apartment and nose around. This necessitated that I come up with a half-baked plan.

I got a batch of phony real estate papers together and tacked them underneath the clasp on a standard clipboard. I ran off a bunch of literature associated with a rent control group and I was in business. Rent control was a big issue with the New Left. They deplored rent-gouging landlords who screwed over people, and there were plenty of them out there.

For the better part of a week I knocked on doors in the neighborhood.

I hit the occupants with an extended rap about my belonging to a tenants' advocacy group whose sole purpose was to demonstrate, by the actual collection of real estate data, that poor and elderly people were being displaced in certain neighborhoods in Jamaica Plain by young people and college students who were able to pay a higher combined rent than single persons and families.

They fell for it like a ton of bricks. Jamaica Plain had more than their share of left-leaning students who had a huge sympathy for the problem. I went into apartment after apartment. Most of the residents allowed me to physically inspect their apartments and they leveled with me about the amount of rent they were paying and the number of people who were sharing it.

The commune guys were no different. Before the week was out they had laid out the welcome mat. They permitted me free access to the entire apartment enabling me to count the number of rooms and check out the closet space. Surprisingly enough, three of the commune members, who were sitting in the kitchen taking turns sucking on a cheap bottle of wine, allowed me to be alone while I peered into their personal living spaces and ruffled around their closets.

The apartment was filthy rotten. Clothes and personal items were strewn about everywhere. Un-eaten portions of food lay rotting on the floors and an army of cockroaches were having a field day. I was happily ready to vacate the place when I hit the jackpot.

Amidst all the squalor and clutter I spotted a double-barreled shotgun lying upright alongside a long black bag in the corner of the last bedroom closet I searched. I suspected that the bag contained additional firearms and theorized that the gun that I was looking at had been mistakenly left out. I had completed the initial part of my assignment - I had verified Lynch's information and I was ecstatic.

Now I had to figure out just what the commune members might have intended to do with the weapons. I decided to make a verbal comment on my discovery for two reasons: the first was to deflect suspicion away from me in the event that they were aware of my find and were testing me, and the second was to pump these crumbs for more information.

"Hey, you dudes getting ready to fight the revolution?" I asked, half joking.

"Yeah man," one of them responded. "We already shot a pig but we only wounded him. It was in the papers." The others laughed.

"The next time we'll take better aim," one of the others chimed in.

It was obvious that they were half tanked, but still in all, I was astonished by their openness. Had it gotten this bad I asked myself? Had the hate and violence become so much a part of the national fabric that these left wing nut bags weren't even bothering to conceal their crimes from a stranger anymore? Even if they were giving me a line about the wounded cop they made no effort to hide their violent intentions.

To make matters worse there was a case still open on a wounded Boston Cop. No one had ever been arrested for the Dick McEachern shooting in the Boston Common. The shooting had been investigated but was never confirmed. A few of the brass hated Dick so badly that they secretly refused to believe his story. Instead, they preferred to suspect that the incident might have been the result of a self-inflicted accidental discharge.

Once the trio's conversation lapsed into drunken gibberish I politely thanked them for their cooperation and made my exit. I promised that I would return with the results of the study, thus leaving the door open for another bout. I didn't waste any time after I left the apartment. I called Lynch at his house and requested that he remain there because I was on the way over. Twenty minutes later I pulled up and parked next to his small white colonial on Friendship Road. I gave him the information and he passed it on to the Criminal Investigations Division the next day. They never bothered to get back to me. I reasoned that the detectives assigned to the unit were attempting to develop enough probable cause to apply for a search warrant, or maybe they had some other game plan. As it turned out nothing ever happened and nothing ever would because a week later the apartment was abandoned.

I bumped into Leo Bordier that summer. I think it was on Newbury Street in the Back Bay. I was on some sort of assignment, although I can't recall the details. He told me he had been living on Pembroke Street before moving to a third floor apartment at 66 Westland Avenue. He was living right in the middle of a lot of action - everything from hustler activity to student disruptions. He commented that he didn't like the amount of prostitution that was occurring in his neighborhood. Otherwise, he looked prosperous and happy.

He was accompanied by an older woman whom he introduced as his wife. She was kind of a schoolmarm type and nothing like the volatile and glamorous women he had married previously. I could see that she was protective and fiercely loyal to Leo. She was also well educated and a devotee of good literature. That, I thought, made her a good companion for my friend.

Leo told me he was in the comic book business and that things were going really well. He remarked that he had collected old comic books all of his life and now he was making a good living at his hobby by operating a mail order service out of his apartment. Our chat harkened me back to our early State Hospital conversations about the character 'Superman.'

Leo had been obsessed with phantasmagoric stories about strong men and Superman was the epitome of such lore. He said that Neitshe's concept of the 'Overman' was the root inspiration of the modern day super hero.

Leo had continued his writing and was quietly confident that his work would eventually be published. By this time he had written several novels and had come close once, but the publishing house had burned down just after he had signed a contract. His faith in himself and his art would eventually be rewarded, but that was still more than a dozen years away.

Leo was among the most inspirational sources I had ever known, a muse of the highest order, and I was delighted to have run into him. He never went back to the booze, he said. He explained that what I had regarded as his 'overstay' at Boston State Hospital was simply the additional time he needed to mend.

Leo entranced me - he always had. He had learned to manage. He had found a place to deposit his pain and another place to extinguish his nightmares. They would no longer dominate his life. Perhaps I could learn from him.

I told him that Beverly and I were splitting up. He knew Beverly - he had met her through Michael and me. I was never sure what he thought about her though I sensed he was uncomfortable around her. He looked down just for a moment and then raised his head and gazed at me. His dark eyes were stippled with empathy. He knew my distress and for a fleeting instant I sensed his own deep grief about his failed marriages. "Your pain will pass," he said. He encouraged me not to worry excessively about the kids, assuring me that the simple fact of a divorce could never change our close relationship.

"Because parenthood is stamped in time" he said.

Leo's message was comforting. His deep melodious words washed through me like a spiritual ablution and left me with an inner sense of peace.

Unfortunately Leo's words didn't stop Beverly and me from continuing to plunge into a downward spiral. Things were getting worse as the days wore on. Curiously enough, Beverly became obsessive concerning my movements. On at least one occasion she followed my car - she even dragged one of her relatives in on the tail.

I believed that Beverly's perfidy knew no bounds once I learned that she had enlisted the services of one of my pals to spy on me and reveal information about my personal life. She wanted to know what I was doing and with whom I was doing it. I didn't have anything to hide but the knowledge of my friend's betrayal sickened me. He had gone to such lengths that even Beverly had to warn me about not trusting anyone. Many years later her father confided in me that this Judas had attempted to hit him up for enough money to put a tap on my telephone.

I have always believed that one who would betray a friend is the greatest of violators. Dante consigned such people to the innermost circle of Hell, where the flames were the deepest and hottest. I remember thinking, when I learned about my friend's treachery, that such a punishment would be fitting and proper for him but I knew he wasn't in it alone.

Beverly's jealous rage was triggered once she learned that I was dating another woman. The woman was Kay, a twenty-seven year old divorcee with two kids who was employed as a waitress in the Captain's Bar, an expensive piano bar in one of Boston's most elegant hotels.

The Statler, as it was known back then, was an elitist watering hole for a few selective cops, mostly from headquarters. I pretty much avoided the place because of my undercover role. Conversely, Gerry knew everyone in the hotel; he did details there and one night when I happened to be with him he introduced me to Kay.

She worked the lounge with a couple of other waitresses who were about the same age as she. One of them was Ruth, a long legged beauty and the other was Samantha, a dark eyed exotic woman who could well have modeled for the original bust of Maximus Cleavage. The women were all attractive (you needed to be a knockout to work in the Captain's bar) but it was Kay who caught my eye. She would have caught any guy's eye.

Kay was a curvaceous and stunning champagne blonde and it took me a couple of weeks to summon up the courage to ask her out. I was curiously delighted when she agreed. I had no idea what she could possibly see in a reject like me. Despite all the attention patrons showered on her in the lounge, none of their adulation seemed to faze her - she blew them away like toy soldiers. She even sloughed off a baseball player from the Red Sox. He tried his best to date her, but he never got to first base.

Kay said she liked me because I was straight and never ordered drinks at the bar while I was working. (She didn't know anything about Mike Russo at the time.)

Our first date consisted of an eight hour day trip to Provincetown, a picturesque fishing village and eccentric enclave located at the very tip of Cape Cod and about one hundred and twenty miles from Boston. After paying for a full tank of gas I only had enough money to purchase one meal when we finally arrived. I lied to Kay and told her that I wasn't hungry, but she knew otherwise and insisted on sharing her food with me.

I got to know her pretty well that day and I was impressed with the devotion she had for her two boys. Danny and Scott were at the center of her life, just as Kim and Kristin occupied mine. Kay lived with her elderly parents and two children in a double-decker in a nearby city. Keeping her family healthy and together were her highest priorities.

Our lives would dovetail together like two perfectly fitted parts of an interlocking puzzle. Puzzles are not always completed, but for the next two years our fulfilling relationship would buttress us against the stings of a harsh world.

Thirty-Nine

I t began like any other ordinary night of routine intelligence gathering, with my eyeballing an overloaded MIT bulletin board advertising everything from projected student actions to Aquarian encounters with myriad spiritual gurus, and it culminated with the convergence of a flow of events that would forever alter my perception of political authority.

It was late in October. I remember the time well because it was shortly after my divorce had become final. During the nasty six months waiting period the rancor between Beverly and I had grown so bitter that I experienced a deep sense of relief when the legalities were finally over. I had struggled to come to terms with what had happened and when the day finally arrived the sociologist in me couldn't resist capturing what I believed at the time to be the essence of our marital conflict. I penned a small note to myself:

Thursday, October 21, 1971 - Divorce: An action precipitated by a need, spurned on by neglect, colliding with the moral and legal norms of a social system.

Had I been able to arrive at a less theoretical and more visceral understanding of our dilemma, I would have calculated for the influence of upbringing and the effects of my own personal brand of police-conditioned objective reality on Beverly's synthetic world of wish fulfillment and fantasy. Our worlds were incompatible, polar opposites so to speak, the beast and the beauty, the boor and the belle, an irreconcilable duo, mutually antagonistic and foredoomed from the start.

I wrote Beverly a long anguished letter, sort of a Marital Bill of Attainder, chronologically listing all of my grievances against her. I began with our extra-marital agreement which, as I asserted, she never intended to keep, and ended with the final date of the divorce itself. The letter was steeped in charges of duplicitous behavior and spousal betrayal and when I was finished I felt spent. I carefully placed it in a large envelope and sealed the rear flap. I could not continue to live with the torrid anger and suffocating resentment I felt towards Beverly, so I stuffed some of that animus in the envelope too. I discharged a long distressing cathartic sigh of release and began the process of putting the pieces of my life back together. I was back on ground zero - I had been there before.

I never mailed the letter; my distrust of Beverly ran too deep. I feared that she would find some way to use it against me. I have always believed that one should never write anything down of a personal nature that one does not want the whole world to see. (That's what's making this part of my story so tough in the telling.)

The ocean has a way of putting things in perspective. It can also act as a sedative. My problems seemed to pale whenever I returned to my new home on Shore Drive and gazed into its eternal immensity. Sometimes, in stormy weather, the gargantuan house would tremble and shake, right down to its massive foundation, and enormous waves would cascade over the break-wall and lick at the windows of our second floor apartment. More money also helped me adjust to my new life as a divorced parent. I had gotten a twenty dollar a week raise and Tim Moran assigned me to instruct two full-year courses at Northeastern. Ray LaVirtue, one of my former college classmates and then Director of the Law Enforcement Program at Bristol Community College, reached out from Fall River and offered me another one. The community college was located over sixty miles away and the lectures were three hours long but it paid almost twice as much as Northeastern.

I was able to pay off my car loan with the insurance settlement I received from the accident. Plus, I had enough cash left to buy a new 1971 gleaming red automatic Volkswagen Super Beetle, complete with two metal studded winter tires.

Eventually I was able to purchase another bicycle. I transported it on a permanent bike rack that I had installed on the rear of my VW and I was back in business.

I came to enjoy the simplicity and freedom of my new life. Beverly and I were no longer married and I liked it that way, but I still hadn't fully come to terms with the anguish of being separated from my children. That would take a lot more time.

The divorce contract stipulated that I would have visitation rights on Saturday and Tuesday afternoons and any other such time as we both agreed. Beverly never interfered with my right to see the kids and come hell or high water I never missed an opportunity.

And you can take the 'high water' part literally. One Saturday morning, after a raging storm, I awakened to a neighborhood immersed in two feet of water. My VW was actually floating down the street. It took a couple of hours for the water to recede, another hour to get the car started and two more to make my way through the flooded tangle of roadways, but in the end I salvaged my visitation day. Seeing the kids on my allotted days became standard operating procedure (as did my weekly alimony and child support payments).

I hardly ever entered my Pine Street house and I always took the kids somewhere, even if it was just for a hotdog and coke at a nearby Woolworth's Five and Ten Cent store. In the beginning that was about all I could afford. My aunt picked up a lot of the slack too. She often took the girls for the weekend. And, as she had always been able to do so well, she entertained them with her endless tales and escorted them on trips to Boston on the 'flying trains' (elevated subway cars).

I made every effort not to change their lives, but, as anyone who has ever been divorced knows, my efforts were foredoomed to failure. Divorced children invariably suffer for the sins of their parents - Kimberly and Kristin would be no different. That's who I was thinking about that night while scanning the collage of notices tacked on the MIT bulletin board - my kids. I was preoccupied with the array of morbid possibilities that might beset the children of divorced parents, everything from loneliness to child abuse. Kristin had referred to me on my last visit as "Uncle Daddy." I feared she had already begun to blur the distinction between a father and an uncle.

Tacked between two informational leaflets concerning a conscientious objector service and a women's collective, I observed a handout promoting a civil disobedience demonstration at the John F Kennedy Building scheduled for Monday, November 8, at 1:00 PM. That was one juicy peace of information! The JFK building was the seat of federal power in Boston and according to the small print on the bottom half of the leaflet, the People's Coalition for Peace and Justice had planned an unlawful action for that day. Now I had to dig up the rest of the info.

I left the university and scooted over to 173A Mass. Avenue in Cambridge, the main office of the People's Coalition for Peace and Justice. I didn't waste any time in getting there. It was getting late and I knew the office would be getting ready to close up for the night. As it turned out, I sandwiched in just enough time to pick up another leaflet and get a couple of answers to some hastily asked questions. I spent the remainder of the week tracking down the rest of the information.

I learned the plan called for a two-fold action containing both overt and covert components. The overt strategy consisted of a noon rally on the Boston Common followed by a march and demonstration at the John F Kennedy building. The twenty-seven story federal tower had been a magnet for protest actions of all kinds since its dedication on September 9, 1966. The cops routinely handled demonstrations there. The overt part of this action was no big deal.

It was the protest organizer's secret plan that preoccupied me and caused me to fret. If they were successful this would be like no other action previously attempted. And it was simply this - to attract as many individuals as possible to participate in a 6:30 AM blockade of the seven doors leading into the massive federal office building.

This would be an attempt to shut down government itself, by preventing the four thousand employees who staffed the twenty federal agencies housed in the building, from going to work. The participants would form a tightly compressed human chain in front of each entrance thereby discouraging both employees and customers from entering the building.

As I would learn, the protestors did not intend to resist arrest but would try to impede the process by going limp and refusing to cooperate if the cops moved in on them. There would be no violence, no pushing, no threats, no-nothing, just passive civil disobedience. I devoted the next couple of weeks to collecting pieces of information, establishing tactics, identifying participants and projecting increasingly refined estimates of strength for both actions. The organizers believed they could pull this off if they could just beat the cops to the scene - hence the 6:30 AM call to assemble.

They naively believed they could get the jump on the cops by keeping this information from them. In this respect their cover was already blown. I was squeezing them like a rubber duck and as a result I was able to brief the department on their every move. That of course, didn't guarantee we wouldn't have trouble.

I became pathetically more uncomfortable as the day of execution neared. Things were going badly in the country. The war was droning on in spite of everyone's best efforts to stop it. Whatever short-lived jubilance the anti-war movement had experienced as a result of the recent negative war polls had long since passed. As a dark depression descended on the whole of the anti-war movement, greater feelings of hopelessness and despair crept across the land.

I was deeply affected by this struggle. My own values were being challenged to the core. The thin line I skated, between myself and my creation, Mike Russo, was being tested constantly and I was ravaged by the conflicting loyalties that each personality engendered - one for cops the other for the protestors.

The government was suffocating in a burgeoning web of deceit and students and other anti-war activists were being driven to more extreme levels of contentious behavior. The government, the cops, the anti-war organizers, and the students, the liberals, the conservatives, the academicians and the soldiers, the hawks and the doves - the whole bloody mess of them were engaged in a widening argument. It was as though they were all spinning around out of control like runaway planets in an expanding solar system. My ability to bridge the gap between the cops and the demonstrators, never very remarkable to begin with, was hanging on a vanishing thread.

I still believed that communication with the police officers in the street could make a difference and with that in mind I sent up the following request:

From: Phillip M. Vitti, Patrolman/Agent, Intelligence
         Division.

To: John J. Donovan, Deputy Superintendent,
         Commanding, Intelligence Division.

Subject: Recommendation for Briefing Officers at the
         Department Roll Calls

SIR:

This Officer respectfully recommends that the Officers and men of the city's districts, especially those who would be effected by major or minor demonstrations of either a peaceful or violent nature, be advised in advance (during roll calls) of what they might expect concerning the number of persons expected to demonstrate, possible behavior of demonstrators, names of sponsoring groups, names of leaders (if necessary), past histories of individual or group's tactics and the purpose of the demonstration.

The adoption of such a procedure would establish the legitimacy of the Intelligence Division throughout the City's District Stations and would work to better implement lines of communication between the Intelligence Division and the Patrol Force.

This procedure would not only enhance the flow of communication but would also expand the intelligence pool with respect to planned community actions. It would also work to refine the Department's logistical response to proposed demonstrations and curb excessive police behavior.

The Officers assigned to the Intelligence Division would be willing to provide these briefings.

Respectfully submitted,
Phillip M Vitti

I don't know at what level of the chain of command that this recommendation was trashed, but it ended up in the circular file with the rest of the nonsense submitted by young upstart patrolmen. I never heard anything from it.

Forty

T¹ **he dissident training for the** civil disobedience exercise, scheduled to take place early on Monday morning, began about eighteen hours prior to the actual action. Hundreds of people moved in shifts, around the clock, at three principal locations to learn the philosophy and techniques of civil disobedience. The main sessions took place at the Paulist Center at 5 Park Street in Boston, an urban radical Catholic Church aligned with a number of New Left causes, most especially the plight of the grape workers; at the Unitarian Church on Arlington Street at the opposite side of the Boston Common, a church recognized among movement people for its (unsuccessful) invocation of the medieval Right of Sanctuary for draft evaders; and at the Old Baptist Church in Cambridge, a progressive Protestant institution, also in sympathy with New Left causes, especially women's issues.

I started to get itchy late Sunday afternoon. I buzzed Jimmy Lynch and told him that I was coming in.

"I can't sit around the house, Sarge," I explained. "I don't care about overtime - we just forecast the biggest fucking civil disobedience demonstration in the city's history since the colonists dumped tea in the Boston Harbor and I want to follow it through."

I didn't have to explain that I was obsessed with the possibility of an exaggerated forecast and both the professional and personal embarrassment that would certainly follow. Nor did I have to voice my deep concern for the reputation of the department and the safety of the cops and the demonstrators in the event of a miscalculation. I didn't want to take the chance of missing a scrap of information, no matter how slight, that could be critical.

Lynch knew all that. He knew about the divorce too, and how badly I was feeling about the kids. He also understood my restlessness and my need to get out of my empty apartment. Jimmy Lynch knew a lot of things about me and I welcomed his quiet reassurance at those painful junctures of my life. We knew a lot about each other. We had grown close over the years.

After a thoughtful pause, Lynch agreed that I should work and promised to make up the time, one way or the other - that meant comp time. I couldn't have cared less. There was a battle shaping up and I was obsessed with the outcome.

For the rest of the day and night and early into the next morning I hustled between the two cities of Boston and Cambridge, stopping at every conceivable location that might afford me the slightest scintilla of information that would help me predict the action proposed for the Government Center in the early morning. I spent a great deal of time in the Paulist Center where the training sessions were continuing throughout the night and early morning.

The physical aspect of the training centered on the tactical application of civil disobedience itself. Individuals, organized into groups of six to a dozen people, were taught to form a human chain by sitting down next to each other and linking arms. These small groups were for training purposes only - the actual exercise would be conducted on a much wider scale.

The trainees were instructed that in the event of arrest they should not resist the police, but instead fall limp and be willing to be dragged by their hands and feet to the wagon. They were admonished not to volunteer any information to the police, and if arrested they were not to answer any questions the police might ask, other than their names. There was protracted discussion concerning the rights of arrested persons. Each individual was handed a supply of small red capsules containing detailed instructions on what to do if arrested and was urged to distribute them among the protestors the following day, especially to those who had not benefited from the prior night's training.

The educational aspect of the training was devoted to an examination of the philosophical underpinnings of civil disobedience. These, the organizers said, were the techniques of Mahatma Gandhi, Martin Luther King and Henry David Thoreau. Even the philosophy of Saint Thomas Acquinas was said to have played a role.

One speaker pointed out that Gandhi had spent the better part of his life defying governmental discrimination against Indians in South Africa and political repression by the English in India. "Though he had spent many years in jail," the speaker said, "in the end he transformed a nation through his unmitigated devotion to the principles of civil disobedience."

King, who was an adherent of Gandhi and non-violent civil disobedience, had sparked demonstrations and boycotts all over the country, especially in the South where he disobeyed laws that he considered to be unjust. Thoreau, though a bit more remote in time, was another guy that the speaker commented had risked arrest and imprisonment for his failure to pay taxes - a personal act in opposition to slavery. (Although a friend bailed him out after only one night, his action coupled with his writings, formed the basis for much of the social protest of the Vietnam Era.)

The speaker concluded, "These men offered their freedom, their bodies and their lives to bring about justice. They offered the ultimate sacrifice, themselves, to make thing better for others." There was no questioning this guy's solid commitment to this unlawful form of protest. Judging from the expressions on the faces of the trainees when he finished, he had made his point.

The three churches were filled with the politics of protest. I found a fourth community church front on Charles Street, a few streets away from the Paulist Center, offering educational training on the rationale of civil disobedience. All of them were doing their thing.

However, the Paulist Center carried the heaviest action - the place was humming. The night chapel was alive with the music of protest. The disciples stepped to its rhythm and were lifted by its melody onto another level of human awareness, beyond the pale of risk and fear, to a place where might was never right and war was always wrong. Unyielding human will alone would inevitably overcome the indomitable power of government.

The battle was shaping up. The metamorphosis was taking place.

The arena was being prepared. Soon the forces of right, buried in ancient antediluvian notions of moral supremacy, would collide with the establishment's need for order and the preservation of power.

DAWN

Daybreak arrived and I was already beat. I had worked for most of the night and early morning, stopping only briefly to catch a few zzzs in my cramped car. I had parked the little bug around the corner from Charles and Beacon Streets, about half way between the Paulist Center and the Unitarian Church. It was a strategically good geographical point for moving between the two churches and the twenty-four hour Hays and Bickford's restaurant on Washington Street.

I had loaded up on java all night long and spent some down-time in the restaurant talking with a couple of guys leftover from the Forties who were hanging around the joint. They amused me with their swagger and colorful Runyonesque type banter. They seemed trapped in a time warp that had effectively insulated them from the upheaval of the Sixties. I had a real caffeine buzz on by the time I hit the street.

When I reached Government Center there were several hundred demonstrators already blocking the front door. According to schedule, the assemblage had gathered on the Boston Common at 6:30 AM before marching the short distance to the Government Center. There were several hundred participants - more would join the resistance as the day wore on. They were not prepared for the multitude of cops who had taken positions around the building.

There were more than three hundred uniformed police officers showing and still more in reserve. The cops had been drawn from every district in the city and some of the officers had been working thirty-six hours straight covering a series of mini-actions that had preceded this big one. The Tactical Patrol Force was there also, sitting in police busses in full regalia, waiting to move out if in the event they were needed. The district cops resented this. The way Sergeant Detective Buddy Evans - a tough, steadfast and reliable District 9 (Roxbury) cop would eventually put it, "The TPF were fucking the duck while the district cops had to pick up the slack."

The marchers were dismayed and puzzled by the presence of so many cops. After all, the civil disobedience part of the protest had been secretly planned to catch the 'fuzz' by surprise. The sponsoring groups had widely advertised a 1:00 PM action to take place outside the JFK Building. This fractional mis-information had been based on a doubled-edged strategy designed partially to provide early afternoon reinforcements for the nucleus of war resistors. The sponsors' primary aim, however, was to prevent the police department from cordoning off the area before the core of early morning protesters could assemble and pack themselves into tight little knots in front of the several doors leading into the building.

The organizers should have known better! Their plans were already blown, right down to the nitty-gritty details. I felt a beam of pride for having discovered their hidden agenda. It was a good piece of intelligence that would enable the police department to ensure that the operation of government would continue. That alone justified my efforts.

I gave Jimmy Lynch a final briefing. He was thankful for the detailed information which he hurriedly relayed to the Bureau of Field Service. Just before he hung up he commented, "You do good work, Phil."

I felt pleasantly relieved - the whole thing was going down according to plan. The biggest part of my job was over. Now it would be up to the rest of the intelligence team to swing into action. Peter, Gerry, Pat, Dapkas and Cox would run the street operation. Their plan was to coordinate the arrest of the leaders with the actions of the Bureau of Field Service. I could relax a little.

To better monitor the ground action the Intelligence Unit had set up a surveillance camera on the second floor of One Center Plaza, an eight story, crescent shaped brick and mortar retail and office complex overlooking the main entrance of the JFK. This provided a good vantage point to survey the crowd below. The circular shape of the building, enhanced by its many rectangular windows arranged in close proximity to each other, lent it the appearance of an alien spacecraft sitting in the middle of a huge city complex.

The Intelligence Officers, each of whom possessed a remarkable knowledge of known social agitators, took turns manning the camera. Binoculars were used to pinpoint suspected leaders.

When an officer spotted a known protest leader in the crowd he was expected to transmit the information to the command post that was set up

474

not far from the periphery of the demonstration. Channel 1 was specifically cleared for this action. It was a well-planned and methodically executed proactive police strategy - the best one yet. Large postal trucks were lined up on both sides of the main entrance to the building to channel protestors into a manageable area. The trucks had been moved into play during the early morning hours.

A makeshift booking area was set up inside an office on the bottom floor of the building itself to expedite the booking process. Wagonloads of prisoners would be successively delivered through a remote service entrance where they would be booked, fingerprinted and photographed. In order to avoid clogging the district police station cells it was decided, ahead of time, to release all but the most unruly prisoners on personal recognizance.

The brass believed that busting the leaders would discourage the others from following in their belligerence. However, the brass was wrong and so was I! There were no leaders! That should have been clear to me from the night before. The signs were present. In fact, they were staring me right in the face, but I missed them.

Even during the training sessions the opposition already had begun to melt into a solid mass of resistance. Now it had formed into one single interconnected press of human flesh and will, pitted against a three hundred and sixty-eight foot pinnacle of steel and concrete, surrounded by a protective circle of helmeted police officers.

It was too late to brief Jimmy Lynch or Warren Blair about that now. The operation was well underway.

The morning started off damp and cold - the pavement had long since released its summer warmth. The number of demonstrators had swelled to more than one thousand strong and most of them had assumed a sitting position in front of the main entrance with the intention of blocking federal workers, customers and deliverymen from entering the building. The protestors sat there, grim faced and determined, facing stern looking police officers from the Canine Unit who were assisted by their ninety-pound German Shepherd partners.

Teams of police officers moved through the congregation escorting federal employees and people with government business into the building. The protestors offered no resistance - they simply sat still with their arms locked together. They rocked from side to side chanting and singing songs such as *Kumbaya* and *We Will Overcome*.

By mid-morning a few arrests had been made. Intelligence Officers guided uniformed police officers through the crowd and picked off the best known of the protesters. Howard Zinn was among the first to go - he fell limp and refused to cooperate. A big beefy cop reached down and pulled him straight up by the hair of his head and yanked him away from the others. A wretched look of pain and horror crossed Zinn's face and he was gone - a significant link of the human chain had been extricated.

Howard Zinn had expected to be arrested. He was a prime police target. A colorful protagonist of the saga of the New Left and a political Guru to anti-war activists, he had been dammed by conservatives, cops and college deans, who charged that he was guilty of having deliberately misguided college students by encouraging them to engage in unlawful political protests. From the students' point of view, he was one of the most popular political science teachers at Boston University, an easy grader who possessed a refined eloquence and burned with deep political passions. His melodic voice emanated with a serene quality and his tall thin frame and angular features bestowed on him the appearance of a modern day Abraham Lincoln (albeit, a comedic one at times.)

I had read some of his stuff and listened to a few of his speeches and, although I disagreed with most of his fundamental notions, I had come to admire his courage. He was a hard core recalcitrant and was constantly at odds with the Boston University administration. Silber and Zinn were on opposite ends of the political spectrum and the differences between them added to the passionate rhetoric of the times. He was a ball breaker and I liked him for that reason.

I never shared my fondness for Zinn with my colleagues - not Jimmy Lynch, and certainly not Gerry. They would have carted me away. Nor could I share my feelings with Peter - he had already kidded me about going over to the other side and that revelation would have cemented his suspicion.

Howard Zinn was not the only well-known professional to be arrested. A District Court Judge named Sullivan was busted also. I guessed that he was either a flake or one highly committed individual to have risked his position that way. I supposed that was precisely what made these people stand out, their willingness to sit on a cold street for several hours, subjecting themselves to ridicule and incarceration for their beliefs. They were different from many of mainstream movement people whom I had experienced over the years. These were not the revelers, the phonies, the groupies, the draft dodgers, the chronic malcontents, the 'sickos' or the Canada flocking cowards.

These protestors were a different breed. They were generally non-violent, rational, civilized and thoughtful people who were willing to pit themselves against constituted authority. They risked arrest and professional damage to end what they sincerely believed was a malevolent war, spurned by a flawed political system, which was destroying lives, wasting resources, depleting the land and grinding up the nation.

It was starting to grind me up, too. Perhaps I had been in the business too long: too much undercover, too many rallies, too many speeches, too many actions, too many radicals, not enough sleep and an overload of coffee.

I scanned the crowd and my attention fixed on a canine cop standing guard at the front door of the building. His uniform was crisp and clean and his boots were brightly polished. His face was expressionless and devoid of emotion as he stood there gazing out at the crowd.

A skinny kid with a long thin beard and dark piercing eyes was sitting squarely in front of him. The kid had been sitting in the same spot for almost two hours. I thought his bony ass must have been cold. The officer's dog was snarling and pulling at the short leash. The dog came within two inches of biting the protester on the nose. The officer never let on that he was acutely conscious of the dog's position or the distance between the animal and the protester. Nor did the kid complain or alert the officer to the imminent danger of his being bitten by the dog. The kid never flinched or moved a single inch back on the sidewalk. He was determined to hold his ground.

The officer maintained his professional demeanor and held on tightly to the leash, taking care not to injure his silent challenger. These men were engaged in a serious contest of wills and neither one of them showed any signs of giving in.

I was standing only a few feet away from these antagonists, staring intently at the both of them. I was mesmerized by the drama that was being played out - the dog was barking loudly and growing more aggressive by the moment. The cop screwed up the leash one more turn curling it up around his left wrist but still neither man would acknowledge the other. I wouldn't have risked a plug nickel on predicting the outcome of this cowboy's game of bluff.

I spotted Gerry approaching from my right rear. I knew that he was ready to give me a message. Over the course of time we had learned to communicate with one another cryptically and quickly. My ears perked up and the mental receptors in my brain began the process of filtering out background noise from the crowd, readying itself for his transmission. Gerry stood behind me momentarily and squeezed out his tight-lipped communiqué.

"That canine cop has a son in Vietnam," he whispered. Gerry was never one to miss the pathos and irony in a human situation and apparently he wished to share this little piece of melodrama with me.

That did it! The epiphany struck! I felt like I was being hit right through the center of my heart with a lightning bolt. The profound incongruity of these two antagonists sharing this same tortured place, fixated with the same dark preoccupation, triggered a flood of conflicting emotions in me. Both of these men, **the blue man and the beard,** desperately wished for the war to be over - one for the love of his son, the other for the love of humankind. Two mutual combatants seeking the same end, juxtaposed in a pathetic confrontation sparked by an un-winnable war, over which neither one had any control. It was a lugubrious piece of street theater.

My mind shifted back to my early years at the State Hospital - to the middle of that mad suffering place - to that place of personal freedom and intellectual awakening - to that place of simplicity and isolation - to that place of helping and hope - to that place of ideas - to that place before I would be chewed up by the tri-headed beast of corruption, greed and violence - to that place before I married and screwed up my life - to that place before the death of Andrianna. To this place - to this cold wretched place - to this place of conflict, defiance and provocation - to this place where I would suffer the ultimate confrontation - a confrontation within and against myself - an internal battle waged for my very soul. God, I was going mad!

An ambulance screeched to one of the side doors and a federal employee, a woman suffering a heart attack, was removed from the building. No one attempted to impede her transportation by stretcher through the crowd, but the presence of so many bodies piled up in front of the door slowed her progress to the waiting ambulance just the same.

The crowd surrounding the protesters was getting bigger by the minute. Some were drawn by curiosity to the spectacle being played out in the shadow of the Federal Building. Others were there to support their comrades - a few even sat down next to them. As one violator was arrested another would take his place on the pavement. A cadaverous looking old lady assumed a street position in front of a robust and athletic, wavy-haired guy. I wondered if she had enough life left in her to make it through the day. This was the most singularly committed, politically diverse crowd that I had witnessed since becoming a member of the Intelligence Division. All types comprised the group, from conservatively dressed engineers to way out rag-tag 'yippie whackos' who likened the Federal Building to a giant, pork piercing phallic symbol. The nucleus of resistors sitting on the pavement was ringed by scores of stand-up supporters who agreed, in principle, with the purpose of the action: to bring an end to the war in Vietnam - **Now! Now! Now!** One of them was Christine Carey, a cute mini-skirted state employee from the nearby Leverett Saltonstall Building, herself a college student, moved by the deaths of so many of her friends. Meg Buckley was another, a newly graduated nurse working at the Carney Hospital in Dorchester. She was tall, shapely and pretty with long dark hair falling to her hips. She saw, in every crowd of Vietnam War protesters, an opportunity to pray for the safe return of her brother Billy. It was as though these civil dissidents were themselves a bullhorn to God.

My emotions began to churn like an overheated mixer. They shifted between anger, depression, elation and confusion.

The ground underneath me seemed to tremble and for a prolonged moment of time I literally did not know who I was, Phil Vitti or Mike Russo, the Marine-cop or the teacher-radical. An intensifying well of feeling began to force its way up through my guts, swelling my passions and imperiling my judgment. Emotions threatened to overwhelm me. I was becoming engorged with grief and desperately needed to bare my soul to someone, to anyone, someone who knew me and who might understand the source of my anguish.

I managed to disengage myself from the first ring of spectators overlooking the demonstrators. I maneuvered my way through the crowd, being careful to avoid eye contact with any of the cops I knew, especially the intelligence guys. I passed a woman who looked like Andrianna Tranquillo. Her face was ashen white and absent of any expression. She was just standing there, staring straight ahead.

I walked up the stairs to the second floor of One Center Plaza and zeroed in on a pay phone. I called Beverly. She picked up the phone and said hello. I paused for a moment, hesitating for only an instant, and spoke quietly into the mouthpiece.

"Beverly it's me. I'm feeling really bad. I'm at a demonstration at the JFK building and I'm experiencing a lot of doubt. I'm not sure what I stand for or whose side I'm on. I'm not even sure who I am anymore. I'm tired - I haven't had much sleep. I don't mean to bother you, but I don't know who else I can talk to. You're the one who has been with me since I started to work undercover. Perhaps this confusion will pass - perhaps--"

"What's the matter with you?" she interrupted, the tone of her voice piqued with impatience. "I've never heard you talk like this before. Are you all right?"

She sounded cold and distant. I might as well have been speaking to her through a kettledrum. She was clearly miffed at me for having called her. I probably interrupted her cleaning regimen.

"Nothing, Beverly, nothing. I'm sorry I disturbed you. Say hello to the kids for me." I carefully placed the phone back into its resting place.

My heart throbbed and my throat tightened - my chest pounded and my head ached. I stumbled into a men's room and was blissfully relieved to learn that it was vacant. I entered the most distant cubicle, sat on the closed hopper and buried my face in my hands. The silence slowly enveloped me. I don't know how long I remained there but it was for a very long time. It was a good place to be - a good place to hide out. I didn't want anyone to see me crying.

Epilogue

I **have no further memory of** the day's events. I would learn almost three days later that things got pretty rough sometime in the late afternoon, just before the federal employees were released from work. The cops moved en masse into the crowd and scores of persons were arrested. There were injuries reported on both sides.

I was changed on that day, and I knew in my essence that I would never be a silent voice on the department. Eventually I regained my equilibrium and refocused my efforts back to intelligence gathering. It was a good thing I did because, as luck would have it, several months later I inadvertently stumbled upon some urgent information that a woman's collective had planned to derail a train headed into Boston in opposition to President Nixon's interdiction of Vietnam. Preliminary plans had already been carried out by the time I had learned of the plot. Fast action prevented the city of Cambridge from having to deal with a major catastrophe.

Domestic intelligence gathering died a slow death following the end of American involvement in Southeast Asia beginning in June 1972, when the U.S. ended their combat role in Vietnam and languishing into January 1973, following a cease-fire agreement entered into by the main warring parties. The war had been the incendiary ejecta that had fed the flames of social protest. Without it, the peace and justice movement dissolved into the crap-trap of history.

In July 1974, I was awarded my Detective's Rating. It was the proudest day of my career. I was reassigned to work with the department's elite Organized Crime Unit where I would be exposed to a no less intriguing but more conventional sort of criminal investigation. In 1985, following successive promotions, I would return to head both the Intelligence and Organized Crime Units as a Deputy Superintendent, where I would once again experience the horrible sting of foul politics---but that's another story.

To the Boston Police Department --- Thanks for the memories.